Lecture Notes in Artificial Int

Edited by J. G. Carbonell and J. Siekman

Subseries of Lecture Notes in Computer Science

Ipke Wachsmuth   Günther Knoblich (Eds.)

Modeling Communication with Robots and Virtual Humans

Second ZiF Research Group International Workshop
on Embodied Communication in Humans and Machines
Bielefeld, Germany, April 5-8, 2006
Revised Selected Papers

 Springer

Series Editors

Jaime G. Carbonell, Carnegie Mellon University, Pittsburgh, PA, USA
Jörg Siekmann, University of Saarland, Saarbrücken, Germany

Volume Editors

Ipke Wachsmuth
University of Bielefeld, Faculty of Technology
33594 Bielefeld, Germany
E-mail: ipke@techfak.uni-bielefeld.de

Günther Knoblich
University of Birmingham, School of Psychology
Edgbaston, Birmingham B15 2TT, UK
E-mail: g.knoblich@bham.ac.uk

Library of Congress Control Number: 2008923959

CR Subject Classification (1998): I.2.9, I.2, J.4, K.4.3, H.5, I.6

LNCS Sublibrary: SL 7 – Artificial Intelligence

ISSN   0302-9743
ISBN-10   3-540-79036-5 Springer Berlin Heidelberg New York
ISBN-13   978-3-540-79036-5 Springer Berlin Heidelberg New York

Springer is a part of Springer Science+Business Media

springer.com

© Springer-Verlag Berlin Heidelberg 2008
Printed in Germany

Typesetting: Camera-ready by author, data conversion by Scientific Publishing Services, Chennai, India
Printed on acid-free paper   SPIN: 12253173   06/3180   5 4 3 2 1 0

Preface

Embodied agents play an increasingly important role in cognitive interaction technology. The two main types of embodied agents are virtual humans inhabiting simulated environments and humanoid robots inhabiting the real world. So far research on embodied communicative agents has mainly explored their potential for practical applications. However, the design of communicative artificial agents can also be of great heuristic value for the scientific study of communication. It allows researchers to isolate, implement, and test essential properties of inter-agent communications in operational models. Modeling communication with robots and virtual humans thus involves the vision of using communicative machines as research tools. Artificial systems that reproduce certain aspects of natural, multimodal communication help to elucidate the internal mechanisms that give rise to different aspects of communication. In short, constructing embodied agents who are able to communicate may help us to understand the principles of human communication.

As a comprehensive theme, "Embodied Communication in Humans and Machines" was taken up by an international research group hosted by Bielefeld University's Center for Interdisciplinary Research (ZiF – Zentrum für interdisziplinäre Forschung) from October 2005 through September 2006. The overarching goal of this research year was to develop an integrated perspective of embodiment in communication, establishing bridges between lower-level, sensorimotor functions and a range of higher-level, communicative functions involving language and bodily action. The present volume grew out of a workshop that took place during April 5–8, 2006 at the ZiF as a part of the research year on embodied communication. The goal of this workshop was to explore how artificial agents can advance our understanding of key aspects of embodiment, cognition, and communication.

It turned out that the goals of roboticists and virtual human researchers are quite similar with regard to mechanisms underlying intelligent, communicative behavior as illustrated in some of the contributions of the book. For instance, feedback signals and expressive gestures receive equal attention as means of communicating with embodied virtual agents as well as robots. Behavior control programs devised for the coordination between different robots can also support coordination in virtual humans. Conversely, insights from virtual humans research may be extended to conversational robots, for instance, on how to utilize corpus data for the control of communicative behavior in robots.

The present volume reflects the emerging dialogue between robotics research and research on virtual humans. It contains a selection of 17 articles authored by researchers from 11 countries. In addition to artificial intelligence research on communicative agents, the chapters also provide an interdisciplinary perspective from linguistics, behavioral research, theoretical biology, philosophy, communication psychology, and computational neuroscience. The topics include studies on human multimodal communication; the modeling of feedback signals, facial expression, eye contact, and deception; the recognition and comprehension of hand gestures and head movements; communication interfaces for humanoid robots; the evolution of cognition and language; emotion and social appraisal in nonverbal communication; dialogue models and methodologies; Theory of Mind and intentionality; complex systems, dynamic field theory, and connectionist modeling.

We are very grateful to the authors of the articles in this volume as well as to the international reviewers who provided very helpful input. We hope that the results of their hard work will be perceived as a timely and inspiring reference for an interdisciplinary audience of researchers and practitioners interested in multimodal communication and cognitive interaction technology. Further, we would like to express our thanks to Manuela Lenzen, Marina Hoffmann, and the whole ZiF team. They worked tirelessly to make the workshop a successful and lively event. Thanks also to Mo Tschache, Isabelle Szydlowski, Marion Kämper, and Christian Becker-Asano for their support in preparing the book.

December 2007

Ipke Wachsmuth
Günther Knoblich

Notes

Web pages for the ZiF research year providing further information and links can be accessed under http://www.uni-bielefeld.de/ZIF/FG/2005Communication/.

A related book is published as: *Embodied Communication in Humans and Machines* (I. Wachsmuth, M. Lenzen, G. Knoblich, eds.), Oxford University Press, 2008.

Reviewers

Table of Contents

From Annotated Multimodal Corpora to Simulated Human-Like Behaviors

Matthias Rehm and Elisabeth André

Augsburg University, Institute of Computer Science
86159 Augsburg, Germany
{rehm,andre}@informatik.uni-augsburg.de
http://mm-werkstatt.informatik.uni-augsburg.de

Abstract. Multimodal corpora prove useful at different stages of the development process of embodied conversational agents. Insights into human-human communicative behaviors can be drawn from such corpora. Rules for planning and generating such behavior in agents can be derived from this information. And even the evaluation of human-agent interactions can rely on corpus data from human-human communication. In this paper, we exemplify how corpora can be exploited at the different development steps, starting with the question of how corpora are annotated and on what level of granularity. The corpus data can be used either directly for imitating the human behavior recorded in the corpus or rules can be derived from the data which govern the behavior planning process. Corpora can even play a vital role in the evaluation of agent systems. Several studies are presented that make use of corpora for the evaluation task.

Keywords: Multimodal interaction, embodied conversational agent, behavior modelling, multimodal corpora.

1 Introduction

A number of approaches to modeling the behaviors of embodied conversational agents (ECA's) are based on a direct simulation of human behaviors. Consequently, it comes as no surprise that the use of data-driven approaches which allow us to validate design choices empirically has become increasingly popular in the ECA field. To get insight into human-human conversation, researchers rely on a large variety of resources including recordings of users in "natural" or staged situations, TV interviews, Wizard of Oz studies, and motion capturing data. Various annotation schemes have been designed to extract relevant information for multimodal behaviors, such as facial expressions, gestures, postures and gaze. In addition, there has been increasing interest in the design of annotation schemes to capture emotional behaviors in human-human conversation. Progress in the field has been boosted by the availability of new tools that facilitate the acquisition and annotation of corpora.

The use of data-driven approaches provides a promising approach to the modeling of ECA behaviors since it allows us to validate design choices empirically.

I. Wachsmuth and G. Knoblich (Eds.): Modeling Communication, LNAI 4930, pp. 1–17, 2008.
© Springer-Verlag Berlin Heidelberg 2008

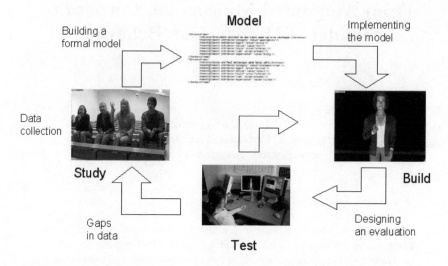

Fig. 1. Development cycle for embodied conversational agents

Nevertheless, the creation of implementable models still leaves many research issues open. One difficulty lies in the fact that an enormous amount of data is needed to derive regularities from concrete instantiations of human-human behavior. In rare cases, we are interested in the replication of behaviors shown by individuals. Rather, we aim at the extraction of behavior profiles that are characteristic of a group of people, for example, introverts versus extroverts. Furthermore, the resulting ECA behaviors only emulate a limited amount of phenomena of human-human behaviors. In particular, the dynamics of multimodal behaviors has been largely neglected so far. Last but not least, there is the danger that humans expect a different behavior from an ECA than from a human conversational partner which might limit the potential benefits of a simulation-based approach.

The methodological approach for modeling communicative behavior for embodied conversational agents is well exemplified by Cassel's Study-Model-Build-Test development cycle [8]. Figure 1 gives an overview of the different steps in this development cycle. To build a formal model for generating realistic agent behaviors, data of humans that are engaged in a dialogue with other humans are collected. In most cases, formal models are not built from scratch. Rather, the data analysis serves to refine existing models found in the literature. The resulting models of human-human conversational behavior then serve as a basis for the implementation of ECAs that replicate the behaviors addressed by the models. To evaluate the resulting system, experiments are set up in which humans are confronted with ECAs following the model. Depending on the outcome of such experiments, the developers might decide to acquire new data from humans so that the existing models may be refined.

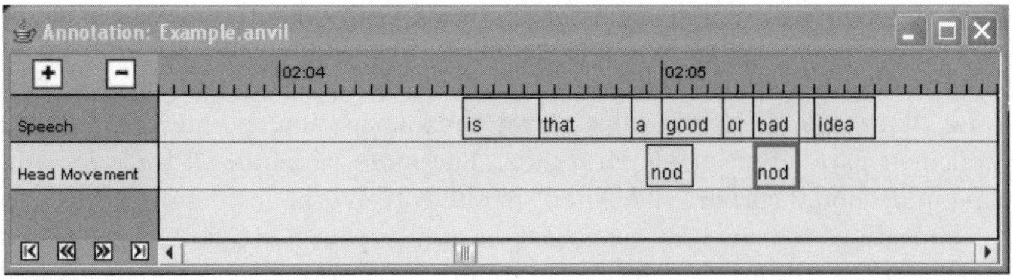

Fig. 2. Information of different modalities is annotated in parallel on a temporal score

In the rest of this article, we exemplify how the single steps of the development process have been realized by ECA researchers. First we will provide an overview of existing corpus-based work that has been conducted in order to get insight on multimodal human-human dialogue with the aim to replicate such behaviors in an embodied conversational agent. We will present several approaches to bridge the gap from corpus analysis to behavior generation including copy-synthesis, generate-and-filter as well as first attempts to realize trainable generation approaches. Finally, we will discuss several empirical studies that have been conducted with the aim to validate models derived from a corpus.

2 Multimodal Corpora for Studying Human Behavior

It is undeniable that a rich literature on human communicative behavior exists covering such diverse areas as dialogue management (e.g. [2]) gesture use (e.g., [26]; [20]) or gaze behavior (e.g., [4]; [19]). But for the explicit task of emulating human communicative behavior by an embodied conversational agent, this literature is often deficient in one way or another. This is due to the fact that the proposed theories and models were of course not created with the generation task in mind and thus often consider only one modality or lack crucial information, e.g. about the synchronization of different modalities, making it sometimes necessary to collect a completely new corpus for deriving this information.

Corpus work has a long tradition in the social sciences where it is employed as a descriptive tool to gain insights into human communicative behavior. Due to the increased multimedia abilities of computers, a number of tools for video analysis have been developed over the last decade allowing for standardized annotation of multimodal data.

2.1 Annotating Multimodal Information

A corpus is a collection of video recordings of human (or human-agent) communicative behavior that is annotated or coded with different types of information. A multimodal corpus analyses more than one modality in a single annotation, e.g. speech and gesture, and ideally explicates the links and crossmodal relations between the different modalities. Which kind of information is coded in a given corpus is defined in an annotation scheme that specifies the coding attributes and values. Figure 2 gives an impression of a very simple annotation board that codes utterances and head movements. Each modality has its own layer in a data format that resembles a musical score i.e. the information on different modalities is coded in parallel on a temporal axis. The more widely used tools for annotating multimodal corpora like Anvil[1] or the Nite Workbench[2] support tailoring the annotations scheme to a given task often using an XML format that is proprietary to the given tool. The annotated data is also generally given in XML format allowing for accessing the information by simply parsing the XML tree.

There is no limit on the number of annotation layers one can define to describe communicative behavior. Speech, gestures, gaze or facial expressions are good candidates for which information can be annotated on different levels, such as the spatio-temporal course of actions, semantic content, or communicative function. Depending on the research area, a great number of annotation schemes are available focusing on these different levels of annotation. Basically, we can distinguish between *how* the information in this channel is realized at the signal level and *what* kind of information is realized. How the information is realized often includes the temporal course of an action in a given channel, for gestures e.g. the distinction between preparation, stroke, and retraction phases (see below). What kind of information is realized often includes categorizing the elements of a specific channel and emphasizing the communicative function of the modality by coding e.g. what kind of feedback is given by a specific gaze behavior. Whereas the how level of annotation supports the extraction of concrete animation parameters for an agent and information about the temporal synchronization of modalities, the what level allows us to derive information concerning crossmodal functional relations that are of relevance to the behavior planning process.

Elaborate annotation schemes exist (for an overview see e.g. [23]) ranging from gesture analysis (e.g. [15]; [26]), over general movement analysis (see e.g. [24]) to the coding of facial expressions (e.g. [12]). If they are suitable for the task of modeling the communicative behavior of an agent — be it at the concrete level of controlling the animation or at the more abstract level of planning appropriate multimodal behavior — has to be decided from case to case based on a given agent system.

The MUMIN corpus focuses on the analysis of gestures and facial displays which accompany communicative phenomena, such as feedback, turn-taking or sequencing ([3]), and is a good example of a multimodal corpus that was not created with the generation of multimodal output in mind. While not focusing on the generation task, the corpus shows how different modalities converge in their contribution to communicative functions. Feedback, turn management, and sequencing constitute communicative functions that are not bound to a single modality, such as speech, but are inherently multimodal in face to face communication. Gestures and facial displays convey such information and are only annotated if they play a relevant role for feedback, turn management or

---

[1] http://www.anvil-software.de/

[2] http://nite.nis.sdu.dk/

sequencing. Turn management for example consists of the three attributes turn-gain, turn-end, and turn-hold. Turn-gain can have the values turn-accept and turn-take distinguishing between a situation where the turn is freely offered by the other participant and accepted and a situation where the speaker takes the turn although the other participant was not finished yet. For each modality, these functional attributes are annotated allowing for a multimodal analysis of communicative phenomena, i.e. an analysis of the correlations between the different modalities in performing the functions. The shape and dynamics of the facial displays and gestures are only roughly annotated with the aim to characterise and distinguish the non-verbal expressions. Gestures e.g. are annotated only by handedness (single vs. double) and trajectory (a number of simple trajectories was defined).

The standard annotation scheme for the coding of facial expressions is the facial action coding system (FACS, e.g. [12]). The basic parameter of FACS is an action unit which corresponds to a facial muscle. A facial expression can thus be described as a vector of activated action units. This scheme is very successful for describing human facial expressions, but suitable only to a limited extent for the generation of multimodal behavior because in general the animation of facial expressions for agents does not correspond directly to facial muscles. A different approach takes into account one of the current animation standards (MPEG-4). MPEG-4 defines a number of facial animation parameters that correspond to reference points in the face, such as the middle of the right eyebrow. Karpouzis et al. [18] describe how these reference points and their movement can be recognized automatically allowing for automatically anntotating facial expressions in a format that is directly suitable for the animation of a virtual character [34].

A special case is Laban movement analysis [24] which is a detailed description scheme first introduced to describe dance movements. This scheme was successfully utilized in the EMOTE model [11] to control the gestural behavior of a virtual character (see Sec. 3). Attempts to exploit this scheme also for the annotation of multimodal corpora were only a limited success due to the many dimensions which make the annotation far too tedious to be reliable [17].

2.2 Multimodal Corpora for ECA Design

So far we have described approaches that annotate information on different levels, such as the signal or the functional level, and that use corpora to achieve quite diverse goals. In the following, we will concentrate on corpora that have been collected with the goal of generating appropriate communicative behavior in virtual agents and exemplify the still diverse annotation approaches with the annotation of gesture use in human communication.

Basically, we can distinguish between a direct use of corpus data e.g. to generate animations that directly correspond to the behavior found in the data, and an indirect use of corpus data, for example to extract abstract rules that govern the planning and generation process. The direct use calls for annotations that can be mapped onto instructions for a generation component. An example includes the annotation of facial expressions using the MPEG-4 standard from

which facial expressions with an MPEG-4 compliant agent system are generated.
Rule derivation for controlling the behavior planning process on the other hand
requires annotations that refer to a more abstract functional level. An example
is the annotation of categories of facial expressions, such as smiles or frowns, and
their communicative function ideally linked to other modalities, such as speech.

Kipp et al. [22] suggest an annotation scheme for gestures that draws on the
distinction between the temporal course of a gesture and its type and relies on
a gesture typology introduced by McNeill [26]. The temporal course of the gesture is described by a *phase layer*. Gesture phases are preparation, hold, stroke,
and retraction. Generally, the hands are brought from a resting position into the
gesture space during preparation. The stroke is the phase of the gesture that car-
ries/visualizes its meaning. Afterwards, the hands are brought back to a resting
position during the retraction phase. Because gestures are often co-expressive
with the speech channel, sometimes a hold is necessary. A hold is a break in the
gesture execution if e.g. the utterance has not yet proceeded to the word which
should be accompanied by the gesture. What kind of gesture is realized has to
be annoted in a second layer, the *phrase layer*. Following McNeill, Kipp et al.
distinguish between adaptors, beats, emblems, deictic, iconic, and metaphoric
gestures. Adaptors comprise every hand movement to other parts of the body,
such as scratching one's nose. Beats are rhythmic gestures that may emphasize
certain propositions made verbally or that link different parts of an utterance.
Emblems are gestures that are meaningful in themselves, i.e., without any utterance. An example is the American "OK"-emblem, where the thumb and first
finger are in contact at the tips while the other fingers are extended. Deictic
gestures identify referents in the gesture space. The referents can be concrete,
for example, when somebody is pointing to the addressee, or they can be abstract, for example, when somebody is pointing to the left and the right while
uttering the words "the good and the bad". Iconic gestures depict spatial or
shape-oriented aspects of a referent, e.g., by using two fingers to indicate someone walking while uttering "he went down the street". Metaphoric gestures at
last visualize abstract concepts by the use of metaphors, e.g. by employing a box
gesture to visualize "a story". This is an example of the conduit metaphor that
makes use of the idea of a container — in this case a container holding information. The goal of Kipp et al. is the imitation of gestural behavior by a virtual
agent. To achieve this goal, information on the spatial layout of the gesture is
also indispensable and coded in terms of attributes, such as handedness, straight-
ness of trajectory, start and end positions for the stroke, three-dimensional hand
position and elbow inclination.

The proposed scheme has the advantage of an economic balance between
coding effort and generation effect. Using the different phase categories for annotating gestures with movement information means that in the ideal case a
gesture is coded by three categories (preparation, stroke, retraction). The information of the spatial layout is annotated in a way that corresponds to traditional
keyframes of animation. Thus, the data derived from the corpus can more or less

be directly used to control the gestural behavior of a virtual character resulting in an imitation of the recorded human behavior.

Abrilian et al. [1] as well as Chafai et al. [10] annotate instead the expressivity dimensions of gestural activity focusing on how a gesture is accomplished and not on what kind of gesture is used. They employ six parameters to rate the movement quality of the gestures (and of head and torso movements) in the investigated clips: activation, repetition, spatial extent, speed, strength, and fluidity. All parameters are annotated continuously between two values. Activation e.g. ranges from passive to active, speed from slow to fast, and fluidity from jerky to fluid. The annotation revealed correlations between the different parameters. For example, highly active gestural movements are often observed together with repetitive and strong movements. Chafai et al. link their expressivity parameters — fluidity, power, spatial expansion, repetition — to the above mentioned gesture phases that describe the different movement phases of a gesture. They analyse the temporal course of these parameters allowing to pinpoint irregularities and discontinuities that are interpreted as pragmatic functions in the ongoing interaction. Irregular and discontinuous movements are interpreted as attentional clues for the addressee that provide information about relevant parts of an utterance.

To sum up, the information on a different level than the actual gesture can serve useful for the generation task. The found regularities about the temporal course of the parameters and the correlations between them allow to derive rules for the generation of an agent's behavior. Moreover, expressivity parameters are not bound to a single modality, and the consistent use of a parameter, such as fluidity, over the different modalities, such as gesture, head and body movement, supports the coherent generation of believable behavior.

Rehm and André [31] describe an annotation scheme that analyzes gestures also on a more abstract functional level. The SEMMEL corpus was created to capture the relation between linguistic and nonverbal strategies of politeness. When humans interact with each other, they risk continuously threatening the face of their conversational partners, for example by showing disapproval or by putting the other person under pressure. To mitigate such face threats, humans usually rely on various politeness strategies. The seminal work by Brown and Levinson [5] contains a rich repertoire of linguistic means of politeness, but ignores multimodal aspects. Therefore, Rehm and André decided to collect their own corpus. To code politeness strategies, they follow Walker et al.'s [35] categorization into direct, approval-oriented, autonomy-oriented, and off-record strategies. In direct strategies, no redress is used, the speaker just expresses his concerns. Approval-oriented strategies are related to the positive face needs of the addressee, using means to approve of her self-image. Autonomy-oriented strategies on the other hand are related to the negative face wants of the addressee, trying to take care of her want to act autonomously. Off record strategies at last are the most vague and indirect form to address someone, demanding an active inference on the side of the addressee to understand the speaker. The coding of strategies uses a simplified version of Brown and Levinson's hierarchy

Fig. 3. Snapshot from the SEMMEL corpus. Above the video is displayed, below the annotation board.

distinguishing between seven different approval-oriented, five different autonomy-oriented, and four different off-record strategies. The coding of gestures follows Kipp's approach (see above). Accordingly, two gesture layers are distinguished: the gesture phase layer and the gesture phrase layer.

The aim of this annotation scheme was to derive information about the functional co-occurence of linguistic politeness strategies and gesture use to inform the behavior planning process of an embodied conversational agent (see Sec. 3). A statistical analysis revealed a correlation between gesture types and linguistic politeness strategies. The more indirect the strategy, the more abstract gestures (metaphoric) were used. This correlation is utilized in an overgenerate-and-filter approach to agent behavior selection (see [31] and Sec. 3).

Poggi et al. ([29]; [7]) realize a multimodal score that integrates both signal and functional level information in a single annotation scheme. Apart from the signal type and signal description which specifies the surface features of a movement, the meaning type and meaning description as well as the function of a signal are annotated. The meaning description of a gesture is an interpretation of what can be seen e.g. raising the right hand is interpreted as *just wait, be careful*. To classify the meaning type, a semantic typology is established that distinguishes between content information, information on the speaker's mind, and self presentation (information on the speaker's identity). The function at last represents the information contribution of a signal relative to other modalities. The function of a gesture is given in comparison to the co-expressive speech signal. Five different functions are annotated. Repetition denotes that speech and gesture bear the same meaning, addition is used if additional information is given by the gesture, substitution, if a word is omitted, but its information is given by the gesture, contradiction describes the fact that contradicting information is revealed on the speech and on the gesture channel, and independence indicates that speech and gesture co-occur, but relate to different parts of the communicative plan.

Thus, Poggi et al.'s scheme explicitly codes the relations between different modalities (here exemplified for speech and gesture) on a functional level. This information is employed to model how different modalities are coordinated during the behavior planning process.

The presented list of corpora is necessarily incomplete and was selected to highlight the advantages and challenges of using multimodal corpora. These challenges include on the one hand the question of how to utilize corpus data for the control of non-verbal communicative behavior in virtual agents (or robots). This is dwelled upon in the next section. A second challenge is the question of how to discover what kinds of links exist between modalities (temporal, spatial, functional, semantic/conceptual) and how they are represented. Kipp et al. [22] give an example that this is no trivial problem. They discovered in their data that the often claimed temporal synchronicity between words and co-expressive gesture (e.g. [26]) is not as strict as they thought. Thus, other mechanisms than purely temporal relations seem to be necessary to synchronize these two modalities that are correlated on a conceptual level.

3 Multimodal Corpora for Modeling Human Behavior

To derive implementable models from empirical data, ECA researchers have analyzed various aspects of multimodal human behavior in an annotated corpus, such as the frequency of specific behaviors, the transitions between them, their co-occurrence with other behaviors as well as expressivity parameters, such as fluidity. The approaches may be distinguished by the level of the annotations (signal level versus functional level) from which models are built, the extent to which the context of a multimodal behaviour is taken into account and the employed generation mechanism which may involve a direct or indirect use of the corpus (see Sec. 2).

Some researchers generate ECA behaviors directly from motion capturing data. For instance, Stone and colleagues [33] recorded a human actor that was given a script capturing multimodal behaviors that were anticipated as relevant to the target domain. Multimodal ECA behaviors were then generated by recombining the speech and motion samples from the recorded data. The technique produces more naturalistic behaviors than techniques that synthesize behaviors from scratch. However, the approach requires a mechanism to sequence behaviours in a coherent manner. Furthermore, the question arises of how to cope with situations for which appropriate motion capturing data and speech samples are missing. To allow for variations in the performance of an ECA, data have to be collected for different kinds of situation, personality, emotion etc. The problems may be compared to problems occurring when using a unit selection approach to synthesize speech.

Another approach is to control an agent by high-level expressivity parameters. For instance, the EMOTE system by Chi et al. [11] is based on dance annotation as described by Laban (see Sec. 2). The system is able to modify the execution of a given behavior by changing movement qualities in particular the Laban principles of effort and shape. Pelachaud and colleagues made use of six dimensions of expressivity that were derived from perceptual studies [28] (see Sec. 2.2). The advantage of both methods is that they enable the modulation of action performance at a high level of abstraction. Furthermore, they rely on a small set of parameters that may affect different parts of the body at the same time. The hypothesis behind the approaches is that behaviors that manifest themselves in various channels with consistent expressivity parameter will lead to a more believable agent behavior. Pelachaud and colleagues extract the setting of the expressivity parameters from the corresponding annotations in the corpora. They realized a so-called copy-synthesis approach which replays the annotations in the corpus using an ECA and corresponds to a direct use of a corpus.

Others perform a statistical analysis of human data to derive rules that guide the generation process. For instance, Foster and Oberlander [14] conducted experiments with a majority-choice and a weighted-choice model for the generation of facial displays. In the first case, the facial display that occurred the largest number of times in a given context is chosen. In the latter case, a random choice is made where the choice is weighted according to the relative frequency of facial displays. Context was either defined as non-existing making use of frequencies calculated over the whole corpus, as simple e.g. by considering the words in the sentence or the semantic classes of the words, or extended by taking into account also specific contextual clues like pitch-accent specifications.

Statistical models may be easily combined with an over-generate-and-filter approach as proposed in the BEAT system (e.g. [9]). The basic idea is to annotate text with plausible gestures based on rules that are derived from studies of human-human dialogue. Since it may happen that the initially proposed multimodal behaviors cannot co-occur physically, modifiable filters are then applied to trim the gestures down to a set appropriate for a particular character.

An example of an over-generate-and-filter approach includes the work by Kipp [21] who allow for different degrees of automation in behavior generation. The human author has the possibility to completely pre-author scripts that are annotated with instructions for a gesture generator. In addition, the human author may devise rules that may be used to automatically generate annotated scripts. Finally, machine learning methods are employed to derive further rules. At runtime, all rules that fire are applied to an utterance. After that process, an utterance may contain a lot of non-verbal actions which may not occur simultaneously. The system then applies a filtering approach where manual annotations are preferred over automated ones.

Rehm and André [31] make use of an over-generate-and-filtering approach to enhance natural language utterances with suitable gestures making use of a gesticon and rules derived from the statistical analysis described in Sec. 2.2. In the first step, a probabilistic process selects a gesture type (iconic, metaphoric, etc.) based on the statistical results of the corpus study. For instance, deictic gestures may be given a higher priority than iconic gestures when suggesting non-verbal behaviors for approval-oriented strategies. The enriched natural language utterance is passed on to the animation engine. Since non-verbal behaviors are generated independently of each other, the system may end up with a set of incompatible gestures. The set of proposed gestures is therefore reduced to those gestures that are actually realized by the animation module. The findings of corpus studies may not only inform the generation, but also the filtering of gestures. For instance, iconic gestures may be filtered out with a higher probability than metaphoric gestures when realizing off record strategies.

Another question is to what extent the context in which specific multimodal behaviors occur should be taken into account when generating multimodal behaviors. One extreme would be to simply determine the frequency of multimodal behaviors, such as certain kinds of gesture. In this case, the context would not be considered at all. Instead non-verbal behaviors would be chosen based on the frequency with which they occur in the corpus. A more context-sensitive approach would be to consider the context provided by the words, by the semantic class of words or by the communicative strategy used. Kipp [21] introduces rules based on keyword spotting to annotate utterances with gestures. Rehm and André define rules that are based on the relative frequency of gestures in combination with certain strategies of politeness. Foster [13] discusses a complete representation of context which is not just defined by linguistic features, but that captures all aspects of a multimodal utterance including intonation, facial displays and gestures. Most approaches neglect the temporal context in which multimodal behaviors occur. An exception includes Kipp who proposed an approach relying on bigram estimations in order to derive typical sequences of two-handed and one-handed gestures.

Usually, rules for selecting multimodal behaviors are manually extracted from a corpus. Kipp [21] discusses the use of machine learning techniques to derive rules automatically. Unfortunately, such an approach requires a large amount of data - especially if the context in which a rule may be applied is captured as well. Therefore, Kipp [21] does not rely on recordings of humans, but on manually authored presentations. Unlike most previous work, he does not emulate multimodal human-human communicative behavior, but tries to derive design guidelines of human animators.

Fig. 4. Greta realizing an iconic vs. a metaphoric gesture

4   Evaluation of Corpus-Based Approaches to Generation

The question arises of how to evaluate ECAs whose behaviour is driven by empirical data. One possibility is to investigate to what extent the derived models enable a prediction of human-like behaviours. Such an approach has been used to evaluate the performance of an approach to the data-driven generation of empathetic facial displays by Foster and Oberlander [14]. To compare the performance of the models against the corpus, they employed 10-fold-cross-validation. For each fold, 90% of the data were used to derive a behavior model and 10% of the data were used to validate the models. For each sentence, they measured precision and recall by comparing the predicted facial displays with the actual displays in the corpus and then averaged the scores across the sentence. Their evaluation revealed that majority-choice models resulted into higher precision and recall than weighted-choice models. A similuar evaluation methods was proposed by Kipp who partioned his corpus into a training (60%) and a test test(40%) and measured precision and recall for manual annotations of non-verbal behaviors. Instead of comparing predicted behaviors with actual behaviors, Buisine and colleagues [6] conduct a perceptive evaluation where humans judge to what extent the replayed behaviors by the agent ressemble the original behaviors. In particular, they investigated whether humans are able to detect blends of emotions in an embodied agent.

Of course, a great similarity to human-like behaviors or to pre-authored behaviors does not necessarily mean that the resulting agent is positively perceived by a human observer. To shed light on this question, perception studies are performed which compare how human observers respond to ECAs whose behaviors are informed by an empirical model in comparison to ECAs with randomized multimodal behaviors. Garau and colleagues [16] as well as Lee and colleagues [25] investigate the effect of informed eye gaze models on the perceived quality of communication. Both research teams observed a superiority of informed eye gaze behaviors over randomized eye gaze behaviors. Rehm and André [31] investigated whether a gesturing agent would change the perceived politeness tone compared to that of the textual utterances and whether the subjective rating is influenced by the type of gestures (abstract vs. concrete). They presented subjects with two variants of utterances including criticism: one in which the criticism was accompanied by a gesture of the concrete, and the other one in which the criticism was accompanied by an abstract gesture (see Fig. 4). The subjects then had to rate the perceived tone of politeness. Their studies revealed that the perception of politeness depends on the graphical quality of the employed gestures. In cases where the iconic gesture was rated as being of higher quality than the metaphoric gesture, they observed a positive effect on the perception of the agent's willingness to co-operate. In cases where where the iconic gesture was rated as being of lower quality than the metaphoric gesture, they observed a negative effect on the perception of the agent's willingness to co-operate. That is well designed gestures may strengthen, but badly designed gestures weaken pragmatic effects. The studies by Foster and Oberlander [14] enable a direct comparison of prediction-based evaluation methods and perception-based evaluation methods. Foster and Oberlander investigated how a talking head that was driven by different variants of a generation algorithm was perceived by human observers. They observed that humans seem to prefer behaviors that follow a weighted-choice model over behaviors that follow a majority-choice model. They conclude that humans prefer non-verbal behaviors that reflect more of the variations in the corpus even if the non-verbal behaviors that accompany specific sentences did not correspond to the non-verbal behaviors in the corpus. The results of their studies show that a perception-based evaluation method may indeed lead to different results than a prediction-based evaluation method. Furthermore, they noticed that the users' opions regarding the acceptability of facial displays may vary systematically. In particular, they observed interesting gender-specific differences. All preferences for the weighted-choice models were expressed by the female subjects while the male subjects did not have any preference at all or seem to slightly prefer the majority-choice models.

Besides asking users directly for their impression of the agent, researchers investigated whether an agent that is based on an empirically driven model changes the nature of the interaction. Garau and colleagues [16] found that model-based eye gaze improved the quality of communication when a realistic avatar was used. For cartoonish avatars, no such effect was observed. A study by Nakano and colleagues [27] revealed that an ECA with a grounding mechanism seems to encourage more non-verbal feedback from the user than a system without any grounding mechanism. Sidner and colleagues [32] showed that users are sensitive to a robot's conversational gestures and establish mutual gaze with it even if the set of communicative gesture of the robot is strongly limited.

In contrast to the work above, Rehm and André [30] focus on a direct comparison of human-agent and human-human interaction. The objective of their work was to investigate whether humans behave differently when interacting with an agent as opposed to interacting with another human. As a first step, they focused on gaze behaviors as an important predictor of conversational attention. To this end, they recorded users interacting with a human and a synthetic game partner in a game of dice called Mexicali (see Fig. 5). The scenario allowed

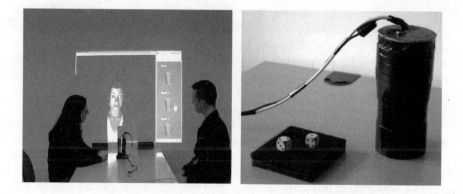

Fig. 5. The Gamble system and the CamCup

them to directly compare gaze behaviors in human-human with gaze behaviors in human-agent interaction. On the one hand, they were able to confirm a number of findings about attentive behaviors in human-human conversation. For instance, their subjects spent more time looking at an individual when listening to it than when talking to it - no matter whether the individual was a human or a synthetic agent. Furthermore, the addressee type (human vs. synthetic) did not have any impact on the duration of the speaker's gaze behaviors towards the addressee. Even though the game was in principle playable without paying any notice to the agent's nonverbal behaviors, the users considered it as worthy of being attended to. While the users' behaviors in the user-as-speaker condition were consistent with findings for human-human conversation, we noticed differences for the user-as addressee condition. People spent more time looking at an agent that is addressing them than at a human speaker. Maintaining gaze for an extended period of time is usually considered as rude and impolite. The fact that humans do not conform to social norms of politeness when addressing an agent seems to indicate that they do not regard the agent as an equal conversational partner, but rather as a (somewhat astonishing) artefact that is able to communicate. This attitude towards the agent was also confirmed by the way the users addressed the agent verbally.

5   Conclusion

Annotated multimodal corpora serve as useful tools for developing embodied conversational agents with a rich repertoire of multimodal communicative behaviors. We have seen how corpora are employed in the study of human behavior with the aim of simulating human communication. Different approaches were presented on how the information derived from such corpora is utilized to control the behavior generation process for an agent. And finally we have exemplified that corpora can even play a role in evaluating human-agent interactions.

Although the use of corpora in the development process of embodied conversational agents has increased significantly, a number of open research issues remain. Standardized schemes are not easy to establish due to the different levels of granularity possible in the annotation process. Despite of new annotation tools, the collection and annotation of corpora is still cumbersome and time-consuming. A great challenge for the future is therefore de-contextualization of multimodal data and their automated adaptation to a new context.

References

1. Abrilian, S., Martin, J.-C., Buisine, S., Devillers, L.: Perception of movement expressivity in emotional tv interviews. In: HUMAINE Summerschool (2006)
2. Allwood, J., Nivre, J., Ahlsén, E.: On the semantics and pragmatics of linguistic feedback. Journal of Semantics 9, 1–26 (1992)
3. Allwood, J., Cerrato, L., Jokinen, K., Navarretta, C., Paggio, P.: The mumin annotation scheme for feedback, turn management and sequencing. In: Gothenburg Papers in Theoretical Linguistics 92: Proceedings from The Second Nordic Conference on Multimodal Communication, pp. 91–109 (2005)
4. Argyle, M., Cook, M.: Gaze and mutual gaze. Cambridge University Press, Cambridge (1976)
5. Brown, P., Levinson, S.C.: Politeness — Some universals in language usage. Cambridge University Press, Cambridge (1987)
6. Pelachaud, C., Martin, J.-C., Niewiadomski, R., Abrilian, S., Devillers, L., Buisine, S.: Perception of Blended Emotions: From Video Corpus to Expressive Agent. In: Gratch, J., Young, M., Aylett, R.S., Ballin, D., Olivier, P. (eds.) IVA 2006. LNCS (LNAI), vol. 4133, pp. 93–106. Springer, Heidelberg (2006)
7. Caldognetto, E.M., Poggi, I., Cosi, P., Cavicchio, F., Merola, G.: Multimodal Score: an ANVIL Based Annotation Scheme for Multimodal Audio-Video Analysis. In: Proceedings of the LREC-Workshop on Multimodal Corpora, pp. 29–33 (2004)
8. Cassell, J.: Body Language: Lessons from the Near-Human. In: Riskin, J. (ed.) The Sistine Gap: History and Philosophy of Artificial Life, University of Chicago Press, Chicago (in press)
9. Cassell, J., Vilhjalmsson, H., Bickmore, T.: BEAT: The Behavior Expression Animation Toolkit. In: Proceedings of SIGGRAPH 2001, Los Angeles, CA, pp. 477–486 (2001)
10. Chafai, N.E., Pelachaud, C., Pelé, D.: Analysis of gesture expressivity modulations from cartoon animations. In: Proceedings of the LREC-Workshop on Multimodal Corpora (2006)
11. Chi, D., Costa, M., Zhao, L., Badler, N.: The EMOTE Model for Effort and Shape. In: Proceedings of SIGGRAPH, pp. 173–182 (2000)
12. Ekman, P., Rosenberg, E. (eds.): What the Face Reveals: Basic & Applied Studies of Spontaneous Expression Using the Facial Action Coding System (FACS). Oxford University Press, Oxford (1998)
13. Foster, M.E.: Issues for corpus-based multimodal generation. In: Proceedings of the Workshop on Multimodal Output Generation (MOG 2007), pp. 51–58 (2007)
14. Foster, M.E., Oberlander, J.: Data-driven generation of emphatic facial displays. In: Proceedings of the 11th Conference of the European Chapter of the Association for Computational Linguistics (EACL), pp. 353–360 (2006)

15. Frey, S., Hirschbrunner, H.P., Florin, A., Daw, W., Crawford, R.A.: A unified approach to the investigation of nonverbal and verbal behavior in communication research. In: Doise, W., Moscovici, S. (eds.) Current Issues in European Social Psychology, pp. 143–199. Cambridge University Press, Cambridge (1983)
16. Garau, M., Slater, M., Vinayagamoorthy, V., Brogn, A., Steed, A., Sasse, M.A.: The Impact of Avatar Realism and Eye Gaze Control on Perceived Quality of Communication in a Shared Immersive Virtual Environment. In: Proceedings of the SIGCHI conference on Human factors in computing systems, pp. 529–536 (2003)
17. Höysniemi, J., Hämäläinen, P.: Describing children's intuitive movements in a perceptive adventure game. In: Martin, J.-C., Os, E.D., Kühnlein, P., Boves, L., Paggio, P., Catizone, R. (eds.) Multimodal Corpora: Models Of Human Behaviour For The Specification And Evaluation Of Multimodal Input And Output Interfaces, pp. 21–24 (2004)
18. Karpouzis, K., Raouzaiou, A., Drosopoulos, A., Ioannou, S., Balomenos, T., Tsapatsoulis, N., Kollias, S.: Facial expression and gesture analysis for emotionally-rich man-machine interaction. In: Sarris, N., Strintzis, M. (eds.) 3D Modeling and Animation: Synthesis and Analysis Techniques, pp. 175–200. Idea Group, USA (2004)
19. Kendon, A.: Some functions of gaze direction in social interaction. Acta Psychologica 32, 1–25 (1967)
20. Kendon, A.: Gesture — Visible Action as Utterance. Cambridge University Press, Cambridge (2004)
21. Kipp, M.: Creativity meets Automation: Combining Nonverbal Action Authoring with Rules and Machine Learning. In: Gratch, J., et al. (eds.) IVA 2006. LNCS (LNAI), vol. 4133, pp. 230–242. Springer, Heidelberg (2006)
22. Kipp, M., Neff, M., Albrecht, I.: An annotation scheme for conversational gestures: How to economically capture timing and form. In: Proceedings of the LREC-Workshop on Multimodal Corpora, pp. 24–27 (2006)
23. Knudsen, M.W., Martin, J.-C., Dybkjr, L., Ayuso, M.J.M., Bernsen, N.O., Carletta, J., Heid, U., Kita, S., Llisterri, J., Pelachaud, C., Poggi, I., Reithinger, N., van Elswijk, G., Wittenburg, P.: ISLE Natural Interactivity and Multimodality Working Group Deliverable D9.1: Survey of Multimodal Coding Schemes and Best Practice (2002), URL(07.02.07): http://isle.nis.sdu.dk/reports/wp9/D9.1-7.3.2002-F.pdf
24. Lamb, W., Watson, E.: Body Code: The Meaning in Movement. Routledge & Kegan Paul, London (1979)
25. Lee, S.P., Badler, J.B., Badler, N.I.: Eyes alive. In: Proceedings of the 29th annual conference on Computer graphics and interactive techniques, pp. 637–644 (2002)
26. McNeill, D.: Hand and Mind — What Gestures Reveal about Thought. The University of Chicago Press, Chicago, London (1992)
27. Nakano, Y.I., Reinstein, G., Stocky, T., Cassell, J.: Towards a Model of Face-to-face Grounding. In: Proceedings of the Association for Computational Linguistics, Sapporo, Japan, July 1–12, pp. 553–561 (2003)
28. Pelachaud, C.: Multimodal expressive embodied conversational agents. In: Proceedings of ACM Multimedia, pp. 683–689 (2005)
29. Poggi, I., Pelachaud, C., Magno Caldognetto, E.: Gestural Mind Markers in ECAs. In: Gesture-Based Communication in Human-Computer Interaction, pp. 338–349. Springer, Heidelberg (2004)
30. André, E., Rehm, M.: Where Do They Look? Gaze Behaviors of Multiple Users Interacting with an Embodied Conversational Agent. In: Panayiotopoulos, T., Gratch, J., Aylett, R.S., Ballin, D., Olivier, P., Rist, T. (eds.) IVA 2005. LNCS (LNAI), vol. 3661, pp. 241–252. Springer, Heidelberg (2005)

31. Rehm, M., André, E.: Informing the design of agents by corpus analysis. In: Nishida, T., Nakano, Y. (eds.) Conversational Informatics, John Wiley & Sons, Chichester (2007)
32. Sidner, C.L., Lee, C., Kidd, C., Lesh, N., Rich, C.: Explorations in engagement for humans and robots. Artificial Intelligence 166(1–2), 140–164 (2005)
33. Stone, M., DeCarlo, D., Oh, I., Rodriguez, C., Stere, A., Lees, A., Bregler, C.: Speaking with Hands: Creating Animated Conversational Characters from Recordings of Human Performance. ACM Transactions on Graphics 23(3), 506–513 (2004)
34. Tsapatsoulis, N., Raouzaiou, A., Kollias, S., Cowie, R., Douglas-Cowie, E.: Emotion Recognition and Synthesis based on MPEG-4 FAPs. In: Pandzic, I., Forchheimer, R. (eds.) MPEG-4 Facial Animation, pp. 141–167. John Wiley & Sons, Chichester (2002)
35. Walker, M.A., Cahn, J.E., Whittaker, S.J.: Improvising Linguistic Style: Social and Affective Bases for Agent Personality. In: Proceedings of AAMAS 1997, pp. 96–105 (1997)

Appendix: Where to Find Multimodal Corpora

Some of the corpora mentioned in this article can be accessed by interested researchers. The specifics concerning data protection and access regularities vary from corpus to corpus. A good starting point to search for available multimodal corpora is the website of the Humaine Association (former Humaine Network of Excellence): http://emotion-research.net/wiki/Databases. Mostly linguistic corpora are available from the European Language Resources Association (ELRA, http://catalog.elra.info/) or from the Lingustic Data Consortium (LDC, http://www.ldc.upenn.edu/).

At last, we would like to mention explicitly three exemplary corpora. The AMI corpus contains around 100 hours of multiparty meeting interactions and is freely accessible (http://corpus.amiproject.org/). The Smartkom corpus is a German corpus of a Wizard of Oz experiment on human-computer interactions in an information kiosk scenario. There is a service charge for accessing this corpus (http://www.bas.uni-muenchen.de/Bas/BasSmartKomHomeeng.html). The CUBE-G corpus contains around 20 hours of culture-specific interactions from Germany and Japan in three standardized scenarios (first meeting, negotiation, status difference). Information on this corpus can be found under http://mm-werkstatt.informatik.uni-augsburg.de/projects/cube-g/.

Modeling Embodied Feedback with Virtual Humans

Stefan Kopp[1], Jens Allwood[2], Karl Grammer[3],
Elisabeth Ahlsen[2], and Thorsten Stocksmeier[1]

[1] A.I. Group, Bielefeld University, P.O. Box 100131, D-33501 Bielefeld, Germany
{skopp,tstocksm}@techfak.uni-bielefeld.de
[2] Dep. of Linguistics, Göteborg University, Box 200, SE-40530 Göteborg, Sweden
{jens.allwood,elisabeth.ahlsen}@ling.gu.se
[3] Ludwig Boltzmann Inst. for Urban Ethology, 1090 Vienna, Austria
karl.gramer@univie.ac.at

Abstract. In natural communication, both speakers and listeners are active most of the time. While a speaker contributes new information, a listener gives feedback by producing unobtrusive (usually short) vocal or non-vocal bodily expressions to indicate whether he/she is able and willing to communicate, perceive, and understand the information, and what emotions and attitudes are triggered by this information. The simulation of feedback behavior for artificial conversational agents poses big challenges such as the concurrent and integrated perception and production of multi-modal and multi-functional expressions. We present an approach on modeling feedback for and with virtual humans, based on an approach to study "embodied feedback" as a special case of a more general theoretical account of embodied communication. A realization of this approach with the virtual human *Max* is described and results are presented.

Keywords: Feedback, Virtual Humans, Embodied Conversational Agent.

1 Introduction

In communication two or more interlocutors change turns to contribute information that is new to the other. This process is not a ping-pong of turns with one interlocutor contributing information and the other passively receiving it. Rather, information is simultaneously and continuously shared between speaker and listener; whenever we listen to somebody in an interaction, we produce expressions like "hmmm", "yes" or "mh" to give feedback on whether the information contributed by the speaker is really shared. Such feedback is essential for communication. Without it a human dialog quickly breaks down [31] and simply by giving it properly one can create the illusion of a dialog partner listening.

Originally the term "feedback" stems from the cybernetic notion by Wiener [30] and describes "processes by which a control unit gets information about the effects and consequences of its actions". Since feedback words are often produced during the speaker's contribution, Yngve [31] has introduced the term "back-channel" to emphasize this permanent bi-directionality of human communication. Other terms and

I. Wachsmuth and G. Knoblich (Eds.): Modeling Communication, LNAI 4930, pp. 18–37, 2008.

definitions that have been put forth for different nuances of feedback are "listener responses", "acknowledgers", "response words", "conversational grunts" or "roger function" (e.g., [1,28]). A comparative classification of feedback is difficult because analyzing its semantic/pragmatic content is fairly complex and involves several different dimensions: a "yes" can mean agreement as well as indifference, a "no" may signal surprised agreement one time and disagreement the other time. For the German "hm" feedback, Ehlich [9] counts nine different meanings in a transcribed dialog. Obviously, linguistic feedback involves a high degree of context dependence with regard to features of the preceding communicative act, such as the type of speech act (mood), its factual polarity, information status, or evocative function (cf. [2]). Often it directly responds to cues that speakers emit in order to clarify the dialog status, e.g. by gazing at the listener or by producing certain prosodic features [27,20].

Allwood et al. [2] assume that feedback is a central functional subsystem of human communication. It consists of those methods that allow for providing, in unobtrusive ways and without interrupting or breaking dialog rules, information about the most basic communicative functions in face-to-face dialogue. In detail, feedback consists of unobtrusive (usually short) expressions whereby a recipient of information informs the contributor about her/his ability and willingness to communicative (have *contact*), to *perceive* the information, and to *understand* the information [2]. That is, feedback serves as an early warning system to signal how speech perception or understanding is succeeding. A feedback utterance at the right time can communicate to the speaker that she should, e.g., repeat the previous utterance and speak more clearly, or use words that are easier to understand. A further possible function of feedback is to communicate whether the recipient is *accepting* the main evocative intention about the contribution, i.e. can a statement be believed, a question be answered, or a request complied with. Furthermore, feedback can indicate the emotions and attitudes triggered by the information in the recipient.

Clearly, the essential role of feedback in natural communication makes it a crucial issue in the development of artificial conversational agents. However, the conception and implementation of computational simulations of natural communicative feedback so far remained a tough, but also very timely modeling challenge, for the high degree of interactivity and responsiveness needed requires the realization of concurrent, incremental processes of perception and production of multimodal, multi-functional expressions. In this paper, we start with a review of the techniques that have been previously employed to enable feedback for virtual or robotic agents. We then propose a more general approach to "embodied feedback" that considers feedback a special case of a more general theoretical account of embodied communication. Based on this, we present a computational model of an embodied feedback system with the conversational virtual human *Max*, and we give examples of communicative feedback behaviors that become possible this way.

2   Previous Approaches to Modeling Feedback

Almost every existing conversational agent system has, implicitly or explicitly, modeled aspects of communicative feedback. Much work has been directed to the presentation of emotional feedback, usually given though continuously adapted facial expressions of the agent that often are combined with prosodic cues. Such feedback can either express the agent's own emotional state, and how it changes over the course of dialogue [4], or it can be used to intentionally convey affective states like commiseration. In the Greta character [17], thematic and rhematic parts of a communicative act are assigned an affective state, yielding performative facial expressions that are drawn from large lexicons of codified behavior. Heylen et al. [12] utilize affective feedback to support learning effects with the tutoring system INES, taking into account elements of the student's character, the harmfulness of errors made, and the emotional effects of errors. AutoTutor [10] is another example of a so-called pedagogical agent that deliberately employs positive ("Great!"), neutral ("Umm"), or negative feedback ("Wrong") to enhance learning by the student. Feedback is modeled as a special kind of dialogue moves that lead from one knowledge goal state (e.g., get the student to articulate the expectation under focus) or dialogue state (e.g., the student just expressed an assertion as her first turn in answering the question) to another, and that are triggered by fuzzy production rules.

Earlier systems have already acknowledged feedback as integral part of communicative behavior, stressing its importance e.g. for managing the flow of conversation. The Gandalf system [23] employs pause duration models to generate agent feedback, i.e. verbal back-channel utterances or head nods were given after a silent pause of a certain duration (110ms) in the speaker's utterance. Gandalf simulated turn-taking behavior by looking away from the listener while speaking, returning his gaze when finishing the turn. The REA system [7] also used a pause duration model and employed different modalities for feedback (head nods, short feedback utterances): when the dialog partner has finished a turn, she nodded; if she did not understand what was said to her, she raised the eyebrows and asked a repair question. Like Gandalf, Rea looked away at the beginning of her turn and returned the gaze to the listener when a turn change is intended. BodyChat [24] was a system that demonstrates the automation of communicative behaviors in avatars for users that communicate via text. Their avatars automatically animate attention, salutation, turn-taking, back-channel feedback and facial expression, as well as simple body functions such as the blinking of the eyes. Feedback behavior selection was boiled down to rules such as "RequestFeedback by Looking or RaiseEyebrows", "GiveFeedback by Looking and HeadNod". Beun & van Eijk [5] propose a model to generate elementary feedback sequences at the knowledge level of dialogue participants. Based on an explicit model of the mental states of the dialogue partners, they state dialogue rules to enable a computer system to generate corrective feedback sequences when a user and a computer system have different conceptualizations of a particular discourse domain.

In the last few years, several systems tried to improve on *predicting* the right time for feedback. Ward and Tsukahara [29], noticing that feedback is often interlaced into pauses between two words or phrases of the speaker, describe a pause-duration model that also incorporates prosodic cues based on the best fit to a speech corpus. It can be stated in a rule-based fashion: After a relatively low pitch for at least 110ms, following at least 700ms of speech, and given that you have not output back-channel feedback within the preceding 800ms, wait another 700ms and then produce back-channel feedback. Takeuchi et al. [22] augment this approach with incrementally obtained information about word classes. Fujie et al. [10], in addition to analyzing prosody information to extract proper feedback timing, employ a network of finite state transducers, including one that maps recognized words onto content for possible feedback before the end of the utterance. Their model is implemented in the conversational robot ROBISUKE that also uses short head nods for feedback.

The effects of modeled feedback behaviors have been tested in evaluation studies from early on. In experiments with the Gandalf agent, the presentation of content-related feedback (successful question answering or command execution) together with so-called envelope feedback such as gaze and head movement for turn-taking/-giving or co-verbal beat gestures were found to lead to smoother interactions with fewer user repetitions and hesitations. Additionally, the language capability of the system, though being identical to the other conditions, was rated higher [6]. Other evaluation studies showed that the commonly used models are able to predict feedback only to a limited extent. Cathcart et al. [8] evaluated three different approaches: (1) the baseline model simply inserts a feedback utterance every n words and achieves a accuracy of only 6% (n=7); (2) the pause duration model gives feedback after silent pauses of a certain length, often combined with part-of-speech information, and achieves 32% accuracy; (3) integrating both methods increased accuracy to 35%.

Gratch et al. [11] describe a recent experiment on multimodal, yet purely nonverbal agent feedback and its effects on the establishment of rapport. Their "Rapport Agent" was built to elicit rapport while listening and giving feedback to a human who is telling a previously watched cartoon sequence. This system analyzes the speaker's head moves and body posture through a camera and implements the pitch cue algorithm of [29] to determine the right moment for giving feedback by head nods, head shakes, head rolls and gaze. Compared to random head moves and posture shifts the system seems to elicit an increased feeling of rapport in the human dialog partners: subjects used significantly more words and told longer recaps with the Rapport Agent. Further, subjects' self-report evaluation showed higher ratings of the agent's understanding of the story and a stronger feeling of having made use of the agent's feedback. One caveat, though, is that random feedback is obviously a very low baseline for it will constantly create situations of odd and disturbing agent behavior (although, remarkably, about one quarter of subjects in the random condition felt they were given useful feedback). Correspondingly, subjects were equally likely to find the rapport-inducing avatar more helpful (40%) or more disturbing (another 40%) than the random feedback (where most subjects judged they were "not sure").

In summary, with the exception of the systems originating from Gandalf, previous modeling attempts have mainly relied on rules that state on a behavioral level how to map speaker events onto feedback reactions by the system, and evaluation studies have revealed shortcomings of this approach. We propose that embodied feedback must also be conceptualized and structured in terms of more abstract functional notions, which can be meaningfully tied to events occurring within a listener as she actively attempts to perceive, understand, and respond to a speaker's contribution.

3   Framing Embodied Feedback

As part of the research year on "Embodied Communication" at the Center for Interdisciplinary Research [25], we embarked on a more comprehensive feedback model based upon a general theoretical account of embodied communication. This approach emphasizes that communication is a highly dynamical, co-constructive, multimodal, and multi-level process, taking place between two interlocutors with similar embodiments. It is this embodiment that allows agents to be expressive in many different ways and on different levels of speed, awareness, or intentionality. Further, their congruent embodiments enable them to ground perception and understanding of physical expressions of the other in own bodily experiences. Feedback as an aspect of human communication shares all these characteristics.

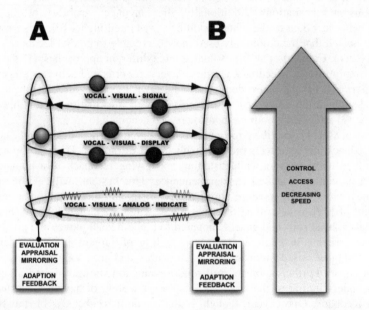

Fig. 1. General outline of the embodied feedback model. While speaker **A** is contributing information, employing multimodal behaviors at different levels of speed, awareness, or communicative intentionality, listener **B** is responding with multiple, simultaneous feedback expressions at the same levels (see text for explanations).

Figure 1 illustrates our overall view on embodied feedback as it can takes place between two communicators, A and B. Vocal as well as visual expressions can run in both directions on different concurrent levels of communication (thus subsuming the classical notion of backchannels). Both, speaker and listener employ these levels and thereby operate upon different time scale as well as with different degrees of communicative intentionality and awareness. In order to frame our account of embodied feedback more concretely we start with considering the dimensions that can be applied in order to characterize and distinguish the various expressions involved. We consider the following to be most relevant in this context.

Types of expression or modality
Feedback is obviously more than just a verbal phenomenon. Listeners employ non-verbal means like posture, facial expression, gaze, gesture, posture or prosody to give feedback, often in combination with verbal backchannels. For example, prosodic and

temporal features carry information about how successfully the recipient has integrated the information into her existing body of knowledge [9], head nods and jerks frequently accompany and can even change the function of verbal feedback [13].

Types of function/content of the expressions
Every expression, considered as a behavioral feedback unit, has two functional sides. On the one hand it can evoke reactions from the interlocutor, on the other hand it can respond to evocative aspects of a previous contribution. Note that responding to evocative aspects does *not* mean that the listener only produces feedback in direct reaction to explicit cues by the speaker. Instead, we stress here that feedback is not purely reflexive but is often also triggered by some internal state changes of the listener. Nevertheless, these state changes are caused by, and thus responsive to, the contribution of the speaker. In this sense giving feedback is mainly responsive, while eliciting feedback is mainly evocative. Each feedback behavior may thereby serve the four basic responsive feedback functions described above [2]: contact (C), perception (P), understanding (U), and acceptance/ agreement (A). In addition, further emotional or attitudinal information (E) may be expressed concurrently, e.g. by an enthusiastic prosody and a friendly smile, or by affect bursts like a sigh, a yawn or a "wow" [18].

Degrees of intentional control and awareness
In communication, agents are causally influencing each other. Such causal influence might to some extent be innately given and function independently of awareness and intentional control of the sender, e.g. when blushing. Other types of causal influence are learned and then automatized, i.e. with less intentional control but still potentially amenable to it (e.g. smiles or emotional prosody). Still other forms of influence are correlated with higher degrees of awareness and/or intentional control. Consequently, we assume that feedback information concerning the basic functions (C, P, U, A, E) can also be given on many levels of communicative intentionality. In order to simplify matters, we distinguish three levels from the point of view of the sender [1]: (i) *Indicated* information is information that the sender is not aware of, or intending to convey, but is seen as an indexical (i.e., causal) sign. (ii) *Displayed* information is intended to be "showed". (iii) *Signaled* information is intended to be recognized by the recipient as being displayed. In this respect, feedback can range from explicit signals to implicit, unintentional indicators of how information processing is unfolding, where we regard linguistic feedback as being signals by convention.

Types of reception
We assume that feedback results from a two-stage process of appraisal and evaluation of information in the receiver: First, an unconscious "appraisal" is tied to the occurrence of perception, emotions and other primary bodily reactions. If perception and emotion is connected to further processing involving meaningful connections to memory, then understanding, empathy and other cognitive attitudes, like surprise or hope, may arise. Secondly, this stage can lead to a more aware "evaluation" concerning the evocative functions (C, P, U) of the preceding contribution and especially its main evocative function (A), which can be accepted, rejected or met with some form of intermediary reaction (e.g. modal words like *perhaps, maybe*). We use the term "reactive" when the behavior is more automatic and linked to earlier stages of receptive processing, and the term "response" when the behavior is more aware and linked to later stages.

Degree of continuity
Feedback information can be expressed in analog ways, such as prosodic patterns in speech, continuous body movements and facial expressions, which evolve over stretches of interaction. It may also be more digital and discrete, such as feedback words, word repetitions or head nods and shakes. Normally, analog and digital expressions are used in combination.

4   A Computational Model of Embodied Feedback

The previously described theoretical account indicates what aspects a computational model needs to address and to integrate in order to be able to achieve simulation of natural feedback. Previous approaches, as discussed in Sect. 2, tend to focus on the mechanistic aspect of feedback in that it is solely reflexive to the behavior of the speaker. This notion has been proven successful to keep a conversation going, and thus may suffice for a pure story-listening system. But it is clearly insufficient for a truly conversational agent that is to hold up its end of a dialogue and to respond in a reasonable way to a statement made or a questions asked by its human user. The feedback of such an agent should reflect in a faithful and immediate manner its internal state, as it will come to bear in its next utterance anyway, thus being able to serve as an early warning system. We argue that the more abstract functional notions described above can help to conceptualize feedback behaviors and their potential causes in order to facilitate its modeling within a communicative agent.

In this section, we present such a computational modeling attempt for the virtual human *Max*. We first describe the Max system and the most relevant features of its general architecture as well as its dialog model (see [15] for more detailed explanations). We then devise a multimodal feedback system (for German) along the lines of our theoretical framework, and we present an approach to computationally model it for simulating embodied feedback with Max.

4.1   The Virtual Human Max

Max is a virtual human under development at the A.I. Group at Bielefeld University. The system used here has been applied as an information kiosk in the Heinz-Nixdorf-MuseumsForum (HNF) since January 2004. HNF is a public computer museum in Paderborn (Germany), where Max engages visitors in face-to-face small-talk conversations and provides them with information about the museum, the exhibition, and other topics (on average, about 30 conversations a day). Visitors enter typed natural language input to the system using a keyboard, whereas Max responds with synthetic German speech along with nonverbal behaviors like manual gestures, facial expressions, gaze, or locomotion [15].

Max is designed as a general cognitive agent, based on an architecture that runs perception, action, and deliberative reasoning in parallel and connected on multiple levels. All processes, whatever level in the architecture they belong to, can exchange information either via multi-agent message passing or via a direct routing of data along connections between input/output fields.

Perception and action are connected through a reactive component in which numerous behaviors run continuously, concurrently, and under varying influence by cognitively higher levels. Such behaviors implement reactive loops like gaze tracking the current interlocutor or secondary behavior like eye blink and breathing. A behavior realization component, being part of the action layer of the architecture, is in charge of realizing requests from other components and fusing them into coherent agent behavior. This includes the step-wise realization and blending of chunks of multimodal utterance, for which it combines the synthesis of prosodic speech and the procedural animation of emotional facial expressions, lip-sync speech, and co-verbal gestures, with the scheduling and synchronous execution of the implied verbal and nonverbal behaviors [14].

Reasoning and deliberative processing take place in a cognition component that determines when and how the agent acts. This decision making is driven by both the internal goals and intentions the system is having, and the incoming events which, in turn, may originate either externally (user input, persons that have newly entered or left the agents visual field) or internally (changing emotions, assertion of a new goal etc.). It is carried out by a BDI interpreter, which continuously pursues multiple, possibly nested plans (*intentions*) to achieve goals (*desires*) in the context of up-to-date knowledge about the world (*beliefs*). It draws on a dynamic knowledge base that comprises the agent's currents beliefs, goals and intentions, a model of the ongoing discourse and a model with basic facts about the current interlocutor.

All capabilities of dialogue management, language interpretation and behavior selection are represented as plans: so-called skeleton plans constitute the agent's general dialogue skills like negotiating initiative or structuring a presentation. These plans are domain-independent. They are adjoined by a larger number of plans that basically implement condition-action rules. These rule plans are used to define both the broad conversation knowledge of Max (e.g., the dialogue goals that can be pursued, possible interpretations of input, small talk answers) as well as his more detailed knowledge about specific presentation contents or general world knowledge. Such condition-action rules test either user input or the dynamic memories (beliefs); their actions can alter dynamic knowledge structures, raise internal goals and thus invoke corresponding further planning, or trigger the generation of an utterance. The latter happens by choosing a template of a communicative act (words plus conversational function), refining its performative aspects with further semantic-pragmatic information, and marking up the focused words. The action layer of Max comprises a behavior planning that selects further nonverbal behaviors (body gestures, head gestures, facial expressions) based on the conversational function.

Using these rule plans, the deliberative component interprets an incoming event, decides how to react depending on current context, and produces an appropriate response. Thanks to its general capabilities of pursuing and managing plans, Max is thereby able to conduct longer, coherent dialogues and to act proactively, e.g. to take over the initiative, instead of being purely reactive as classical chatterbots are. In its current state, Max employs roughly 900 skeleton plans and about 1.200 rule plans of conversational and presentational knowledge; see [15] for concrete examples.

Finally, Max is also equipped with an emotion system [4] that continuously runs a dynamic simulation to model the agent's emotional state, which is then transmitted within the architecture. That way, the current emotional state continuously modulates subtle aspects of the agent's behavior such as pitch, speech rate, and variation width of the voice, or the rate of breathing and eye blink. The current emotion category (e.g. happy, angry, sad, etc.) is mapped onto Max's facial expression, and it is sent to the deliberative component where a belief is formed about every significant emotional state. That is, Max becomes aware of his current emotional state and can include it in further deliberations. The emotion system, in turn, receives input both from the perception and the deliberative component. For example, seeing a person or achieving a goal triggers a weighted positive stimulus, while detecting obscene or politically incorrect wordings in the user input lead to negative impulses on Max's emotional system.

4.2 A Feedback System for Max

As with the generation of general conversational behavior, feedback requires a prescriptive model that predicts *which* vocal or non-vocal expressions are suitable and *when*, by formulating conditions upon the selection and triggering of the single feedback behaviors. As we have noted earlier, this model must cover both the more reflexive functions of feedback, when listeners on different levels of awareness react to cues produced by the speaker, and the more declarative functions of feedback, when listener by themselves inform about the success or failure of their evaluation/appraisal of what a speaker is contributing. Based on the theoretical model that captures and refines both kinds of functions, we define the potential sources (or causes) of feedback by Max as follows:

- ± Contact (C): always positive, unless the visitor or Max leaves the scene
- ± Perception (P): positive as long as the words typed in by the user are known to the system. This evaluation must run incrementally in a word-by-word fashion, while the user is typing in.
- ± Understanding (U): positive if the user input can be successfully interpreted, i.e. Max can derive a conversational function by having found an interpretation rule that fires under current context condition. This evaluation should, also, run incrementally word-by-word whilst the user is typing in.
- ± Acceptance (A): the main evocative intention of the user input must be evaluated as to whether it complies with the agent's current beliefs (convictions), desires, or intentions.
- Emotion and attitude (E): the emotional reaction of the agent is caused by positive/negative impulses that are sent to the emotion system upon detection of specific events as described above, e.g. when appraising the politeness or offensiveness of user input. All C, P, U evaluations can be fused into an assessment of the (un-)certainty of the agent about the current locution.

What behavior repertoire is needed to fulfill each of these functions in the positive or negative case? Based on the results of an analysis of the most frequent words in spoken German, we conceive of a basic feedback system for Max to encompass the following verbal-vocal expressions (English translation in parentheses): "Ja" (yes), "mhm", "nn", "genau" (exactly), "nein" (no), "ne" (no), "doch" (however, still), "und?" (and?), "was?" (what?), "wie bitte?" (pardon?), "ich weiß nicht" (I don't know), "ich verstehe nicht" (I don't understand), "was meinst du?" (what do you mean?). These expressions can be combined with each other and/or can be repeated (self-repetition). Likewise, they can be combined with a repetition of the speaker's contribution (other-repetitions) or a reformulation of it.

Often overlooked, vocal backchannel expressions like "mhm" or "nn" must be generated with appropriate prosodic cues, which contribute decisively to the conveyance of the main feedback function as well as attitudinal or emotional coloring. Recent studies [21,26] demonstrate that the interpretation of a backchannel significantly changes, e.g., with the position of the peak, with interaction effects of the combination with pitch and duration. However, only few prosodic backchannels receive unambiguous interpretations, underlining the importance of discourse context and the accompanying non-vocal expressions. The most important embodied feedback expressions are head nod, shake, head tilt, and head protrusion, each with different numbers of repetitions and different movement qualities. Further, the agent should have facial display of emotions as well as epistemic attitudes like surprise or (un-)certainty (e.g. frown), showing up immediately as they arise when interpreting an ongoing contribution. Finally, gaze as basic turn-taking and grounding cue [16] and emblematic manual gestures like shrug are to be incorporated. In the next section we will present an approach to endowing Max with the ability to employ some of these nonverbal behaviors along with the abovementioned vocal backchannels for giving appropriate feedback at appropriate places.

4.3 Architecture and Realization

A conversational agent with feedback capability is expected not only to deliver correct backchannels, but also to show them at the right places and times during the speaker contribution. In a linguistic context delays can have the potential to modulate the meaning of the following utterance—especially in the case of feedback expressions that are supposed to immediately provide information on, e.g, the intelligibility or acceptability of a speaker statement. As a consequence it is absolutely vital for an implemented feedback model to cut latencies to the minimum and to avoid giving feedback at the wrong moments in conversation. We follow Thórisson [23] in that correct and relevant feedback generation in human-like agents should result from a correct and *incremental* functional analysis of a multimodal action, as long as generated behaviors are executed at the time they are relevant. The model that we present here thus strives to simulate and integrate the mechanisms of appraisal and evaluation distinguished in Sect. 3, operating on different time scales and levels of awareness or automaticity. These processes can all feed into reaction response dispositions and then trigger the aforementioned agent feedback behaviors.

Figure 2 shows an overview of the proposed model of embodied feedback and how it is interweaved with Max's general architectural set-up. The model comprises four general stages for detecting, processing, planning, and producing multimodal feedback behavior, connected on two layers. The planning layer consists of dedicated processes that are running to keep track of the contact, perception, and understanding listener states of the agent and, based on this information, decide which feedback behavior to generate and when. Input processing continuously updates the listener states and sends important events directly to a feedback planner. For example, if the gaze has moved and the speaker now directly looks at the listener (Max), this may be a hint that feedback is expected. Results of feedback planning are abstract requests for expressions of different functions. A generation module maps them along with information about the current listener states onto specifications of suitable multimodal behaviors that are then realized by a set of modality-specific generators.

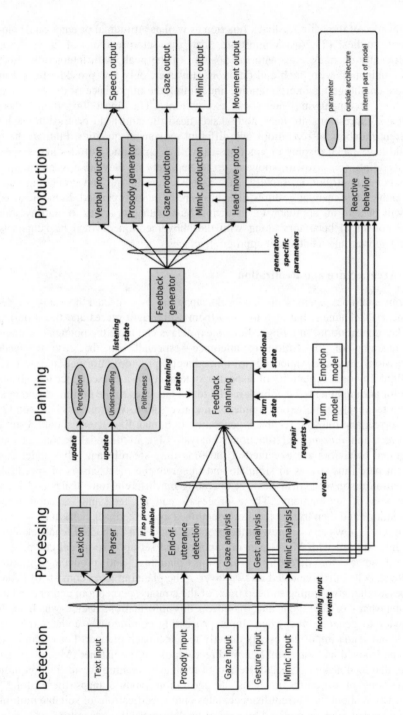

Fig. 2. Overview of the system architecture for generating embodied feedback. All Processing and Planning modules operate incrementally upon incoming user input.

Our current implementation comprises explicit numerical parameters to quantify the agent's listener state in terms of contact, perception, and understanding evaluations. Perception has continuous values between one (1.0) for excellent, flawless perception of the received verbal events and zero (0.0) for completely incomprehensible input. Understanding has values between one (1.0) for complete understanding of the incoming utterances in the phrasal context and zero (0.0) for an unintelligible input. With each new user input, both variables start with the value 1.0. Importantly, perception and understanding are unidirectionally linked such that a lowering of perception will always result in a lowering of understanding, but not vice versa as it is sometimes possible to infer the meaning of an only partly perceived contribution from context (thus having high understanding with low perception).

The emotional state of Max is directly affected by appraisal of the user input, when an interpretation rule determines a praising or an insulting phrase (not included in Figure 2 for sake of clarity). Being simulated independent, the emotional state influences the planning of feedback behaviors, and it directly triggers behavioral outlets of emotions. For instance, emotional appraisal can asynchronously send impulses to the emotion system, which runs a continuous dynamic simulation and affects the facial expression of Max several times a second. To this end, and as nowadays common in agent architectures, the planning layer is augmented with a reactive layer of feedback generation. This layer is constituted by direct connections from the input processing units to the production units, as provided by Max's architectural framework. This pathway allows for incorporating feedback behaviors that function independently of awareness and intentional control of the sender, e.g. blushing, as well as behaviors that are only potentially amenable to awareness and control, like smiles or emotional prosody. In addition, the planner delegates control of behaviors with a longer duration (e.g. raising the eyebrows as long as input is not understood) to this layer. Behaviors using this path support the rest of the generated feedback instead of replacing it.

Input processing

In order to produce intra-phrasal feedback, incoming events must be evaluated as soon as possible and in an incremental fashion. Since we are dealing with typed language input, single words are the minimal unit of verbal input processing. Two modules, the lexicon and the parser accomplish verbal processing. The "Lexicon" processes every newly entered word by, first, trying to determine its word class (adjective, noun etc.) using part-of-speech tagging [19]. A possibly required process step is stemming, removal of morphological inflection, of the text events whose sophistication varies with the language used. Second, a lexicon lookup is done for the resulting lemma. If the lookup fails, perception (and, consequently, understanding) is lowered by a constant amount. This amount is bigger for a content word than for a function word, i.e. not having perceived correctly a noun is worse than having missed an article. Note that if the word could be found, the perception parameter is not increased again but stays at the same level (initially 1.0).

The "Parser" component is a means of directly controlling the understanding parameter. Ideally, it would evaluate incoming words for their potential fit into the currently constructed syntactic-semantic structure. In the current state of the system, this is implemented by probing the applicability of interpretation rules after each newly entered word. That is, it is checked with the dialog engine whether the currently available input is interpretable by the system under the current context conditions (represented by Max's beliefs). For example, the input "24 yeers" would normally result in low perception and understanding values as the word "yeers" is unknown. However, if the system has asked the user about her age just before, the detection of numeric input will result in an interpretation that the user is informing the agent about her age. If a conversational function could be determined, as in this case, understanding is generally increased.

One of the most important aspects when it comes to determining the right moment for giving feedback is end-of-utterance (EOU) detection. Purely textual input as Max uses it at the moment can be considered an impoverished input for EOU detection, which usually draws on prosodic information. An implementation must thus try to gain as much information as possible from the words flowing into the system. As feedback often occurs on phrase boundaries, a possible way would be to use an incremental parser that can signal the upcoming probable completion of a phrase. Currently, end of utterances are simply signaled by enter-pressed events. In addition, appropriate places for feedback are found using the part-of-speech tags supplied by the lexicon. Feedback after e.g. articles is very improbable, while feedback after content words like nouns or verbs is more appropriate. Processing of user prosody, gaze, gesture or facial expression are mapped out but currently not implemented. That is, Max currently gives feedback solely based on verbal input.

Table 1. Rules for the event-based generation of perception and understanding feedback

Perception		
After NPs	Match in Lexicon	"mhm", slight nod, silent prosody
After pauses		"mhm", slight nod
After contribution	Match in lexicon	"mhm", nod
	No match in lexicon	"was?", "wie bitte?", repetition of unknown word
	No match for 2nd time after negative perception FB	"mhm", nod
Understanding		
After pauses	Match in lexicon and matching interpretation rule(s)	"mhm", "ja", "ich verstehe", slight head nod, word repetition
After contribution or pauses	Match in lexicon and matching interpretation rule(s)	"mhm", "ja", "ich verstehe", head nod, word repetition
After contribution or pauses	No matching interpretation rule	"was meinst du damit?", puzzled look
	Word not in lexicon and no matching interpretation rule	"Was?", "wie bitte?", "ich habe nicht verstanden", "ich verstehe nicht", puzzled look, other word repetition

Feedback planning

The feedback planner controls the production of multimodal feedback and is only active while the agent is in the listening state as well as in turn-transition phases (indicated by the turn state). Feedback planning reacts to events from input analysis as well as to significant changes in the listener state variables. Generally, thus, the simulation of communicative feedback calls for a combination of an event-based model with a "reservoir" model. The former can be modeled following a rule-based approach that explicitly states contextual or conventionalized conditions for a specific feedback behavior. The latter must couple the generation of feedback behaviors to how perception and understanding is gradually decreasing. We adopt a probabilistic approach that can capture these not so clear-cut, less aware causal-effect structures obtained from empirical data. The current rule-based part of the planner is based on a linguistic analysis of the German feedback system and defines which expressions from our basic feedback system can be used to provide feedback on perception and understanding in an appropriate, context-sensitive way (see Table 1).

After every new word flowing into the system, the probabilistic component of the planner computes the probabilities of all single backchannels that Max could give. In detail, the planner draws a Bayesian inference in order to calculate the conditional probability $P(B|U=x)$ of the feedback behavior B, given that the current understanding level is x, according to equation (1).

$$P(B|U=x) = P(U=x|B)P(B) \, / \, P(U=x) \qquad (1)$$

That is, $P(B|U=x)$ is expressed in terms of three other probabilities. $P(U=x)$ is the a priori probability of successful understanding of the currently provided user input. This probability is taken to be identical to the understanding value determined by the input processing as described above. $P(B)$ is the a priori probability of behavior B being used for giving feedback. This probability is set differently depending on whether the human pauses, continues with, or ends her contribution. Finally, $P(U=x|B)$ is the conditional probability that an agent performing the feedback behavior B has a certain level x of understanding. In our current implementation, which aims to explore whether communicative feedback can be modeled for virtual humans in this way, $P(B)$ and $P(U|B)$ are predefined by hand as educated guesses. An empirical study is underway that will inform the setting up of these values [3]. Figure 3 shows the probabilities $P(U|B)$ for several backchannel behaviors. They are approximated as piecewise linear distributions over the possible values of U. Note that it may be appropriate for one ECA to give a lot of feedback, while another agent may be intended to be more shy and thus to give less. This can be modeled easily by setting the a priori probabilities $P(B)$ accordingly.

Since both the rule-based and the probabilistic mechanism need to be integrated, the model seeks for a behavioral combination that suits the currently requested feedback functions best. The feedback planner and generator therefore have to deal with the more general question of how feedback categories can be combined. The functions are not disjunctive in the sense that, although positive understanding feedback implies successful perception, negative understanding can override positive perception or contact.

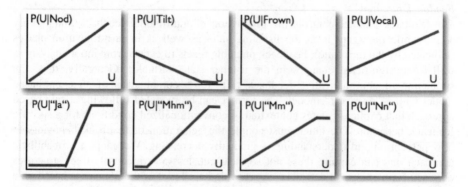

Fig. 3. The approximated probability distributions P(U|B) for several feedback behaviors B. "Vocal" (top right) is the general probability of vocal feedback, the bottom row contains the single distributions for vocal backchannels.

One can think of a resolution method, e.g., where behaviors are picked from the repertoire by order of priority, with higher levels of evaluation (understanding) having higher priorities than lower appraisals (e.g. perception). In our current implementation, the different types of planning and generating feedback simply work in parallel, yet in a cascaded fashion. Lower processes are faster and trigger behavior earlier than higher processes. The lower processes may thus gain temporary access to effectors. In result, Max will at first look certain and nod due to positive contact and perception evaluations, but then start to look confused once a negative understanding evaluation has barged in, eventually leading to a verbal request for repetition or elaboration like "wie bitte?".

Results of feedback planning can be either specific requests for verbal feedback, along with prosodic features, or more abstract specifications of weighted to-be-achieved feedback functions that also make explicit the different types of communicative intentionality discussed above (e.g. "signal-positive-understanding" or "display-negative-perception"). The latter allow the generator module to compose a multimodal feedback expression by drawing on modality-specific behavior repertoires and test relevant constraints, e.g., for the availability of required effectors. The output of this generation step is an XML behavior specification in MURML that combines all required information regarding, e.g., head movements and prosodic verbal output. This specification is sent to the *Articulated Communicator Engine* [14], which realizes the production stage in Fig. 2 by employing a set of concurrent, modality-specific behavior generators. Verbal and prosody production build on a text-to-speech component that has been extended to enable the on-demand generation of verbal backchannels with characteristic pitch contours. Currently, six different pitch contours with a variable duration, hesitation (time ratio between first phone and remaining phones), and raising slope parameters are possible. Beyond the scope of this paper, combinations of these parameters where found in user studies to reliably indicate boredom, anger, agreement or a happy mood, on top of the same verbal feedback signal "ja" (see [21]). Mimic production controls eyebrow raises, lip-sync speech animation, and a weighted facial display of basic emotions. Gaze and head behaviors are realized by means of procedural animation.

5 Generation Examples

The model described in Sect. 4 was realized in Max. It enables him to give embodied feedback based on incrementally processing the verbal input as the user is typing it in. Table 2 contains two examples to demonstrate the embodied feedback given by Max over time; Fig. 4 shows snapshots of the corresponding non-vocal backchannels. In Table 2, the last row of each sub-table contains the text inputted by the human user word by word. The rows above indicate when Max has produced verbal, head, or eyebrow feedback, in addition to the continuous evolvement of the understanding status of the agent in the top row.

Table 2. Examples of Max's feedback behaviors produced on typed language input. The inputs (given in the bottom rows) develop from left to right; see text for translations and explanation.

Underst.	1.0	0.8	0.8	0.6	0.6	1.0
Verbal						"Ja, ich bin begeistert."
Head		Tilt		Tilt		Nod
Browes					Frown	
Human	"Bielefeld	ist	eine	tolle	Stadt"	

Underst.	1.0	1.0	0.8	0.8	0.8	0.4	0.4	0.4
Verbal						"Wie bitte?"		
Head						Nod	Tilt	Tilt
Browes								Frown
Human	"Bielefeld	liegt	direkt	am	Totoburger	Wald	glaube	ich"

The first input phrase (English translation: "Bielefeld is a great city.") is understandable for Max, albeit two words ("Bielefeld" and "tolle") are unknown to the POS tagger in the Lexicon. Perception drops slightly, thereby increasing the probability of negative feedback (head tilt and frown, as can be seen from the negative slope of the probability curves in Fig. 3). In result, two head tilts and a frown occur. Yet, Max was able to interpret the input, which resets the understanding level to 1.0 and results in vocal feedback "Ja" preceding the verbal response "Ich bin begeistert" ("I'm delighted") produced by the rule-based component (Table 1).

The second sentence (translating to "Bielefeld is located close to the Totoburger Forrest") serves as an example for a more problematic perception and understanding, the reason being that "Totoburger" is a wrong, completely unknown word. At first, Max follows attentively with successful understanding – the probabilistic component did not trigger any positive feedback here due to the generally smaller prior probabilities of backchannels during continuing input. Upon reception of the word "Totoburger" however, perception drops significantly and this results in frequent vocal as well as non-vocal feedback.

Fig. 4. Examples of embodied feedback in the virtual human Max. From left to right: Head tilt and frown, vocal feedback, and nodding in a positive mood.

6 Conclusions

In this paper, we presented work towards an account of communicative embodied feedback and, in particular, towards the modeling of more natural feedback behavior of virtual humans. The computational model we have presented extends the architectural layout commonly employed in current embodied conversational agents. At large, it can be considered a row of individual augmentations of the classical modules for interpretation, planning, and realization, affording an incremental processing of the incoming input. One main innovation in this respect was to refine the step size and time scale at which these stages processes input, along with a suitable routing of information via the deliberative or the reactive pathways. One main shortcoming of the interactions currently possible with Max is the need to type in the input, which for instance may result in people focusing their attention on their typing activity and not noticing online feedback given by Max. While spoken language recognition is easily possible in laboratory settings, we want to keep the system as robust as possible in the museum scenario, which affords us with great opportunities for evaluating our models. We are thus planning to stick to the typed input but will discard the need to press enter upon completion of an utterance. Thus, instead of explicitly transmitting the input to the system, Max is to inform the human about having received sufficient information by employing his now developed feedback capabilities. Additional, future work will address the inclusion of additional input modalities like prosody or gesture, which will require new models for an incremental segmentation and processing of more analog aspects of communication.

Our model further represents a new approach to the context-sensitive selection and placement problems of feedback behavior. The feedback planner reacts to both feedback eliciting cues as well as significant changes in the listener-internal assessments of the current perception, understanding, and agreement states. It thus combines a „shallow" feedback model covering mainly conventionalized mappings, largely akin to most previous systems, with a deeper, theoretically grounded model that accounts for processes of appraisal and evaluation and their effect on the continuously evolving listener states. These states are assumed to capture some of the relevant factors that give rise to responsive functions of feedback expressions and that can be mapped onto different expressions and modalities to realize these functions.

The modeling and simulation work described here is only one line of research we pursue in order to gain a better understanding of the human feedback system and its underlying mechanisms. In other work, our theoretical approach provides the basis of a framework for analyzing empirical data on embodied feedback in natural interactions (Allwood et al., submitted). We have started to design a coding scheme and a data analysis method suited to capture those features that are decisive in this account (such as type of expression, relevant function, or time scale). Both lines of research, the empirical and the simulative, are meant to converge. For example, the corpus analysis can directly inform our predictive feedback model by providing transition probabilities for the feedback planner. The other way around, the computational modeling yields observable simulations that can be compared with real data to scrutinize the theoretical assumptions.

A mandatory next step will be to conduct an evaluation of the Max's behavior. For one thing, it remains to be shown that it succeeds to serve as an early warning system, which can indeed increase the efficiency and naturalness of human-agent interactions by evoking those repairs from speakers that compensate for the very problems Max is facing with their contributions. Another interesting, more general question along the same line is whether different dimensions of feedback bear different effects on persons interacting with Max (their behavior and attitudes towards Max).

References

1. Allwood, J.: Linguistic Communication as Action and Cooperation. Gothenburg Monographs in Linguistics 2. Göteborg University, Department of Linguistics (1976)
2. Allwood, J., Nivre, J., Ahlsén, E.: On the semantics and pragmatics of linguistic feedback. Journal of Semantics 9(1), 1–26 (1992)
3. Allwood, J., Kopp, S., Grammer, K., Ahlsen, E., Oberzaucher, E., Koppensteiner, M.: The analysis of embodied communicative feedback in multimodal corpora – a prerequisite for behaviour simulation. Journal of Language Resources and Evaluation (to appear)
4. Wachsmuth, I., Becker, C., Kopp, S.: Simulating the Emotion Dynamics of a Multimodal Conversational Agent. In: André, E., Dybkjær, L., Minker, W., Heisterkamp, P. (eds.) ADS 2004. LNCS (LNAI), vol. 3068, pp. 154–165. Springer, Heidelberg (2004)
5. Beun, R.J., van Eijk, R.M.: Conceptual Discrepancies and Feedback in Human-Computer Interaction. In: Proc. Dutch directions in HCI, ACM Press, New York (2004)
6. Cassell, J., Thórisson, K.R.: The Power of a Nod and a Glance: Envelope vs. Emotional Feedback in Animated Conversational Agents. Int J. Applied Artificial Intelligence 13(4–5), 519–538 (1999)
7. Cassell, J., Bickmore, T., Billinghurst, M., Campbell, L., Chang, K., Vilhjálmsson, H., Yan, H.: Embodiment in Conversational Interfaces: Rea. In: Proc. CHI, pp. 520–527 (1999)
8. Cathcart, N., Carletta, J., Klein, E.: A shallow model of backchannel continuers in spoken dialogue. In: Proc. European Chapter of the Association for Computational Linguistics (EACL10), pp. 51–58 (2003)
9. Ehlich, K.: Interjektionen, Max Niemeyer Verlag (1986)

10. Fujie, S., Fukushima, K., Kobayashi, T.: A Conversation Robot with Back-channel Feedback Function based on Linguistic and Nonlinguistic Information. In: Proc. ICARA Int. Conference on Autonomous Robots and Agents, pp. 379–384 (2004)
11. Marsella, S.C., Morency, L.-P., Gratch, J., Okhmatovskaia, A., Lamothe, F., Morales, M., van der Werf, R.J.: Virtual Rapport. In: Gratch, J., Young, M., Aylett, R.S., Ballin, D., Olivier, P. (eds.) IVA 2006. LNCS (LNAI), vol. 4133, pp. 14–27. Springer, Heidelberg (2006)
12. Nijholt, A., Heylen, D., Vissers, M., op den Akker, R.: Affective Feedback in a Tutoring System for Procedural Tasks. In: André, E., Dybkjær, L., Minker, W., Heisterkamp, P. (eds.) ADS 2004. LNCS (LNAI), vol. 3068, pp. 244–253. Springer, Heidelberg (2004)
13. Houck, N., Gass, S.M.: Cross-cultural back channels in English refusals: A source of trouble. In: Jaworski, A. (ed.) Silence-Interdisciplinary perspectives, pp. 285–308. Mouton de Gruyter, Berlin (1997)
14. Kopp, S., Wachsmuth, I.: Synthesizing multimodal utterances for conversational agents. Computer Animation & Virtual Worlds 15(1), 39–52 (2004)
15. Kopp, S., Gesellensetter, L., Krämer, N., Wachsmuth, I.: A conversational agent as museum guide – design and evaluation of a real-world application. In: Panayiotopoulos, T., Gratch, J., Aylett, R.S., Ballin, D., Olivier, P., Rist, T. (eds.) IVA 2005. LNCS (LNAI), vol. 3661, pp. 329–343. Springer, Heidelberg (2005)
16. Nakano, Y., Reinstein, G., Stocky, T., Cassell, J.: Towards a Model of Face-to-Face Grounding. In: Dignum, F.P.M. (ed.) ACL 2003. LNCS (LNAI), vol. 2922, pp. 553–561. Springer, Heidelberg (2004)
17. Poggi, I., Pelachaud, C., de Rosis, F., Carofiglio, V., De Carolis, B.: GRETA. A Believable Embodied Conversational Agent. In: Stock, O., Zancarano, M. (eds.) Multimodal Intelligent Information Presentation, Kluwer, Dordrecht (2005)
18. Scherer, K.R.: Affect Bursts. In: van Goozen, S., van de Poll, N.E., Sergeant, J.A. (eds.) Emotions: Essays on Emotion Theory, pp. 161–193. Lawrence Erlbaum, Mahwah (1994)
19. Schmid, H.: Improvements in Part-of-Speech Tagging With an Application To German (1995), http://www.ims.uni-stuttgart.de/ftp/pub/corpora/tree-tagger1.pdf
20. Shimojima, H., Koiso, M., Swerts, Katagiri, Y.: Mouton de GruyterAn Informational Analysis of Echoic Responses in Dialogue. In: Proc. ESSLLI Workshop on Integrating Information from Different Channels in Multi-Media-Contexts, pp. 48–55 (2000)
21. Stocksmeier, T., Kopp, S., Gibbon, D.: Synthesis of prosodic attitudinal variants in German backchannel "ja". In: Proc. of Interspeech 2007, Antwerp, Belgium (2007)
22. Takeuchi, M., Kitaoka, N., Nakagawa, S.: Timing detection for realtime dialog systems using prosodic and linguistic information. In: Proc. of the International Conference Speech Prosody (SP 2004), pp. 529–532 (2004)
23. Thórisson, K.R.: Communicative Humanoids: A Computational Model of Psychosocial Dialogue Skills. Ph.D. thesis, MIT (1996)
24. Vilhjálmsson, H.H., Cassell, J.: BodyChat: Autonomous Commumicative Behaviors in Avators. Agents, 269–276 (1998)
25. Wachsmuth, I., Knoblich, G.: Embodied communication in humans and machines - a research agenda. Artificial Intelligence Review 24(3-4), 517–522 (2005)
26. Wallers, A.: Minor sounds of major importance - prosodic manipulation of synthetic backchannels in swedish. Master's thesis, KTH Stockholm, Sweden (2006)
27. Ward, N.: Using prosodic cues to decide when to produce back-channel utterances. In: Proceedings of ICSLP, pp. 1728–1731 (1996)

28. Ward, N.: Prosodic features which cue backchannel responses in English and Japanese. Pragmatics 32, 1177–1207 (2000)
29. Ward, N., Tsukahara, W.: Prosodic features which cue back-channel responses in English and Japanese. Journal of Pragmatics 32, 1177–1207 (2000)
30. Wiener, N.: Cybernetics and Control and Communication in the Animal and the Machine. MIT Press, Cambridge (1948)
31. Yngve, V.H.: On getting a word in edgewise. In: Papers from the 6th Regional Meeting of the Chicago Linguistics Society, University of Chicago, pp. 567–578 (1970)

The Recognition and Comprehension of Hand Gestures - A Review and Research Agenda

Timo Sowa

Elektrobit Corporation, Am Wolfsmantel 46, 91058 Erlangen, Germany
timo.sowa@elektrobit.com

Abstract. In this paper I review current and past approaches towards the use of hand gesture recognition and comprehension in human-computer interaction. I point out properties of natural coverbal gestures in human communication and identify challenges for gesture comprehension systems in three areas. The first challenge is to derive the meaning of a gesture given that its semantics is defined in three semiotic dimensions that have to be addressed differently. A second challenge is the spatial composition of gestures in imagistic spaces. Finally, a third technical challenge is the development of an integrated processing model for speech and gesture.

Keywords: gesture comprehension, gesture recognition.

1 Introduction

When people talk, their speech is usually accompanied by gestures of the hands and arms. These coverbal gestures and synchronous speech are assumed to express the same meaning at the same time, but the modalities differ considerably in that speech packages content linearly in symbolic form, while gesture embodies meaning and depicts it in 3D space [42]. Many gesture researchers consider speech and coverbal gesture as surface realizations of a common "idea unit", produced by an integrated, multimodal system of communication [33,43,34]. Similarly, a tight coupling of the two modalities is assumed for language comprehension [1,13].

Due to the ubiquity and expressive power of gesture in communication, it has also received attention as a means to communicate with computer systems, embodied virtual agents, or robots [22,64,5]. The goal of this paper is to survey the research on hand gesture recognition and comprehension in human-computer interaction (HCI) and to relate technical achievements to the current knowledge on coverbal gesture in human communication. Particular attention will be given to the notion of gesture semantics and the implications for computational approaches that aim to model the meaning of natural gestures for HCI. In the first part of the paper, I will review gesture input for HCI with an emphasis on speech and coverbal gesture integration. In the second part, I will point out properties of coverbal gestures in everyday communication not yet touched upon in computer systems and sketch ways of addressing them computationally. Finally, I

I. Wachsmuth and G. Knoblich (Eds.): Modeling Communication, LNAI 4930, pp. 38–56, 2008.
© Springer-Verlag Berlin Heidelberg 2008

will summarize the agenda for the development of future gesture comprehension systems.

2   Gesture Recognition and Comprehension in HCI

In human-computer interaction the term *gesture input* refers to a range of different interaction styles, many of which have little or nothing in common with coverbal gestures observed in human communication. Some of these input techniques, e.g. in the form of 2D-pen strokes on a screen, are as old as the first graphical user interface. However, it is only since the 80s that hand gestures have been employed in prototypical interfaces with the outspoken aim of making interaction with a computer more natural [5]. In the following sections, I will sketch the current state of affairs for the different sub-tasks involved in gesture recognition, beginning with body movement tracking, followed by gesture classification using pattern recognition, gesture segmentation, and concluding with multimodal systems that combine gesture and speech input.

2.1   Sensing Technology

The processing chain from gestural expression to interpretation begins with the capture of the signal via sensing devices. In a broad sense, signal capturing can be divided in two dimensions, active vs. passive and invasive vs. non-invasive sensing methods. Active sensors capture movement and posture information by themselves – they are little pieces of electronics. Passive methods use markers which are captured by other means. Invasive methods use active devices or passive markers mounted on the user's hands and arms. A frequently used and quite accurate device for measuring hand posture is the dataglove. Datagloves contain goniometers to measure the flexion of hand and finger joints either based on fiber optics or on electrical conductance [71,35]. Most types measure the proximal and middle finger joints. Additionally, some models capture the distal joint, finger abduction, thumb rotation, palm curvature, and wrist flexion.

Several invasive methods for hand position and orientation tracking are available. Mechanical approaches using exoskeletons or arrangements of levers attached to the hands and arms as, for instance, the Phantom device [9], are reliable, but also cumbersome. Electromagnetic tracking systems use pulsed fields emitted from a central sender unit, that can be measured by small receivers attached to the user (Fig. 1, left). Benefits of this technique are barrier-free movement and the absence of any occlusion problems. Active sensing is in general more obtrusive than the use of passive markers, since sensor data has to be retrieved, which is often done via cables or a radio transmitter (cf. Fig. 1, right, for an example of a passive, marker-based system). To minimize occlusion problems in marker-based system, data from several cameras with different viewing angles can be combined.

Non-invasive sensing methods are usually based on computer vision [61]. The first task for a vision-based gesture input system is to determine the configuration of the body (particularly the hands and arms) in space. For most natural

Fig. 1. Motion tracking devices: active sensor-based (left) and passive marker-based (right). (from [58])

gestures, only the hands (and possibly the head) play a role for the determination of meaning (in some gestures, however, other body parts such as the upper/lower arms are semantically relevant). Hence, body configuration recognition is often simplified to just include hand and head position tracking. With appropriate long-sleeved and dark clothing, tracking can be accomplished with skin color segmentation of the video image [45,56]. Full-body tracking methods usually rely on a-priori or adaptive body models in 2D or 3D [26,12]. The detection of hand-shape is particularly difficult in vision-based systems. Comprehensive overviews of gesture recognition in computer vision including the problem of hand-shape recognition can be found in [50] and [68]. Note that some vision-based recognition approaches do not use information on the limbs' configuration at all. Instead, they directly classify gestures from the video image.

Generally speaking, using invasive or non-invasive sensing methods is a matter of trade-off between algorithmic complexity of signal capturing on the one hand and accuracy and obstructiveness on the other. Obstructiveness from marker-based to non-contact, vision-based methods decreases. However, freedom of movement comes at the expense of accuracy and simplicity of the algorithms.

2.2   Gesture Recognition

In human-computer interaction the term *gesture recognition* is most often used in the sense of pattern classification. Under the classification paradigm, a given sequence of preprocessed input data acquired from the sensing devices is allotted one class c_i of a pre-defined set of classes $C = c_1, \ldots, c_m$. The classes depend on the demands of the target application. Thus, as Benoit et al. [3] put it, "[the recognition of] 2D or 3D gestures is a typical pattern recognition problem. Standard pattern recognition techniques, such as template matching and feature-based recognition, are sufficient for gesture recognition" (p. 32). Semantic processing is outside the scope of gesture recognition, and I will use the term *gesture comprehension* for systems that include a semantic layer.

Most pattern matching approaches for gesture recognition are based on training, which means that a set of training samples containing movement input data is collected and manually alloted the correct class. In the training phase, these examples are used to adjust the internal parameters of the model such that the recognition rate improves. A popular, training-based technique for gesture recognition are hidden markov models (HMMs) [53]. They model a continuous process as a series of discrete states with state-change probabilities. HMMs are well suited for the classification of time-varying signals that fulfill the Markov property: the probability of a state in the future only depends on the current state, but not on past states. A helpful feature of HMMs is their ability to compensate time and amplitude variances which improves the robustness for interpersonal movement differences. HMMs have been applied for the classification of dataglove- and accelerometer-based input [24], for gesture classification on difference images [54], or for input data that represents the angles of the joints and end-effectors in the human kinematic chain [49]. Further training-based approaches include artificial neural networks, used for data-glove and motion tracker input [62], and combinations of HMM and neural network classifiers [15].

2.3 Gesture Segmentation

Gestures are meaningful segments in the continuous stream of bodily movement. A gestural movement, also called *gesture phrase*, usually has a certain temporal structure consisting of subsequent phases [33,34]. Within a phrase, only a single phase, called the *stroke* or *expressive phase*, is meaningful. Other phases serve different purposes, e.g. to make the hand ready for a stroke *(preparation phase)*, or to move it back to a rest position *(retraction phase)* among others. In natural movement, there is also non-gestural activity such as body posture transitions (someone changing his rest position from hands on lap to arms folded), or adjusting the clothes. A gesture comprehension system has to filter the stroke portion out of the movement and has to distinguish gesture phrases from non-gestural movements. This (difficult) task is commonly called the *gesture segmentation problem* [23]. In HMMs the segmentation problem can be solved within the model by introducing separate states for each stroke phase to be detected and common states for the optional preparation and retraction phase. With a cyclic HMM containing "garbage" models parallel to the model of the gesture phrase, the rejection of non-gestural movements is possible [49]. These model-inherent segmentation techniques are feasible because of the limited, and pre-defined set of gestures. An unknown movement phase that precedes or succeeds a stroke is a preparation or retraction. Any other movement that does not fit the trained gesture classes can be assigned to the "garbage" model.

Explicit segmentation, external to the recognition model, is facilitated by certain kinematic properties or *segmentation cues* in the movement [39]. The transition between hand/arm movement and pause is an easily detectable segmentation cue exploitable for different kinds of input data. It has been used for vision-based input by computing the change of an image from one frame to the next [25], or in tracking-based systems for the detection of hand movement alone [37], or combined hand and finger movement [24]. Based on the idea that intentional gestures will require effort, hand tension has been suggested as a segmentation cue and employed in glove-based systems [23,21]. Hand tension is the deviation of the joint angles in the hand from a "normal", relaxed position. A fully stretched or rolled finger, for instance, deviates strongly from a relaxed middle position and causes a lot of tension. Another cue based on the idea that gesture coincides with effort is the overall torque at the arm joints caused by gravity when a person maintains a certain body posture [58]. Effort in movement can also be measured as the activity of a body segment in terms of momentum, kinetic energy, and force. Local minima of these properties have been used as segmentation cues that signal a segment border [30]. Kinetic energy was used as a segmentation cue in [4].

2.4   Gesture and Speech

In the following sections, systems using gesture input in the context of speech (and vice versa) are examined. They are usually called *multimodal systems*, because they integrate input information from more than one communicative modality. Multimodal speech and gesture systems come in three flavors, depending on the purpose and the processing stage at which the modalities are conjoined.

Gesture Facilitates Speech Recognition. Systems of the first flavor focus on speech recognition and comprehension, while they treat gestures as facilitators that contribute contextual information for speech input processing. Gestural information is exploited for different purposes. Qu and Chai describe a speech recognition system that uses pointing gestures on a 2D screen to improve speech recognition performance [52]. Their approach is based on salience modeling for pointing gestures. It is assumed that pointing increases the salience of the target in a communicative situation. The higher salience causes a priming effect increasing the chances of recognizing a word connected to the target. Qu and Chai model the priming effect at two different steps in the speech recognition engine. For the first solution they modified the word probability in the language model[1] by a term that depends on the pointing position. For an alternative approach, they applied a standard language model, but re-ranked the output of the recognition system, the n-best list of the most probable words, according to the salience model. In both cases, the additional information provided by gesture is "consumed" and the system's output is the recognized spoken utterance.

Gesture is not only exploited for speech recognition, but also as a facilitator in later stages of the speech processing pipeline. One important task of a comprehension system during semantic processing is the determination of coreference, i.e. the question whether two linguistic expressions refer to the same entity. Eisenstein and Davis examined the relationship between coreference and positional/kinematic features of the hands [17]. They found a significant connection between coreference of two noun phrases and features such as the distance

---

[1] A speech recognizer usually relies on two data sets: an acoustic model and a language model. The acoustic model provides the probability of recognizing a certain phoneme sequence given that a certain word was uttered. The language model reflects the probability that a given sequence of words is followed by a certain word in a multiword utterance.

between the positions of the hands in focus measured when the phrases were uttered or use of the same hand. In addition to verbal information, such gestural features can thus be used as predictors for coreference and contribute to linguistic processing.

Gestures were also applied as facilitators for sentence unit (SU) detection in spontaneous speech. The determination of SUs may improve speech recognition and subsequent processing stages such as parsing. Chen, Liu, Harper, & Shriberg as well as Eisenstein and Davis suggested multimodal approaches for SU detection based on Hidden Markov Models incorporating gestural cues [10]. While Chen et al. used hold and effort features automatically extracted by vision-based hand detectors, Eisenstein and Davis hand-coded gesture phrases and phases and used phase boundaries for SU prediction. While both approaches failed to yield statistically significant improvements using a gesture-enhanced SU detection model, follow-up work by Chen, Harper, & Huang demonstrates an improvement over speech-only SU detection by using a maximum entropy approach instead of an HMM [11].

Speech Facilitates Gesture Recognition. The second flavor of multimodal speech-gesture input systems focuses on gesture recognition and treats speech as a facilitative factor. Sharma et al. created an HMM-based system to recognize continuous gestures in narrations of a TV weather anchorman [57]. Their system could distinguish three gesture types typical for the weather domain: pointing gestures, contour gestures (enclosing an area with a movement), and area gestures (sweeping over an area). A keyword recognition system trained on frequent words (this, here, east, west, storm, region etc.) was running in parallel to the gesture recognizer. Using the keyword/gesture type co-occurrence likelihood from a corpus evaluation, Sharma et al. were able to improve the classifier's performance.

Improving gesture recognition with speech also works with the suprasegmental information contained in the speech signal. Kettebekov, Yeasin & Sharma describe a gesture recognition system that exploits prosodic cues to differentiate meaningful phases of pointing and contour gestures, preparation, and retraction phases of gestural movements [36]. They implemented two different approaches: In the first approach prosodic cues are considered as features in an HMM-based recognizer. For the second approach, they employed a Bayesian network. Both prosody-supported methods yield significantly better recognition results than the gesture recognizer alone, whereas the Bayesian network performed better than the augmented HMM model.

Integration of Gesture and Speech. There are several generic approaches towards the integration of input information originating from different modalities. Commonly, two main subtypes of these multimodal architectures are distinguished [47]. First, there are *feature-level*, or *early fusion* approaches in which the recognition of information from one modality is supported by another modality and vice versa in a pre-semantic stage. Feature-level fusion can be applied if the modalities are physically or temporally strongly coupled such as (acoustic) speech signals and (visual) lip shape information. Second, *semantic-level*, or *late fusion* approaches combine semantic information derived independently from the different modalities. Gesture and speech integration is usually considered on the semantic level. The underlying idea of semantic-level fusion is to end up with a common meaning specification of a multimodal command or interaction which is executed by the computer.

A frequently applied semantic-level fusion method is to consider the meaning specification as a frame structure of attribute-value pairs [66,46,60]: First, the input from each modality is evaluated and it produces partially filled frames. Corresponding frames are then integrated until all attribute slots are filled with values and the application command is thus fully specified.

In simple frame-based multimodal integration approaches all partially filled frames are structured equally and the attribute values are simple "scalar" data types such as symbols or numbers. Therefore, they cannot model complex structured commands. An integration method that employs substructures within frames and thus allows to build up structural hierarchies was proposed in [29,27,14]. The fusion mechanism is based on the unification of typed feature structures (Fig. 2). For each structural unit and sub-unit, such as a pointing gesture or an object creation command, there is a typed feature structure describing the sub-features needed for completion. An object creation command, for example, needs a type and a location to be complete. The location could be provided via pointing.

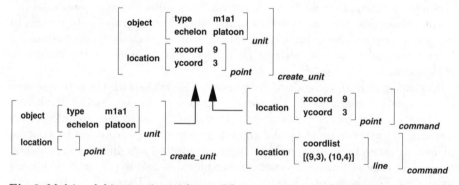

Fig. 2. Multimodal integration with typed feature structures: Speech input (lower left) is unified with one of two alternative interpretations of a gesture performed with a pen (lower right) to a common feature structure.

In order to cope with the uncertain nature of unimodal information sources, the unification approach can be extended by allowing multiple alternative input and output interpretations tagged by their respective recognition probabilities as suggested in [31]. The speech and gesture recognizers in their system prototype, for instance, provide an n-best list of the most probable input hypotheses for each modality. The probability of a multimodal integrated feature structure is computed based on the probabilities of the input hypotheses.

An alternative approach based on finite-state machines (FSM) was proposed in [28]. Multimodal grammars are modeled with FSMs consisting of one input tape for each modality and an output tape containing the meaning of the multimodal speech-act after parsing. According to the authors, the advantages of the FSM approach over unification grammars are less complex formalisms and better integratability with speech recognition systems.

A similar, but more flexible approach in which temporal constraints can be expressed explicitly was described by Latoschik [39]. He represents multimodal grammars with augmented transition networks enriched by temporal information at each node (tATN). The state transitions model lexical input (words), temporal tests on the presence of gesture attributes, like "user was pointing", and allow for logical negation and conjunctions of attributes.

Grammar-based approaches such as unification or FSMs impose a (more or less rigid) structure on multimodal input. In an alternative approach that is less susceptible to violations of structure, each input modality was encoded including the context as attributed relational graphs [8]. The nodes represent possible reference objects, while the arcs stand for temporal or semantic relations between the referents. Multimodal integration is thus expressed as a graph matching problem. The matching algorithm tries to maximize the overall fit of the modality-specific graphs.

A common challenge for all semantic-level integration methods is the *correspondence problem* originally defined for the combination of linguistic and visual information [59]. Applied to gesture and speech integration, its central issue is how to correlate chunks of information from one modality to the other. Usually, temporal proximity is employed as a cue to determine corresponding input information. Grammar-based integration methods either implicitly consider temporal proximity coarsely by the linear ordering of input events, or via explicit temporal constraint or integration rules. In [63] an integration method based on the idea of communicative rhythms is described. A regular pulse defines temporal windows within which multimodal input events are assumed to correlate.

Interpretation of Pointing. The value of gestural pointing in speech-based interfaces has been recognized early on in the HCI community. "Put-that-there" is the first natural language interface that incorporated pointing in 3D space [5]. The system could interpret instructions for object creation, manipulation, and deletion such as "create a blue square there" or "move this to the right of the square" while the user was pointing to a large screen. Whenever a demonstrative was encountered, the pointing direction was evaluated to resolve the reference. The direction was captured with a position/orientation tracker mounted at the user's wrist. The interpretation of the pointing depends on the type of demonstrative. A reference to an object (*this, that*) is resolved by the object closest to the spot pointed at. A location reference (*here*) is resolved by the x, y-coordinates from pointing. More recent approaches consider pointing in fully immersive 3D environments and with more natural gesture forms. In [39] pointing gestures are also used for object and location references, but they are recognized based on the hand-shape and are integrated with speech if a pointing hand-shape co-occurs with a demonstrative based on a multimodal grammar (see above). Pointing references are interpreted using lists that order all visible objects according to the proximity to the pointing ray at any point in time. Using the referent list, the system considers more than one possible alternative as the correct referent, and may integrate deictic reference by gesture with reference by verbal description to come up with the best combined choice. In [38] and [37] a pointing cone was used that preselects possible object or location references.

In addition to free-hand pointing in a 3D environment, 2D pointing using the mouse or other devices has been used in multimodal systems. Typically, a pointing gesture in 2D is interpreted as reference to an object of the application domain as in [44], but there are also cases of speech-dependent interpretation, for instance as a point or line in a map-based application [14]. In [7], pointing is interpreted as an attentional signal that controls the focus stack and thus indirectly influences the interpretation of speech. Still, other complex cases of pointing, such as pars-pro-toto pointing (pointing to the part but referring to the whole), can be observed in everyday human interaction and were modeled in prototypical applications [65].

3   Challenges for Technology

Given this landscape of technical approaches towards gesture and speech input processing, I will now consider three areas of interest for coverbal gesture recognition and interpretation. The following issues should be considered in more detail when designing computational systems.

3.1   Three Semiotic Dimensions of Meaning

The task of a gesture comprehension system is to determine the meaning of gestures – but what exactly is the meaning of a gesture? In current and past engineering approaches, we have seen that gesture meaning can be a position on a screen, an ordered list of reference objects computed from a pointing ray, an abstract model of shape, a style of movement, etc. In most cases, however, the issue of meaning is not touched upon, because the systems stop at the recognition stage. In contrast to words, the meaning of gestures is more difficult to access, because if we consider gestures as signs in the sense of Peirce [51], we will realize that gestures acquire meaning in three different ways, or in three different semiotic dimensions. Each of these dimensions must be accounted for in order to build an adequate model of gesture meaning.

Peirce divides signs into three classes. His trichotomy of signs reappears as one fundamental principle of differentiation in almost any classification schema for gestures [16,70,42,18]. According to [51, 2.304], "[a] sign is either an *icon*, an *index*, or a *symbol*. An *icon* is a sign which would possess the character which renders it significant, even though its object had no existence". It refers to something by similarity between its representamen and the object. Thus, it can be said that meaning is an inherent part of the icon. Peirce continues: "An *index* is a sign which would, at once, lose the character which makes it a sign if its object were removed, but would not lose that character if there were no interpretant." That is to say, an index needs context to signify, since the object is a part of that context. The link between representamen and object of an index is physical, no mental instance (interpretant) is needed for representation. Signposts are typical indices in this sense, since they indicate the driving or walking direction and become meaningless deprived of context. Finally Peirce defines a *symbol* as "a sign which would lose the character which renders it a sign if there were no interpretant." Symbols are signs which have a conventionalized meaning in a social group or class. The meaning of a symbol therefore depends on a mental, not physical, connection to its object. Each word, perhaps with the exception of onomatopoeia, is a symbol.

The Peircean trichotomy of signs is applicable to gestures, too. It would naturally lead to iconic gestures, indexical or deictic gestures, and symbolic gestures. Though in Peirce's wording the three classes seem to be mutually exclusive, they are in fact not. Each single gesture can signify at the same time in the iconic, deictic[2], and symbolic dimension of meaning. Consider, for instance, someone referring to a nearby pole by "pointing" to it while moving the hand up and down. This gesture signifies in the deictic dimension, because it links to the visible world and the reference (the pole) could not be determined without this context. Yet, with the movement, a part of the gesture's meaning is inherent in the gesture itself (something like longitudinal extent), and thus signifies in the iconic dimension.

A computational model that extracts meaning from the iconic dimension must provide a means to detect the similarity between the gesture's physical form and the referent. The term *similarity* is not to be taken in a pictorial sense here, since gestures are no pictures of their referents. They simply cannot be, because the hands' capabilities of depiction in space are limited, and have to be compensated for by depiction in time. We also have to keep in mind that the referent of (the iconic dimension of) a gesture is usually not a physical object that is depicted by the gesture. Computational approaches, in particular those dealing with graphical environments, may suggest that view, because reference resolution to determine the target object of some operation has been a focal application domain in gesture-based systems. Gesture may refer to properties, experiences, or relations that are important and newsworthy at the moment of speaking. These could include, for instance, a certain geometric property of an object, a way to handle it, a capability of this object, all of which are somehow associated with the object. Detecting similarity means that the bodily action has to be associated with its referent via some analogical link mediated by experience. The kind of experience required to understand iconicity could be visual or practical. The interpretation of the deictic aspect of a gesture requires the availability of an appropriate contextual model to which the gesture refers. In multimodal systems, this was always a model of the visual context, i.e. either of the real world, or the model underlying the artificial world created by computer graphics. However,

---

[2] Deictic is used synonymously for indexical.

this is not the only context a gesture could refer to deictically as the following section will show. So for a computer system to understand gestural deixis, the correct contextual model has to be chosen. The symbolic dimension is perhaps the easiest to handle with a computer system, since it only requires a fixed association between gesture form and some internal representation of meaning.

3.2   Deixis All over the Place

So far, gestures have been discussed and considered as detached signs in the spatial medium that signify in three semiotic dimensions. Computational approaches towards gesture comprehension take on these dimensions by interpreting the spatial sign, possibly in the context of speech. Yet, besides the verbal context there is the spatial context of the gesture that contributes to meaning. Despite its significance for the formation of meaning, the spatial context has not attracted much attention in the human-computer interaction community. Gestures are not only signs in the spatial medium, but they may acquire meaning through space and, at the same time, they may structure their own medium by imposing meaning on space. This process of setting up and referring to spatial meaning (which is inherently deictic since it requires a context) may be iterative: gestures may thus refer to the context other gestures have brought into existence. This deictic potential is present in all gesture types, not only in gestures commonly called deictics.

One variety of gestures building up a spatial context can be found in narrative discourse. As McNeill points out, successive gestures in action descriptions often employ space in a coherent way [42]. The right field of the gesture space, for instance, may be reserved for one character in the narration, while the left field represents another. The placement of gestures in either field then implies the character. Abstract semantic values such as time or episodes can also be bound to specific portions of space. In such examples, the semantically "loaded" area, which I will call *referent space* henceforth, is discrete. Emmorey et al. describe cohesive depictions of spatial content in a continuous referent space via iconic gestures [19]. They consist of "three or more successive gestures that are used to convey structural features of the environment" (p. 160). The spatial relations between gestures may quantitatively reflect corresponding relations between their referents. Thus, referent space may map almost linearly to the space depicted. Liddell describes similar patterns of spatial organization in sign language. Such mental spaces co-exist with grammatical structures [41,40]. A special strategy for depicting spatial relations with coverbal gestures is to anchor the position of one referent with one hand (e.g. a certain place or landmark) and to use the other hand successively to indicate further referents in relation to the first (see [37] for a system using such two-gesture combinations). Usually the non-dominant hand is used as the anchor and is often held while the dominant hand performs further gestures. The first gesture in such a spatially coherent sequence may even set up a reference coordinate system as observed in descriptions of complex, structured objects [20,58]. The first gesture, often performed bimanually, introduces a coarse outline of the object in space, while successive gestures elaborate the description by depicting details or parts relative to this frame of reference. Again,

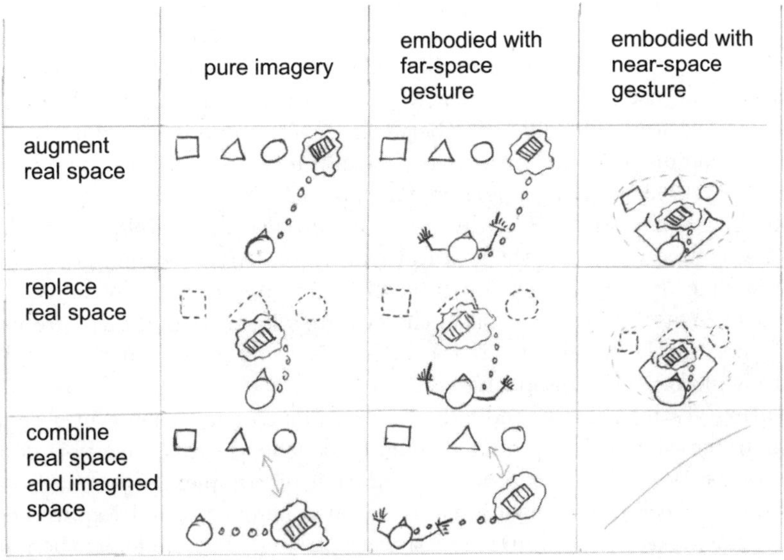

	pure imagery	embodied with far-space gesture	embodied with near-space gesture
augment real space			
replace real space			
combine real space and imagined space			

Fig. 3. Different types of imagination and explication via gestures and speech

the maintenance of the reference frame with the non-dominant hand is typical for these depiction strategies.

In all these cases, gestures set up a spatial context that is maintained for some time and is used to place subsequent gestures within. They represent a form of deixis without a static, visually accessible context, comparable to what Karl Bühler called "Deixis am Phantasma" of which he distinguished three subtypes [6]: the first is characterized by a referent space as an augmentation of real space with an imagined object, for instance, if someone is looking at the empty window ledge in the living room and imagines a vase of flowers placed upon it. The second type involves a change of origo, the center of a speaker's coordinate system defining *here, now,* and *I.* A speaker or listener in a communicative situation may mentally transfer his/her origo with respect to time, place, and person, such as in any description of distant places. Here, the referent space completely replaces real space. The third main type is characterized by referring to a distant, currently inaccessible referent without a shift of origo. Pointing into the direction of one's home town illustrates this type.

Bühler's analysis applies in the same vein to referent spaces which are not purely imagistic, but externalized by gesture as a material, though ephemeral, carrier as illustrated in Fig. 3. The first row depicts an augmentation of the real space by referent space, the second illustrates a replacement of real space by referent space, and the third row shows a combination of both spaces.

Bühler's three types of deixis to invisible and purely imagistic referents are illustrated in the first column of Fig. 3. In the first row, the visible environment is augmented by an imaginary object, in the second row, the imaginary object or scene does not relate to the current environment, but replaces it, and in the third row, the imaginary referent exists and is referred to from the current situation, but is not visibly accessible. Columns two and three illustrate how gesture can be used by the speaker to structure space and impose meaning in the three situations. The difference between the situations depicted in the second and third column is in the area used to locate imagistic entities. In the second column imagistic entities appear in far space. In the third column, they are located in gesture space. The difference in physical accessibility of these two areas has consequences for the gestural realization. Areas beyond gesture space are accessible only by projection typically using pointing gestures. When the referent is created in gesture space, the gesture's location and form are usually more immediately connected to the referent's properties such that an iconic gesture is more likely to appear.

Treating gestures not as individual signs, but as components in a coherent spatial frame of reference could be highly beneficial for application domains where properties such as spatial configuration or complex, structured objects are in focus. Technical realizations of spatial coherence would require keeping track of the location of gestures in gesture space and thus modeling the referent space. In order to assess meaning, the mapping between referent space and the world has to be determined. First steps in this direction were taken in [37,58]. A serious problem is the differentiation of one referent space from another, a task that resembles the segmentation problem for individual gestures, but on a higher processing level. For how long do successive gestures cohere in a common spatial frame of reference, where does a frame of reference dissolve, and where does another one begin? One cue in gesture form is the use of the non-dominant hand that explicitly signals the maintenance of spatial coherence in the cases mentioned above. Is has to be examined whether there are other structural cues exploitable in gesture comprehension systems.

3.3   Integrated Multimodal Language Comprehension

Current psycholinguistic thinking promotes the idea of an integrated system for language comprehension comprising verbal and non-verbal activity likewise. Psycholinguistic studies show that language comprehension is facilitated by the visibility of coverbal gestures (cf. [2] for an overview). It is assumed that all pieces of nonverbal communicative activity and speech contribute to compound messages. These messages are brought about and comprehended by a multi-modal system of communication in which speech and gesture are processed in a tightly integrated fashion [1,13]. This idea finds support in neurocognitive studies demonstrating a semantic dependency of gesture and speech input processing. When subjects are confronted with speech and gesture stimuli, electrophysiolog-ical responses differ for semantically matching and mismatching stimulus pairs [32,48]. Another experiment demonstrates an electrophysiological effect of iconic gestures on the processing of speech even if attention was distracted from gesture [69]. Recent results from fMRI studies lend further support to the integrative theory by showing that both action and language recruit overlapping parts of the brain in multimodal comprehension tasks [67]. Together, these results are taken as evidence for a common semantic processing of both modalities.

Given the psycholinguistic and neurocognitive findings on the relevance of non-verbal signals in face-to-face communication, we may maintain the working hypothesis that language comprehension is essentially multimodal. This paradigm could be adopted for the design of computational models of gesture and speech comprehension. Research and multimodal system engineering may profit from this idea in two respects: By moving towards an architecture built alongside insights from cognitive science, multimodal systems may provide a platform to test and to refine models of comprehension. At the same time, better recognition performance and increased robustness can be expected, if we build systems where the global-imagistic visual and the linear-segmented verbal sides disambiguate each other and influence each other's course of processing during comprehension.

The survey of gesture and speech input systems distinguished three classes of approaches described in the literature: gesture facilitates speech recognition, speech facilitates gesture recognition, and gesture and speech integration. The former two areas have only attracted attention in the past 7-8 years, while the latter has quite a long tradition in research. All hand gesture and speech integration approaches are so-called late-fusion models [47], where the meanings of the modalities are determined independently from each other and merged in a later processing step. A big challenge, but also a chance for system builders would be to integrate the facilitative function of gesture for speech and vice versa in a gesture-speech integration model. This approach would get us closer to a truly interactive and closely-coupled mechanism for multimodal comprehension. Yet, the models of mutual facilitation described in 2.4 are based on statistics and do not consider semantics yet.

In accordance with a more interactive model of comprehension, the information of one modality could be used to influence the recognition and meaning formation process in the other modality and vice versa. Imagine speech-based interaction with a system in a noisy environment or over a distance (e.g. distant communication with a mobile robot). An instruction by the human interlocutor such as "turn around" could be accompanied by an iconic gesture that expresses the idea of rotation, for instance, a circular movement of the hand. An instruction to pick up a small object could be accompanied by indicating a small size with a small distance between the tip of the thumb and the index finger. In such cases, the iconic information present in gestures could be exploited to increase the chances of recognizing the correct words co-expressive with the gestural idea ("turn around", "small"). An implementation of these properties would require a conceptualization of the gesture in an appropriate spatial format which in turn activates words that correspond to the spatial idea ("around" would be linked to the spatial concept of circular movement). This strategy leads to a partial disintegration of the modular structures in the system. The speech recognition system, for instance, cannot be a separate module in the multimodal system any longer, but has to be broken up to allow gestural information to enter the system. Successful cross-modal facilitation also relies on a deep semantic model of the domain in which words that imply some spatial meaning are linked to various spatial representations into which iconic gesture input can be transformed [55].

In analogy to the facilitation of speech recognition, gesture recognition and segmentation could in turn benefit from semantic processing of speech. Note that such reciprocal backlinks from semantic processing to recognition might require a revision of earlier hypotheses (initial speech recognition leads to a semantic process which in turn links back to gesture recognition – but gesture recognition has already built up a hypothesis). Eventually, such a system architecture will have less in common with a modular multimodal system that leads from gesture and speech input to a common interpretation, than with a dynamic system getting input from two sides that stabilizes and zeroes in on a solution.

4 Conclusion

I have laid out challenges for gesture recognition in three areas: the semiotic domains, deixis in imagistic space, and an integrated processing approach for gesture-accompanied speech. The review of the computational approaches still shows a huge gap between gesture recognition and comprehension technology in human-computer interaction and the potential of coverbal gesture as a carrier of meaning in human communication. The majority of systems still focus on gesture recognition as a pattern classification problem. Only a few systems model the semantic dimensions of deixis and iconicity, and those are limited to specific domains. Modeling gestural deixis in imagistic spaces will open the door to advanced gesture-based applications and conversational interfaces that do not rely exclusively on the perceivable world as a context model. In particular, the augmentation of real space by an imagined space anchored in gestures opens up a new area of research with applications that connect visual perception, imagery, and deixis. Bound to an integrated multimodal processing approach comprising models for gestural deixis and iconicity is the prospect that cross-modal facilitation can produce more robust systems for speech and gesture understanding. Besides building computational models more in line with current research in cognitive science, early integration may avoid the cumulation of recognition errors leading to unstable systems.

Acknowledgments. This work was supported by a research grant from the German Academic Exchange Service (DAAD). The author is indebted to the anonymous reviewers for their helpful comments.

References

1. Bavelas, J., Chovil, N.: Visible Acts of Meaning: An Integrated Message Model of Language in Face-to-Face Dialogue. Journal of Language and Social Psychology 19(2), 163–194 (2000)
2. Beattie, G.: Visible Thought: The New Psychology of Body Language. Routledge, London (2003)

3. Benoit, C., Martin, J.-C., Pelachaud, C., Schomaker, L., Suhm, B.: Audio-Visual and Multimodal Speech-Based Systems. In: Gibbon, D., Mertins, I., Moore, R. (eds.) Handbook of Multimodal and Spoken Dialogue Systems: Resources, Terminology and Product Evaluation, pp. 102–203. Kluwer, Dordrecht, The Netherlands (2000)

4. Bers, J.: A Body Model Server for Human Motion Capture and Representation. Presence: Teleoperators and Virtual Environments 5(4), 381–392 (1996)

5. Bolt, R.: "put-that-there": Voice and gesture at the graphics interface. Journal of Computer Graphics 14(3), 262–270 (1980)

6. Bühler, K.: Sprachtheorie. In: Gustav Fischer, Jena, Germany (1934)

7. Burger, J., Marshall, R.: The Application of Natural Language Models to Intelligent Multimedia. In: Maybury, M. (ed.) Intelligent Multimedia Interfaces, pp. 174–196. MIT Press, Cambridge (1993)

8. Chai, J., Hong, P., Zhou, M.: A Probabilistic Approach to Reference Resolution in Multimodal User Interfaces. In: Nunes, N.J., Rich, C. (eds.) Proceedings of the 2004 Int. Conf. on Intelligent User Interfaces (IUI 2004), pp. 70–77. ACM Press, New York (2004)

9. Chen, E.: Six Degree-of-Freedom Haptic System for Desktop Virtual Prototyping Applications. In: Proceedings of the First International Workshop on Virtual Reality and Prototyping, Laval, France, pp. 97–106 (June 1999)

10. Chen, L., Liu, Y., Harper, M., Shriberg, E.: Multimodal Model Integration for Sentence Unit Detection. In: Proceedings of the Int. Conf. on Multimodal Interfaces (ICMI 2003), ACM Press, New York (2003)

11. Chen, L., Harper, M., Huang, Z.: Using Maximum Entropy (ME) Model to Incorporate Gesture Cues for SU Detection. In: Proceedings of the Int. Conf. on Multimodal Interfaces (ICMI 2006), pp. 185–192. ACM Press, New York (2006)

12. Cheung, K.-M., Baker, S., Kanade, T.: Shape-from-Silhouette Across Time Part II: Applications to Human Modeling and Markerless Motion Tracking. Int. Journal of Computer Vision 63(3), 225–245 (2005)

13. Clark, H.: Using Language. Cambridge University Press, Cambridge (1996)

14. Cohen, P.R., Johnston, M., McGee, D., Oviatt, S., Pittman, J., Smith, I., Chen, L., Clow, J.: Quickset: Multimodal Interaction for Distributed Applications. In: Proceedings of the Fifth Annual International Multimodal Conference, pp. 31–40. ACM Press, New York (1997)

15. Corradini, A.: Real-Time Gesture Recognition by Means of Hybrid Recognizers. In: Wachsmuth, I., Sowa, T. (eds.) Gesture and Sign Language in Human-Computer Interaction, pp. 34–46. Springer, Berlin Heidelberg New York (2002)

16. Efron, D.: Gesture, Race and Culture. Mouton, The Hague (1941)/1972)

17. Eisenstein, J., Davis, R.: Gesture Features for Coreference Resolution. In: Renals, S., Bengio, S., Fiscus, J.G. (eds.) MLMI 2006. LNCS, vol. 4299, pp. 154–165. Springer, Heidelberg (2006)

18. Ekman, P., Friesen, W.: The Repertoire of Nonverbal Behavior: Categories, Origins, Usage and Coding. Semiotica 1, 49–98 (1969)

19. Emmorey, K., Tversky, B., Taylor, H.: Using Space to Describe Space: Perspective in Speech, Sign, and Gesture. Spatial Cognition and Computation 2, 157–180 (2000)

20. Enfield, N.: On Linear Segmentation and Combinatorics in Co-Speech Gesture: A Symmetry-Dominance Construction in Lao Fish Trap Descriptions. Semiotica 149(1/4), 57–123 (2004)

21. Wachsmuth, I., Fröhlich, M.: Gesture Recognition of the Upper Limbs - From Signal to Symbol. In: Wachsmuth, I., Fröhlich, M. (eds.) GW 1997. LNCS (LNAI), vol. 1371, Springer, Heidelberg (1998)
22. Harling, P., Edwards, A. (eds.): Progress in Gestural Interaction: Proceedings of the Gesture Workshop 1996. Springer, Berlin Heidelberg New York (1997)
23. Harling, P., Edwards, A.: Hand Tension as a Gesture Segmentation Cue. In: Harling, P., Edwards, A. (eds.) Progress in Gestural Interaction: Proceedings of the Gesture Workshop 1996, pp. 75–87. Berlin Heidelberg New York, Heidelberg (1997)
24. Hofmann, F., Heyer, P., Hommel, G.: Velocity Profile Based Recognition of Dynamic Gestures with Discrete Hidden Markov Models. In: Wachsmuth, I., Fröhlich, M. (eds.) Gesture and Sign Language in Human-Computer Interaction, pp. 81–95. Springer, Berlin Heidelberg New York (1998)
25. Howell, A., Buxton, H.: Gesture Recognition for Visually Mediated Interaction. In: Braffort, A., Gherbi, R., Gibet, S., Richardson, J., Teil, D. (eds.) Gesture-Based Communication in Human-Computer Interaction, pp. 141–152. Springer, Berlin Heidelberg New York (1999)
26. Huang, Y., Huang, T.: Model-Based Human Body Tracking. In: Proceedings of the 16th International Conference on Pattern Recognition (ICPR 2002), vol. 1, pp. 10552–10556. IEEE Press, Washington (2002)
27. Johnston, M.: Multimodal Unification-Based Grammars. In: Ali, S., McRoy, S. (eds.) Representations for Multi-Modal Human-Computer Interaction, AAAI Press, Menlo Park (1998)
28. Johnston, M., Bangalore, S.: Finite-State Methods for Multimodal Parsing and Integration. In: Proceedings of the ESSLLI Summer School on Logic, Language, and Information, Helsinki, Finland (August 2001)
29. Johnston, M., Cohen, P., McGee, D., Oviatt, S., Pittman, J., Smith, I.: Unification-Based Multimodal Integration. In: Proc. of the 35th Annual Meeting of the Association for Computational Linguistics, Madrid, pp. 281–288 (1997)
30. Kahol, K., Tripathi, P., Panchuanathan, S.: Gesture Segmentation in Complex Motion Sequences. In: Proceedings of the International Conference on Image Processing (2), pp. 105–108. IEEE Press, Rochester, New York (2002)
31. Kaiser, E., Olwal, A., McGee, D., Benko, H., Corradini, A., Li, X., Cohen, P., Feiner, S.: Mutual Disambiguation of 3D Multimodal Interaction in Augmented and Virtual Reality. In: Proc. of the Fifth Int. Conf. on Multimodal Interfaces (ICMI 2003), pp. 12–19. ACM Press, New York (2003)
32. Kelly, S., Kravitz, C., Hopkins, M.: Neural Correlates of Bimodal Speech and Gesture Comprehension. Brain and Language 89, 253–260 (2004)
33. Kendon, A.: Gesticulation and Speech: Two aspects of the Process of Utterance. In: Key, M.R. (ed.) The Relationship of Verbal and Nonverbal Communication, pp. 207–227. Mouton, The Hague (1980)
34. Kendon, A.: Gesture: Visible Action as Utterance. Cambridge University Press, Cambridge (2004)
35. Kessler, G.D., Hodges, L.F., Walker, N.: Evaluation of the Cyberglove as a Whole-Hand Input Device. Transactions on Computer Human Interaction 2(4), 263–283 (1995)
36. Kettebekov, S., Yeasin, M., Sharma, R.: Prosody Based Audiovisual Coanalysis for Coverbal Gesture Recognition. IEEE Transactions on Multimedia 7(2), 234–242 (2005)
37. Koons, D., Sparrell, C., Thorisson, K.: Integrating Simultaneous Input from Speech, Gaze and Hand Gestures. In: Maybury, M. (ed.) Intelligent Multimedia Interfaces, pp. 257–276. AAAI Press/MIT Press, Cambridge (1993)

38. Wachsmuth, I., Kranstedt, A., Lücking, A., Pfeiffer, T., Rieser, H.: Deixis: How to Determine Demonstrated Objects Using a Pointing Cone. In: Gibet, S., Courty, N., Kamp, J.-F. (eds.) GW 2005. LNCS (LNAI), vol. 3881, pp. 300–311. Springer, Heidelberg (2006)
39. Latoschik, M.: Multimodale Interaktion in Virtueller Realität am Beispiel der virtuellen Konstruktion. In: Latoschik, M. (ed.) DISKI, Infix, Berlin, vol. 251 (2001)
40. Liddell, S.K.: Grammar, Gesture, and Meaning in American Sign Language. Cambridge University Press, Cambridge (2003)
41. Liddell, S.K.: Blended Spaces and Deixis in Sign Language Discourse. In: McNeill, D. (ed.) Language and Gesture, pp. 331–357. Cambridge University Press, Cambridge (2000)
42. McNeill, D.: Hand and Mind: What Gestures Reveal about Thought. University of Chicago Press, Chicago (1992)
43. McNeill, D.: Gesture and Thought. University of Chicago Press, Chicago (2005)
44. Neal, J., Shapiro, S.: Intelligent Multi-Media Interface Technology. In: Sullivan, S., Tyler, S. (eds.) Intelligent User Interfaces, pp. 11–43. ACM Press, New York (1991)
45. Nickel, K., Stiefelhagen, R.: Pointing Gesture Recognition Based on 3D-Rracking of Face, Hands and Head Orientation. In: Proceedings of the Int. Conf. on Multimodal Interfaces (ICMI 2003), pp. 140–146. ACM Press, New York (2003)
46. Nigay, L., Coutaz, J.: A Generic Platform for Addressing the Multimodal Challenge. In: Katz, I., Mack, R., Marks, L., Rosson, M.B., Jakob, N. (eds.) Human Factors In Computing Systems: CHI 1995 Conference Proceedings, pp. 98–105. ACM Press, New York (1995)
47. Oviatt, S.: Multimodal Interfaces. In: Jacko, J., Sears, A. (eds.) The Human-Computer Interaction Handbook, pp. 286–304. Lawrence Erlbaum, Mahwah (2003)
48. Özyürek, A., Willems, R.M., Kita, S., Hagoort, P.: On-line Integration of Semantic Information from Speech and Gesture: Insights from Event-Related Brain Potentials. Journal of Cognitive Neuroscience 19, 605–616 (2007)
49. Lee, S.-W., Park, A.-Y.: Gesture Spotting in Continuous Whole Body Action Sequences Using Discrete Hidden Markov Models. In: Gibet, S., Courty, N., Kamp, J.-F. (eds.) GW 2005. LNCS (LNAI), vol. 3881, pp. 100–111. Springer, Heidelberg (2006)
50. Pavlovic, V., Sharma, R., Huang, T.: Visual Interpretation of Hand Gestures for Human-Computer Interaction: A Review. IEEE Transactions on Pattern Analysis and Machine Intelligence 19(7), 677–695 (1997)
51. Peirce, C.S.: Collected Papers of Charles Sanders Peirce. The Belknap Press of Harvard University Press, Cambridge (1965)
52. Qu, S., Chai, J.Y.: Salience Modeling Based on Non-Verbal Modalities for Spoken Language Understanding. In: Proceedings of the Eighth International Conference on Multimodal Interfaces (ICMI 2006), pp. 193–200. ACM Press, New York (2006)
53. Rabiner, L.: A Tutorial on Hidden Markov Models and Seleted Applications in Speech Recognition. Proceedings of the IEEE 77(2), 257–286 (1989)
54. Rigoll, G., Kosmala, A., Eickeler, S.: High Performance Real-Time Gesture Recognition Using Hidden Markov Models. In: Wachsmuth, I., Fröhlich, M. (eds.) Gesture and Sign Language in Human-Computer Interaction, pp. 69–80. Springer, Berlin Heidelberg New York (1998)
55. Roy, D.: Semiotic Schemas: A Framework for Grounding Language in Action and Perception. Artificial Intelligence 167, 170–205 (2005)
56. Shan, C., Tan, T., Wei, Y.: Real-Time Hand Tracking Using a Mean Shift Embedded Particle Filter. Pattern Recognition 40(7), 1958–1971 (2007)

57. Sharma, R., Cai, J., Chakravarthy, S., Poddar, I., Sethi, Y.: Exploiting Speech/Gesture Co-occurrence for Improving Continuous Gesture Recognition in Weather Narration. In: Proceedings of the Fourth IEEE International Conference on Automatic Face and Gesture Recognition, pp. 422–427. IEEE Computer Society, Washington (2000)

58. Sowa, T.: Understanding Coverbal Iconic Gestures in Shape Descriptions. Akademische Verlagsgesellschaft Aka, Amsterdam (2006)

59. Srihari, R.: Computational Models for Integrating Linguistic and Visual Information: A Survey. Artificial Intelligence Review 8, 349–369 (1994)

60. Thórisson, K.: A Mind Model for Multimodal Communicative Creatures & Humanoids. International Journal of Applied Artificial Intelligence 13(4–5), 449–486 (1999)

61. Turk, M.: Computer Vision in the Interface. Communications of the ACM 47(1), 60–67 (2004)

62. Väänänen, K., Böhm, K.: Gesture-Driven Interaction as a Human Factor in Virtual Environments – An Approach with Neural Networks. In: Gigante, M.A., Jones, H. (eds.) Virtual Reality Systems, pp. 93–106. Academic Press, London (1991)

63. Wachsmuth, I.: Communicative Rhythm in Gesture and Speech. In: Braffort, A., Gherbi, R., Gibet, S., Richardson, J., Teil, D. (eds.) Gesture-Based Communication in Human-Computer Interaction, pp. 277–290. Springer, Berlin Heidelberg New York (1999)

64. Wachsmuth, I., Fröhlich, M. (eds.): Gesture and Sign Language in Human-Computer Interaction. In: Wachsmuth, I., Fröhlich, M. (eds.) GW 1997. LNCS (LNAI), vol. 1371, Springer, Heidelberg (1998)

65. Wahlster, W.: User and Discourse Models for Multimodal Communication. In: Sullivan, J., Tyler, S. (eds.) Intelligent User Interfaces, pp. 45–67. ACM Press, New York (1991)

66. Waibel, A., Vo, M.T., Duchnowski, P., Manke, S.: Multimodal Interfaces. Artificial Intelligence Review 10, 299–319 (1996)

67. Willems, R., Özyürek, A., Hagoort, P.: When Language Meets Action: The Neural Integration of Gesture and Speech. Cerebral Cortex Advance Access, (published December 11, 2006) (2006) doi:10.1093/cercor/bhl141

68. Wu, Y., Huang, T.: Vision-Based Gesture Recognition: A Review. In: Braffort, A., Gherbi, R., Gibet, S., Richardson, J., Teil, D. (eds.) Gesture-Based Communication in Human-Computer Interaction, pp. 103–115. Springer, Berlin Heidelberg New York (1999)

69. Wu, Y.C., Coulson, S.: Meaningful Gestures: Electrophysiological Indices of Iconic Gesture Comprehension. Psychophysiology 42, 654–667 (2005)

70. Wundt, W.: The Language of Gestures. In: vol. 6 of Approaches to Semiotics, Mouton, The Hague, Paris (1900/1973)

71. Zimmerman, T., Lanier, J., Blanchard, C., Bryson, S., Harvill, Y.: A Hand Gesture Interface Device. In: Proceedings of the SIGCHI/GI Conference on Human Factors in Computing Systems and Graphics Interface, Toronto, Canada, pp. 189–192. ACM Press, New York (1986)

Modeling Facial Expression of Uncertainty in Conversational Animation

Matthew Stone and Insuk Oh

Department of Computer Science
Rutgers, The State University of New Jersey
110 Frelinghuysen Road, Piscataway NJ 08854-8019
matthew.stone@rutgers.edu

Abstract. Building animated conversational agents requires developing a fine-grained analysis of the motions and meanings available to interlocutors in face-to-face conversation and implementing strategies for
using these motions and meanings to communicate effectively. In this
paper, we sketch our efforts to characterize people's facial displays of
uncertainty in face-to-face conversation. We analyze empirical data from
human–human conversation and extend our platform for conversational
animation, including RUTH (the Rutgers University Talking Head), to
simulate what we find. This methodology leads to a range of new insights into the structure, timing, expressive content and communicative
function of facial actions.

Keywords: embodied conversational agents, facial displays, face-to-face
conversation, uncertainty.

1 Introduction

Our cooperative conversations are amazingly complex activities. As we talk, we
must contribute appropriate content, we must give each contribution an appropriate emphasis to show why we are making it, and we must support the
interaction by collaborating to ensure that we are understood. With all this to
do, it's no wonder that words alone are not enough.

Research has shown that people canuse nonverbal behaviors as an integral part
of their face-to-face conversations [1,2,3]. For example, coverbal gesture can help
contribute content to the conversation in ways that interlocutors pick up on and
remember [4]. Eyebrow flashes can help to mark emphasis in the accompanying
speech and disambiguate its contribution to the discourse [5]. Even how one
holds one's body [6] and directs one's head [7] can give visible form to one's
efforts to structure and track the conversation, and can help to support the
robust dynamics of natural communication.

In this paper, we explore the use of animation and simulation as a methodology that can help to characterize this rich repertoire of expressive behaviors. Our
investigation focuses on the facial displays that interlocutors can use to signal
their certainty or uncertainty about their contributions to face-to-face conversation. In fact, as part of a broader investigation, we have found that interlocutors

I. Wachsmuth and G. Knoblich (Eds.): Modeling Communication, LNAI 4930, pp. 57–76, 2008.

do have behaviors at their disposal that can accurately indicate their level of
certainty to viewers, and reproducing those behaviors can allow viewers to infer an animated agent's level of certainty too [8,9,10]. However, these behaviors
are quite complex, involving the orchestration of many fine-grained expressive
movements that play out over time in synchrony with a spoken utterance. They
include emblematic displays with relevant meanings, such as the "facial shrug"
meaning *I don't know*, which is performed by raising the eyebrows and using
the muscle at the chin to raise and project the lower lip. But they also include specific combined uses of signals with other emotional and conversational
meanings, spanning subjects' eyes, eyebrows, mouth shape and head pose. In
these utterances, it seems that uncertain speakers dramatize their cognitive effort for their interlocutors, as they formulate contributions to conversation word
by word, and showcase their appraisal of that effort as problematic, difficult or
comical. Viewers infer speakers' uncertainty indirectly, by tracking the cognitive
effort and appreciating the appraisal. The multifaceted and dynamic nature of
uncertainty communication poses a substantial challenge for creating embodied
conversational agents with the rich expressive capabilities that people use.

The specific contribution of this paper is to describe how we have extended
the capabilities of our face animation system RUTH (Rutgers University Talking
Head) [11] to support the study of such specific, naturalistic facial movements as
performed in synchrony with coverbal speech.[1] We begin in Sec. 2 by exploring
how people communicate uncertainty face-to-face, and how we are combining
observational research, computer animation, and psychological studies to characterize how this communication works. We also describe some of the difficulties
we encountered in using the original version of RUTH, within this methodology,
to animate the kind of complex naturalistic behaviors that speakers use to communicate uncertainty. In Sec. 3, we explain how the empirical data we wanted
to model led to substantial revisions in the capabilities of the animation system
and the way the animation interfaces with utterance representations and dialogue architecture. Finally, as we discuss in Sec. 4, the data also gives us reason
to reconsider more general design principles for future animated agents.

Our presentation reports one aspect of a broader project. In addition to the
data analysis and animation research we describe here, this project also included
validation experiments to document viewers' interpretations of recorded utterances and of RUTH animations. We can only summarize these other ingredients
of the project here, and we refer interested readers to [10], which summarizes our
evaluation of RUTH, and to [8], which describes all our experiments in detail.

2   Communicating Uncertainty Face-to-face

Both speakers and their audience are sensitive to uncertainty in conversation.
When they are uncertain, speakers give answers more slowly, and are more likely
to use rising intonation, to qualify their statements with hedges, and to provide

---

[1] The updated version of RUTH is available for research use at
   http://www.cs.rutgers.edu/~village/ruth

commentary evaluating their search for information [12]. Listeners can recognize these cues from recorded speech [13]. This uncertainty shows itself in the nonverbal cues that speakers use as well. A recent survey [14], elaborating a common-sense inventory that goes back at least to Darwin [15], proposes that such cues can include frowns, sideward eye movements, lip-pouting, lip-pursing, tensed mouths, side-to-side head-shakes, head tilts, self-touch gestures, hand-behind-head cues, palm-up gestures, and the shoulder-shrug. Such "expressions of uncertainty"—nonverbal signals that can be interpreted as giving evidence about speakers' uncertainty or related states such as confusion—count as some of the most frequent displays in American conversation [16]. And their interpretations are robust. Swerts and Krahmer [17,18], for example, found that eyebrow movements, smiling, diverted gaze, and marked facial expressions were reliable visual cues that speakers produced and addressees used to distinguish responses where speakers felt confident in the information they were providing from those where speakers did not.

It is less clear how expressive nonverbal behaviors manage to succeed in drawing out these interpretations. The subjective meaning of uncertainty is hotly debated in the communication literature [16,19], but in typical cases, uncertainty seems to combine both cognitive and affective components [20,19]. The cognitive state of uncertainty is one's judgment that, for all one knows, a question of interest could have more than one possible resolution, each with a substantial probability associated with it. Uncertainty carries affective meaning because it usually involves a secondary judgment that one *should* know how things are. Recognizing that one's ignorance is a problem may trigger a range of emotions, such as discomfort, fear, anger, or embarrassment. The subjective complexity of uncertainty suggests that specific expressions might convey uncertainty indirectly, by signaling specific ingredients of the cognitive or affective state associated with an interlocutor's uncertainty.

We can illustrate the potential for these nuances of interpretation by considering eyebrow movements as signals of uncertainty. From descriptive work [21,14] and perceptual work [17,18] we know that speakers can use brow raises and frowns to convey their uncertainty. But these actions are used in many other situations; they have very general meanings. Brow raises can signal surprise or interest, and are used conversationally to emphasize noteworthy information. Frowns can signal anger or difficulty, and are used conversationally when information needs serious consideration. For such underspecified meanings to convey uncertainty as effectively as they do, the intended interpretation must be cued somehow, perhaps by how the speaker performs the behavior, when the speaker performs it, or what else the speaker does at the same time. In our data, for example, some uncertain speakers showed a brief frown as a reaction to a difficult question, before formulating a response. Others combined a frown with eyelid tightening while delivering the response, as in Fig. 1, as if to dramatize with a complex collection of movements the difficulty of getting their contribution "into focus". Still others accompanied delimited intonation units highlighting uncertain information in their answers with extended brow raises, delivered with a head pose and gaze direction that seemed to engage the interlocutor. This delivery seemed to convey uncertainty by indicating the speaker's specific expectation that their contribution was provisional and might require further back-and-forth. In each of these cases, a fine-grained analysis of the utterance suggests hypothetical principles that might derive a specific interpretation of uncertainty from the more general meanings of raises, frowns and other behaviors in context. We need to confirm such principles empirically, so we need closer descriptive and perceptual investigations of the nonverbal communication of uncertainty. This goal motivates our effort to recreate and adapt specific patterns of observed movement on an animated character, so that we can present viewers with systematically varied conversational displays and obtain judgments about them.

Of course, in investigating uncertainty communication through animation, we also aim to lay the groundwork for embodied conversational agents that can convey their uncertainty over the course of a conversation. People constantly show their level of understanding and perceive others' level of understanding through a variety of audiovisual channels, and thereby adapt their contributions to make sure they can be understood [7,22,17,18]. Theoretical accounts suggest that this ability is crucial to interlocutors' success in avoiding, detecting, and resolving misunderstandings, and in reaching mutual understanding [23,24]. In effect, interlocutors in conversation often have only probabilistic information about what their partner meant or what they might best contribute in response. In these situations, interlocutors' nonverbal cues can reveal not only that they are uncertain, but also how the uncertainty makes them feel, and what consequences it might have for the interaction. These appraisals of conversational process can help focus interlocutors' joint effort towards resolving the uncertainty as the conversation proceeds.

Embodied conversational agents are also likely to have probabilistic information about what their partner meant or what they should contribute in response. In fact, agents face particular uncertainty because of the difficulty of automatic speech recognition and because of the incompleteness of practical models of the world and the limitations of models of human users. Uncertainty has therefore received particular attention for human–computer interaction, for example in tutorial dialogue [25,26].

One output for our research, then, may be a repertoire of behaviors for agents to use in such uncertain contexts. Concretely, in the simplest case, a probabilistic dialogue manager could specify its uncertainty about a planned move as part of the input to generation. In response, the generator would select words and embodied actions not only to convey the specified content but also to convey the specified uncertainty. It might do this by selecting facial displays to perform in synchrony with the units of the utterance using a pattern that we have seen an individual communicator use in natural conversation and that we know viewers tend to interpret accurately. In this way, our empirical investigation may lead to systems that can signal their own uncertainty and recognize their interlocutors', and consequently interact more robustly with people.

2.1   Visual Communication of Uncertainty

We designed and carried out a series of experiments to identify illustrative examples of behavior that reliably communicate speakers' uncertainty. Full details about the experiments can be found in [8]. The investigation deliberately narrows in on the empirical prerequisites for our central theoretical and computational problem: how to generate and interpret specific patterns of behavior as conveying uncertainty. The narrow focus has implications for the kinds of conclusions we can draw. Our experiments cannot characterize how people tend generally to show uncertainty, or even what signals of uncertainty are most common in natural conversation. Nor can they establish differences across individuals or across cultures in how interlocutors express uncertainty. We do not have enough data to address these issues. They represent important unresolved problems for future work.

We began by collecting a corpus of speech and video of subjects engaged in a face-to-face interaction designed to elicit a range of contexts and degrees of uncertainty. Subjects spoke in an informal conversation with an experimenter, and discussed a familiar topic, Rutgers University. Along the way, the experimenter asked a series of questions about the university drawn from the University's frequently-asked questions website. At key questions, the experimenter also asked subjects how certain they were of their answer on a scale of zero to one hundred. We used this self-report as a ground truth measure in correlating speaker behaviors and viewer judgments with subjective uncertainty. In fact, however, a number of prior experiments have shown that subjects' meta-cognitive judgments about whether they know an answer correlate closely with whether they do in fact know [12,13,17].

For further analysis, we focused on two questions that elicited a wide range of different certainty responses: *Who is the current Rutgers University president?* and *Do you know in what year the University was chartered?*.[2] We first aimed to discover whether subjects' responses showed reliable cues to their level of certainty [9,8]. Following [13,17], we presented recordings of answers to new judges, who rated how certain the speaker seemed in their response. Each judge was assigned to one of four conditions for the experiment: in different conditions, judges rated the text transcript of the speaker's response, the video (no sound), the audio (no video), or both video and audio. In keeping with the results of [17], we found that judges' ratings of a speaker's apparent certainty correlate quite closely with the certainty the speaker themselves reported—as long as judges get at least the video or the audio from a recording of the subject's original delivery. For example, the correlation between an individual judge's rating of recorded video and the speaker's self-reported uncertainty was 0.796 (Spearman's ρ correlation, $p < 0.01$ by two-tailed permutation test). However,

---

[2] The latter question might seem somewhat obscure to outsiders, but the Rutgers campus is festooned with flags and monuments commemorating the founding of the University in 1766. So students definitely feel this is something they *should* know, even if they can't always come up with the exact year.

with our examples, judges were not able to recognize a speaker's uncertainty merely from the text transcript of what was said.

We then wanted to investigate whether we could reproduce the visual cues to uncertainty on an animated agent, and use those cues to communicate the agent's uncertainty. We therefore created (silent) animations with RUTH that reproduced subjects' deliveries in our test items as closely as possible. As we describe presently, this process required substantial revision to RUTH. Once we had these videos, we showed them to new sets of judges, under three different conditions, and found that their ratings of RUTH's apparent certainty also correlate quite closely with the subject's reported certainty. See [10]. To start, the correlation between an individual judge's rating of a fully-realized RUTH animation and the speaker's self-reported uncertainty in the utterance from which the recording was derived was 0.635 (Spearman's ρ correlation, $p < 0.01$ by two-tailed permutation test). Moreover, by manipulating the elements of the animated performance and running corresponding ratings conditions, we were able to show that both facial movements (displays of affect) and head and eye movements (manifestations of cognitive state) seem to contribute to viewers' judgments. A second group of judges saw RUTH animations which reproduced the head and eye movements of the original performance, along with lip movements for synthetic speech. Their ratings correlate with self-report only at 0.541 (Spearman's ρ correlation, $p < 0.01$ by two-tailed permutation test). A final group saw RUTH animations which omitted the head and eye movements, but included lip movements and other expressive movements of the face. Their ratings correlate even less with self-report, at 0.405 (Spearman's ρ correlation, $p < 0.01$ by two-tailed permutation test). These results are consonant with the idea that viewers' attributions of uncertainty are inferences from speakers' meta-level signals both about their cognitive effort and about their affective state. Now that we know that RUTH animations can be interpreted like videos of people, and can vary the information they contain, we can refine our perceptual experimentation in future work to test this idea more precisely.

2.2   Starting Point: RUTH

Our focus in this paper is on the process of encoding human behaviors onto RUTH, and the particular lessons we learned by developing a representation of the performance of specific embodied utterances that bridges the fields of communication, linguistics, and computer animation. Although we have always aimed at such a synthesis in developing RUTH [11], we had never before attempted to realize animations that faithfully reproduced such complex signals of interactional and expressive state from qualitative specifications. So our initial starting points—our initial prototype of RUTH, and a FACS coding of people's behaviors in specific utterances—were further apart than we anticipated.

RUTH [11] is a real-time facial animation system that animates conversational facial displays and head movements in synchrony with speech and lip movements. RUTH's animation primitives include arbitrary point-based deformations of an underlying polygonal mesh. RUTH has no dynamical models of the action of muscles or the motion of the skin. Deformations for active motions are represented as vector offsets to mesh vertices and are summed linearly to determine the shape of the face at a particular frame of animation. RUTH handles head movements by applying rotations and translations to part of the model; the effect fades out across the neck to maintain smooth geometry. The eyes also rotate in place. For animating speech, RUTH uses a coarticulation model based on dominance functions [27,28,29] to capture the fact that different speech sounds are visible to different degrees and for different durations during articulation. RUTH is designed for use both with recorded and synthetic speech. The interface in either case is raw audio data paired with a symbolic specification of phoneme timings. We have instrumented the Festival speech synthesizer [30] to output phoneme timing information directly to RUTH; for recorded speech, we label phoneme timings by hand or use speech-recognition software to compute a forced alignment with the text transcript.

To explore the relationship between nonverbal actions and speech, RUTH offers a high-level specification of utterance realization in which qualitative nonverbal behaviors are timed in synchrony with the prosodic structure of utterances. RUTH assumes the ToBI model of English intonation [31], and uses the timestamps of accented syllables and of breaks between phrases as possible synchronization points between speech and gesture. Short behaviors (such as a nod) can synchronize with an accented syllable. Longer behaviors (such as raised eyebrows) can synchronize with a phrase as a whole; in this case, key milestones in the time-course of the animated behavior are timed to coincide with the beginning of the phrase, the first accented syllable in the phrase, the last accented syllable in the phrase, and the end of the phrase. In the resulting animations—as in people's natural utterances—units of prosodic structure coincide with units of gesture and prominent syllables coincide with the most prominent phases in the realization of accompanying behaviors [21,32,1,3].

We prototyped RUTH using a small collection of recordings of scripted utterances, mostly from the domain of broadcast news. Our initial design captured only the most frequent behaviors from these recordings. In particular, we started with those behaviors that signal discourse structure and emphasis, rather than those that express affect or help manage interaction. The prototypical display of emphasis is a symmetrical movement of the brows, highlighting an individual word or an extended phrase. See also [5]. Speakers may use raised eyebrows or, less commonly, a frown. Brief movements of the head offer a more general clue to the function of a word or phrase in the ongoing discourse. A downward nod on a word or phrase is the most common case, but speakers can also avail themselves of a range of other behaviors, including head raises, tilts, and turns, to mark what is said with a particular prominence or contrast.

2.3 Data and Analysis

We selected ten interaction segments from our data set for in-depth analysis. We transcribed all spoken words and obtained timings for individual phonemes in the speech by using the Praat speech analysis program (www.praat.org) to hand-correct an automatic alignment of sound and transcript. Two trained coders used the Facial Action Coding System (FACS [33]) to characterize the movements of the face. The coders worked independently then met to work out a consensus labeling. Agreement statistics for this process are not available, but both coders had passed the FACS reliability test, and preliminary assessments of their work were in keeping with published reliability statistics for FACS, with agreement on presence or absence of individual behaviors over 0.8 [33]. FACS specifies specific criteria to assess the type, intensity, and timing of facial movement into categories that can be reliably assessed by viewers. An inventory of types of facial action are considered, such as, for example, *eyelid tightening*, action unit 7, which achieves a squinting look that, in conversation, can convey doubt, and *chin raise*, action unit 17, which results in a pouting effect that is part of the classic "facial shrug" emblem shown in Figs. 4(b) and 4(c). FACS guidelines describe the degree of each appearance change as an intensity level from smallest (A) to greatest (E). Time denotes the duration of a movement, from the onset where the motion is first visible, to the apex where it reaches its maximum intensity level, to the offset where the motion is last visible. One of the most important aspects of using FACS to extend the behavioral repertoire of conversational agents is its comprehensiveness—it measures all visible facial movement, not just that presumed to be associated with emotion or cognitive states—and thus it allows for discovery of relationships between movement and psychological states [34].

We used an event-based coding, which means that we marked the durations of actions and their peak of intensity, rather than giving a frame-by-frame classification of action and intensity. We departed from the typical event-based coding in FACS, however, in allowing coders to identify an interval for the apex over which an action peaks, rather than just a single frame. This is important for conversational displays because they are often consciously held for an extended interval; it also anticipates our goals of linking the annotations to the time course of an animation and to events in the synchronous speech.

To code head pose and eye direction, we developed our own rough categorization of the appearance of the subject. (We found the FACS coding for head and eyes, which directly describe individual degrees of freedom for moevemnt, somewhat counterintuitive and difficult to use.) We coded the apparent tilt of the subject's head as a clock direction, so that for example 12 is straight up, 1 slightly to the left, 11 slightly to the right, and so forth. Then, we coded the intensity and direction of the subject's eyes and nose as another clock direction (e.g. 3 is turned to the left, 9 to the right, N for straight ahead), judged with respect to the natural axis of the subject's head, which was perhaps tilted away from the vertical. We didn't explicitly mark forward and backward motion, but we did attempt to reconstruct it later when realizing specific movements in animation.

The overall annotation we did can be summarized in a behavioral map [35], showing the different layers and components of a person's aggregated behavior in one schematic table. Figure 1 offers one example. This overview of the utterance helps to suggest how speakers demonstrate their uncertainty in multimodal presentations. It also showcases the complex expressions and fine-grained structure of movement we were confronted with in looking at facial signals in natural conversation.

The additional snapshots in Figs. 2 to 6 are also taken from natural utterances from this data set, or from RUTH animations based on them. The examples suggest the diversity of expression found even in these few examples. In them, we saw elements of the emotional displays for surprise, happiness, fear, sadness, anger and disgust, as well as a range of other emblematic displays particularly involving mouth movements. Many familiar action units were used frequently, including raising and lowering of the brows, widening and tightening of the eyelids, smiles, and facial shrugs. But these actions were realized in many different combinations—individual displays often showcased one affective or emblematic meaning with movements around the eyes (e.g., surprise, effort) and another, unrelated meaning (e.g., ignorance, smiles) through movements around the mouth. Overall we saw no less than fifteen qualitatively different patterns on the face, and each of these could be further modulated in different ways by the intensity and asymmetry of different movements, as suggested already in Fig. 1. The only expression to be really repeated across utterances was the simple enjoyment smile many speakers showed while laughing (usually making a joke of their own ignorance). In a very real sense, each of the other expressions in our data set is unique. This flexibility shows how far we are from a general account of the meanings and behaviors of face-to-face conversation, and indicates why it is important and difficult to investigate nonverbal communication through conversational animation.

3   Design Rationales for Extensions

The behavioral analysis described in Sec. 2.3 gave us a new sense of the expressive power required to faithfully describe individual utterances such as that mapped in Fig. 1. To investigate such utterances in RUTH, we needed to give the animation system comparable expressive power. Two major changes were required: a new approach to head pose, as described in Sec. 3.1, and a new inventory of facial actions, as described in Sec. 3.2. As we illustrate here, this expressive power gives us much of the resources we need to reproduce specific patterns of nonverbal behavior in RUTH, but as Sec. 4 and Sec. 5 underscore, we are still a long way from reproducing all the behaviors we observed in animation, and from giving a general account of their meanings and interpretations.

3.1   Head Pose

We did not account for posture shifts in the initial specification of RUTH. Head movements were treated as excursions from a fixed neutral position. Utterances always began in the neutral position and finished in the neutral position. This simple scheme sufficed for the monologue data which guided our initial design.

The naturalistic data we collected, however, made it clear that posture shifts are an important element of conversational behavior. Interlocutors seem to use

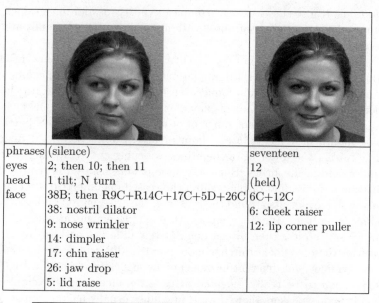

phrases	(silence)	seventeen
eyes	2; then 10; then 11	12
head	1 tilt; N turn	(held)
face	38B; then R9C+R14C+17C+5D+26C	6C+12C
	38: nostril dilator	6: cheek raiser
	9: nose wrinkler	12: lip corner puller
	14: dimpler	
	17: chin raiser	
	26: jaw drop	
	5: lid raise	

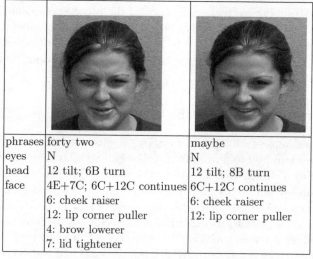

phrases	forty two	maybe
eyes	N	N
head	12 tilt; 6B turn	12 tilt; 8B turn
face	4E+7C; 6C+12C continues	6C+12C continues
	6: cheek raiser	6: cheek raiser
	12: lip corner puller	12: lip corner puller
	4: brow lowerer	
	7: lid tightener	

Fig. 1. A map of one subject's behavior in a specific interaction, as we annotated it. The top row shows representative images tracing out the subject's embodied interaction. The words are broken out into phrases: we have first the initial silence while the subject planned her response; then the answer, demarcated into three short phrases that help to set off *seventeen* as a sure answer and mark *forty-two* as one possibility, open for further discussion. The head and eye movements and facial actions are synchronized with these phases in the presentation of the utterance and, as the detailed coding suggests, integrate a complex range of behaviors.

these posture shifts to dramatize the status of their participation in the conversation. Of course, the current state of empirical research is not far enough along to support a scientific description of exactly how these behaviors function in conversation. Instead, we will try to convey our intuitions that these behaviors have relatively transparent meanings by considering examples such as those in Fig. 2 and offering the impressions that we have as viewers.

While not speaking or formulating an utterance, participants often adopted a characteristic "listening" pose, with the head brought forward and posed slightly lower, in a kind of pantomime of attention and deference. The first two images from the left of each row of Fig. 2 shows listening poses from synthesized utterances. Participants often marked their efforts to search for information or plan an utterance by repositioning the head and eyes to look upward and away, as illustrated in the third image in each row of Fig. 2. They adopt distinctive poses for the delivery of planned utterances, and thereby embody the attitude with which the material is contributed: raising themselves and facing directly forward in confident deliveries; orienting their face slightly sideways but their eyes directly forwards, as if in anticipation of a skeptical response, to proffer controversial suggestions; or tilting their head on tentative replies as if to invite a collaborative response. The rightmost image in each row of Fig. 2 show speaking poses. Speakers often mark disfluencies by abrupt head movements, for example to resume the kinds of attitudes seen in utterance planning.

It is useful to describe such behaviors as posture shifts rather than as excursions for three reasons. First, successive movements adopt a distinct series of poses without any return to a neutral resting position. A speaker may move directly from a listening pose, to a planning pose, to a sceptical delivery, without ever adopting or even passing through a neutral rest position facing the interlocutor with the head held high. Second, there seems to be no intrinsic limit to the duration of a posture shift, and accordingly no expectation that an interlocutor who adopts a distinctive pose must soon end it. A listening attitude, for example, can last indefinitely. It's not a delimited excursion—it is in effect a change in what counts as the agent's neutral state. Finally, the qualitative meaning of the behavior follows from the position adopted, and not the trajectory or excursion that the speaker effects. The examples of Fig. 2 illustrate this. Our discussion narrates the import of these behaviors by interpreting where a speaker has placed their head as they deliver their contribution, without reference to where their head has been or where they might put it next.

Our conclusions align with those of Vilhjálmsson, Cassell and colleagues [36,6], who study the posture shifts that agents manifest on their bodies as a whole. What we say about the face, in dramatizing the state of an interaction and dramatizing the attitude with which an interlocutor contributes to the discourse, mirrors, in the small, the same kinds of orienting behaviors that also play out on people's shoulders and hips.

Posture shifts continue to align very closely with the prosodic structure of utterances. We do find posture shifts in periods of silence, of course. They are part of how people signal their participation in the conversation as they listen and

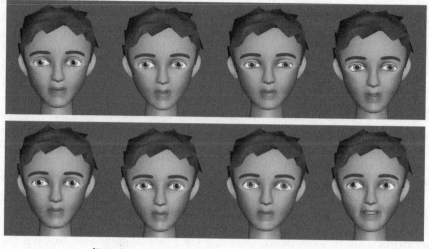

listening   planning   speaking

Fig. 2. Posture shifts on the head in the delivery of embodied utterances. Each row shows four images drawn from our realization of a specific interaction from our data set—two listening poses, a planning pose, and a speaking pose. The sequence begins with a neutral listening pose, followed by an attentive pose synched up with the prosodic excursion at the end of the question-asking utterance and marked, among other things, by a lowering of the head. The subject then turns away in utterance planning, and finally adopts a distinctive final pose to deliver their response. These are good examples of posture shifts, as opposed to nods, shakes, or other conversational head gestures, because these motions meaningfully target particular poses one after the other, without returning to a neutral rest.

plan their utterances. But posture shifts that occur along with utterances seem to align in only one of two ways. Most posture shifts are timed so that the head adopts its new pose at precisely the same moment as an accompanying prosodic event. (In our analyses, precisely the same moment refers to the interval of a single frame of video, or about 0.03 seconds.) Although some such posture shifts are timed to align with the beginning or the end of an utterance, they most often coincide with the most prominent accented syllable in a phrase. For example, in returning after looking away in thought, speakers generally face back forward again in time with the delivery of the main accent of the contribution they have planned. This alignment is perhaps somewhat surprising and does add to the analytical difficulty of distinguishing between posture shifts and movements like nods that are meaningful as excursions. Finally, of course, we do find some posture shifts that begin with distinctive prosodic events. This particularly fits two cases: disfluencies, where the speaker must wait until the disfluency occurs to signal it and recover from it; and the ends of utterances, where the resumption of a listening pose is usually effected in the subsequent silence. These patterns of timing are consistent with our earlier model [11] and with much other research in nonverbal communication in assuming a close relationship between the timing of utterances and the timing of coverbal behaviors.

3.2 Facial Displays

We omitted a wide range of facial movements in the original specification of RUTH. We worked primarily with eyebrow movements and assumed movements were performed symmetrically on both sides of the face. This fit the data we originally worked with—factual content delivered in a dispassionate style—but probably did so only because that data offered few cases where speakers depicted the emotional content of what they said or dramatized their attitude in presenting it. Our new experiment elicited a wide range of additional displays.

Our subjects used many of the elements of prototypical emotional expressions. However, these seemed less signs of felt emotions than icons that marked speakers' appraisals of their own contributions to conversation. As suggested in Fig. 3, this showed both in the forms of the behaviors and—at least impressionistically— in their meanings. The behaviors had a stylized form; they typically involved only part of the realization of a true emotion, and were often realized much more intensely on one side of the face than the other. And the interpretation of the behaviors seemed specifically tied to the ongoing communicative activity. For example, one subject displayed the characteristic nose scrunching and lip raising of disgust, just on the right side, and thereby seemed to convey not genuine revulsion at the proceedings, but rather a lighthearted indication that her contribution to the conversation was, as it were, a bit fishy. Figure 3(b) shows our realization of this display in RUTH. In another utterance, a different subject showed part of the signature of fear—specifically the left lip stretcher motion that pulls the lip down and to the side—midway through utterance planning, as though to signal her concern that she might be unable to provide needed information. Figure 3(c) shows this display in RUTH.

Facial behaviors that go beyond our original model show up in expressions unrelated to the emotions as well. Realizations of such expressions are presented in Fig. 4. A commonly-seen case is the "facial shrug", formed by pressing the lips together and raising the chin, arching the upper lip and allowing the lower lip to bulge outward. A realization in RUTH appears as Fig. 4(b). The expression, like a shoulder shrug, is a conventional signal of ignorance. Another case is the emblem of "holding oneself back", lowering the jaw but keeping the mouth closed and tight using a dimpler behavior, often with the lips sucked slightly in. RUTH's version is shown in Fig. 4(a). Speakers who use this emblem while looking away in silence, for example, create the impression that they are worried they might blurt out something wrong—they are reconsidering their utterance, rather than thinking or planning it from scratch.

To represent these examples, we had to extend the range of motion of our character. Where a motion can play out separately on different sides of the face, we introduced separate controls for the two sides. At the same time, we added motions for widening the eye in surprise (the FACS upper lid raiser), and tightening the eyelid to squint (the FACS lid tightener); for wrinkling the

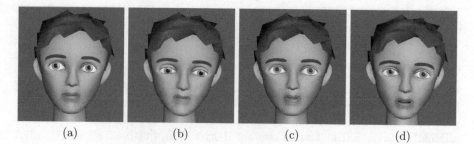

(a)   (b)   (c)   (d)

Fig. 3. People adapt the expressions of emotions to provide feedback about the state of the conversation. In (a), the wide eyes and lowered jaw of surprise combine with a gesture pulling the lip to the right—perhaps emblematic of chewing over something tough—to suggest that the speaker is working through a tough surprise. In (b), the lip raiser on the right evokes disgust, and hints that the utterance being planned will be unsatisfying. In (c), the lip is pulled down on the left, drawing on the basic expression of fear, again conveying the speaker's negative appraisal of the projected outcome of their search for the right thing to say. Example (d) gives another, more striking example of a conversational facial gesture colored by fear. All four examples are based on subjects' behavior after being asked a question but before providing an answer; they show the subject acknowledging their understanding of the question and attempting to formulate a satisfactory response.

nose and for raising the lip, as in disgust; for lowering the lower lip (the FACS lip corner depressor) and stretching the lips downward and outward (the FACS lip stretcher), as in fear; and for raising the chin. In a number of cases, these behaviors no longer combine together in the linear way presupposed by our underlying animation engine. To keep the animation believable, we therefore created separate primitives to describe key behaviors in combination. These cases typically involve treating motions with lips closed differently to corresponding motions with lips open, to take into account the changes in deformation as the lips start to press against one another.

4   Future Extensions and Issues

Our detailed analysis of particular utterances has left us with a more concrete sense of the gaps between human behaviors and the animations of RUTH, even as we have extended it. For one thing, there are a range of miscellaneous movements that we saw in human conversation but have not implemented in RUTH, including among others sucking in the lips, licking the lips, and blowing out air through tense lips in a sigh of frustration. These are difficult to animate with RUTH's current architecture of prespecified deformations in linear combination; more so than the other behaviors we have animated these motions depend closely on the physical dynamics of force and contact across the face. However, these motions do fall into the important category of *manipulators* [37] some of which should probably be included in any agent's behavioral repertoire. Agents need

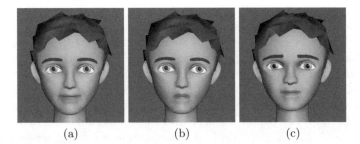

(a)   (b)   (c)

Fig. 4. Not all expressions get their meaning by reference to emotion. The pose in (a) is our rendering of an emblem for "holding oneself back", with the jaw low and mouth stretched. (We have not animated RUTH sucking the lips in, another common ingredient of this emblem.) This speaker seems to be zeroing in on the required information—in contrast to the situation in (b), where the speaker raises the chin (and the lower lip along with it), as part of an emblem of ignorance: the "facial shrug". Image (c) shows a facial shrug on the lower face colored by elements of surprise and fear across the eyes, a pose that works as an ensemble to portray ignorance and its associated negative affect. The snapshots of (a) and (c) are again taken from the interval between question and answer, while (b) accompanies a hesitation at a moment of difficulty in completing an answer.

to fidget when distracted or uncomfortable. This is one of the most common indicators of difficulty in conversation (at least in our data).

Even for those FACS action units which we included in RUTH's repertoire, there are significant differences between how they look on human faces and how they look on RUTH. Figure 5 shows a pair of contrasts that illustrate the limitation of RUTH's model in reproducing conversational displays. Most human faces have permanent infraorbital furrows (below the lower eyelid) or nasolabial furrows (adjacent to the nostril wings) that become more prominent in many actions and can sometimes be crucial in allowing viewers to recognize them [33]. However, RUTH does not yet show changes in skin marks such as lines, wrinkles, and furrows. Animating such changes goes beyond the resources of RUTH's current design, which handles smooth deformations but not these

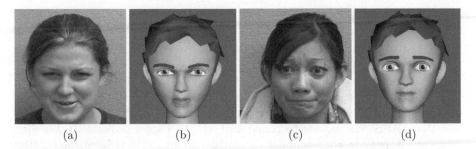

(a)   (b)   (c)   (d)

Fig. 5. The absence of wrinkles and other appearance changes in RUTH animations may color the meaning of RUTH's displays and make them more difficult for viewers to recognize.

other appearance changes. However, by leaving out these movements, we may have made RUTH's facial expressions much harder to recognize.

Let us look at the example of Fig. 5. When we make side-by-side comparisons between the actual human expression and RUTH's implementation, we can see that missing skin marks can be a critical issue. In the left pair of images, there are crucial wrinkles on the bridge of the subject's nose and around the subject's mouth. These help to show that the upper face portrays an emblem of disgust, and that the lower face overlays a smile over the dimpler and chin raise of a facial shrug. Without these indicators of the specific combination of action units that lead to this facial expression, the RUTH implementation is more ambiguous. In particular, unlike the photo, it is compatible with a straightforward expression of anger. In the same manner, the third image portrays the subject as apologetic, which is close to sadness. The RUTH version, without the brow wrinkles to indicate the involvement of the frowning muscle, and without the chin wrinkles that indicate that the mouth pose is a deliberate use of a facial shrug emblem, is more readily interpreted as surprise or fear. Our perception experiment showed that the difference between the original human facial expression and RUTH implementation is not large. However, these examples illustrate the possibility that the missing cues and marks can actually alter how displays are interpreted.

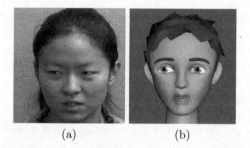

(a)   (b)

Fig. 6. Animation should lead to the same visual impression as the original video. That may mean exaggerating the human motions on RUTH. In this figure, the reorentation of RUTH's eyes involves a comparable rotation in space as the original example but does not give as strong an impression of looking away.

One way to compensate may be to exaggerate RUTH's expressions over the original human data. In fact, when an ECA coder reads the annotations without watching original video, it is still very difficult to know exactly how much movement responds to each intensity level. After all, FACS is designed to annotate observable movements from the face, not to provide specifications for computer implementation. Therefore, ECA researchers have to make an inference as to how that FACS code should be coded into RUTH. Figure 6 shows RUTH with eyes turned away to the same degree as the human subject. Nevertheless, the expressiveness from the human subject appeared to be relatively stronger. The slight and yet perceivable difference could be in part due to the simple physical difference in its appearance. For example, RUTH's eyes are relatively bigger than those of humans, thus diluting the effect of the same amount of movement on RUTH.

5 Conclusion

In this paper, we have explored the complex behaviors that interlocutors use to convey uncertainty face-to-face. These behaviors reveal movements of the head and eyes that signal the state of the conversation and the cognitive activity that the speaker is engaged in, and diverse expressive movements across the face that convey the speaker's appraisal of their efforts to contribute to conversation. Through the analysis of these behaviors, we have articulated a clearer understanding of the capabilities that face animation systems should support to reproduce people's signals of uncertainty in perceptual studies and prototype conversational agents. Some of these new requirements are realized in a new implementation of RUTH, the Rutgers University Talking Head.

The revised implementation of RUTH synthesizes a range of insights from across the science of communication. We have drawn on the Facial Action Coding System (FACS [33]) in broadening the animation inventory of our agent by implementing an extended range of qualitatively different movements. We have drawn on previous animated agents, and the literature on speech prosody, such as [31], to describe how those movements are aligned in time with the prosodic structure of speech.

Our methodology embraces psychological techniques for human-subjects investigations of the interpretation of embodied utterances. In addition to integrating our new animations into conversational systems, we have also begun to take our new animations into the lab and evaluate them. In future work, we hope to repeat the cycle of data collection, synthesis and perceptual studies to get a broader and more precise fix on the ways people communicate face-to-face. For example, we would like to assess whether the behaviors that we have identified are representative or common, and to find behaviors that are. Similarly, we would like to confirm that these behaviors have general meanings and interpretations across individuals, while getting a better handle on the ways nonverbal behaviors vary across individuals. On the one hand, we would like to run additional perceptual studies of the component motions of complex communicative actions, to understand how interlocutors' understanding of individual motions combines together to yield a coherent interpretation of embodied utterances. On the other, we would like to follow up on the hypothesis that differences in nonverbal behavior, like differences in choices of words, arise because different people take different approaches to co-constructing the conversational context and correspondingly choose to convey different information. The diverse possibilities for future work illustrate the generality and power of the methodology we have described for combining observational, computational and psychological techniques to understand face-to-face conversation and extend the behavioral repertoire of conversational agents.

Acknowledgments. Thanks to the organizers and audience of the workshop on *Modeling Communication with Robots and Virtual Humans*, to the Gesture Focus Group at SUNY Stony Brook, and to the anonymous reviewers of this chapter. We are grateful for the assistance of Mark Frank and Doug DeCarlo at various stages of this research. Our work was supported in part by NSF HLC 0308121, CCF 0541185, and HSD 0624191, and by Stone's Leverhulme Trust Visiting Fellowship at the University of Edinburgh 2005–2006. We thank Autodesk Alias for the use of Maya modeling and animation software.

References

1. McNeill, D.: Hand and Mind: What Gestures Reveal about Thought. University of Chicago Press, Chicago (1992)
2. Bavelas, J.B., Chovil, N.: Visible acts of meaning: An integrated message model of language in face-to-face dialogue. Journal of Language and Social Psychology 19(2), 163–194 (2000)
3. Engle, R.A.: Toward a Theory of Multimodal Communication: Combining Speech, Gestures, Diagrams and Demonstrations in Instructional Explanations. PhD thesis, Stanford University (2000)
4. Cassell, J., McNeill, D., McCullough, K.E.: Speech-gesture mismatches: evidence for one underlying representation of linguistic and nonlinguistic information. Pragmatics and Cognition 6(2) (1999)
5. Krahmer, E., Ruttkay, Z., Swerts, M., Wesselink, W.: Pitch, eyebrows and the perception of focus. In: Symposium on Speech Prosody (2002)
6. Cassell, J., Nakano, Y., Bickmore, T.W., Sidner, C.L., Rich, C.: Non-verbal cues for discourse structure. In: Proceedings of the Annual Meeting of the Association for Computational Linguistics (ACL 2001), pp. 106–115 (2001)
7. Nakano, Y.I., Reinstein, G., Stocky, T., Cassell, J.: Towards a model of face-to-face grounding. In: Dignum, F.P.M. (ed.) ACL 2003. LNCS (LNAI), vol. 2922, pp. 553–561. Springer, Heidelberg (2004)
8. Oh, I.: Modeling Believable Human-Computer Interaction with an Embodied Conversational Agent: Face-to-face Communication of Uncertainty. PhD thesis, Rutgers University (2006)
9. Oh, I., Frank, M., Stone, M.: Face-to-face communication of uncertainty: expression and recognition of uncertainty signals by different levels across modalities. In: ICA International Communication Association (2007)
10. Stone, M., Oh, I.: Understanding RUTH: Creating Believable Behaviors for a Virtual Human Under Uncertainty. In: Duffy, V.G. (ed.) HCII 2007 and DHM 2007. LNCS, vol. 4561, pp. 443–452. Springer, Heidelberg (2007)
11. DeCarlo, D., Revilla, C., Stone, M., Venditti, J.: Specifying and animating facial signals for discourse in embodied conversational agents. Computer Animation and Virtual Worlds 15(1), 27–38 (2004)
12. Smith, V.L., Clark, H.H.: On the course of answering questions. Journal of Memory and Language 32, 25–38 (1993)
13. Brennan, S.E., Willams, M.: The feeling of another's knowing: prosody and filled pauses as cues to listeners about the metacognitive states of speakers. Journal of Memory and Language 34, 383–398 (1995)
14. Givens, D.B.: The Nonverbal Dictionary of Gestures, Signs and Body Language Cues. Center for Nonverbal Studies Press (2001)

15. Darwin, C.: The Expression of the Emotions in Man and Animals, John Murray, London (1872)
16. Rozin, P., Cohen, A.B.: High frequency of facial expressions corresponding to confusion, concentration and worry in an analysis of naturally occurring facial expressions in americans. Emotion 3, 68–75 (2003)
17. Swerts, M., Krahmer, E.: Audiovisual prosody and feeling of knowing. Journal of Memory and Language 53(1), 81–94 (2005)
18. Krahmer, E., Swerts, M.: How children and adults produce and perceive uncertainty in audiovisual speech. Language and Speech 48(1), 29–53 (2005)
19. Ellsworth, P.C.: Confusion, concentration and other emotions of interest. Emotion 3, 81–85 (2003)
20. Brashers, D.E.: Communication and uncertainty management. Journal of Communication 51, 477–497 (2001)
21. Ekman, P.: About brows: Emotional and conversational signals. In: von Cranach, M., Foppa, K., Lepenies, W., Ploog, D. (eds.) Human Ethology: Claims and Limits of a New Discipline: Contributions to the Colloquium, pp. 169–202. Cambridge University Press, Cambridge (1979)
22. Clark, H.H., Krych, M.A.: Speaking while monitoring addressees for understanding. Journal of Memory and Language (50), 62–81 (2004)
23. Paek, T., Horvitz, E.: Conversation as action under uncertainty. In: Proceedings of the 16th Conference on Uncertainty in Artificial Intelligence (UAI), pp. 455–464 (2000)
24. DeVault, D., Stone, M.: Scorekeeping in an uncertain language game. In: BRANDIAL: Proceedings of the 10th Workshop on the Semantics and Pragmatics of Dialogue, pp. 64–71 (2006)
25. Liscombe, J., Hirschberg, J., Venditti, J.J.: Detecting certainness in spoken tutorial dialogues. In: Proceedings of Interspeech (2005)
26. Forbes-Riley, K., Litman, D.J.: Analyzing dependencies between student certainness states and tutor responses in a spoken dialogue corpus. In: Dybkjaer, L., Minker, W. (eds.) Recent Trends in Discourse and Dialogue, Springer, Heidelberg (2007)
27. Löfqvist, A.: Speech as audible gestures. In: Hardcastle, W.J., Marchal, A. (eds.) Speech Production and Speech Modeling, pp. 289–322. Kluwer, Dordrecht (1990)
28. Cohen, M.M., Massaro, D.W.: Modeling coarticulation in synthetic visual speech. In: Thalmann, N.M., Thalmann, D. (eds.) Models and techniques in computer animation, pp. 139–156. Springer, Heidelberg (1993)
29. King, S.A.: A facial model and animation techniques for animated speech. PhD thesis, The Ohio State University (2001)
30. Black, A., Taylor, P.: Festival speech synthesis system. Technical Report HCRC/TR-83, Human Communication Research Center (1997)
31. Silverman, K.E.A., Beckman, M., Pitrelli, J.F., Ostendorf, M., Wightman, C., Price, P., Pierrehumbert, J.: ToBI: A standard for labeling English prosody. In: Proceedings of the International Conference on Spoken Language Processing, pp. 867–870 (1992)
32. Bull, P., Connelly, G.: Body movement and emphasis in speech. Journal of Nonverbal Behavior 9(3), 169–187 (1985)
33. Ekman, P., Friesen, W.V., Hager, J.C.: Facial Action Coding System (FACS): Manual and Investigator's Guide. In: A Human Face, Salt Lake City, UT (2002)
34. Cohn, J.F., Ekman, P.: Measuring facial action. In: Harrigan, J.A., Rosenthal, R., Scherer, K.R. (eds.) The New Handbook of Nonverbal Behavior Research, Oxford, pp. 9–64 (2005)

35. Frank, M.: Research methods in detecting deception research. In: Harrigan, J.A., Rosenthal, R., Scherer, K.R. (eds.) The New Handbook of Methods in Nonverbal Behavior, Oxford (2006)
36. Vilhjálmsson, H., Cassell, J.: BodyChat: autonomous communicative behaviors in avatars. In: Proceedings of the International Conference on Autonomous Agents (Agents 1998), pp. 269–276 (1998)
37. Ekman, P., Friesen, W.V.: The repertoire of nonverbal behavior: Categories, origins, usage, and coding. Semiotica 1(1), 49–98 (1969)

The Evolution of Cognition —
From First Order to Second Order Embodiment

Malte Schilling and Holk Cruse

Department of Biological Cybernetics and Theoretical Biology, University of
Bielefeld, P.O. Box 10 01 31, D-33501 Bielefeld, Germany
mschilli@techfak.uni-bielefeld.de, holk.cruse@uni-bielefeld.de

Abstract. The capability to behave autonomously is assumed to rely
fundamentally on being embedded into the current situation and in the
own body. While reactive systems seem sufficient to address these aspects
to assure ones surviving in an unpredictable environment, they clearly
lack cognitive capabilities as planning ahead: The latter requires internal
models which represents the body and the environment and which can
be used to mentally simulate behaviours before actually performing one
of them. Initially, these models may have evolved in reactive systems
to serve specific actions. Cognitive functions may have developed later
exploiting the capabilities of these models.

We provide a neuronal network approach for such an internal model
that can be used as a forward model, an inverse model and a sensor
fusion model. It is integrated into a reactive control scheme of a walking
machine, enabling the system to plan its actions by mentally simulating
them.

Keywords: Embodiment, Internal Model, Mental Simulation, Recurrent Neural Network, Cognitive Control.

1   First Order Embodiment

The long term goal of a behavioural biologist, a psychologist, and to some extent
also of a roboticist is to understand the mechanisms underlying intelligent behaviour in animals including humans. Traditional Artificial Intelligence, inspired by
the analysis of logical thinking and rationality has shown considerable progress:
Intelligence was considered as a high-level process on a Knowledge Level [1]
which relies on using knowledge encoded in a symbolic representation and being closely connected to language and communication. While being successful
on specific high-level tasks, it was however found to reach limits way before approaching the adaptivity of even "simple" animals, as for example insects. For
an insect, the chance to survive in an unpredictable world is still by orders of
magnitude higher than for any yet sophisticated robot. As insects are not assumed to apply explicit logical rules or symbolic reasoning, the research strategy
has been changed to study and understand the way how such simple systems—
ranging from strictly sensor driven reactive systems to behaviour based systems
which allow some form of internal state—may operate.

I. Wachsmuth and G. Knoblich (Eds.): Modeling Communication, LNAI 4930, pp. 77–108, 2008.

The "behaviour based" approach, mainly put forward by Brooks [2], proposed to avoid the application of a central internal representation. Such systems are constructed as bottom-up approaches, starting on the lowest level with simple reflexes without any form of an internal state, but allowing also complex behaviours which rely on internal states or dynamical transformations of sensory signals, but which are usually realised in a distributed form of representation. The overall performance emerges as an effect of the interactions between all the active behaviours. Nonetheless, even the "reactive" systems in the strict sense—meaning without any form of an internal state—are able to solve tasks which were supposed to require intelligence. Experiments performed following this approach questioned the dominant concept of intelligence at that time and changed the understanding of the term. It is now assumed that intelligent behaviour can arise out of simple processes that are interacting with each other. Intelligence could be thought in this way as an emergent property of the system, which can only be ascribed from the observers point of view when concentrating on the complex overall behaviour. The behaviour of these systems does not rely on an internal symbolic representation of the world, instead they use the "world as its own [best] model" (Brooks [2], p. 139), relying only on information channels using analogue, subsymbolic signals. By using the world as its own model one circumvents the problem of a prioris [3], namely deciding what to represent and how to update the representation. Instead, the robot is situated directly in the environment [4]. And, in the first place, while behaving in the environment the robot has not to select its actions relying on an abstract representation of its configuration provided by sensory modules. Instead the robot is embodied and its behaviours arise in the interaction with the environment. These strictly reactive systems can easily been augmented by allowing internal states as are motivations (see (Maes [5]) for an early example) and learning (e.g., [6,7,8,9], to name just a few).

During the last years simple reactive systems [1] have been studied that were able to show an astonishing adaptive and flexible behaviour. Among these are, for example, studies of orientation and navigation in ants [11,12] and our own work in studying the walking behaviour of stick insects [13,14,15,16]. By these and many other studies [17] the notion of embodiment and situatedness has been put forward. As a consequence research in this field turned at first away from high-level intelligence phenomena as communication, but concentrated in a bottom-up manner on the fundamentals of intelligence focussing on a lower level, i.e., more on acting and interactions with an environment than on communication.

According to Brooks [2] situatedness means that the robot acts in a real world and not in a simulated environment. Embodiment means that the robot has an own body and own sensors to be able to directly experience the reactions of

---

[1] From now on, we will use the term reactive system in a broad sense as usually used in Cognitive Science in order to distinguish these systems from cognitive ones [10]. Included are reactive systems in the strict sense, i.e., without any internal state, as well as systems with internal states, but no predictive and cognitive capabilities. Thus, reactive systems as considered here include behaviour based systems.

the environment to its own actions. As we will later introduce a second type of embodiment, we will use here the term first order embodiment ("1E", following Metzinger [18]). Correspondingly, being situated in a real world may be termed first order situatedness ("1S"). Seen from the brains point of view, already embodiment is a kind of situatedness, as the brain is situated in the body [19]. Therefore, both notations might be combined to "1SE" and termed first order embeddedness (the term embeddedness has been used before by Mataric [20] as a substitue for situatedness but already in a more general sense as she has also related this term to embodiment (Mataric in [19]): "embodiment is a form of situatedness."). 1SE allows the grounding of a brain or a brain-like system into its physical (sensory and actuator related) properties, leading to intelligent behaviour as a consequence of a form of self-organization, which arises at the lowest levels.

2   From First Order to Second Order Embodiment

Although research concerning the abilities of such reactive systems is still at its beginning, it is obvious that some higher functions depend on some form of internal representation and cannot be reached by these systems. A reactive system is not able to plan ahead. This capability requires some kind of internal representation of at least some aspects of the world. This internal model could then be used for simulating different actions and for thinking based on the results of such imagined actions. It appears to be plausible that the basis of these models is formed by a model of the own body [21] which may later be extended to include properties of the environment. Such internal models must be grounded in the body itself and continuously adapted to reflect the functional properties and changes of the body: They must be embodied—therefore, we call this second order embodiment: Second order embodiment (according to Metzinger [18]) is the formation of a functional internal representation of—as a first step—the own body. Again including situatedness, second order embeddedness (2SE) also allows for representation of the environment. This representation emerges out of interaction between the own body and the environment and allows for intelligent behaviour by using this model, e.g., to mentally simulate and evaluate behaviour or to use the internal models serving specific actions, for which they may have evolved in the first place. From our point of view, we call the model as such simulated or second order embeddedness, because the body and some aspects of the environment are simulated in such a way that the model represents the critical physical properties in sufficient detail. To make a system a cognitive one (what, following McFarland and Bösser [22], we define as a system which is able to plan its actions in advance), the embodied internal model as such is not sufficient. Rather planning ahead requires the ability to apply actions to such models being decoupled from the body [23]. In other words, a "manipulable" model [21,10] is required which can be deployed by the controller for mental simulation while the body itself is detached from the controlling system. The selection of an appropriate action can be guided in this way by considering different actions, inferring their consequences only in the model and then choose the most suited one. Internal models are therefore a prerequisite for cognitive functions. Initially, these internal representations may have evolved in different contexts. As an example we want to mention three different aspects of internal models [24] which can be found even in simple animals and are usually ascribed to reactive systems:

- **Sensor Fusion Task:** Animals are—in contrast to robots—equipped with a wide variety of sensors. Many of these provide redundant information which could be exploited to cancel out disturbances and noise. The connections between supplementing sensors describe how these signals relate to each other. Thereby, these connections may form some kind of internal model [25,26].

  For example, if we have a closed mechanical chain, for instance both hands of a human holding a rigid stick, just measuring the joint angles and calculating the position of both hands may lead to inconsistent results due to measurement errors. If we had a mechanical model of these arms (and the stick) that allows to represent all geometrically possible positions, and only these, then feeding the measured joint angle values into this model would lead to a solution with smaller errors, because the geometrical constraints would in part cancel out the effects of the individual measurement errors.

- **Inverse Kinematic Function:** Reaching movements—in animals as well as humans—are usually aimed at a visible target. While the target position is defined in an egocentric three dimensional space, the position of the target and the movement to reach the target must be described in terms of joint positions and displacements. Some kind of transformation between these two reference systems is needed which translates the position in space into joint angles. An inverse model performs such transformations [27,28]. Aimed movements are not only found in mammals, but even insects perform such movements (an example is the targeting behaviour in the stick insect [29,30,31]).

  If the controlled arm or leg contains extra degrees of freedom (DoF), i.e., more joints than necessary for the solution of the task, there is not only one, but there are many solutions. Therefore, the controller, i.e., the brain, has to select one out of these many possible solutions. In such a case, an inverse model could be needed already in reactive systems.[2]

- **Forward Kinematic Function:** Forward models convert a joint configuration into a location in space. For fast goal-directed movements like the reaching movements just described, the delay of proprioceptive feedback might be too slow to account for an adaptive control of the movement. A possible solution for a fast prediction of the real feedback could be provided

---

[2] An alternative solution, avoiding the problem to determine the contribution of the joints individually, has been proposed by Bernstein [32] in the way that the relations between different joints are fixed. This indeed simplifies the problem but on the cost of not being able to exploit the possibilities given by the existence of many DoFs.

by a forward model [33,34] because forward models could be used to determine spatial location when joint angles are given. Combined with an inverse model, a possible error can be detected faster compared to relying only on proprioceptive feedback.

A forward model could also be used to predict the effect of a behaviour without actually performing it [35]. Therefore, a forward model can be used by a system to plan ahead. If the ability to predict is complemented by the ability to use these predictions as a basis to decide on what behaviour will be performed, the system is not anymore a reactive system, but can be termed a cognitive system. Therefore, if evolution has equipped a brain of a reactive system with such a network, the step to exploit the predictive capabilities of this network and thereby to become a cognitive system appears to be a small one.

Thus, reactive systems may use internal models for different tasks, for sensor fusion or as a pairwise combination of inverse and forward model for the control of fast goal-directed movements. In addition, cognitive systems may exploit the existence of forward models and use them for prediction.

One approach for the application of internal models in movement control is to introduce a specific model for each separate task. In contrast, we propose a way how one internal model can accomplish all tasks mentioned, namely the sensor fusion task, the inverse modelling and acting as a forward model. This unified model is based on a neural structure representing the geometry of the body segments. Therefore, this model can only provide geometrically possible solutions, even if constraints are applied. The model itself behaves like an autoassociator: when providing incomplete information to the model, it performs a pattern completion and provides consistent values for the missing parameter. The model can therefore be used for inverse, forward or any mixed kinematic problem including the sensor fusion task.

To address the question if and how such a model could be realized, we want to introduce a simple recurrent neural network approach, which shows the required behaviour. The essential principle for the integration of redundant and complementing information is the calculation of mean values: therefore, this approach is termed the Mean of Multiple Computation principle. At first, we will show how such a model can be used as a forward or an inverse kinematic model and then want to hypothesize about an extension including dynamic parameters. Afterwards, we want to discuss findings from psychology and neurology and the implications of these findings for the structure of the internal models. These observations concern the disintegration of the internal model used to explain certain mental disorders, and to account for some strange phenomenological experiences.

3   MMC — An Internal Model

How could a neuronal model look like that serves as an inverse kinematic body model, i.e., solves the inverse (kinematic) task but can still exploit all available DoFs? In the following section a solution for this problem will be explained and we will describe later that this network is also a solution for both other tasks, the sensor fusion problem and the forward problem. To this end we describe a recurrent neural network (RNN) that represents a geometrically described body. In this model, movement of, for example, the hand to a goal position occurs, metaphorically spoken, by fixing a thread to the hand and pulling it in the direction of the goal position like the hand and arm of a puppet (von Kleist [36]). To describe this principle, Mussa Ivaldi et al., [37] has introduced the term "passive motion paradigm". This neuronal model can be used for controlling the real arm by exploiting the joint angles of the model as control signals to move the real arm.

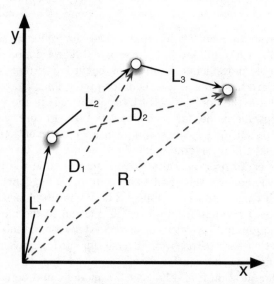

Fig. 1. Graphical representation of a planar (2D) arm consisting of three segments, upper arm (L_1), lower arm (L_2), and hand (L_3). Vector R points to the position of the end effector (tip of the hand). D_1 and D_2 represent additional diagonal vectors.

We will explain the model using a simple linear and 2D version first and later generalize this to non-linear and 3D cases. Fig. 1 shows a planar arm consisting of three segments, upper arm L_1, lower arm L_2, and hand L_3, controlled by three joints: shoulder, elbow, and wrist joint described by joint angles. The shoulder is situated at the origin of a x-y coordinate system. In addition to vectors L_1, L_2, and L_3 we have introduced diagonal vectors D_1 and D_2 and, most important, an end effector vector R. This vector determines the position of the tip of the hand. In the following we explain how this vector graph can be used to form a set of equations which constitutes a weight matrix of a neural network. First, we determine several equations formed by vector triangles: The complete graph consists of several triangles which each forms a closed polygon chain. The vectors complement each other to zero.

$$L_1 + D_2 - R = 0$$
$$L_1 + L_2 - D_1 = 0$$
$$D_1 + L_3 - R = 0$$
$$L_2 + L_3 - D_2 = 0 \qquad (1)$$

Any of these equations can be solved for each of the variables which it is containing. After this is done, all equations determining a given variable are used to form a system consisting, in this simple example, of two equations. In equation 2 this is shown for the variable L_1 as an example.

$$L_1 = R - D_2$$
$$L_1 = D_1 - L_2 \qquad (2)$$

In this way we obtain six systems of two equations each. This procedure is called multiple calculation of the same variable.

As a next step the two values determining the same variable are taken to calculate their mean value (therefore Mean of Multiple Computation, MMC). As a result, we obtain for each variable one equation which describes the variable by its different geometric relationships with respect to the other variables given by the topology of the manipulator. The resulting equations for each variable can now be written as a weight matrix for a neural network. To establish the weight matrix each vector must be decomposed into its x- and y-component which leads to sets of corresponding linear equations. In this 2D example we have two identical nets, one for each component. For 3-dimensional cases we only have to introduce a third identical network representing the z-component.

Until now, we considered a network with no self-excitation, i.e., all recurrent connections being turned off and the diagonal elements of the connection matrix are all set to zero. As a next step, we will feed the current values back into the network, which, in addition, allows to introduce a damping factor at the diagonal of the weight matrix. This self-excitation leads to smoother transitions in the network and prevents oscillations. Thus, the calculated mean values are used as an entry for the equations to calculate the mean values a second time. This procedure will be iterated for a given number of times (Fig. 2 shows the resulting recurrent neural network).

What are the properties of this system and how can it solve inverse and forward kinematic problems? In general, if all variables fulfil a geometrically correct arrangement of the vectors forming the closed chains, the system will be stable over time and always determine the same values. If, however, any disturbance occurs—assume, for example, that only one value is changed and therefore does not match the geometrical constraints—this deviation will spread over the other variables during the following iterations. Due to the calculation of the mean value, the other variables will compensate the disturbance and the network relaxes over time in a way that the vectors, although being changed, again form a geometrically closed graph [38]. For example, provided with a new target position R for the endpoint of the manipulator, the network is in a "non-harmonic" state, meaning that the different calculations for the variables lead

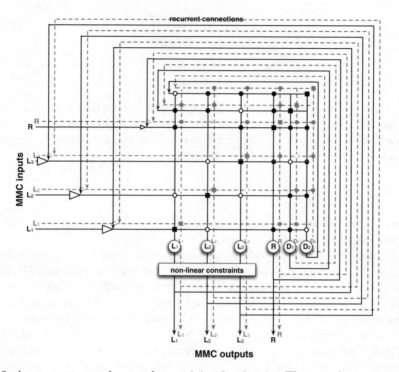

Fig. 2. A recurrent neural network containing 2 x 6 units. The complete net consists of two identical linear neworks, one for the x-components (black lines) and the other for the y-components (grey lines) of the vectors. The units represent the components of the six vectors L_1, L_2, L_3, D_1, D_2, and R of the planar arm (see Fig. 1 for graphical illustration). If an input is given, the corresponding recurrent channel is suppressed (symbolized by the open arrow heads). For details see text.

to different results. In other words, the network represents an inconsistent state. During relaxation the network reaches a stable state by minimising the overall variance of the different computations of all variables—it approaches an attractor of the network. At the same time the other vectors, in particular the vectors representing the arm segments, will follow the new vector R and then adopt a new position fulfilling the desired conditions.

Thus, the MMC model solves the inverse kinematic problem. However, during approximation the length of the vectors may change. For the diagonal and end effector vectors this is not a problem, but the vectors representing arm segments should usually not change their length. It becomes therefore necessary to prohibit changes of the length of these vectors. To this end the model can be expanded by a non-linear part which allows to keep segment length constant. Such constraints are applied to the system after each iteration step. These constraints can act on segment length, but in the same way can deal with working ranges of joints or any other constraint and requirements of the manipulator. These constraints often involve transformation to specific representations or other reference coordinate systems. The transformations connect the different networks by combining information from more than one network. For example, to obtain the length of a segment or a joint angle, we need the x-value and the y-value: The two components of one vector have to be combined to calculate the length of the vector or to calculate the angle of the vector with respect to a baseline, for example the x-coordinate. If the calculated length deviates from the desired length, this value can be corrected before it is fed back for the next iteration (either by a "soft" correction or by rigidly replacing the deviating value by the correct one). Of course, for the new values new x- and y-components have to be computed before these values can be given back into the network. This requires the introduction of other non-linear functions.[3]

The capability of this network to solve the inverse kinematic problem will be illustrated by two examples, one that is characterized by obtaining an infinite number of possible solutions, the other characterized by having no solution at all. For such a practical application, the network has to be connected to the outer world via sensory input. As described, Fig. 2 shows a MMC network for the three joint, 2D arm. Therefore, two parallel linear networks (black lines, broken grey lines for the x- and the y-components, respectively) are used, which are connected by non-linear functions (box) at the output. The 2 x 6 units (two components, six vectors) are connected by weights depicted by dots and squares. The weights depicted by dots basically correspond to the summed weights, determined by equation 1 and 2, as long as the diagonal weights (squares) are zero. If these diagonal weights, described by $d/(d+1)$ with d called damping factor, deviate from zero, the other weights have to be normalized by $(d+1)$.

To deal with the inverse kinematic problem, the, for example visually given, positions of the desired vector R has to be provided as sensory input in the form of the vector components R_x and R_y. A simple example is illustrated in Fig 3 a) and b). The initial position of the arm, represented by a relaxed network, is disturbed by giving a new R vector as external input (the new desired position is marked by a cross). When an input is given to the network this input suppresses the recurrent connection for this unit. These units are therefore called "suppression units" (in Fig. 2 symbolised by the open-arrow heads.).[4] The network is now disturbed by the external input R. The different computations for one variable lead to different results. As an approximation—according to the MMC principle—the mean value is used as an output. Nevertheless, after some iterations the network relaxes to a stable attractor state, in which the variance of the different equations is minimised. If there is a solution (a possible posture for reaching the target) the variance approaches zero and the network represents the solution. Using the output values, the "virtual" movement of the simulated arm is shown for each iteration (Fig. 3 a). Fig. 3 b) shows the time course of

---

[3] Computation of joint angles from angles defined relative to the baseline requires a coordinate transformation which are simple in the 2D case, but more complicated in the 3D case [38,39].

[4] Another "softer" solution is to calculate the mean value between input and recurrent signal.

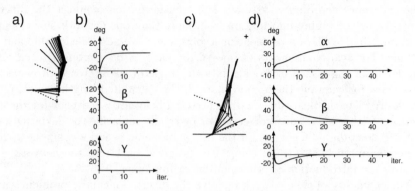

Fig. 3. Solution of the inverse kinematic problem. A planar arm with three segments (i.e., one extra DoF) should point to a given position, marked by a cross, starting from an initial configuration (dotted lines). In a) and b) a situation is shown in which one of the infinite numbered possible solutions is chosen. Part c) and d) of the figure show another situation: the cross is situated outside the workspace of the arm, therefore there is no solution possible. Nevertheless, the network solves the task "as good as possible". a) and c) Movement of the arm. b) and d) Time course of the joint angles (α – shoulder, β – elbow, γ – wrist). Abscissa: number of iterations.

the three joint angles. As can be seen, the arm approaches the desired goal (the velocity profile is described by a decreasing exponential function, but other solutions are possible). The net has found one of the many possible solutions thus solving the inverse kinematic problem.

A more tricky case is given in Fig. 3 c) and d) in the same format as used in Fig. 3 a) and b). Because the desired target position is now situated outside the workspace of the arm, there is no solution to the problem. As there is no solution, a simple, traditional controller would of course not find a solution. Our network, however, "tries to do its best": as qualitatively described by the paradigm using the puppet arm moved via the pulling thread, the simulated arm moves to the target as far as it is geometrically possible, finally pointing straight into the direction of the goal position.

We should note here that the trajectory of the MMC driven arm—as shown in Fig. 3 a) to d)—does in general not correspond to trajectories observed in human reaching movements as the latter show more straight paths. Therefore, when applying a MCC net to describe human arm movements in more detail, additional information is required concerning the shape of the path the end effector is following (for examples see proposals given by Kindermann et al. [40], or Brüwer and Cruse [41]). If such a path for the movement of the end effector is given, individual points of the path could be used as endpoints for local R vectors. This problem becomes obvious in a specific situation that cannot be solved in a straight forward manner by the concept of pulling the hand with a thread. Assume, as shown in Fig. 4 that the thread (fine dotted line) pulls the tip to the goal, but due to joint limitations the shoulder cannot turn further counterclockwise and the elbow cannot be more flexed. In other words the arm would be moved to the limits of its workspace although a geometrical solution is possible (as shown by the dashed arm). In such a case, and similarly when the arm has to cope with obstacles in the workspace, an expansion becomes necessary to find an appropriate trajectory. A simple solution is possible by providing obstacles and likewise borders of the workspace with some kind of repelling potential functions which not only push the arm segments away from the limits [42], but also constrain the pulling thread to stay within the free workspace. The latter is indicated by the coarsely dotted line in Fig. 4.

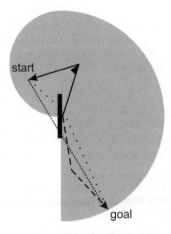

Fig. 4. Application of the passive motion paradigm to a two-segmented planar arm. The shoulder joint is limited to ± 90° (illustrated by the vertical black bar). The elbow joint is restricted in its counter-clockwise movement as indicated by the black triangle. The resulting workspace of the arm itself is depicted by the grey area. Pulling the arm by a thread attached to the tip in the direction of the goal position (fine dotted line) would lead to a blockage of the arm. If the virtual thread is constrained to stay within the workspace (coarsely dotted line), the arm could reach the goal position.

Until now, we applied the MMC principle only to simple 2D examples described in Cartesian coordinates. But other solutions are possible: The principle has been used to describe the 3D body geometry of a hexapod walker, dealing with 18 degrees of freedom and 19 nodes [43,44]. The latter is critical because when connecting each of these 19 nodes with every other node the complexity of one overall network would be too high. The number of possible triangles increases exponentially with the number of nodes. To cope with this problem the model of the walker is divided into two layers (Fig. 5): On the lower layer (Fig. 5 b) each leg, which consists of three joints and three nodes, is represented in joint coordinates in an angular space [17]. This layer can therefore directly be connected to sensors providing the joint angles, as can be found in insects. Angular values at the output can be used to drive the joint actuators. On the top layer only the footpoint of a leg and the hip of a leg are represented leading to 13 nodes and vectors (Fig. 5 a). These vectors are expressed in Cartesian

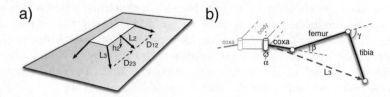

Fig. 5. The MMC body model for the six-legged walker is divided into two layers. The upper layer (a) represents the body and the six legs, which are, however, only represented by a vector connecting hip and tip of the leg (e.g., L_2 for the right middle leg or L_3 for the right hind leg). In addition the z-component of L_2 (h_2) is shown and two vectors (D_{12} and D_{23}) connecting the end points of the middle leg with the ipsilateral front leg and hind leg, respectively. The lower layer contains six networks, each representing one leg (b). Both layers are connected via the shared leg vectors (in the example L_3). α, β, and γ denote the three joint angles.

coordinates as used for visual input, for example, and as needed for a connection to a model of the environment. The two layers can be connected through transformation layers which consist of simple feedforward networks computing the local transformation from angular space to a vector in Cartesian space and vice versa [43].

Generally spoken, MMC networks can be connected through common variables which mediate between the two networks. It is sufficient to introduce an equation which includes the relevant variables from both networks. This equation expresses variables of each of the network in terms of the other and couples the dynamics of the both networks.

MMC networks can not only contain equations describing postures and static relations, but can be extended to include variables of any type. As an example, we extended the MMC network described by introducing equations for the velocity of the nodes (not shown in Fig. 2). This extension requires to introduce temporal aspects. However, time is not used explicitly as a variable. Instead, we compare the current value of a variable with its value in the preceding time step. This position difference over one time step represents velocity. The introduction of velocities into the network makes it possible to generate not only exponentially decreasing velocity profiles (e.g., in Fig. 3) which are unnatural, but to produce bell-shaped velocity profiles as can be observed in human hand movements or saccadic eye movements. In a similar way it is possible to introduce dynamic variables including accelerations or forces.

The geometrical constraints described so far are assumed to be given by the segment lengths only. However, as has been mentioned earlier, mechanical limitations of a joint could be similarly addressed in the framework given by this network. If an angle value determined by the network moves beyond its mechanically allowed range, this value is reset to a possible value before it is given to the net for the next iteration (again, hard or soft ways of correcting the angle value are possible [38]).

We have explained how the MMC net is able to solve the inverse kinematic problem in order to control motor output. Interestingly, this network can also be used to solve problems related to perception. To give a simple example, regarding three vectors forming a triangle, the angles should sum to 180 degrees. However, measurement data may deviate from this value due to measurement errors. If these sensor data are given as input to a MMC network representing a triangle, the network necessarily relaxes to a correct triangle. This means that the angular values represented by the network output generally show a smaller error than the input data. In this way different sensory input values can be lumped together, also providing a simple solution for the sensor fusion problem: If several sensor values are given for the same item, some kind of mean value between all sensor data is determined which at the same time fulfils the geometrical constraints. Correspondingly, the network is able to complete incomplete patterns. If, in the case of our three joint arm (e.g., Figures 2 and 3), for example, only the endpoint of the hand, i.e., the R vector, and one angle, say the shoulder angle, is given, the network at its output provides a complete set of angle values, i.e., provides also a value for the elbow angle and for the wrist angle. Furthermore, if there are two possible solutions (in this example only if the joint ranges were not limited) the net selects one of these two solutions, thus being able to disambiguate ambiguous situations. Thus, the MMC network can be used to solve the inverse kinematic problem and to solve tasks related to the sensor fusion problem.

Obviously, the MMC net can also represent a forward model. As described above, the network acts as an autoassociator. Therefore, it does not matter which variables are provided as input, the network tries to complete the pattern to form a consistent solution. In any case, the net can be used as a forward model, if the variables representing the arm segments L_1, L_2, and L_3 (or the joint angles) are applied as input. Therefore, the network relaxes to the posture given by these input variables and provides the end position. Correspondingly, mixed problems can be solved by the network.

In summary, the basic MMC cycle consists of two steps. On the one hand, we have the linear and parallel computation of one variable in different ways and the calculation of the mean value. This represents the numerical approximation given by the topology of the manipulator which is encoded in the network. On the other hand, we apply constraints on the provisional results which restrict the variables to specific values and enforce them to be in agreement with certain internal and external requirements. These requirements can be rather complex: They may not act only on one variable, but rather on relations or geometric relationships between the variables and therefore require transformations. In general, these constraints introduce some sort of non-linearity. This network can be used to solve inverse, forward or mixed kinematic problems and to cope with the problem of sensor fusion. If an exact solution is not possible, the network approximates the solution by minimising the variance of the equations. It has been proven, that, from any given starting position, the linear network converges to a stable and geometrically correct final state. Forward and mixed kinematic tasks can be solved by providing different input to the network and exploiting its autoassociator capabilities.

Both properties described for the MMC net—the ability to find a solution for inverse kinematic problems in a system with extra degrees of freedom and the ability to improve perception by applying pattern completion allowing for sensor fusion or disambiguation—are properties that could well be exploited by reactive systems and may therefore be found in such systems, i.e., in systems that do not show the ability to plan ahead.

4   Interconnection of Internal Sub-models

In this section, we want to put forward a hypothesis on how internal models might be interconnected. To account for this hypothesis, we will discuss different experimental data from different areas which can be explained by the holistic coupling of perceptual and motor elements as proposed here.

Let us assume that our body model does not consist of one monolithic network as implicitly assumed up to now, but of several basically independent sub-networks, similarly as there are several homunculi found in the human brain. Each of these sub-networks may represent a specific kind of information, like, for example, proprioceptive feedback providing information about the own posture or visual information relating our body to an environment and complementing the information about our own body. Other examples discussed are networks that process information concerning the physical self and networks responsible for representing the self in a more abstract way [45]. In a normal subject these sub-nets are interconnected and the information is integrated through these connections between the different sub-networks, which provide overlapping information. The interconnected sub-networks are forming one unique RNN being, as we speculate, the basis of our bodily experiences. Specifically, it has been proposed by Cruse [21] that a subjective (phenomenal) experience is elicited when the RNN approaches its attractor state. Note that this view differs from the assumption that there are different models or pairs of models in the brain serving different behaviours and functions. The different sub-networks discussed here might on this stage not be involved in behaviour-specific processing or control, but address different modalities or different aspects of movements or body configurations (like posture and velocity) or with respect to different reference coordinate systems. These networks are only part of the overall body model, in which they are integrated to form a consistent impression of the current situation and the current body configuration, using the redundant information to minimize errors in different modalities (to address the task of sensor fusion).

To analyse the relation of the sub-networks and their integration, we want to discuss some disorders and observations, which commonly are related to problems with ones own body model in general. These malfunctions may affect the ability of the subject to perceive, to plan and to act in an environment. From our point of view, some of these malfunctions can be explained by problems concerning the integration of information of the different sub-networks. We assume that the connections between the sub-nets could be weakened by some influences as, for example, stress. In this case, the corresponding body models may adopt their "own life", which could explain the disintegration into several models being experienced by the subject. Let us begin with a case that requires considerations of only one network representing, for example, an arm.

Human subjects suffering from missing limbs, arms or legs, may experience phantom sensations, which means that they have a lively feeling of the missing limb [46]. As this phenomenon can be observed in subjects, who lost the limb by means of an accident or a medical amputation, but also by subjects, who have been born without one or more limbs [47], an innate neuronal representation of the body model has been assumed to exist [48].[5]

A spectacular case has been reported by Ramachandran et al. [49]. In a patient suffering from phantom sensations in the amputated left arm, a lively subjective experience of moving this non-existing left arm could be elicited when the intact right arm was both actively moved and seen in a mirror such that the mirror image of the right arm appeared at the position where the left arm would have appeared if it had been intact. Based on our assumptions, this observation could be interpreted in the following way: usually the model of the arm is in a relaxed and therefore subjectively experienced state, for example, pointing straight to the left. No change of the state is possible because there is no sensory input. In the experiment, the visual input providing information concerning the position of the arm arising from the sensation of the non-existing arm appears to be sufficient to activate the model of the left arm. According to our hypothesis, this activation in turn would lead to a new subjective experience.

Another interesting observation is the so called Pinocchio illusion [50]. If a healthy subject bends his/her elbow and the biceps muscle is stimulated by high frequency vibrations, most subjects experience the elbow joint to be stretched, although the joint is fixed.[6] If these subjects, at the same time, hold their nose with two fingers, subjects eventually experience their nose being elongated. This can easily be simulated by an MMC-based body model if we assume that the length of the vectors describing head, upper arm, and lower arm are fixed, whereas the length of the nose is not (or is at least less strictly fixed compared to the other segments). If we apply a starting configuration as depicted in Fig. 6 (bold arrows) and now increase the value of the elbow angle corresponding to the sensory input being elicited by the biceps vibration (broken black arrows), the nose vector will be lengthened (broken grey arrow), because this is the only possibility to satisfy all geometrical constraints. It has sometimes been observed that instead of the nose, the fingers holding the nose seem to increase their lengths [50]. In the framework of the RNN model this observation would mean that also the corresponding finger vector is not fixed, and is in this case "weaker" than the representation of the nose vector.

---

[5] This assumption does of course not exclude that the representation could be changed due to learning.

[6] This effect is due to stimulation of the muscle spindles.

Fig. 6. The Pinocchio illusion can be explained by an MMC network as a body model used for the sensor fusion task and involved in the generation of ones own sensation of the body posture. The starting position of the arm is illustrated by black arrows (the arrow connecting shoulder and nose is not shown). When the elbow angle appears to increase—following a biceps stimulation—the arm is felt to assume a new position (dotted black arrows). As a consequence, the MMC net has to elongate the vector representing the nose (grey dotted arrow) to adjust for the movement.

As the MMC network only adopts positions that are geometrically possible, this type of body model is also suited to explain results given by Shiffrar [51]. In one experiment the subject was given two temporally subsequent pictures to elicit the phenomenon of apparent motion (Fig. 7). If the time delay is very short, subjects experience a movement along the shortest path between both figure sections, in agreement with the well-known apparent motion paradigm (Fig. 7, black arrow). If, however, the delay is increased to the duration the actual only possible movement would need, subjects have the impression that the apparent movement follows a longer path, that path being the mechanically only possible one when performed by a human arm (Fig. 7, grey arrow). This observation could be explained if we assume that the visual input drives a body model that represents the mechanical limitations of the real arm and therefore can only find a solution to the problem that is geometrically possible.[7]

Even more strange findings are the so called out-of-body experiences (OBE) reported from subjects suffering from impaired processing at the temporoparietal junction [52] or from healthy subjects under specific stress conditions.[8] In a typical case a subject, when reclining in a horizontal position with an

---

[7] As has been mentioned earlier (see Fig. 4), to explain this movement we need an expansion in such a way that the "pulling thread" is constrained to stay within the workspace.

[8] In Metzinger (2003, especially chapter 7 of [53]) a thorough discussion of the before mentioned phenomena, ranging from phantom sensations to out-of-body experiences, can be found which addresses these in much more detail. The survey is guided by the issue of how these phenomena relate to models of one self (or, as he refers, to the self-model), but the question is approached from a different perspective. Thus Metzinger's research is complementing our own view. In addition, the characteristics of our model seem to be in agreement with his argumentation.

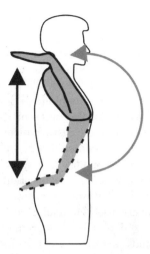

Fig. 7. Perception of apparent motion seems to be based in the application of a body model. When two pictures (person with arm in upper position, full lines, and person with arm in lower position, broken lines) are presented within a short time frame, an apparent motion along the black arrows is perceived which cannot be explicated. If the time delay in the presentation of the two pictures is in the range of the real, possible movement, the apparent motion follows the path depicted by the grey arrows.

upward directed view, experiences his/her body but at the same time experiences him/herself to fly above the lying body in a horizontal position, viewing downwards and observing the own real body. Similarly, some marathon runners when under strong dehydration report to view themselves from a bird's eye view. This at first sight quite esoteric phenomenon has now been studied in more detail and neurophysiological deficits correlated with these phenomena have been found [52] and have been related to body perception and body schema in general [54]. Recent experiments assured the relation of out-of-body experiences to sensory processing [55,56]. In the first experiment, the experience of a conscious self, which is normaly localized in the own bodily borders, was affected by providing a participant with conflicting visual and somatosensory information through the visual dislocation of the seen own body in a virtual reality. As a consequence, the participants mislocalized themselves towards the virtual body, indicating that bodily self-consciousness is based on the integration of multisensory information. Our assumption—that our body model consists of several basically independent networks and that the connections between these sub-nets could be weakened by some influences—provides a possible explanation for all these phenomena: Usually, we experience a coherent picture of our body which is the result of the integration and a form of mediation of the different sub-networks. But in loosening the interrelations of the sub-networks of the body model, the corresponding body models may adopt their "own life". This could explain the disintegration into several models being experienced by this subject [57]. Corresponding effects may lead to phenomena observed in schizophrenia or after damage to the parietal lobes.

Taken together, we propose a model that allows for control of movements, for perceiving movements of human-like behaviour and for imagining movements, as proposed by Jeannerods simulation theory [35,23]. Furthermore, observations in healthy or disabled persons could be explained. Some effects may result from problems arising in the integration of the different sub-networks. It seems that a malfunction of one sub-network or the disturbance of one sub-network in such a way that it is providing faulty or contradictory information does not lead to a complete breakdown of the body model. Instead, the other sub-networks can compensate for the error, preserving still a consistent bodily experience, even if this is a strange one. We assume that only in extreme cases of disagreement the integration between the sub-networks is weakened and the body model falls apart leading to the impression of different models as maybe the case in schizophrenia. Interestingly, even the most severe cases of problems in the integration into a body model can be found in healthy subjects (Pinocchio illusion as a mild case, and out-of-body experience as an extreme case). While the weakening of the interconnections is not part of the model as presented here, the other phenomena mentioned could be easily described by MMC sub-networks which are integrated to form the body model by computing the mean value following the MMC principle.[9]

To conclude, we hypothesize that a body model is formed by different sub-networks. These sub-networks are not related to specific tasks, but represent diverse aspects concerning the bodily situation. The information represented by these sub-networks is integrated to form a bodily experience (and connected to this maybe the impression of a self), usually for cancelling out errors of the sub-networks. A problem in one sub-network therefore only disturbs the overall impression of the bodily experience (maybe leading to strange experiences), but does not lead to the collapse of a bodily experience as such.

5   Walknet — From Reactive to Cognitive Systems

In the above sections, we have introduced a network architecture that, in principle, could be used for different tasks as are sensor fusion and finding solutions for inverse and forward kinematic problems. In the following, we will explain, how a reactive, insect-like controller, termed Walknet [15,16], can be expanded by such a network to reach the ability to plan ahead, i.e., to become a cognitive system. This goal will be reached by extending the reactive system by a MMC net used for sensor fusion in order to improve the quality of the data provided by the different sensors. We then will show how this model could be further exploited as a forward model which can be used to plan ahead. In another extension, we exploit the property of the MMC network to form an inverse model.

---

[9] We should mention here that we do not intend to propose such MMC networks are actually used by the brain. Rather, these models are discussed here to illustrate the feasibility of the concept of the interplay and integration of different sub-networks.

This extension allows to dramatically simplify the reactive part. The MMC net solves a large part of the task, of the reactive controller, but still can be used for planning ahead if necessary.

The reactive network, Walknet (see Fig. 8), is able to control hexapod walking at different speeds, allows for negotiating curves, walking over obstacles [44] and, with minor extensions still on the reactive level, even allows the system to climb over very large gaps [58]. Walknet allows to control 6 legs with 3 joints each, i.e., a mechanical system with 18 DoFs. It represents a biologically inspired control structure: Its structure and function is obtained from experiments with the stick insect. The network is composed of six local control structures—called selector—which decide locally about the state of each leg (if it is in swing or in stance mode). These modules are implemented as neural networks. The selector-nets that switch behaviour between the two leg states are in turn controlled by peripheral sensory influences, like the position or the load of the controlled leg (Fig. 8, PEP, load). In addition, these controllers are coupled through a set of local coordination influences which govern the phase relationships between neighbouring pattern generators. Thus, gaits are not predetermined explicitly, but emerge as a result from the local coordination rules (in Fig. 8 denoted by numbers 1, 2, 3).

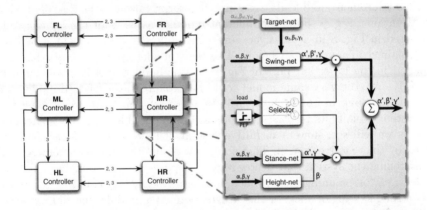

Fig. 8. General architecture of a reactive controller, Walknet, that is able to control six-legged, insect-like walking. The complete system (left part of the figure) consists of six basically independent controllers, one for each leg (FL/FR left/right front leg, ML/MR left/right middle leg, HL/HR left/right hind leg). Each leg controller contains several modules (right part): a swing-net and a stance-net to control swing and stance movement, respectively. A height-net for regulating body ground distance during stance, a target-net for determining the anterior extreme position of the swing movement, and a selector-net that decides at what time the swing-net or stance-net has access to the motor output (α', β', γ'). α, β, and γ denote the three joint angles of a leg (see Fig. 5 b). Influences (1, 2, 3) that change the posterior extreme position of the leg to coordinate the quasi-periodic movements of the legs (shown on the left side of the figure) act only between neighbouring legs, prolonging or shortening the stance phase.

The control of the movement of the individual leg is generated through two independent control modules which are implemented as neural networks, responsible for controlling the three joints of the leg during swing movement or stance movement, respectively. The selector-net modulates the output of these two networks—called swing-net and stance-net—and selects the appropriate one to drive the joints of the walker. The stance movement is a retraction of the leg: the leg is moved backwards using an about constant velocity in the alpha joint, while the beta joint and gamma joint are controlled by the height-network: this neural net maintains the distance between body and ground. The swing-net is a neuronal implementation for the control of the joint velocities during the swing phase. As an input it mainly uses the current joint angles and target angles produced by an additional neural network—called target-net—which transforms a suitable position of the leg, the anterior extreme position (AEP), into joint angles. As an output the swing-net provides joint velocities as a control signal for the joints. Information determining the end position of swing or stance, AEP, or posterior extreme position (PEP), are given to swing-net or stance-net via the already mentioned connections coming from neighbouring legs (for details see [15,16]).

As mentioned above, as a first step, this reactive system will be equipped with a body model that is used to increase the quality of the sensor data (e.g., angle measurement) and leads to an unique interpretation in the case of ambiguous situations. Fig. 9 shows the different modules as used for the leg controller presented in Fig. 8 in a, however, somewhat different arrangement which will be explained in more detail below. The body model used for sensor fusion is depicted in the lower left part of Fig. 9. If this body model is constructed by an MMC net, the very same model could be exploited as a forward model, too. How is this done in our architecture? In this first approach, we assume that the system exploits its reactive elements as far as possible, and only switches to the—as we will see, slower—cognitive system, if there are problems not being solved by the reactive system. Therefore, first of all, we require an "emergency" signal telling the system that it now requires to use its body model as a forward model, i.e., for planning ahead. Such emergency situations could be a particularly strong loading of a leg, or the "frustration" of a module that did not arrive at its goal after a very long time, or, to name a third example, that a leg, according to the reactive controller, is switched to swing state, but nevertheless the load sensor still monitors ground contact. If an emergency signal is released, the switch routing the motor output either to the actuators or the body model (Fig. 9, switch 1) should be changed to now drive only the latter. This means that there is no further body movement.[10] Correspondingly, the sensor signals should not influence the body model. Therefore switch 2 (Fig. 9) is opened, too. The motor output can now drive the body model. If the reactive system would just

---

[10] Collapsing of the legs is prohibited as the actuators are controlled via negative feedback controllers, the reference input of which is represented by an integrator [59]. So switching off the input simply fixes the reference input and therefore maintains leg position while still being able to react to actual disturbances.

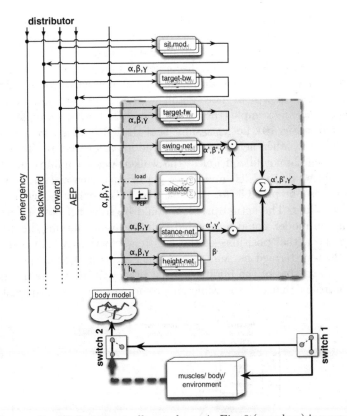

Fig. 9. The reactive Walknet controller as shown in Fig. 8 (grey box) is augmented first on the reactive level by the ability to walk either forward or backward. This requires an additional channel in the distributor-net and an additional target-net (for backward walking). Second, an internal model is introduced which may at first be used to solve the sensor fusion problem, but could then also be used to plan ahead. For planning ahead, in addition to the body model, a switch (switch 1) is needed which routes the control signal either to the body or to the body model (in the former case the body model is used for sensor fusion only). A second switch (switch 2) disconnects the sensor signal from the body model in order to allow the system being able to plan ahead. The switches are triggered by an emergency sensor (this connection is not shown). This sensor in addition starts the search for a new situation model that is able to provide a solution to the actual problem (see also Fig. 10).

continue to control the behaviour then the simulated body would actually run into the problem indicated by the emergency signal. How could this be avoided? A simple possibility is to randomly change the parameters of swing-net and/or stance-net and so to "invent" other movements. The forward model can then be used to test the consequences of this invention. To this end the body model has to be equipped with "virtual" emergency sensors in an analogous way. If the invention was not successful, another solution will be searched for and tested. This procedure, which may, according to S. Freud, be termed "probehandeln"

[60,61], or thinking, will be continued until a solution is found that really solves the problem. A solution is characterized by the fact that the "virtual" emergency sensors are not anymore signalling problematic situations. This information is used to move the switch back, i.e., disconnect the motor output from the body model and to drive the real actuators, thereby coping with the actual problem.

To explain this concept in more detail, we will consider the following emergency situation as an example (the complete process for the example is schematically depicted in Fig. 10). Let us assume that the left hind leg has reached a rear position while the other neighbouring legs adopt a forward position such that the left hind leg cannot lift off unless the walker looses equilibrium. A sensible solution would be that the left middle leg performs a rearward swing movement. This however is not possible for the reactive walker when being in the mode of forward walking. The actual problem could be solved if now a new module, called situation model, could be created that, as input, obtains the information concerning the actual positions of the legs (e.g., forward walking and specific sensors activated, termed as "emergency" in Fig. 9) and as output would initiate a backward step of the middle left leg by activating the target-net of the reactive controller that is responsible for providing targets in rearward walking.

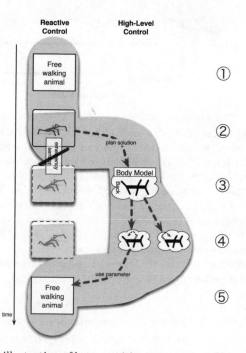

Fig. 10. Schematical illustration of how cognitive processes could be used to cope with a problem that cannot be solved by the reactive system. When the free walking system (1) runs into an impasse as determined by an emergency sensor (2), continuation of walking is interrupted. Instead the body model (3) is activated to search for a solution and the body is decoupled from the control processes. Different possibilities are simulated (4). If a suitable solution is found, this will be applied to continue walking (5).

But how can a new solution be found by this system? We assume that a new solution is normally found by testing a new combination of already existing behavioural elements. The invention of a completely new behaviour is not possible using the architecture proposed (and we assume that even in human beings such an event occurs, if at all, only very rarely). To be able to test new combinations, a not too small number of basic behaviours must already exist. In the case of walking these elements might include the capability of each leg to walk forward or rearward or to walk sideways or in curves. In order to explain how such situation models can be learned and be used, a specific architecture has to be described first. This architecture, as depicted in Fig. 9, consists of two parts, a distributor and a set of situation models, most of which are "innate", corresponding to the modules already described as parts of Walknet in Fig. 8 (target-net, swing-net, stance-net, selector-net, height-net). The distributor (left vertical lines in Fig. 9) corresponds to the set of input channels already used for the swing and the stance modules as shown in Fig. 8, but may also contain other channels, that transport signals provided by other modules, for example values of AEP or PEP of the different legs, or to be more specific, angular components of these positions (for simplicity, only one channel is shown, the AEP as an example). Whereas Walknet, as shown in Fig. 8, is only designed for being able to walk forward, the architecture given in Fig. 9 allows for forward or backward walking. This makes it necessary to introduce two additional distributor channels, one for forward and a second for backward walking. Furthermore, we need two types of target-nets, one for forward walking and another for backward walking. To install a new situation model, i.e., a module that does not belong to the reactive version of Walknet, first of all a random connection is selected that connects any unit of the distributor to one unit of the situation model layer (Fig. 9, uppermost part). These situation models are given as RNNs, the weights of which are zero at the beginning. Learning the weights of the recurrent net is performed following the proposal of Kühn et al. [62,63] who introduced the delta-rule acting within a neuron which therefore is able to act on a local level. The output of the situation model projects back to the distributor-net and has, via another random choice, to search for a contact to any of the units of the distributor-net. If this connection is not successful, which will be indicated by the virtual emergency sensor, a new search is necessary. If successful, the connection should be stabilized. In our example this would mean that when accidentally the unit for backward walking is chosen, it connects to this unit, which, in the reactive net, represents the backward walking influence to the left middle leg (Fig. 9, upper part). Because a purely random search had to cope with quite a large search space, this space has to be limited by heuristics, for example exploiting knowledge concerning the morphological neighbourhood first. The new "ideas" represented in the form of situation models can then be given, via the reactive network, to the motor output thus solving the actual problem. Furthermore, if the same situation, defined by the sensor input and motor context having been learnt in the form of a situation model, reoccurs at a later time, this situation model is immediately activated. Thereby the situation will be solved without further "thinking", i.e., without searching for a new solution.

In this approach we exploit two aspects of our holistic body model. One aspect concerns the capability of being used for smart perception. It receives measured angle values as input and provides corrected angle values as output. The other, more important aspect, concerns the capability of such a network to be used as a forward model and therefore to be able to plan ahead. The third aspect discussed earlier, namely exploiting its ability to be used as an inverse model, has not yet been applied here because the reactive controller being derived from behavioural and neurobiological studies from insects does not require application of an inverse model. This is possible because the extra DoFs of the insect body (18 joints, minus 6 DoFs describing the position of the body in space) can be determined by additional constraints as for example controllers acting on each leg determining the body ground distance. If, however, a body had to be controlled that is, for example, equipped with legs having more than 3 DoFs (as is the case for many crustaceans, but also some insects), such inverse models would be helpful (but not necessary, see above, [32]).

In the remaining part of this section, we will briefly sketch a modification of the controller in which the functionality of the internal model as an inverse model will be exploited. In this version, the inverse model becomes a core part of the controller architecture. The complete function of the stance-net is taken over by the MMC body model (Fig. 11). The height-net is replaced by a fixed input to the z-component of the leg vector activated during stance (see Fig. 5). Furthermore, the x-component of the v-vector[11] controls the corresponding motor output, which via the ground contact sensor also depends on load. Therefore, an explicit stance-net is not anymore necessary. Similarly, the swing-net can be replaced by a transient input to the levator muscle of the β-joint (or in MMC coordinates to the z-component representing the leg height during swing). Finally, instead of using the target-nets, we, during swing, set the length of that vector to zero, which connects the tip of the swinging leg with the tip of the anterior neighbour. Regarding a middle leg in forward walking this is vector D_{12} in Fig. 5, connecting the tip of the middle with the front leg. During backward walking, correspondingly vector D_{23} should be set to zero when the middle leg is swinging. However, we still need the selector-net to switch between swing and stance mode. In order to exploit the properties of sensor fusion, the sensor signals directly drive the MMC net, whereas the selector does not receive its PEP input directly from the angle sensors, but in the form of an "efference copy" from the MMC net (Fig. 11). As in the earlier version (Fig. 9), switch 1 and switch 2 have to be opened in order to allow for planning ahead. Furthermore, the channels determining forward or backward walking are not only required

---

[11] This is the velocity vector along the body-axis which is not shown in Fig. 5 and only briefly mentioned in the introduction of the MMC networks. The velocity vector is provided in an extended version of the MMC network and represents the change of position between consecutive iteration steps. In this case, it describes the movement of the leg.

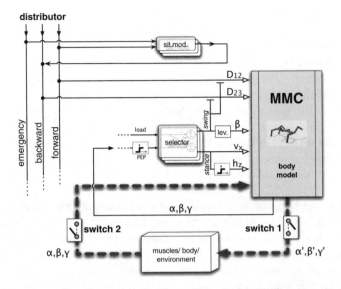

Fig. 11. A leg controller that exploits the ability of the MMC net to be used as an inverse model. We still need the selector-net. However, stance-net and swing-net are dramatically simplified. Target-nets are replaced by an input from the distributor to, during swing, set vector D_{12} (see Fig. 5) to zero for forward walking (or $D_{23} = 0$ for backward walking). This connection is only active during the swing phase (connections with a crossbar at the end). To allow for sensor fusion, the raw sensor data are directly given to the MMC net and only its output values are used to drive the selector-net, for example.

on the local leg level. Rather we need such influences also to control the other legs and, in particular to control the coordination influences acting between the legs. Direct, reflex-like pathways that do not pass the body model are not shown explicitly in Fig. 11.

6   Conclusion

There is now an impressive amount of results available based on quite different approaches, be this experimental psychology, neurology, brain imaging studies, or basic neurophysiology, that agree, to quote a review paper of Jeannerod [35] (p. 10) that "processes as intending, imaging, observation/imitating and performing an action share, at least in part, common structural and functional mechanisms". Or as Gallese and Lakoff [64] have stated in a recent review (p. 458): "Imagination is mental simulation, carried out by the same functional clusters used in acting and perceiving". Therefore, phenomena that at first sight appear to be quite different as are perception, control of action, talking about an action [65,66,67], and imagination of an action, and thereby the ability to think, now appear to be a function of one and the same system. Internal models seems to be a core component of this system. For this purpose, we have proposed a

RNN which is of MMC type. In general, this network can be used for pattern completion and sensor fusion, as a forward model, an inverse model and as any mixed version of forward and inverse models. The body model comprises a holistic model realized by a recurrent neural network consisting of sub-networks and being able to serve all three functionalities mentioned. Interestingly, the individual neurons of this network cannot be addressed as being motor or sensory, but, comparable to the canonical neurons found in monkey brains [68], are active in both sensory and motor tasks. We use this model basically as a model of the own body, but objects of the world, for example items to be grasped, or tools to extend the body geometry, could be integrated into this network. This holistic network could also be the basis for an explanation of phenomena as phantom sensation, the Pinocchio illusion or OBEs.

Generally, our hypothesis is based on the speculation that cognitive systems might have evolved from systems which had to control a geometrically complex body, i.e., a body with many serially arranged DoFs. To exploit these extra DoFs, such systems require an inverse model of the body [10]. We further speculate that, after an inverse model and an internal model in general had been developed, as a second evolutionary step the possibility had been evolved to switch off the connection to the muscles deliberately to be able to run the body model independently and to use it as a manipulable model.[12] Of course, just being able to switch off this connection is not the only prerequisite to become a system being able to plan ahead. We require a signal that is used to decide whether the reactive mode or the cognitive mode should be activated ("emergency sensor") and we require a further system that can evaluate the results provided by the prediction system. In addition, we need, apart from emergency sensors, the ability to spontaneously generate new "ideas", i.e., new behavioural elements and to store them if they have shown to be successful. We have proposed a specific, and simple, neuronal network architecture that is able to deal with these problems. Thus, the step from simple reactive systems to systems with cognitive capabilities seems to be smaller than is often assumed.

To close this gap, we have integrated the MMC network into a larger framework. This extension comprises a major step towards our long-term goal, namely to develop a biologically inspired, i.e., strictly neural, architecture that is based on reactive systems but can be expanded to form a cognitive system. The idea is to apply a minimal amount of given ("innate") structures and allow the system to grow in a self-organized way. Thus, we aim to propose a framework that might be suited to explain how cognitive properties might have evolved from a purely reactive system.

In the first approach (Fig. 9) we did not exploit the capability of the MMC net to serve as an inverse model. This means that in this approach we applied some kind of "evolutionary short-cut". Actually, we do not believe that a model to be used as a forward model or as a system for sensor fusion had been evolved directly to improve the capabilities of a reactive system. However, we could imagine

---

[12] Interestingly, echopraxia [69] seems to be related to this ability to decouple the body. Patients suffering from echopraxia appear not to be able to activate this "switch".

that in a reactive system an inverse model might have evolved, if segments with many degrees of freedom already existed, because it is a direct advantage to exploit these DoFs independently [10]. Therefore, the second approach introduced here (Fig. 11) might be better suited to serve as a guideline for a hypothesis describing how a cognitive system might have been evolved out of a reactive system. In this second approach, we went one step further. The model became the core component of the architecture, connecting control of action, sensing and planning ahead. On the one hand (as shown in Fig. 11), the sensory information is directly fused by the model and given back to the reactive controller afterwards, while at the same time the model serves as an inverse model in determining trajectories for the movement using the information from the reactive controller as an input. On the other hand, the model can serve mental simulation by decoupling the body. Instead of using the loop through the world, the model works on the data fed back via the recurrent connections of the MMC net using the network as a forward model.

An important extension of the network architecture proposed concerns the introduction of situation models forming a procedural memory learned by the individual. The situation models—as proposed here—consist of simple RNNs termed MSBE nets [62]. The neurons of these networks show a striking similarity to mirror neurons [68,70] as they are activated by the sensory and the motor aspect of a specific task, and can be interpreted as not to represent a specific motor command but the goal to be reached by the task. In our examples, we use information from kinesthetic or proprioceptive receptors, in this aspect differing from the cases studied in monkeys [71] where visual or auditory sensory inputs have been investigated.

Whereas local learning rules are available to learn the situation models [62,63], it is still open how an MMC network can be learnt from scratch. Currently, we have developed procedures to learn the linear part of an MMC net [72]. However, it will be a future project to extend this procedures to non-linear MMC nets. Although interesting per se, the ability to learn the basic structure of the body model may not be necessary for biological systems, because these structures might already be genetically predetermined [47,48]. A further open problem deals with the question as to how the storage containing the situation models had to be structured if the number of individual situation models becomes very large. The feasibility of this approach has finally to be verified by testing it on a robot, behaving in a real environment and coping with unknown problems.

The connection of higher cognitive functions to more basal functions as motor control or sensory processing has, as mentioned, found much support in brain research on monkeys as well as humans using brain imaging techniques. This notion has been further extended in the last years by work showing on a structural level that these same brain areas are also involved in language production and therefore communication (e.g., [73,65,64]). It appears that execution, imagination and thinking, as well as speaking about an action share partially the same neural substrate and are based on similar mechanisms. It has been proposed [74] that neurons in the mirror system, which have been found active in the mentioned cases, code knowledge of actions more in terms of a meaning and the goal of the action.

In this system similar neural activation patterns can be evoked by producing, observing, thinking or talking about an action. The usually so called sensory-motor system is in this way involved and utilised in thinking about an action as a form of mental simulation. On a later evolutionary stage [75] it may be used in language production and comprehension to map utterances to meaning by simulating the corresponding action [64]. Feldman and Narayanan proposed an exciting concept based on this assumption that uses principles of motor control in language production and language comprehension [76,77,78]. The general idea is that neural networks, that can be used for motor control, could be utilised for language production, too. This includes application of aspect (past tense, progressive form) as well as metaphors. This idea complements our approach in providing a connection from basic controller structures—called x-schemas in their case—to language understanding. Our approach offers a way of how to connect such control schemas to the notion of having an actual body and being embedded into a situation as well as the notion of grounding of internal models for planing ahead by using these control structures. The approach of Feldman and Narayanan could bridge the gap to higher-level cognition, namely language and communication. So, while not dealing here with communication as such, the long term goal of our approach is to understand intelligent processes growing from bottom up to higher level functions and in the end to communication. The abilities reported have shown not to be only some additional and separate form of "motoric" intelligence, but to be strongly related to higher level cognition and to constitute their fundamentals. Or, as Narayanan has stated in order to describe the connection of the basic sensory-motor system to language [78]:

"Talking the talk is [and we would like to add *'just'*] *like walking the walk."*

Acknowledgements

This work has been supported by the EC-IST SPARK project and by the Deutsche Forschungsgemeinschaft (DFG, grant Cr 58/11-1).

References

1. Newell, A.: The Knowledge Level. Artificial Intelligence 18(1), 87–127 (1982)
2. Brooks, R.A.: Intelligence without reason. In: Myopoulos, J., Reiter, R. (eds.) Proceedings of the 12th International Joint Conference on Artificial Intelligence (IJCAI 1991), Sydney, Australia, pp. 569–595. Morgan Kaufmann publishers Inc., San Mateo (1991)
3. Verschure, P., Althaus, P.: The study of learning and problem solving using artificial devices: Synthetic epistemology. Bildung und Erziehung 52(3), 317–333 (1999)
4. Brooks, R.A.: Intelligence without representation. Artificial Intelligence 47, 139–159 (1991)
5. Maes, P.: A bottom-up mechanism for behavior selection in an artificial creature. In: Proceedings of the first international conference on simulation of adaptive behavior on: From animals to animats, pp. 238–246. MIT Press, Cambridge (1990)

6. Verschure, P., Voegtlin, T., Douglas, R.: Environmentally mediated synergy between perception and behaviour in mobile robots. Nature 425, 620–624 (2003)
7. Parisi, D., Cecconi, F.: Learning in the Active Mode. In: Proceedings of the Third European Conference on Advances in Artificial Life, London, UK, pp. 439–462. Springer, Heidelberg (1995)
8. Beer, R.D.: Dynamical approaches to cognitive science. Trends in Cognitive Sciences 4(3), 91–99 (2000)
9. Sutton, R., Barto, A.: Reinforcement Learning: An Introduction. MIT Press, Cambridge (1998)
10. Cruse, H.: The Evolution of Cognition: A Hypothesis. Cognitive Science (27), 135–155 (2003)
11. Wehner, R.: Desert ant navigation: how miniature brains solve complex tasks. Journal of Comparative Physiology A 189, 579–588 (2003)
12. Möller, R., Lambrinos, D., Roggendorf, T., Pfeifer, R., Wehner, R.: Insect strategies of visual homing in mobile robots. In: Webb, B., Consi, T. (eds.) Biorobotics - Methods and Applications, AAAI Press / MIT Press (2001)
13. Bläsing, B., Cruse, H.: Stick insect locomotion in a complex environment: climbing over large gaps. The Journal of Experimental Biology 207, 1273–1286 (2004)
14. Bläsing, B., Cruse, H.: Mechanisms of stick insect locomotion in a gap-crossing paradigm. Journal of Comparative Physiology A: Sensory, Neural, and Behavioral Physiology 190, 173–183 (2004)
15. Dürr, V., Schmitz, J., Cruse, H.: Behaviour-based modelling of hexapod locomotion: Linking biology and technical application. Arthropod Structure and Development 33(3), 237–250 (2004)
16. Schilling, M., Cruse, H., Arena, P.: Hexapod walking: an expansion to Walknet dealing with leg amputations and force oscillations. Biological Cybernetics 96(3), 323–340 (2007)
17. Pfeifer, R., Scheier, C.: Understanding Intelligence. MIT Press, Cambridge (2001)
18. Metzinger, T.: Different conceptions of embodiment. Psyche 12(4) (2006)
19. Mataric, M.: Situated Robotics. In: Encyclopedia of Cognitive Science, Nature Publishing Group, Macmillan Reference Limited, Basingstoke (2002)
20. Mataric, M.: Behavior-Based Robotics. In: Wilson, R., Keil, F. (eds.) MIT Encyclopedia of Cognitive Sciences, pp. 74–77. MIT Press, Cambridge (1999)
21. Cruse, H.: Feeling our body - the basis of cognition? Evolution and Cognition (5), 162–173 (1999)
22. McFarland, D., Bösser, T.: Intelligent behavior in animals and robots. MIT Press, Cambridge (1993)
23. Hesslow, G.: Conscious thought as simulation of behaviour and perception. Trends in Cognitive Sciences 6(6), 242–247 (2002)
24. Wolpert, D., Ghahramani, Z., Flanagan, J.: Perspectives and Problems in Motor Learning. Trends in Cognitive Sciences 5(11), 487–494 (2001)
25. Wolpert, D., Ghahramani, Z., Jordan, M.: An internal model for sensorimotor integration. Science 269(5232), 1880–1882 (1995)
26. Frith, C.D., Blakemore, S.J., Wolpert, D.M.: Abnormalities in the Awareness and Control of Action. Philosophical Transactions of the Royal Society of London: Biological Sciences 355, 1771–1788 (2000)
27. Wolpert, D., Kawato, M.: Multiple paired forward and inverse models for motor control. Neural Networks 11(7–8), 1317–1329 (1998)
28. Stringer, S., Rolls, E.: Hierarchical dynamical models of motor function. Neurocomputing 70, 975–990 (2007)

29. Cruse, H.: The control of the anterior extreme position of the hindleg of a walking insect. Physiol.Entomol. 4, 121–124 (1979)

30. Dean, J., Wendler, G.: Stick insect locomotion on a walking wheel: Interleg coordination of leg position. Journal of Experimental Biology 103, 75–94 (1983)

31. Dürr, V., Krause, A.: The stick insect antenna as a biological paragon for an actively moved tactile probe for obstacle detection. In: Climbing and Walking Robots – From Biology to Industrial Applications. Proc. 4th Int. Conf. Climbing and Walking Robots (CLAWAR 2001, Karlsruhe), pp. 87–96 (2001)

32. Bernstein, N.A.: The Co-ordination and regulation of movements. Pergamon Press Ltd., Oxford (1967)

33. Miall, R., Weir, D., Wolpert, D., Stein, J.: Is the Cerebellum a Smith Predictor? Journal of Motor Behavior 25(3), 203–216 (1993)

34. Desmurget, M., Grafton, S.: Forward modeling allows feedback control for fast reaching movements. Trends in Cognitive Sciences 4(11), 423–431 (2000)

35. Jeannerod, M.: To act or not to act: Perspectives on the representation of actions. Quarterly Journal of Experimental Psychology 52A, 1–29 (1999)

36. Kleist, H.: Über das Marionettentheater. In: von Kleist, H., und Briefe, S.W., Bd. 2, hrsg. v. Helmut Sembdner, München 1987, S. 345 (originally appeared in Berliner Abendblättern, 1. Jg., 1810)

37. Mussa-Ivaldi, F., Morasso, P., Zaccaria, R.: Kinematic networks distributed model for representing and regularizing motor redundancy. Biol. Cybern. 60(1), 1–16 (1988)

38. Steinkühler, U., Cruse, H.: A holistic model for an internal representation to control the movement of a manipulator with redundant degrees of freedom. Biol. Cybernetics 79, 457–466 (1998)

39. Roggendorf, T.: Extending the MMC principle: Simple manipulator and posture models (Submitted)

40. Kindermann, T., Cruse, H., Dautenhahn, K.: A fast, three-layered neural network for path finding. Network: Computation in neural systems 7, 423–436 (1996)

41. Brüwer, M., Cruse, H.: A network model for the control of the movement of a redundant manipulator. Biological Cybernetics 62, 549–555 (1990)

42. Arena, P., Cruse, H., Fortuna, L., Patanè, L.: Obstacle avoidance method for a redundant manipulator controlled through a recurrent neural network. In: Proceedings of SPIE Microtechnologies for the New Millennium 2007, vol. 6592 (2007)

43. Schilling, M., Cruse, H.: Hierarchical MMC networks as a manipulable body model. In: Proceedings of the International Joint Conference on Neural Networks (IJCNN 2007), Orlando, FL (2007)

44. Kindermann, T., Cruse, H.: MMC - a new numerical approach to the kinematics of complex manipulators. Mechanism and Machine Theory 37(4), 375–394 (2002)

45. Uddin, L.Q., Iacoboni, M., Lange, C., Keenan, J.P.: The self and social cognition: the role of cortical midline structures and mirror neurons. Trends in Cognitive Sciences 11(4), 153–157 (2007)

46. Brugger, P.: From phantom limb to phantom body. varieties of extracorporeal awareness. In: Knoblich, G., Thornton, I., Grosjean, M., Shiffrar, M. (eds.) Human Body Perception from the Inside out, pp. 171–209. Oxford: University Press, Oxford (2006)

47. Funk, M., Shiffrar, M., Brugger, P.: Hand movement observation by individuals born without hands: phantom limb experience constrains visual limb perception. Experimental Brain Research 164(3), 341–346 (2005)

48. Melzack, R.: Phantom limbs and the concept of a neuromatrix. Trends in Neurosciences 13(3), 88–92 (1990)

49. Ramachandran, V.S., Rogers-Ramachandran, D., Cobb, S.: Touching the phantom limb. Nature 377(6549), 489–490 (2002)
50. Lackner, J.: Some proprioceptive influences on the perceptual representation of body shape and orientation. Brain 111, 281–297 (1988)
51. Shiffrar, M.: Movement and event perception. In: Goldstein, B. (ed.) The Blackwell Handbook of Perception, pp. 237–272. Blackwell Publishers, Oxford (2001)
52. Blanke, O., Mohr, C., Michel, C.M., Pascual-Leone, A., Brugger, P., Seeck, M., Landis, T., Thut, G.: Linking Out-of-Body Experience and Self Processing to Mental Own-Body Imagery at the Temporoparietal Junction. J. Neurosci. 25(3), 550–557 (2005)
53. Metzinger, T.: Being No One. The Self-Model Theory of Subjectivity. MIT Press, Cambridge (2003)
54. Blanke, O., Landis, T., Spinelli, L., Seeck, M.: Out-of-body experience and autoscopy of neurological origin. Brain 127(2), 243–258 (2004)
55. Lenggenhager, B., Tadi, T., Metzinger, T., Blanke, O.: Video Ergo Sum: Manipulating Bodily Self-Consciousness. Science 317(5841), 1096–1099 (2007)
56. Ehrsson, H.: The Experimental Induction of Out-of-Body Experiences. Science 317(5841), 1048 (2007)
57. Blanke, O., Ortigue, S., Landis, T., Seeck, M.: Stimulating illusory own-body perceptions. Nature 419(6904), 269–270 (2002)
58. Bläsing, B.: Crossing large gaps: A simulation study of stick insect behavior. Adaptive Behavior 14(3), 265–285 (2006)
59. Cruse, H., Kühn, S., Park, S., Schmitz, J.: Adaptive control for insect leg position: Controller properties depend on substrate compliance. Journal of Comparative Physiology A 190, 983–991 (2004)
60. Freud, S.: Formulierung über die zwei Prinzipien des psychischen Geschehens. In: Gesammelte Werke, Bd. VIII, pp. 229–238 (1911)
61. Freud, S.: Die Verneinung. In: Gesammelte Werke, Bd. XIV, pp. 9–15 (1925)
62. Kühn, S., Beyn, W., Cruse, H.: Modelling Memory Functions with Recurrent Neural Networks consisting of Input Compensation Units. I. Static Situations. Biological Cybernetics 96(5), 455–470 (2007)
63. Kühn, S., Cruse, H.: Modelling Memory Functions with Recurrent Neural Networks consisting of Input Compensation Units. II. Dynamic Situations. Biological Cybernetics 96(5), 471–486 (2007)
64. Gallese, V., Lakoff, G.: The Brain's concepts: the role of the Sensory-motor system in conceptual knowledge. Cognitive Neuropsychology 22(3–4), 455–479 (2005)
65. Pulvermüller, F.: Words in the brain's language. Behavioral and Brain Sciences 22, 253–336 (1999)
66. Hauk, O., Johnsrude, I., Pulvermüller, F.: Somatotopic representation of action words in human motor and premotor cortex. Neuron 41, 301–307 (2004)
67. Glenberg, A.M., Kaschak, M.P.: Grounding language in action. Psychonomic Bulletin and Review 9, 558–565 (2002)
68. Rizzolatti, G.: The mirror neuron system and its function in humans. Anat. Embryol. 210(5–6), 419–421 (2005)
69. Brugger, P., Blanke, O., Regard, M., Bradford, D., Landis, T.: Polyopic heautoscopy: Case report and review of the literature. Cortex 42(5), 666–674 (2006)
70. Fogassi, L., Ferrari, P.F., Gesierich, B., Rozzi, S., Chersi, F., Rizzolatti, G.: Parietal lobe: From action organization to intention understanding. Science 308(5722), 662–667 (2005)

71. Kohler, E., Keysers, C., Umiltà, M.A., Fogassi, L., Gallese, V., Rizzolatti, G.: Hearing Sounds, Understanding Actions: Action Representation in Mirror Neurons. Science 297(5582), 846–848 (2002)
72. Cruse, H., Hübner, D.: Selforganizing memory: Active learning of landmarks used for navigation (Submitted)
73. Rizzolatti, G., Arbib, M.: Language within our grasp. Trends in Neurosciences 21(5), 188–194 (1998)
74. Rizzolatti, G., Fadiga, L., Gallese, V., Fogassi, L.: Premotor cortex and the recognition of motor actions. Cognitive Brain Research 3(2), 131–141 (1996)
75. Hauser, M.D., Chomsky, N., Fitch, W.T.: The Faculty of Language: What Is It, Who Has It, and How Did It Evolve? Science 298(5598), 1569–1579 (2002)
76. Feldman, J.A.: From Molecule to Metaphor: A Neural Theory of Language. MIT Press, Cambridge (2006)
77. Feldman, J., Narayanan, S.: Embodied meaning in a neural theory of language. Brain and Language 89(2), 385–392 (2004)
78. Narayanan, S.: Talking the talk is like walking the walk: A computational model of verbal aspect. In: COGSCI 1997, Stanford, CA, pp. 548–553 (1997)

History and Current Researches on Building a Human Interface for Humanoid Robots

Yosuke Matsusaka

National Institute of Advanced Industrial Science and Technology
1-1-1, Umezono, Tsukuba, Ibaraki 305-8568, Japan
`yosuke.matsusaka@aist.go.jp`

Abstract. In this chapter we overview humanoid robotic research as another thread of ECA research. This chapter consists of two parts: In the first half, we overview the historical research on creating communicative functions for humanoid robots. In these sections, we see how research on realizing a human interface for a humanoid robot has begun and developed, by tracing some very early humanoid robotic research done in 1970. In the later half, we try to survey recent research related to this topic. In these sections, we will have a brief overview of researches, and also, through the process of reviewing, we try to make clear the characteristics of using robots in the ECA research.

Keywords: humanoid robot, communication, survey, ECA.

1 Introduction

In this chapter we overview humanoid robotic research as another thread of ECA research.

In most ECA systems, agents with virtual bodies are used as a research platform. Here, a humanoid robot is a robot which has a human-shaped "physical" body. Because the shapes are similar, humanoid robotic research shares many issues with virtual agent-based ECA researches. But, on the other hand, it also has many characteristics different from the virtual agents. For example, a humanoid robot has a physical body and abilities to share physics in a real world. It can use its hands and body to interact with humans and objects, while this is usually impossible for the virtual agents.

For many years, humanoid robotics research and virtual agent research has done successful research from its own point of view and developed its ideas independently. In this chapter, we would, once again, like to return back to the basic objective of ECA research on using human-shaped agents to human communication research, and try to put together these two independent ideas.

Objective of this chapter is to discuss the issues occurring in ECA research from the humanoid robotics' point of view and introduce some recent ideas developed from this approach.

This chapter consists of two parts: In the first half, we overview historical research on creating communicative functions for humanoid robots. In these

I. Wachsmuth and G. Knoblich (Eds.): Modeling Communication, LNAI 4930, pp. 109–124, 2008.
© Springer-Verlag Berlin Heidelberg 2008

sections, we see how research on realizing a human interface for a humanoid robot has begun and developed, by tracing some very early humanoid robotic research done in 1970s. In the later half, we try to survey recent research that has been done related to this topic. In these sections, we will have a brief overview of researches, and also, through the process of reviewing, we try to make clear the characteristics of using robots in the ECA research.

2   Scope of This Chapter

This chapter is intended to form a bridge between humanoid robotic research and virtual-agent-based research. Intended reader is the one who is working in virtual agent research area and unfamiliar with humanoid robotic research.

Unlike the other overviews of robotic research, this chapter focuses on enhancing differences between virtual agent research and humanoid robotic research by showing examples. From this reason, we give importance to explaining the issues that could be shared between those two (e.g. creation of body, behavior, response, etc...). On the other hand, unlike in normal robotics research overviews, we give less importance to explaining some other topics often focused on in robotic research (e.g. learning algorithms). For this part, only a brief introduction with some references is provided to assist further reading.

3   The History

3.1   Speech Communication Function in WABOT-1

In 1973 the group led by Ichiro Kato developed a robot named WABOT-1 (Figure 1). The project aimed to create completely the function of a human by integrating most-advanced electromechanical technology of the day. WABOT-1 had a human imitated body with two arms and two legs, and by controlling the electric motors, it could walk like the humans do. Kato has given it the term "Humanoid" to denote such human-shaped robot which has human imitated functions[1]. Academic research to develop a human-shaped being by means of electromechanical technology began at that point.

Kato has explained the meaning of doing research on humanoid robots in two ways. One is to create an artificial being that helps humans in their living space. A human-like body is suitable to act in rooms or to use tools, because those rooms and tools are primarily designed for human beings. Also, a human-like body and resulting human-like modes of behavior are easy to understand for human communicators.

The other objective to create such robot is for scientific purposes. The process of creating human functions by means of electromechanical technology give a lot of knowledge to these developers. In order to create these functions, the developer has to investigate the functions of the unknown parts and create correct models. They also have to actually realize the function by implementing the technologies which may sometimes be substitutional compared to those of humans. The developers also have to verify the correctness of the system they have created, by applying the robot to the real-world tests. All these processes make a natural loop of investigation, modeling and verification, and give healthy feedback to research activity itself. In part of Kato's work, not only have they created humanoid robots, but also have they created myoelectric prostheses as for human amputees, based on the knowledge they have acquired by creating the robots.

In WABOT-1, the objective for creating the function of the human is not limited to its physical shape, but the objective has also extended to create an artificial human perception function and communication function. For this objective, speech recognition function is installed for WABOT-1. Voice command input from the user is recognized by using the isolated word recognizer running on the computer connected outside of the robot. The robot could accept a few commands such as "take one step forward". The communication realized by state-of-the-art technology of the 1970s is hardly to be called natural (the users have to wait for several minutes to get the speech recognition result), but creation of a whole featured humanoid robot is actually a very important step to establish the basis of humanoid robotic research.

Some readers may feel strange to hear this story about humanoid robot development at Waseda university by referring to the recent situations. But different from the recent, the research for developing a humanoid robot was considered very unique in 1970, and thus made unique development in very limited research sites. We will pass though those early humanoid researches in this first few sections.

3.2 "Pianist" Robot WABOT-2

After the creation of WABOT-1, Ichiro Kato and the group started thinking about adding "kansei" ability as part of the humanoid robot feature. Kansei is a Japanese term which denotes human feelings or images toward things. The term is sometimes translated as "intuitiveness" or "affectiveness" in English.

Ability to play music is selected as a task to develop this ability. WABOT-2 had two hands with dexterous finders to touch the keyboard (Figure 2). It had a camera on its head to read the scores. It also had speech recognition features, not only for speech command understanding, but also for understanding speech rhythms. By using this speech rhythm understanding function, it can make sessions with human singers.

The project has handled widely spread issues from low level motion control, such as motor control or path planning of the fingers, to high level cognition, such as music understanding or rhythm taking. Those functions are tightly connected to each other to realize the natural and interactive music playing. Here, the cognitive functions and the physical controls are mixed together on the same stage. Such issues on bodily grounded cognitive interactions are also discussed as one of the main objectives in this project.

copyright(c) Humanoid Robotics Institute, Waseda University

Fig. 1. WABOT-1 1973

3.3   Multi Modal Communications and AIs (Waseda and MIT)

At Waseda university in 1990s, two robots were created. Those robots are called 3rd generation robots. One robot is a full body humanoid robot called "WABIAN". The other is a upper torso humanoid robot called "HADALY" (Figure 3). Different from the WABOT-1 or WABOT-2, both robots had two eyes, an expressive face, and gesturable arms.

The robots aimed to get closer to one of the final goals of humanoid robotics research: the home robot. It had several communication functions such as gesture understanding and generation, eye contact detection and expression as well as the speech recognition and understanding to realize a more natural communication with the human.

About the same time, a project at MIT created two robots. One is an upper torso robot called "cog". The other is a head and face robot called "kismet".

The cog robot aimed to realize human-like cognitive development mechanisms implemented using AI. It initially had simple vision and motor control functions

copyright(c) Humanoid Robotics Institute, Waseda University

Fig. 2. WABOT-2 the "pianist" robot

as its primitive, and automatically learns how to accomplish the tasks (e.g. how to reach its hand toward the object) through trials. Learning functions are essential for the robot which has to work at home, required to deal with general tasks.

The kismet robot has been developed as a social interactor. It can produce several facial expressions and uses those expressions to affect human communicators. They have also measured their effectiveness and discussed the strategy to control social relations among the human and the robot (described later in Section 4.2). Skill to affect humans and control social relationship is essential for the robot which has to work together with humans in a human society.

3.4 Beginning of the Party - Arrival of Honda Humanoid

At the end of 1990s, Honda unveiled a humanoid robot they had developed as from the mid-1980s. ASIMO is the world first humanoid robot made by a commercial company. The quality they realized is high enough to make the audience believe that in the near feature such robots will be used at home or in public places.

In early 2000 Sony showed SDR (later called QRIO), a compact humanoid which had the ability to dance. Many other major companies (e.g. PaPeRo for NEC and Wakamaru for Mitsubishi) also joined this movement.

After the 20 years since the humanoid research has started, both the academic and the economic basis for developing a humanoid robot has been stabilized.

copyright(c) Humanoid Robotics Institute, Waseda University

Fig. 3. WABIAN and HADALY

Now, what is the main issue for next 20 years? Communication feature must be one of it, because the humanoid robot has to communicate and collaborate with humans in their living space as a fundamental objective. In the following sections, we introduce some of the ongoing projects to give an overview of the current progress of this research area.

4   Current Research Topics and Questions

In this section we list some of the ongoing research on developing communicative functions for humanoid robots.

4.1   Robot as a Media - Why Physical Robots?

Before entering the main part of the survey, we would like to discuss first the fundamental difference between the humanoid robots compared to virtual human characters to make clear the actual meaning of using such robot as a platform of ECA research. Here, for convenience, we use the term v-ECA to denote "virtual embodied conversational agent" and the term p-ECA to denote "physical (real body) embodied conversational agent". We can come up with many points for discussing this issue. But in this specific chapter, I would like to focus on the following points.

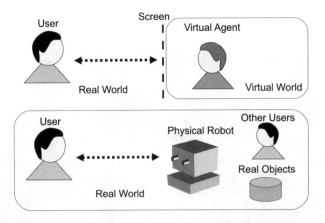

Fig. 4. Difference of v-ECA and p-ECA in terms of sharing the world with a user

Physical interaction: One of the main features we can get by using p-ECA is the ability to make physical interaction with humans. Because the robot has a physical body in real-world and has power driven by motor, it can make physical interaction either with humans or objects.

Three-dimensional expression: In most of the v-ECA researches, 2D displays are used as output devices. In case of robotic systems, the bodies of the robots are observed three-dimensionally. This feature gives several useful effects to human observer. When a user has observed a 3D object, he[she] will perceive two different images of the object from his[her] two eyes respectively. Distance between the eyes gives a certain difference to the view angle and the difference of the observed image gives a user a feeling of depth. The expression supports reality of the 3D object. Moreover, let us think about a case of observing a 3D object from multiple users' points of view. In the single user's case, the distances between the observed images are small. But in a multiple user's case, images are observed very differently between each user. Figure 4 shows an example of the perspective-oriented display shown differently among each user. In Figure 4-a display by the robot is observed as "the robot is pointing to me, talking to user B", while in Figure 4-b display by the robot is observed as "the robot is talking to me, pointing to user A". In Section 4.2 we introduce examples of robotic systems which have used their ability to make perspective-oriented displays to social interactions.

True embedding in the real world (sharing physics, spaces and view points): The robot can share the physics and make a perspective-oriented expression in the real world with human communicators. In addition to this two characteristics, the robot can move around the spaces using its locomotive device. By using this function, it can take its own perspectives by changing its position. Figure 6 explains the example of use of perspective changing. We can easily imagine that the expression in Figure 6-b is much clearer than the expression in Figure 6-a. The robot has freedom to move to any place in the world

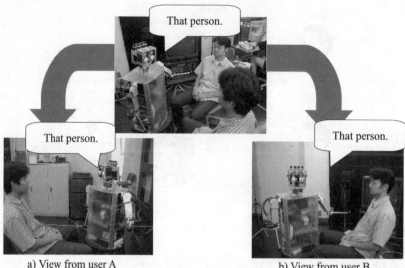

a) View from user A   b) View from user B

Fig. 5. Perspective-oriented display by a three-dimensional robot

to communicate. These features enable the robot to be truly embedded and communicate in the real world.

We will once again discuss these issues in the final section. To have concrete ideas of using robotic systems for communication tasks, we overview concrete examples of the robotic systems which featured communication abilities in the next few sections.

4.2   Communication and the Body

In this section, we overview robotic communication researches by ordering the focus on each part of the body.

Gaze: Humans are known to have very strong sensitivity to gaze. Here we see some studies that tried to realize gaze expression from the robot.

In HADALY and WABIAN, small cameras are installed exactly positioned to the eyes. By using this design, the actual function of the gaze exactly matches the expression of the robot: when the robot controls its camera to capture information of the user, the resulting behavior looks like the robot gazing toward the user. This specific design enables the functional design of the robot to be combined with the expression.

Because gaze expression is strong enough to give a message to the human, the robotic gaze could also be used to control the communication with the human. Kikuchi et al has measured the effect of gaze behavior from the robot to the human interactor, and installed a gaze control strategy of the robot to display to the user whether the robot is currently accepting a command or working for the task[2]. The expression by gaze has worked as a natural way to clarify the internal

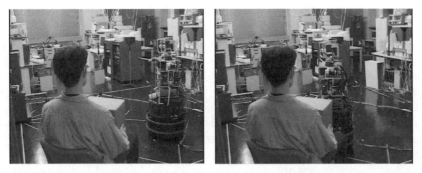

a) Far relation   b) Close relation

Fig. 6. Clarification by perspective change

state of the robot. Matsusaka et al has created a robot which can talk with multiple users by controlling and recognizing the gaze[3]. It can perceive who-is-talking-to-whom, by recognizing the gaze direction of the human communicator. The robot has used its own gaze expression to express who he is talking to.

Shared attention is a term which denotes a state of two or more interactors focusing on a same object. When we think of interaction between a learner and a giver, the learner has to perceive which object or event should be focused on, in order to get a correct piece of information from the giver. The giver has to control the focus of the learner to tell the information correctly. Without this process, it becomes difficult for the learner to guess the exact subject the giver is speaking of so as the exact intent of the giver. Shared attention is considered as an important process to speed up learning. It is important for the robotic system if we consider using a developmental approach to train our baby robot. Nagai has measured an effect of direction and timing of robotic gaze in creation of the shared attention[4]. Imai et al has measured an efficient motion of the gaze when giving direction toward the human[5].

Arms and fingers: An arm is an efficient device to point out the object in the space. One can express the exact direction of the intended object using the pointing gesture without using some words. In some situations, arm gesture is the only way to explain the situation when the situation is too complex to be explained by words. A robotic systems have to communicate with humans in the real world. It needs to have an ability to understand those gestures, because it often has to understand and accept the tasks related to objects and spaces. One of the characteristics of the robotic system compared to v-ECA is that a robot can move by itself. As we see in Figure 6, the robot can control its relative position with the human to make clear the expression. Tojo et al have implemented and measured effects of changing relative positions with objects and humans[6]. Imai et al have measured effects of changing relative positions between humans in direction giving tasks[5].

Facial expressions: Facial expression is one of the richest non-verbal information displays used by humans. Moreover, face is the place where many sensors are located. Takanishi et al has created a humanoid face which has expressive eyes, eyebrows, eyelids, mouth and lips[7]. The face also has cameras on its eyes, touch sensors, smell sensors, and it can generate facial expressions depending on that sensor input. In the system, input from the sensor gives effect to the emotional state of the robot, and the robot produces the facial expression depending on its emotion. Expression of the face has the function to affect the user's emotion toward the robot. Thus, it is possible to control human behavior by means of emotional display. User studies done on evaluating expression generated by the robot and proper design of the emotion spaces are discussed in this project.

Kismet has used facial expression to cope with human caregivers[8]. Kismet is designed to be an infant and has strategies to affect human caregivers to keep giving their care toward itself, in order to enhance its learning process.

Creation of lifelike bodies: There are some works aimed to create a lifelike body of the robot. Kobayashi et al has been creating a realistic human-shaped robot (they have used the term "android" to denote their robot to clarify the difference of research direction from the humanoid robotic research) which uses artificial muscles to realize natural shape and motion[9]. Sarcos is a company which has been creating realistic robotic characters for museums and exhibitions. Hanson Robotics is a company which creates lifelike artificial heads with artificial skins. Ishiguro et al has been creating a body copied from the human's own body. The body is used as a tele-operated "self", and measuring an effect given both to the others and to the own[10].

Artificial skins and elastic muscles: A robot can use a physical body to interact with humans and objects. There is research to develop essential technologies to realize this physical interaction. Takanishi et al has used pressure detection material in multi-layered form to realize artificial skin which can detect stroke and hit distinguishably[7]. Kageyama et al have developed a pressure sensor, based on electromagnetic induction which can easily be embedded in the silicone skin of the robot[11]. Cog and HADALY have an elastic arm which used series elastic actuator and spring-and-damper mechanism respectively[12][13]. The elasticity of the arm is not only important to prevent damaging the human, but also important to make interaction by touching the object using the elastic arm as a sensor.

4.3   Model of Mind

Among many mind models, hieratic behavior generation models are one of the well-used models in both v-ECA and p-ECA, because it has a convenience to realize highly responsive behavior. In this section we focus on this specific approach.

The hieratic behavior generation approach was first introduced by Brooks in creating robot "Genghis"[14]. Such concept initially was developed in the robotic area for generic tasks. Later, it was imported to v-ECA systems for realizing expressive behaviors. Then, it was imported back again to the robotic system for communication tasks. From this reason, there are certain interactions between v-ECA and p-ECA researches.

AIBO(Hieratical + Emotional parameters): In 1999 Sony started selling AIBO, a pet robot. Upon making the robot, they considered deeply on how they could keep entertaining people without them getting bored by the repeating behavior generated from the robot. They decided to choose the hieratic behavior generation strategy for their new concept category "pet robot"[15]. AIBO uses a hieratic model to generate behavior as a response to the sensor input, and it also has internal emotional parameters to set some weighting to those behavior selection criteria. That behavior generation mechanism made possible to create various sorts of behavior which can also work robust to interact with the human and the world. As we know, AIBO has made a successful sales as a robotic pet, not only for its hardware design, but also for its realistic behaviors.

Kismet(Social hieratical): Some researchers have tried to implement a hieratic structure to control a higher level of behavior. In Kismet[8] the relation between the robot and the human (as a caregiver) has been modeled as higher layers of the hieratic behavior model. Those higher level layers provide meta parameters to control the behavior selection mechanisms in the lower layers.

ROBITA(Hybrid production rule): One of the problems we often face when we use a hieratic model is the difficulty of making productive behavior which requires deep planning. Kim et al[16] has used a hybrid approach, which uses production rule in the higher layer to control the meta parameters of the behavior generation mechanism in the lower layer.

JIJO-2 (Bayesian approach): Motomura et al has introduced the Bayesian approach to the robotic behavior generation[17]. The Bayesian approach can incorporate uncertainty in its internal state and it can easily incorporate existing learning algorithms.

4.4   Hardware and Software Architectures of the Mind

Here, we introduce some research done to develop actual hardware to give life to the robotic mind.

In past years, when the computers were so big, the "remote brain" approach was taken as a way to install massive processing power to the compact robot platform[18]. In 1990, after small powerful embedded processors became popular, robotic systems with multiprocessor networks were developed. Bischoff et al used i2c bus for connecting multiple processors inside the robotic body[19]. Yamasaki et al developed a fast network called "responsive link" capable to transfer huge data such as audios and videos[20].

There are also considerations on the software architecture to ease the development of a robotic mind separated in modules. Matsui et al has developed a language called "eus-lisp": a lisp language which has event handling and physics simulation features[21]. Matsusaka et al has used software and hardware architecture which realized transparency between the on-board and outside networks' processing modules[22].

4.5 Learning Algorithms and Semantic Modeling

One of the higher end of human function is probably the ability to learn. Here, we briefly overview some recent prominent researches.

Nakanishi et al has been working on creating imitation learning systems[23]. The robot learns skills of handling an object by observing human examples of handling the object. Knowledge of the dynamics of the own body of the robot is used to recognize the dynamics of handling the object by the human. Nagakubo et al has developed a full body humanoid robot that can learn though imitation and interaction in the real-world[24]. A group led by Ritter has created a robot by combining shared attention mechanisms and imitation learning[25].

Roy has created a vocabulary learning system on an active vision head[26]. The robot has observed an object from multiple perspectives and learned its concept by associating the sensor inputs with the word inputs.

Iwahashi has created a vocabulary learning system on a robot which learns verbs[27]. In this system, the robot implements a Markov chain based algorithm to estimate the state of the input, and has an ability to learn how to symbolize the series of image and motor control input in association with speech. The learning algorithm also has a mechanism to estimate the focus of instruction using the contextual information of the series of past input.

On creation of semantics of the dialog, Ishiguro et al has developed a software which can design exchanges of the dialog in action-state graph[28].

4.6 Applications

Here in this final section, we would like to introduce some real world applications which have featured communication abilities.

Attendant (Office and Museum) robot: In this type of application, the robot moves around the office, engages with the visitors, and interacts with them to exchange information. Jijo-2[29] had a internal database of the map of the office and a database of the activity of the office worker to provide information to the visitors. It updates the data continuously by using Bayesian framework. Project at EPFL[30] has a microphone array based speech recognizer and image recognizer to detect, track and navigate the human. The project has done a long-term working experiment at an exposition site.

The robot as an interactor which interfaces humans with machines: We can think of a humanoid robot, on the one side, as a computer which can easily communicate with other computers, on the other side, as an agent which is designed to communicate with a human.

NEC has been developing a robot named "PaPeRo". PaPeRo is a small size robot which has a bi-wheel mobile platform, and it is capable to follow humans using image and auditory sensors. It also has a speech recognition function to accept human voice commands. The robot is connected to home network using the wireless network, and controls and works together with the other home equipments (e.g. lights, TVs, car navigation).

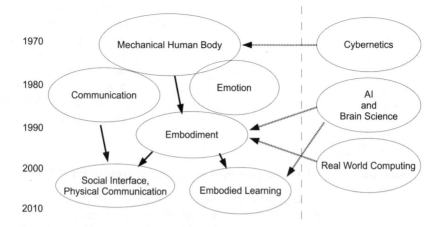

Fig. 7. Schematic overview and relation with other disciplines

The project at NICT and Waseda university has been designing and building an automated home which can work in combination with robots. The robot is expected to be an interpreter to enable human to control the whole function of the home easily.

Robot therapy: A communicative robot is sometimes used as a cure for people. Shibata has been developing a robot called "Paro"[31]. Paro has a soft body and an ability to give a response to physical interaction such as touching. It is expected to be an artificial interactor to cure people depressed by less communication.

Kojima has been creating a special tele-operated robot used for therapy of autistic children[32]. The robot has neither locomotive functions nor arms to manipulate, but it is simple enough so that it almost looks like a single torus. This specific design has shown effectiveness in the therapy by giving the feeling of secureness to the patients.

5 Discussion and Summary

5.1 Schematic Overview and Relation with Other Disciplines

Figure 7 shows the schematic overview of the researches introduced in this chapter. The arrows in the figure indicate a context and a relation of each research.

First, a full mechanical human body was created. Emotion and communication function was added based on a consideration of one of the required functions for a human shaped robot working at home. On adding intelligence to a mechanical human body, the problem of embodiment has introduced as a new concept of AI. The concept of embodiment has later developed a concept of embodied learning, and also combined with the communication function, it has developed the concept of social interface and physical communication.

In addition, relation with other disciplines are shown in the figure. In the 1970s a huge cybernetics movement occurred. Extended from the original concept of the cybernetics introduced in the 1940s, the cybernetics movement in the 1970s has made wide collaborative development including biological science which tried to model the entire living organism as a system. An attempt to create an entire human body as a mechanical system was done on this historical background. Development in AI and brain science in the 1980s and growth of research projects on real-world computing in the late 1990s also gave many effects on development of intelligence for humanoid robots.

5.2 Advantages and Disadvantages of Using a Robot for ECA Research

In this chapter, we have looked through many robotic researches. To summarize these researches, let us go back to the question we have thought earlier: Why has it to be a robot?

As we have seen in Section 4.1 and Section 4.2, a robot has a physical body which can physically interact with the human. Physical interaction has many applications as shown in Section 4.6. We have seen in Section 4.1 and Section 4.1 that visual communication can also be enhanced by using 3D body expression of the robot. Learning is an important function for the robot, because the robot has to acquire the skill through human communication in order to accomplish general tasks in our life space. Facial expression (Section 4.2) and shared attention (Section 4.2) are the important communicative skills to enhance the learning process. Emotional expression has actual power to control the relation with the human (Section 4.2). The model of emotion is discussed often in relation with the model of dynamics in robotic control (Section 4.3). All of the above are the applications which require using real robotic bodies and clearly shows the benefit of using robots as a platform of ECA research.

One of the major difficulties of using a robot to ECA research is the problem of creating hardware. Even to add a small change to the texture of face, p-ECA requires adding new motors and new hardware mechanism. Those developments often require some time as well as money. In addition, because each of the motors requires some physical spaces, there exists a theoretical limit on creating complex expressions. On the other hand, in v-ECA systems, there are no such limits on creating those expressions.

5.3 Future Directions

Although for differences shown in the previous section, we have seen that in many parts especially on mind models or nonverbal expression such as gaze or gestures, p-ECA research shares many issues with v-ECA researches.

Recent development of the virtual display device has realized realistic three-dimensional illusion. Those start to be applied to ECA studies (e.g. [33]). Also a combined approach of v-ECA and p-ECA has also been developed recently. In such systems, texture of the face is projected to a three-dimensional surface of the robotic face and can make a richer expression than the robotic system which only uses the mechanical display. This is the promising technology which can both benefit from v-ECA and p-ECA.

The author believes that in the near future there will be no distinction between v-ECA research and p-ECA research.

References

1. Kato, I.: Homini-robotism. In: In Fifth International Conference on Advanced Robotics, vol. 1, pp. 1–5 (1991)
2. Kikuchi, H., Yokoyama, M., Hoashi, K., Hidaki, Y., Kobayashi, T., Shirai, K.: Controlling gaze of humanoid in communication with human. In: Proc. of Intl. Conference on Intelligent Robots and Systems, pp. 255–260 (1998)
3. Matsusaka, Y., Tojo, T., Kobayashi, T.: Conversation robot participating in group conversation. IEICE Trans. Information and System E86-D(1), 26–36 (2003)
4. Nagai, Y.: Understanding the Development of Joint Attention from a Viewpoint of Cognitive Developmental Robotics. PhD thesis, Osaka University (January 2004)
5. Imai, M., Ono, T., Ishiguro, H.: Physical relation and expression: Joint attention for human-robot interaction. In: Proceedings of 10th IEEE International Workshop on Robot and Human Communication, pp. 512–517 (2001)
6. Tojo, T., Matsusaka, Y., Ishii, T., Kobayashi, T.: A conversational robot utilizing facial and body expressions. In: IEEE Proc. SMC 2000, pp. 858–863 (2000)
7. Takanishi, A., Takanobu, H., Kato, I., Umetsu, T.: Development of the anthropomorphic head-eye robot we-3rii with an autonomous facial expression mechanism. In: IEEE ICRA 1999, pp. 3255–3260 (1999)
8. Breazeal, C., Brian, S.: Infant-like social interactions between a robot and a human caretaker. Adaptive Behavior 8(1) (2000)
9. Kobayashi, H., Ichikawa, Y., Senda, M., Shiiba, T.: Realization of realistic and rich facial expressions by face robot. In: Proceedings of the 2003 IEEE International Conference on Intelligent Robots and Systems, pp. 1123–1128 (2003)
10. MacDorman, K., Ishiguro, H.: The uncanny advantage of using androids in cognitive and social science research. Interaction Studies 7(3), 297–337 (2006)
11. Kageyama, R., Kagami, S., Inaba, M., Inoue, H.: Development of soft and distributed tactile sensors and the application to a humanoid robot. In: Proceedings of IEEE International Conference on Systems, Man, and Cybernetics, vol. 2, pp. 981–986 (1999)
12. Brooks, R., Breazeal, C., Marjanovic, M., Scassellati, B., Williamson, M.: Computation for Metaphors, Analogy and Agents. In: The Cog Project: Building a Humanoid Robot. LNCS (LNAI), Springer, Heidelberg (1998)
13. Morita, T., Iwata, H., Sugano, S.: Design strategies of human symbiotic robot wendy. Journal of Robotics and Mechatronics 13(3), 224–230 (2000)
14. Brooks, R.: Intelligence without reason. In: Proceedings of IJCAI 1991, pp. 561–595 (1991)
15. Sawada, T., Takagi, T., Fujita, M.: Behavior selection and motion modulation in emotionally grounded architecture for qrio sdr-4x ii. In: Proc. of IROS 2004, pp. 2514–2519 (2004)
16. Kim, K., Matsusaka, Y., Kobayashi, T.: Inter-module cooperation architecture for interactive robot. In: Proc. IROS 2002, vol. 3, pp. 2286–2291 (2002)

17. Motomura, Y., Hara, I., Itoh, K., Asoh, H., Sato, T.: Task, situation and user models for personal robots. In: IJCAI 2001 workshop on Reasoning with Uncertainty in Robotics (2001)
18. Inaba, M.: Remote-brained robotics: Interfacing ai with real world behaviors. In: Proc. of 1993 International Symposium on Robotics Research (1993)
19. Bischoff, R., Jain, T.: Natural communication and interaction with humanoid robots. In: Second IEEE International Symposium on Humanoid Robots, pp. 121–128 (1999)
20. Yamasaki, N.: Design and implementation of responsive processor for parallel/distributed control and its development environments. In: Journal of Robotics and Mechatronics, pp. 125–133 (2001)
21. Matsui, T., Asoh, H., Hara, I., Otsu, N.: An event driven architecture for controlling behaviors of the office conversant mobile robot, jijo-2. In: Proc. IEEE-ICRA 1997, pp. 3367–3371 (1997)
22. Matsusaka, Y., Kobayashi, T.: System software for collaborative development of interactive robot. In: Proc. IEEE-HUMANOIDS 2001, pp. 271–277 (2001)
23. Nakanishi, J., Morimoto, J., Endo, G., Cheng, G., Schaal, S., Kawato, M.: Learning from demonstration and adaptation of biped locomotion. Robotics and Autonomous Systems 47, 79–91 (2004)
24. Nagakubo, A., Kuniyoshi, Y., Cheng, G.: The etl-humanoid system – a high-performance full body humanoid system for versatile real world interaction. Advanced Robotics 17(2), 149–164 (2003)
25. Steil, J.J., Roethling, F., Haschke, R., Ritter, H.: Situated robot learning for multi-modal instruction and imitation of grasping. Robotics and Autonomous Systems 47(2–3), 129–141 (2004)
26. Roy, D.: Grounding words in perception and action: Insights from computational models. Trends in Cognitive Science 9(8), 389–396 (2005)
27. Iwahashi, N.: A method for the coupling of belief systems through human-robot language interaction. In: Proc. 12th IEEE Workshop Robot and Human Interactive Communication, pp. 385–390 (2003)
28. Ishiguro, H., Kanda, T., Kimoto, K., Ishida, T.: A robot architecture based on situated modules. In: IEEE Proc. IROS 1999, pp. 1617–1623 (1999)
29. Asano, F., Asoh, H., Matsui, T.: Sound source localization and signal separation for office robot "jijo-2". In: Proceedings of Multisensor Fusion and Integration for Intelligent Systems (1999)
30. Siegwart, R., Arras, K., Bouabdallah, S., Burnier, D., Froidevaux, G., Greppin, X., Jensen, B., Lorotte, A., Mayor, L., Meisser, M., Philippsen, R., Piguet, R., Ramel, G., Terrien, G., Tomatis, N.: Robox at expo.02: A large scale installation of personal robots. Robotics and Autonomous Systems (42), 203–222 (2003)
31. Shibata, T., Tashima, T., Tanie, K.: Emergence of emotional behavior through physical interaction between human and pet robot. In: Proc. of the IARP First Int'l Workshop on Humanoid and Human Friendly Robotics, vol. 4, pp. 1–6 (1998)
32. Kozima, H., Nakagawa, C., Yasuda, Y.: Interactive robots for communication-care: A case-study in autism therapy. In: IEEE International Workshop on Robot and Human Interactive Communication, pp. 341–346 (2005)
33. Altosaar, M., Vertegaal, R., Sohn, C., Cheng, D.: Auraorb: Social notification appliance. In: Conference on Human Factors in Computing Systems, pp. 381–386 (2006)

Typological and Computational Investigations of Spatial Perspective

Martin Loetzsch[1], Remi van Trijp[1], and Luc Steels[1,2]

[1] Sony Computer Science Laboratory - Paris, 6, rue Amyot, 75005 Paris - France
[2] VUB AI Lab, Vrije Universiteit Brussels, Pleinlaan 2, 1050 Brussels - Belgium

Abstract. This paper is part of an ongoing research program to understand the cognitive and functional bases for the origins and evolution of spatial language. Following a cognitive-functional approach, we first investigate the cross-linguistic variety in spatial language, with special attention for spatial perspective. Based on this language-typological data, we hypothesize which cognitive mechanisms are needed to explain this variety and argue for an interdisciplinary approach to test these hypotheses. We then explain how experiments in artificial language evolution can contribute to that and give a concrete example.

Keywords: spatial language, perspective reversal, language games, embodiment.

1   Introduction

Traditionally, the 'language faculty' has been proposed to contain an innate and universal grammar, a view that has been defended by some influential thinkers such as Noam Chomsky and Steven Pinker [1,2]. A different stance is taken by cognitive (e.g. [3]) and functional linguistics (e.g. [4]), two related fields that study the general cognitive mechanisms that underly conceptualization and the functional pressures that explain differences in linguistic behaviour. Recently, a growing number of scientists have been working from a cognitive-pragmatic (or cognitive-functional) angle that combines the insights of both disciplines into a more complete language theory [5].

Our research subscribes to the cognitive-functional approach and therefore starts from the observation that language is a system that has both a functional dimension (linguistic behaviour) and a cognitive dimension (the biological nature or infrastructure of the language faculty), and that understanding language means understanding both dimensions and the correlations that exist between them. As argued in [6], the functional dimension of language can be directly observed in utterances and other forms of linguistic behaviour. The cognitive dimension, on the other hand, remains hidden in the 'black box' of the human mind. This means that the external use of language is the first and most important source of characterizing the inner workings of the mind, but at the same time the functional dimension of language can only be fully understood when

I. Wachsmuth and G. Knoblich (Eds.): Modeling Communication, LNAI 4930, pp. 125–142, 2008.
© Springer-Verlag Berlin Heidelberg 2008

more is known about the cognitive dimension, which implies that we have precise operational models of the information processing that goes on in cognition.

In this article, we first present a brief overview of spatial expressions across languages based on the literature on spatial language and our own study of ten languages[1]. Based on this data, we are able to formulate hypotheses on what cognitive mechanisms and operations are needed to make these kinds of expressions possible. We then present our research method, involving an experimental set-up with embodied communicative agents, that aims to go inside the black box and investigate these mechanisms. This research method is illustrated by an example experiment on spatial language, more specifically on the role of perspective reversal. Speakers of a language are able to use a different spatial perspective than their own in conceptualizing what to say and to explicitly mark this in language when needed. This is clearly present in road instructions (e.g. *Go straight ahead and leave the building to your left*), demonstratives, etc. Although there are obvious differences in how languages express perspective, there can be no doubt about the fact that they all have several ways to do so and that the speakers make abundant use of this facility. In the final section, we discuss the first results and directions for future research.

2   Some Observations of Spatial Language

Spatial language has already received a lot of attention in the past (see [19,20,3] for some groundbreaking research), but most of the studies on space grammars is based on familiar, western languages. This has led to some hasty conclusions, for instance that no language will have prepositions expressing specific shapes of objects such as *sprough*, meaning 'through a cigar-shaped object' [21], or that relative, anthropocentric spatial categories such as *left* versus *right* are universal or central to human spatial thinking [22]. However, recent cross-linguistic explorations have shown that human languages do not only vary in the syntactic structures that are employed to express spatial relations, but also in the set of semantic categories that are shared within a speech community (see [23,24] for a thorough investigation of 'relative' versus 'absolute' spatial expressions). In this section, we provide cross-linguistic examples of spatial expressions and look for cognitive-functional explanations that underly them.

We do not attempt to provide a complete semantic or syntactic typology of spatial expressions (some good reference works are [19,23,25]). Instead, we will give some relevant examples and try to answer the following three questions about spatial expressions that have been under serious debate in the past: (1) are people equipped with primitive spatial categories, (2) what is the semantic (and cognitive) nature of spatial categories across languages and (3) what grammatical

---

[1] A complete overview of this study does not fit the purpose of this paper, so we made a selection of examples that illustrate our needs best. The ten languages and their reference grammars were: Alamblak [7], Dutch [8], Iraqw [9], Ket [10], Malayalam [11,12], Manam [13], North Marquesan [14], Páez [15], South-Eastern Pomo [16] and Zulu [17,18].

items are used by languages to express spatial relations? We then present and define the dimension of spatial communication that we are especially interested in: spatial perspective.

2.1 Spatial Categories

Many observers have assumed that spatial language may give us some insights into spatial cognition and the human mind in general. Starting from a nativist theory of language, or with the limited data of western languages, many scientists have claimed the existence of a universal set of spatial categories. This section suggests the opposite by showing a glimpse of the vast variety in how languages have decided to 'cut up' spatial relations.

Frames of Reference. One of the blackest flies in the ointment for everyone who defends the nativist view of language – whether they are talking about the innateness of syntax or the universality of semantic categories – is the fairly recent discovery of languages that do not use relative spatial categories such as *left* or *right* for locating objects in space. Instead, there are quite a few languages that prefer an 'absolute frame of reference' [23], comparable to spatial categories such as *North* and *South* in English.

The language Manam is a good example: its speakers live on a small island and their spatial language is dominated by two absolute directions (*ilau* 'towards the sea', and *auta* 'inland, towards the interior of the island'). All other directions are expressed by using these two. Across the seaward-inward line, Manam distinguishes between *ata* 'to one's left when facing the sea, and right when facing inland' and its opposite direction *awa*. When needed, the speakers of Manam can even combine these four directions for more precise indications. Adding the suffix *-lo* to the direction indicates motion. Thus the speakers of Manam wouldn't say something like 'The car is parked left of the tree' but rather something like 'The car is parked on the seaside of the tree'. Manam has a very complex and well developed range of spatial expressions, but all of them are based on this strong seaward-inland axis ([13], chapter 9).

(1) *áta*   *i-sóa?i*
    left when facing seaward   3SG.RL-be located
    'He is in the direction left when facing seaward.'

(2) *aúta-lo*   *i-óro*
    inland-MOTION   3SG.RL-go seaward
    'He went in inland direction.'

The choice between different reference frames doesn't mean that they come with a universal set of spatial categories either. As documented in [23], the semantics of absolute spatial expressions can not be reduced to one single system of primitive categories. For example, some of these languages lack words that could be translated as 'left' or 'right' (as relative to a dominant axis). For example, North Marquesan only distinguishes an 'across' axis with respect to its dominant seaward-inland axis. To distinguish which side of this axis is referred to by the speaker, extra landmarks or place names have to be mentioned that help the hearer to find the right direction.

Also strongly related languages that make use of the relative frame of reference, such as English, Dutch and German, do not have spatial expressions that map easily from one to another. One can for instance easily observe the big differences between the formal and semantic properties of their spatial prepositions.

Specific versus Abstract. Traditionally, spatial categories have been regarded as carrying very abstract meaning. The parade example is the aforementioned prediction of Landau and Jackendoff that no language should have locatives like the hypothetical *sprough*, meaning 'through a cigar-shaped object' [21]. The classic counterexample is found in the Californian language Karuk that has a spatial suffix *-vara* with exactly this meaning ([23], p. 63).

When looking at the languages of the world, it becomes clear that the Karuk example is by no means an exception. For instance, South-Eastern Pomo has an inventory of 26 directional morphemes, most of which carry specific information such as the nature of the goal (water, land, etc.), the travel medium, deviations and changes in the motional state, etc. ([16], pp. 55–62, 79–91). The same language also contains motion verb roots that specify the presence or absence of the source of the motion, the relationship between the source and the referent that undergoes the motion (e.g. whether they touch each other or not), and the shape and orientation of the referent (long, standing, lying or vertical). The following example[2] shows how the semantics of the spatial markers specify the source object of the event:

(3) *líl*
     into an enclosed space
     -bò
     crawling motion along a surface, into a long object horizontally
     -t
     IMPERF.
     'He crawled into a tunnel.'

This example contains the directional morpheme *lil-* that specifies that the movement is into an enclosed space. This meaning is combined with the motion verb root *bo-* that specifies that the object is also long and horizontal, so the object that the speaker refers to can be translated as 'tunnel'.

Next to verb roots and suffixes, demonstratives too have been attested to give more specific information when they are used to indicate the relative distance from a referent to the deictic center. They can tell whether the *"referent is visible or out-of-sight, at a higher or lower elevation, uphill or downhill, upriver*

---

[2] The example came without glosses. Based on the information found in [16], we added them ourselves.

or downriver, or moving toward or away from the deictic center" ([26], p. 170, also see [27]).

Example (4) shows an elevational marker in Alamblak, meaning that the referent is in a higher location than the speaker. Examples (5) and (6) show some demonstratives in Manam. As seen before, Manam bases its directions on the dominant seaward-inland axis and combines this with demonstratives so that the speaker can not only express the relative difference of a referent to herself, but also in which direction the referent should be situated. The speakers of Manam are able to express a four-way distance contrast with their demonstratives, ranging from nearby to far away and out of sight.

(4) *fëh-m-ko*
    pig-3PL-up (higher than speaker)
    'pigs up (there)'

(5) *áine   éne   i-tui=túi*
    woman   over there.across 3SG.RL-stand=REDUPL
    'The woman is standing over there (left or right from the seaward-inland axis).'

(6) *i-alále   enáwa-lo   ʔába   i-múle*
    3SG.RL-go   far over there-MOTION again   3SG.RL-return
    enáta-lo
    far over there-MOTION
    'He went way over there (an out-of-sight place in the direction right when facing the sea) and then went back to way over there (an out-of-sight place in the opposite direction).'

In some cases, languages get even more specific. Alamblak has a number of locative words that can only be used with specific referents (e.g. trees, houses, canoes, large natural objects, etc.) ([7], p. 85). The most specific spatial expressions are place names, which are very often constructions that have become fixed names. Example (8) shows a noun phrase from Brabant (a Dutch dialect) that has become the name of a small forrest in the north of Belgium. We will not consider toponymy any further, but it should be noted that the use of place names is a very simple and effective way for people in a local community to talk about their environment.

(7) (a) *rawof*
        'inside' (only with canoes)

    (b) *mëfha*
        'front' (only with canoes)

(8) *drei   boom-ke-s-'   berg-en*
    three   tree-DIMIN.-PL-GEN.   mountain-PL.
    Lit.: 'The mountains of the three small trees.'

Open-class vs Closed-class Subsystems. Traditionally, linguists have made the distinction between an 'open-class' or 'lexical' subsystem of language on the one hand, and a 'closed-class' or 'grammatical' subsystem on the other hand. As argued in [28], the closed-class subsystem determines conceptual structure and should therefore be the focus of research if one wants to investigate the spatial structuring in language. While this distinction is very useful for scientific purposes, it does not capture the complete picture of language.

The distinction between an open-class and closed-class subsystem has been conceived from a static view on language. However, languages are constantly changing and research in grammaticalization shows that closed subsystems are not as closed as they appear to be [29]. This has led to Paul Hopper's notion of 'emergent grammar' [30], that is, grammar is always on the move. The recent development of the collostructional analysis in corpus linguistics allows researchers to detect latent grammaticalization processes that can only be uncovered by looking at large amounts of data [31,32]. The following example (taken from [33], p. 163) shows how the speakers of Thai use the 'open-class' word *maa* 'come' in a serial verb construction to mark the destination of an event.

(9) *thân   cà   bin   maa   krungthêep*
    he   will fly   come Bangkok
    'He will fly to Bangkok.'

When it occurs in serial verb constructions, *maa* cannot be inflected independently for tense, mood, or aspect. A subsequent step in the grammaticalization process could be the re-interpretation of the verb as an adposition. It is widely attested that lexical verbs are a big source of grammaticalization for prepositions, case-markers and other grammatical items.

Thus when looking at actual language data, there seems to be no sharp distinction between lexical and grammatical items. This has been recognized and explicitly addressed by many studies in cognitive linguistics and construction grammar [34,35]. These theories represent linguistic knowledge as a continuum from the lexicon to syntax, which is an important observation for building a model that is in line with what is known about cognition.

Moreover, spatial relations can be expressed by virtually every grammatical item in language: motion verbs, cases (e.g. Finnish distinguishes between the interior locative cases inessive, elative and illative, and the exterior locative cases adessive, ablative and allative), spatial prepositions, adnominals, adverbial phrases, three-place locative constructions (e.g. Alamblak), demonstratives, etc.

2.2   Spatial Perspective

Our main research focus lies in **'spatial perspective'**, that is, how speakers express a scene as perceived by the visual system and how they are able to cope with the different angles from which the different speech participants observe the world. Our notion of spatial perspective more or less corresponds to what Talmy calls the 'perspective point' – the *"point within a scene at which one* *conceptually places one's 'mental eyes' to look out over the rest of the scene"* ([19], p. 217, see also examples (11–12) further down). The following examples give a clear illustration of spatial perspective.

(10) The car is parked on this side of the house.
(11) There are some houses in the valley.
(12) There is a house every now and then through the valley.
(13) The ball rolled from *my left* to *your right*.

In the first example, the speaker means that the car is located on the side of the house at which she is standing. In other words, the scene should be viewed from her spatial perspective. Examples (11) and (12) show how complex spatial perspective can be when it is combined with other cognitive mechanisms. In (11), the spatial perspective is stationary and the scene is viewed from a certain distance, whereas example (12) shows that the same valley can be conceptualized from a viewpoint in which one can see every individual house from up close, following a motion *through* the valley. The last example shows how there can be a **shift in spatial perspective**. Sentence (13) illustrates how the speaker explicitly marks from which viewpoints the hearer has to interpret the locative expressions in the utterance. The source of the ball movement is 'left of the speaker' as seen from the speaker's point-of-view. The target location of the roll-event contains information that should be interpreted from the hearer's own spatial perspective.

Spatial perspective is also shown in deictic markers such as pronouns or demonstratives. Example (14) gives three Japanese demonstratives, of which *sono* explicitly means that the referent should be located near the hearer ([36], cited from [26]). Finally, even if the speaker expresses a spatial relation from her own point-of-view, the hearer often has to perform egocentric perspective reversal to be able to interpret the utterance.

(14) *kono+INFL   sono+INFL   ano+INFL*
       near speaker 'near hearer' 'away from speaker and hearer'

Perspective reversal also occurs when using landmarks to situate a referent or to indicate a direction, which is a complicated matter that also varies from language to language. Given the scope and space limits of this paper, we will not go into this topic now, but we will come back to it in the last section of this paper when we discuss the further steps in our research program. We kindly refer the interested reader to ([23], chapter 3) for a brief overview of the linguistic diversity regarding this subject.

2.3   Conclusions

Based on the cross-linguistic data of our own study and the results of other typological research, we can draw the following conclusions with respect to cognitive mechanisms needed for spatial language:

1. Language users must be able to impose a reference frame on their environment. A reference frame contains a point of view (perspective) from which the world is perceived, and local (i.e. temporary and viewpoint-dependent) or global landmarks. By default the perspective on the scene is the position of the speaker in the world, because the vision system directly produces perceptual features from this position.

2. There is strong evidence that there are no universal spatial categories: every language has its own way of cutting up the perceptual space. This implies that the language faculty should include cognitive mechanisms that allow a group of speakers to create new spatial categories. There are of course trends in languages because spatial categorisation is obviously constrained by the properties of the real world and our embodiment in that world. Spatial categories divide the perceptual continuum into discrete regions, such as left/right, front/back. Some categories are relational in the sense that they discretise the spatial relation between different objects located in the reference frame (as in "the ball left of the box").

3. There is strong evidence for a continuum from specific to abstract categories and from lexical to grammatical items (e.g. [37,38]). Moreover the examples given earlier make it abundantly clear that different languages make different choices with respect to what spatial categories or relations are lexicalised or grammaticalised. This implies that the language faculty must give language users the ability to lexicalise or grammaticalise spatial concepts, as opposed to support the usage of hard-coded lexical or grammatical constructions. If every language user has the capacity to invent their own categories and decide himself which ones to lexicalise or grammaticalise, then there is a risk of incoherence, so language users must also be able to negotiate with each other which linguistic conventions are to be commonly accepted by the group.

4. Finally, it is clear that language users are able to adopt another reference frame than their own. This implies that they are capable of egocentric perspective transformation (EPT), i.e. to compute what the world looks like from another perspective, particularly that of the other participant in the dialogue.

3   The Perspective Reversal Experiment

Psychologists and neuroscientists have made quite a lot of progress to identify cognitive mechanisms that are involved in the language faculty. For example, the capacity to perform egocentric perspective transformation has been shown to be universally present in normal humans [39] and possibly animals [40]. Neurological evidence has shown that it is carried out in the parietal-temporal-occipital junction which is active whenever its function is needed [41]. Egocentric perspective transformation is used in a variety of non-linguistic tasks, such as the prediction of the behaviour of others in navigation [42].

These studies typically identify that humans are capable of a certain cognitive task and where in the brain the processing necessary for this task might be performed, however they do not give a precise detailed operational model of exactly what kind of processing is needed, neither of the information structures that are required, how the information might be obtained by the cognitive agent, nor of the information transformations or the order in which they are executed. [This is like observing that humans are able to fight off bacteria and that the liver is involved in this process but without detailing exactly what metabolic pathways or biochemical processes are actually doing the work.] Today it is however possible to make such precise operational models and advances in Artificial Intelligence and robotics enable us to build sufficiently complex artificial 'agents' that contain implementations of these models and to test out whether they are adequate. This is precisely the research task that we are pursuing in our laboratory.

Our research methodology involves the following steps (see [43]):

1. Pick a feature of language.
2. Look at the linguistic coding of this feature in different languages.
3. Hypothesize which cognitive mechanisms and external factors (functional pressures) are necessary for the emergence of this particular feature.
4. Operationalize the mechanisms in computational processes and endow agents with these mechanisms.
5. Build a scenario of agent interaction, preferably embedded in some simulation of the world. This scenario and the virtual world have to pose the specific communicative challenges that trigger the need for the investigated language feature.
6. Perform a systematic series of simulations, demonstrating that the feature indeed emerges and that the cognitive mechanisms are in fact necessary. Ideally, this is shown by comparing simulations in which the agents do not have these mechanisms at their disposal to simulations in which they are endowed with them.

The remainder of this section gives a concrete example in which some of the cognitive mechanisms needed for spatial language have been worked out. The experiment is described in more detail in [44]. It features robots that roam around freely in an unconstrained office environment and play language games [45] about ball movement events (see figure 1). We consider this experiment only to be the first step, as we restrict spatial cognition for the time being to spatial categories only (not yet relations), and use a purely lexical language, even if there can be multiple words.

3.1   Embodiment

The robots are fully autonomous Sony Aibo ERS7 [46][3]. Based on software developed for robotic soccer [47], a real-time image processing system ([48], see left column of figure 2), probabilistic modeling techniques for the maintenance of a persistent, analog, and egocentric model of the ball and the other robot (see middle column of figure 2), object tracking, locomotion, and obstacle avoidance were built into the robots.

---

[3] Main sensor: 208×160 pixel digital camera, 20 degrees of freedom, 400 MHz Mips processor, distance sensors, microphone, speakers, wireless communication.

Fig. 1. Left: An example scene. Two Aibo robots (robot A and B) observe a ball movement and then describe the scene to each other. Right: The scene at the left seen through the built-in cameras of the two robots.

Behavior control programs [49] were made for coordination between robots. Both robots randomly walk around while avoiding obstacles. Each robot that sees both the ball and the other robot sends an acoustic signal. Robots continue with random exploration until a configuration is reached so that they can establish a joint attentional frame, in the sense of [50] (see below in section 3.2). When both robots are ready to observe the scene together, a human experimenter manually moves the ball. The begin and end point of the trajectory (see right column of figure 2) are recorded and sent to the language system via the wireless network. Continuous values on 12 channels are extracted from such descriptions and put into the world model of the agent. In order to be able to repeat the experiment with the same data in different experimental conditions (and in order to accelerate the process), we recorded about 250 such world models for both robots and used them later on in simulations.

This basic sensory processing achieves the first cognitive mechanism identified earlier, namely the ability to create a reference frame from the viewpoint of the agent with objects located within this frame. In this experiment, there are no global landmarks (although they could potentially be implemented), only local landmarks directly in the field of view of the agents.

We have also made a very concrete operational model of the egocentric perspective transformation that is clearly recognised as fundamental in spatial language (see figure 3). The model is implemented by taking the features (such as angle of movement, position of an object, etc.) and transforming them given the position of another object (such as the position of the other robot in the scene).

3.2 Language Games

A language game is a constrained routinised interaction between two agents. It involves two aspects. First a joint attention frame [50] needs to be established,

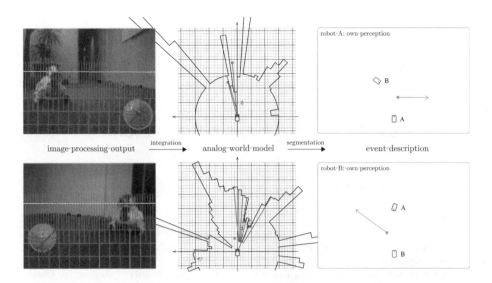

Fig. 2. From images to event descriptions. Left: Real-time model based image processing algorithms scan the camera image along a horizon-aligned grid to detect balls, other players and obstacles. An orange circle denotes a detected ball and black and red dots denote detected obstacles. Middle: The percepts from each camera image are integrated into an analog world model. Green lines denote obstacle percepts, red lines perceived positions of robots. Red squares are hypotheses for the position of the other robot. The filled red square is the estimated position of the other robot, the filled orange circle is the filtered position of the ball. The dark lines around the robot represent the filtered distances to obstacles. Right: Event descriptions extracted from the analog world model.

which means that there must be a shared motivation, a shared communicative goal, and shared attention to the same object in the environment. This joint attention frame is part of the scripts that the robots follow in their interaction. Given a joint attention frame a verbal interaction can take place - which in this case is a description game. One agent describes to another one the most recent event that involves the orange ball. The description must not only be true but also distinctive. Agents then give each other feedback whether the interaction was successful or not.

Apart from the mechanisms to follow the script required to play a game, the agents are endowed with the other cognitive mechanisms that we identified earlier. The first one is the ability to use and create new spatial distinctions to discriminate the 'topic' (the current event) from a 'context' (the previous event). It is based on discrimination trees [51]. Perceptual channels are hierarchically divided into equally sized regions. For example the category `category-4` covers the interval `[0,0.5]` on channel `ball-y2`, meaning that the ball ends right. Whenever distinctive categories cannot be found, the agent extends his ontology by cutting up a perceptual channel into different regions, and progressively they

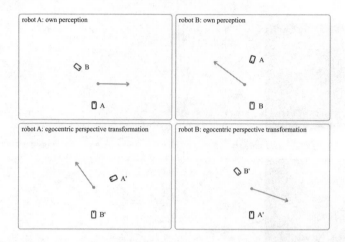

Fig. 3. Egocentric Perspective Transformation. Top row: The event from figure 1 as perceived by robots A and B. Bottom row: The result of egocentric perspective transformation. Both robots are able to construct a description of the scene as it would look like from the perceived position of the other robot.

develop enough categories to make all the distinctions that are needed in this domain. The present experiment does not (yet) endow agents with the ability to deal with relational categories.

Agents use not only their own perspective but also that of the hearer. If the discriminating category works from both perspectives, perspective does not need to be included in the meaning that the speaker is going to express (the perception of that feature of the scene is shared). Otherwise, the meaning must include information from which perspective the categorisation took place. Usually there is more than one way to conceptualize the scene. Categories are ranked based on saliency and score obtained from earlier success in the game. The description with the highest score is used further.

Agents need yet another mechanism, namely the ability to maintain a bi-directional inventory of meaning-form pairs and the ability to extend the inventory either because they need to express a new spatial relation or because they hear a new construction used by another agent. Agents invent new words by combining random syllables if needed.

A game is a success if the hearer knows all the words in the utterance and if the extracted meanings are true and discriminating for the current event. Everything else is a failure. Communicative success is the only measure that drives the coherence of perceptual categories and lexical items among the agents of a population. Each category and meaning-form association has a score that reflects its overall success in communication. After a successful game, the score of the lexical entries that were used for production or parsing is increased by 0.05. At the same time, the scores of competing lexical entries with the same

score	form	meaning
1.00	patide	category-10
1.00	kugizu	category-8
1.00	sotewu	category-11
1.00	remibu	other-perspective
1.00	lipome	category-22
1.00	livego	category-1
1.00	suvuko	category-2
1.00	bezura	category-9
0.95	lopapa	category-3
0.95	votozu	own-perspective
0.85	xapipu	category-6
0.50	fupowi	category-4
0.30	voxuna	category-15
0.25	naxopo	category-16
0.20	bikagi	other-perspective category-8
0.15	nodafo	category-21

Fig. 4. The lexicon of agent 3 after 4412 games

form but different meanings are decreased by 0.05 (lateral inhibition). In case of a failure, the score of the involved items is decreased by 0.05.

3.3   Testing Different Configurations of Cognitive Mechanisms

The main advantage of computational modeling is that we can be very precise in terms of what information processing has to go on to achieve a particular function. But we can do even more because we can test different configurations of cognitive mechanisms to prove why they might have been adopted universally for human languages. This section illustrates this methodology showing that egocentric perspective transformation is not just a luxury which accidentally became used, but is highly useful for increasing the communicative success and decrease the cognitive efforts required by language users.

We tested the dynamics of the evolving communication system for four different configurations of the cognitive mechanisms described earlier. To be able to compare the results, two events from the same set of 250 recorded world models were randomly selected for each interaction.

To show that the implemented cognitive mechanisms do indeed work, we first ran an experiment where both speaker and the hearer don't have the ability to do Egocentric Perspective Reversal but perceive the world from the same point of view (by artificially letting the hearer perceive the same scene descriptions as the speaker). As shown in figure 5a the agents reach more than 90% communicative success after about 1000 interactions. The average lexicon size stabilizes at around 10 words. If, as shown in figure 5b, the speaker and the hearer perceive scenes from different angles and if they are not able to do EPT, they are not able to establish a communication system. Communicative success does not exceed 15% and the average length of the non-aligned lexicons is about 12 words.

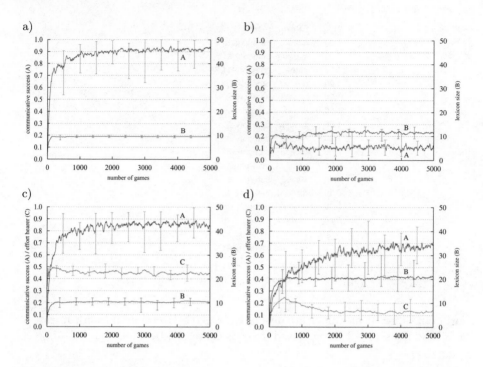

Fig. 5. Experimental results averaged over 10 runs of 5000 language games each in a population of 5 agents: Curve A shows communicative success (fraction of successful games in the last 100 interactions). B is the lexicon size averaged over all agents of the population. C is cognitive effort of the hearer (how often the hearer has to do an additional perspective transformation during interpretation). Experimental conditions: in a), both agents share the same perception and therefore don't have to do perspective reversal. In b), the agents view the scenes from different angles but don't do Egocentric Perspective Reversal. In c), the agents are capable of doing EPT but don't mark it in language. In d), perspective is also marked in language.

In a third configuration, the agents are able to use EPT for conceptualization. That means that the speaker conceptualizes the scene both from his own perspective and the perspective of the hearer. The more salient semantic description is then lexicalized. The hearer immediately adopts the speaker's perspective by performing an EPT on the own world model. If he cannot interpret the utterance in that world model, the own perspective is additionally tried. By doing that, the agents are able to self-organize a communication about ball movements although viewing the scene from different angles, as shown in figure 5c[4]. However, the hearer has to perform additional perspective transformations in interpretations. This is captured in the 'cognitive effort' curve (C) in figure 5c.

---

[4] The fact that the communicative success is slightly less than in the first condition (figure 5a) is the result of noisy perception.

In the fourth configuration, the perspective chosen by the speaker is also marked in language. That means that a perspective indicator (`own-perspective` vs. `other-perspective`) is added to the list of predicates resulting from conceptualization. Note that there is no bias towards a specific way to lexicalize perspective marking. Instead, these perspective indicators are treated in the same way as any other predicate coming out of conceptualization. The fact that single perspective markers emerge is a side effect of the general lexicon process. Given this configuration, the cognitive effort for the hearer significantly drops (figure 5d) as the hearer immediately knows which perspective to use[5].

As the results show, egocentric perspective reversal is an essential prerequisite for communication situated in space. Remarkably, it takes only a few thousand interactions until the 5 agents align their conceptual and linguistic inventories. Whereas in the beginning word meanings tend to be more holistic, as for example the word *bikagi* in figure 4 holistically covers the meaning `other-perspective` `category-8`. Later on, agents start to generalize and perspective is lexicalized separately, e.g. *votozu* for `own-perspective` (figure 4). An example utterance looks like this:

(15) *fupowi*   *remibu*
     other-perspective   category-4

     'ends to your right'

Even though the evolved languages feature multi-word utterances and separate lexical perspective markers (example 15), they are not grammatical. Given this experimental setup, a purely lexical language covers all the communicative needs, but we have already started to experiment with a richer world model that contains opportunities for the agents to recruit additional cognitive mechanisms, including multiple landmarks so that spatial relations become an additional resource in the language game.

4 Conclusions and Further Research

This paper illustrates how different subfields of cognitive science can interact to build a comprehensive theory of spatial language. From linguistics, we get observations of the kinds of how spatial categories and relations get expressed and of the flexibility that is apparently required. Given the evidence, it is clear that spatial concepts are not genetically hard-coded and neither is there a simple universal mapping from spatial cognition to spatial language. Instead there is a lot of variety which necessitates that language users must be seen as creatively expanding and negotiating their repertoire of spatial concepts and their linguistic conventions.

Although psychology and neuroscience can give us hints on the kinds of cognitive capabilities humans have and where approximately in the brain the information processing to achieve these capabilities might be located, it is only by

---

[5] Note that communicative success does not converge as fast as in conditions a) and c) because the learning problem is more difficult.

making concrete detailed operational models that we can actually understand how spatial cognition and language is possible: in contrast to earlier computational work, where spatial cognition, lexicons and grammar are implemented by hand. This paper reported breakthrough experiments showing that the current state of the art in AI and robotics is sufficiently advanced to carry out highly non-trivial experiments that test operational models of spatial language evolution, in other words where agents invent and negotiate a spatial language of their own making. In addition, we demonstrated that egocentric perspective transformation is beneficial for establishing a communication system among agents that are able to see scenes from different spatial perspectives.

Acknowledgements. Our experiments rest on the Fluid Construction Grammar framework [52], to which Nicolas Neubauer and Joachim De Beule have made major contributions. The authors also thank the members of the "GermanTeam" for providing their robot soccer software. This research was funded and carried out at the Sony Computer Science Laboratory in Paris with additional funding from the EU FET ECAgents Project IST-1940.

References

1. Chomsky, N.: Aspects of the Theory of Syntax. MIT Press, Cambridge (1965)
2. Pinker, S., Bloom, P.: Natural language and natural selection. Behavioral and Brain Sciences 13(4), 707–784 (1990)
3. Langacker, R.W.: Foundations of Cognitive Grammar, vol. 1. Stanford University Press, Stanford (1987)
4. Halliday, M.A.: An Introduction to Functional Grammar. John Benjamins, Amsterdam (1994)
5. Nuyts, J.: Brother in Arms? On the Relations Between Cognitive and Functional Linguistics. In: de Mendoza Ibanez, F.R., Pena Cervel, M. (eds.) Cognitive Linguistics: Internal Dynamics and Interdisciplinary Interaction, pp. 69–100. Mouton De Gruyter, Berlin (2005)
6. Nuyts, J.: Aspects of a Cognitive-Pragmatic Theory of Language. In: Nuyts, J. (ed.) On Cognition, Functionalism, and Grammar, John Benjamins, Amsterdam (1992)
7. Bruce, L.P.: The Alamblak Language of Papua New guinea (East Sepik). In: Pacific Linguistics Series C 81, Australian National University, Canberra (1984)
8. Haeseryn, W., Romijn, K., Geerts, G., de Rooij, J., van den Toorn, M.: Algemene Nederlandse Spraakkunst, 2nd, revised edn., Martinus Nijhoff / Wolters Plantyn, Groningen/Deurne (1997)
9. Mous, M.: A Grammar ofd Iraqw. PhD Thesis. Rijksuniversiteit Leiden, Leiden (1992)
10. Werner, H.: Die Ketische Sprache. In: Tunguso Sibirica Band 3, Harrasowitz Verlag, Wiesbaden (1997)
11. George, K.: Malayalam Grammar and Reader. National Book Stall, Kottayam (1971)
12. Andronov, M.S.: A Grammar of the Malayalam Language in Historical Treatment. In: Beitrage zur Kenntnis südasiatischer Sprachen und Literaturen, Harrasowitz Verlag, Wiesbaden (1996)

13. Lichtenberk, F.: A Grammar of Manam. In: Oceanic Linguistics Special Publications 18, University of Hawaii Press, Honolulu (1983)
14. Zewen, F.: Introduction à la Langue des Îles Marquises. Le Parler de Nukuhiva. University of Hamburg, Hamburg (1987)
15. Jung, I.: Grammatik des Paez. Ein Abriss. PhD Thesis, University of Osnabrück, Osnabrück (1989)
16. Moshinsky, J.: A Grammar of Southeastern Pomo. University of California Press, Los Angeles (1974)
17. Canonici, N.N.: Zulu Grammatical Structure, university of Natal - Durban, Natal (1995)
18. Doke, C.M.: Textbook of Zulu Grammar. In: Maskew Miller Longman, Cape Town. Previously published in 1927 by the University of Witwatersrand (1992)
19. Talmy, L.: Toward a Cognitive Semantics, Concept Structuring Systems, vol. 1. MIT Press, Cambridge (2000)
20. Talmy, L.: Toward a Cognitive Semantics, Typology and Process in Concept Structuring, vol. 2. MIT Press, Cambridge (2000)
21. Landau, B., Jackendoff, R.: 'what' and 'where' in spatial language and spatial cognition. Behavioural and Brain Sciences 16, 217–238 (1993)
22. Clark, H.: Space, time, semantics and the child. In: Moore, T. (ed.) Cognitive Development and the Acquisition of Language, pp. 28–64. Academic Press, New York (1973)
23. Levinson, S.C.: Space in Language and Cognition. In: Language, Culture and Cognition 5, Cambridge University Press, Cambridge (2003)
24. Levinson, S.C., Wilkins, D. (eds.): Grammars of Space. Explorations in Cognitive Diversity. Language, Culture and Cognition. Culture and Cognition. Cambridge University Press, Cambridge (2006)
25. Hickmann, M., Robert, S. (eds.): Space in Languages. Typological Studies in Language 66. John Benjamins, Amsterdam (2006)
26. Diessel, H.: Distance contrasts in demonstratives. In: Haspelmath, M., Dryer, M.S., Gil, D., Comrie, B. (eds.) The World Atlas of Language Structures, pp. 170–173. Oxford University Press, Oxford (2005)
27. Diessel, H.: Demonstratives: Form, Function, and Grammaticalization. In: Typological Studies in Language 42, John Benjamins, Amsterdam (1999)
28. Talmy, L.: The fundamental system of spatial schemas in language. In: Hampe, B. (ed.) From Perception to Meaning: Image Schemas in Cognitive Linguistics. Cognitive Linguistics Research, pp. 37–47. Mouton De Gruyter, Berlin (2006)
29. Traugott, E.C., Heine, B. (eds.): Approaches to Grammaticalization. Typological Studies in Language 19, vol. 1. John Benjamins, Amsterdam (1991)
30. Hopper, P.: Emergent grammar. Berkely Linguistics Conference (BLS) 13, 139–157 (1987)
31. Stefanowitsch, A., Gries, S.T.: Collostructions: Investigating the interaction of words and constructions. International Journal of Corpus Linguistics 2(8), 209–243 (2003)
32. Mair, C.: Corpus linguistics and grammaticalization theory: Beyond statistics and frequency?corpus linguistics and grammaticalization theory. In: Lindquist, H., Mair, C. (eds.) Corpus Approaches to Grammaticalization in English, pp. 121–150. John Benjamins, Amsterdam (2004)
33. Blake, B.J.: Case. In: Cambridge Textbook in Linguistics, Cambridge University Press, Cambridge (1994)
34. Kay, P., Fillmore, C.J.: Grammatical constructions and linguistic generalizations: The what's x doing y? construction. Language 75, 1–33 (1999)

35. Goldberg, A.E.: A Construction Grammar Approach to Argument Structure. University of Chicago Press, Chicago (1995)
36. Kuno, S.: The Structure of the Japanese Language. MIT Press, Cambridge (1973)
37. Croft, W.: Radical Construction Grammar: Syntactic Theory in Typological Perspective. Oxford University Press, Oxford (2001)
38. Dryer, M.S.: Are grammatical relations universal? In: Bybee, J., Haiman, J., Thompson, S. (eds.) Essays on Language Function and Language Type: Dedicated to T. Givon, pp. 115–143. John Benjamins, Amsterdam (1997)
39. Shepard, R., Metzler, J.: Mental rotation of three-dimensional objects. Science 3(171), 701–703 (1971)
40. Mauck, B., Dehnhardt, G.: Mental rotation in a california sea lion (zalophus californianus). Journal of Experimental Biology 200(9), 1309–1316 (1997)
41. Zacks, J., Rypma, B., Gabrieli, J., Tversky, B., Glover, G.H.: Imagined transformations of bodies: An fMRI investigation. Neuropsychologia 37(9), 1029–1040 (1999)
42. Iachini, T., Logie, R.H.: The role of perspective in locating position in a real-world, unfamiliar environment. Applied Cognitive Psychology 17(6), 715–732 (2003)
43. Steels, L.: How to do experiments in artificial language evolution and why. In: Cangelosi, A., Smith, A., Smith, K. (eds.) Proceedings of the 6th International Conference on the Evolution of Language, London, World Scientific Publishing, Singapore (2006)
44. Steels, L., Loetzsch, M.: Perspective alignment in spatial language. In: Coventry, K.R., Tenbrink, T., Bateman, J.A. (eds.) Spatial Language and Dialogue, Oxford University Press, Oxford (to appear, 2007)
45. Steels, L., Kaplan, F., McIntyre, A., Van Looveren, J.: Crucial factors in the origins of word-meaning. In: Wray, A. (ed.) The Transition to Language, Oxford University Press, Oxford (2002)
46. Fujita, M., Kitano, H.: Development of an autonomous quadruped robot for robot entertainment. Autonomous Robots 5(1), 7–18 (1998)
47. Röfer, T., Brunn, R., Dahm, I., Hebbel, M., Hoffmann, J., Jüngel, M., Laue, T., Lötzsch, M., Nistico, W., Spranger, M.: Germanteam 2004: The german national robocup team. In: Nardi, D., Riedmiller, M., Sammut, C., Santos-Victor, J. (eds.) RoboCup 2004. LNCS (LNAI), vol. 3276, Springer, Heidelberg (2005)
48. Jüngel, M., Hoffmann, J., Lötzsch, M.: A real-time auto-adjusting vision system for robotic soccer. In: Polani, D., Browning, B., Bonarini, A., Yoshida, K. (eds.) RoboCup 2003. LNCS (LNAI), vol. 3020, pp. 214–225. Springer, Heidelberg (2004)
49. Loetzsch, M., Risler, M., Jüngel, M.: XABSL - a pragmatic approach to behavior engineering. In: Proceedings of the IEEE/RSJ International Conference on Intelligent Robots and Systems (IROS 2006), Beijing, pp. 5124–5129 (October 2006)
50. Tomasello, M.: Joint attention as social cognition. In: Moore, C., Dunham, P.J. (eds.) Joint Attention: Its Origins and Role in Development, Lawrence Erlbaum Associates, Hillsdale (1995)
51. Steels, L.: Perceptually grounded meaning creation. In: Tokoro, M. (ed.) Proceedings of the International Conference on Multi-Agent Systems, pp. 338–344. The MIT Press, Cambridge (1996)
52. Steels, L., De Beule, J.: Unify and merge in fluid construction grammar. In: Vogt, P., Sugita, Y., Tuci, E., Nehaniv, C.L. (eds.) EELC 2006. LNCS (LNAI), vol. 4211, pp. 197–223. Springer, Heidelberg (2006)

Modeling Multimodal Communication
as a Complex System

Kristinn R. Thórisson

Center for Analysis & Design of Intelligent Agents
and Department of Computer Science
Reykjavik University
Kringlunni 1, 103 Reykjavik, Iceland
thorisson@ru.is

Abstract. The overall behavior and nature of *complex natural systems* is in large part determined by the *number* and *variety* of the mechanisms involved – and the *complexity of their interactions*. Embodied natural communication belongs to this class of systems, encompassing many cognitive mechanisms that interact in highly complex ways, both within and between communicating individuals, constituting a *heterogeneous, large, densely-coupled* system (HeLD). HeLDs call for finer model granularity than other types of systems, lest we risk them to be not only *incomplete* but likely *incorrect*. Consequently, models of communication must encompass a large subset of the functions and couplings that make up the real system, calling for a powerful methodology for integrating information from multiple fields and for producing runnable models. In this paper I propose such an approach, *abstract module hierarchies,* that leverages the benefits of modular construction without forcing modularity on the phenomena being modeled.

Keywords: Multimodal realtime communication, computational model, complex natural system, heterogeneous large system, abstract module, theory of dialogue.

1 Introduction

A large number of mental mechanisms play a role in embodied dialogue, from task planning to sentence composition to control of eye gaze from moment to moment. How these are coordinated has to be explained if we want to claim that we understand communication. Examples of what a *complete* theory of dialogue should be able to explain is whether/how some eyeblinks seem to be related to the production of speech content, how it is that sometimes there are less than 50 msec gaps between speaking turns, how facial expressions or intonation can modify the meaning of utterances, and why people look at their hands when doing some types of gestures and not when doing others. Ideally it should also explain how and why communicative and social behaviors are affected in certain ways and not others by certain drugs such as alcohol.

I. Wachsmuth and G. Knoblich (Eds.): Modeling Communication, LNAI 4930, pp. 143–168, 2008.
© Springer-Verlag Berlin Heidelberg 2008

A basic theory of human dialogue presupposes that humans communicate – it is not its role to explain why they communicate in the first place or how such communication systems came about; that is the realm of sociology, biology and evolution science. Suffice it to say that without communication a species has less survival potential, and that the mechanism of reciprocity between individuals of a species must be present for such systems of communication to emerge. Assuming that an individual of a communicating species must have certain basic abilities to perceive and act in ways to communicate in a certain way, we must also postulate certain perceptual and representational capabilities related to communicative interaction.

Among the properties of minds that most greatly seem to influence the commucative apparatus and its operation in realtime dialogue is cognitive capacity. Turntaking is a necessary mechanism to manage the limited processing capacity of a normal human mind in normal operation when processing information-rich content: The reason that we take turns when communicating is that the mind has a limited capacity to generate speech while concurrently hearing and understanding the other speech – attempting to do so for longer than a few seconds is sure to significantly reduce a person's retention and understanding of what was said around her (cf. [1, 2]). Any model of realtime embodied dialogue must therefore take into consideration – in addition to the ability to generate speech, express concepts, gesture and take turns – attentional mechanisms and the inherent capacity of the various cognitive faculties. A necessary and sufficient model of dialogue should in fact be detailed enough that we could build an artificial system that can participate fully in human dialogue. Of course we are not going to build such a system on first attempt, or even second; as we must bring to bear on the task methodologies from several disciplines, this will take significant effort and time.

This paper has two main parts. In the first part I argue that multimodal realtime dialogue shares many characteristics with other complex sytems, such as economies and ecosystems – what we refer to as heterogeneous, large, densely-coupled systems (HeLDs) – and must therefore be studied using some of the same methods as are being developed in these fields. Recognizing this fact may have important implications, in particular, that we need to supplement our efforts with methods from simulation and computational modeling theory. We will start by discussing the claim that embodied multimodal dialogue is a *complex system*, in the sense used by e.g. Simon [3]. Such systems embody/express emergent properties that have been difficult to understand without resorting to large, detailed computational models.

In the second part of the paper I present ideas on the kinds of architectures that might implement such a complex system. In particular, we will discuss how a modeling approach called *abstract module hierarchies* that can overcome many of the difficulties associated with studying complex systems, and how modularity in *implementation* does not have to presuppose modularity at the *cognitive* or *brain* levels. We briefly present two systems exemplifying the use of abstract modules for modeling cognitive and neurocognitive mechanisms. Lastly we will look at arguments for why there might be reason to think that the brain is a modular computing substrate, and thus reason to expect isomorphism between cognitive and brain structures.

2 Complexity of Cognitive Mechanisms

Even the most casual analysis of human realtime communication reveals an intricate complexity of knowledge and behaviors that together define it. First I will briefly review three important sources of complexity, namely interaction at multiple timescales, perception-action loop and multiple information types.

2.1 Multiple Levels of Detail

The full range of dialogue behaviors can be affected by events on many space and timescales, from the emotional impact that a long-winded insult can have on the choice of one's words to the implied surprise of 30 msec noise bursts from clicks of the tongue; from the threat "emanating from" a large fist shaken in one's direction to the effects of Ethanol in alcoholic drinks on outbursts of "honesty".

The shortest and the longest behavioral event in a meaningful dialogue range from 10-40 milliseconds (e.g. tongue click or a quick glance) upwards of several hours, possibly days.[1] Meaningful behaviors thus span at least 4 orders of magnitude of time, even in the simplest cases of multimodal dialogue of meeting and saying "hi" in the hallway. Dialogue participants must keep track of events at the full range of timescales; various kinds of behaviors form clusters at certain timescales, or "bands": eye movements and gaze at the low end (from 40 msec upwards of 1 second for lingering gaze), head, hand and arm movements between 1-2 per second, body movements a bit less frequent, and so on. The perception of each participant of others' behaviors, and their alignment and reciprocation of such behaviors by others, is highly task-dependent, yet bounded by the natural limitations inherent in the body and cognitive capabilities.

Fine-grained analysis of the temporal nature of multimodal action during dialogue, from gaze and upwards, reveals significant repeated and mirrored patterns between dialogue partners [4], a clear sign that the perception and action of each participant is being coordinated to a very fine degree and that interaction behaviors happens at many timescales – gaze is met with gaze, verbal utterance with verbal utterance, gesture with gesture, topics are negotiated, abandoned and revisited. Clearly, tight coordination of such multi-dimensional events requires an intricate underlying architecture, where short- and long-term planning, powerful perception, reactive decisions and fine motor control all come together in a coherent way.

---

[1] As the scale moves towards days, months and years, the category "meaningful dialogue" gets increasingly vague. We could use matching goals to classify a set of communicative events, such as utterances, gaze, facial expression, etc., into a larger communicative event such as interview, collaboration, etc. This method, however, has its limits, for as the size of the overarching goals increases the grouping becomes less obvious. To take an example, just because two people work at the same company, and thus share a positive attitude towards each other, we would hardly classify their greetings every day, over a period of e.g. 20 years, as "communicative event" lasting 20 years, even though their employer provides them with a shared goal and a context for greeting. In spite of its limitations, the method of using goals in the classification is useful in cases where the goals are fairly obvious.

2.2 Perception-Action Loop

Dialogue, and especially multimodal dialogue, is inherently realtime. By *perception-action* loop we mean the continuous, "on-line" ability of living beings to react to something that comes in through their sensors and monitor their own behavior and the environment in a continuous fashion. At the low end the shortest possible voluntary path through this loop in humans, from sensation to action, is bounded by the choice reaction time, 90 ms [5], and at the high-end by the patience of participating in a back-and-forth with someone about a topic or class of topics, as well as the speed at which new thoughts and associations can be generated in relevance to that topic.

An interval of 60 msec, from the time one senses something until they need to give a reply, or take turn, is not sufficient time to contemplate much at all, e.g. infer the major implications of a sentence such as "The Chinese have a vested interest in keeping business open to the West", yet people do show visible and meaningful responses even as the sentence is being spoken. Quick, semi-automatic and fully automatic behaviors, such as fixations and saccades, have been classified as "reactive"; behavior based on deliberate and consciously reportable effort have been termed "deliberative" (cf. [6]). While the distinction seems crude, it has some basis in brain structure [7]. Where reactiveness cannot provide sufficient responses, prediction kicks in: Using various features of speech, gesture, intonation, gaze and so on, people will anticipate what a person is going to do and will act accordingly, to respond, comply, give turn or hand over a tool that was requested. Even the simplest target tracking tasks seem to involve realtime (close-horizon) prediction [8] as does listening to speech [9]. It seems likely that our cognitive apparatus employs several interwoven mechanisms for producing such intricately timed behaviors.

2.3 Multiple Information Types – Numerous Forms of Constraints

Computationally speaking, the data that enter into dialogue are of many types [10, 11], spanning the full spectrum from deterministic to stochastic, continuous to discrete. In fact, the biggest criticism of turntaking research in the last 2-3 decades can be said to be a level of simplification that has had a chilling effect on progress and bound researchers in the shackles of side-effects, arguing over details such as whether there is such a thing as a "turn-constructional unit" and if so, it being sentential [12], syllable-based [13], multimodal (cf. [11, 14, 15]) or content-driven [11]. The situation painfully reminds one of the story about blind men arguing about an elephant[2] – one touches the trunk and concludes that elephants are like snakes, another touches a leg and concludes that elephants are tree-like. The analogy has seldom been so appropriate, as a quick look at a few examples of successful turntaking shows: Efficient task-oriented communication on a noisy factory floor – no possibility to synchronize on syllables or full sentences; successful communication between the deaf (no sound at all); successful communication on the telephone – no multimodal information (although plenty of verbal paraverbal information) – the examples clearly argue against simplistic explanations of turntaking, as for example proposing that phoneme timing is its main perceptual driver [13]. As O'Connell et al. [11] point out, a proper turntaking theory should cover varied situations ranging from debates, to

[2] *Six Blind Men and the Elephant* – poem by John Godfrey Saxe (1816-1887).

lectures, negotiations, task-oriented interactions, media interviews, dramatic performances, casual chats, formal meetings, etc. If such a theory is to provide an understanding of what drives turntaking, then it must provide a way to account for the (several) goals that will be in operation in any conversation – goals pertaining to the individuals' disposition (e.g. a seller who wants to maximize profit), social norms (e.g. no introductions at a store counter), relationships between the participants (e.g. friends who want to stay friendly), purpose of the interaction – the aligned goals between the individuals, i.e. the purpose of the interaction, etc.), cognitive limitations, characteristics and "parameter settings" (e.g. average and maximum speed of understanding what is being said, speed of planning, motivation levels, vested interest), as well as a host of issues related to semantics – from confusing sentences to Freudian slips – which can affect emotions, attitude and other things that influence timing and events in turntaking (see Figure 3). To explain these, however, it does not suffice to propose some simple mechanisms that can generate (some limited amount of) the surface phenomena observed in human dialogue – the mechanisms proposed must explain those and additionally how they interact with the various complexities of perception and direction of attention, the human ability to formulate coherent sentences, to understand them when spoken by others, and their ability to follow social etiquette.

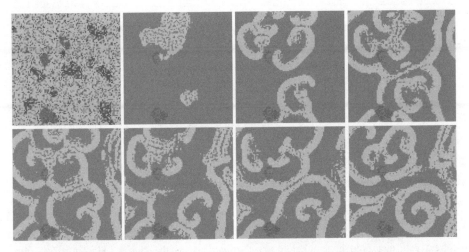

Fig. 1. A grid of 100x100 cells in a cellular automaton, each determining its own state as represented by a color (shown here as one of 4 shades of gray), according to the rules in Figure 2. Spiral patterns will emerge and persist over minutes and even hours of running. The spirals are emergent from the rules: It is difficult, if not impossible, to predict the emergence of such spirals looking only at the rules, partly because they only appear under certain initial conditions, but mainly because it is the interaction between the rules that produces them. Each snapshot taken at the initial state (upper left), and then at 15 second intervals, ordered from left to right, top to bottom.

2.4 Emergence

If scientists of an alien race were to land on Earth to analyze how automobiles operate, they would see numerous different behaviors of these entities: long rows moving slowly in packs, single cars zipping along dirt roads, cars stopped at a red light, single cars parked by houses and rows of cars parked by shopping centers, cars slowing down when approaching intersections, and a few incidences of cars jammed into each other. But as most Earthlings know, such high-level behaviors (the behavior of the whole traffic system within its environment, cities) are all emergent from interactions between several components such as the car's owners, the human laws pertaining to what may and may not be done while operating a motor vehicle – even the long-term goals of the car's owners, e.g. not wanting to die. The observed behaviors of cars are an *emergent* property stemming from the interactions among these complex components. To the aliens' delight, the fact that these components and their interactions are lawful means that observable effects can be classified, labeled and reproduced through manipulations, and modeled at the observable features level – the system's gross-anatomy. To achieve accuracy and breadth in applicability of such a model one must, however, go beyond the surface phenomena and uncover hidden factors. Unless we lived in a perfectly bijective reality, we have to infer the underlying causality and for that we must build on what lies at the next organizational sub-level.

When Light Gray (LG)
1. Turn MG: If there are more than 20 LG cells around and lifetime exceeds 30
2. Turn MG: If there are less than 12 LG cells around and lifetime exceeds 20
3. Turn MG: If number of LG cells around equals 25
4. Turn MG: If lifetime under any circumstance exceeds 60

When Medium Gray (MG)
5. Turn LG: If there are more than 8 LG cells around and their lifetime combined exceeds 80 and there are more than 10 MG cells around

When Dark Gray (DG; only visible in the initial state)
6. Turn MG: If there are more than 3 DG cells around and the sum of their lifetime exceeds 2 and lifetime is greater than 8

Fig. 2. Rule set used for the states (grayscale) in the cellular automaton simulation in Fig. 1. Notice that LG and MG are responsible for the spiral patterns. (*Lifetime* means lifetime of the current cell, measured in simulation steps; *around* means the closest cells, in a 5x5 grid, surrounding the current cell.)

Emergent phenomena have been extensively studied using cellular automata, where simple one, two or three-dimensional grids of cells, decides its own state based on the behaviors of its neighboring cells, according to a set of local rules (cf. [16]). Figure 1 shows an example of such a system: The spirals are an emergent pattern, stemming from a small set of identical rules (Figure 2) local to each square (there are 100x100 cells in this example). The spirals are highly persistent in light of significant disturbances, but are quite sensitive to initial conditions and will not appear in about 10% of cases with randomized initial conditions. These particular rules, however, need to *all* be present for the spirals to form: Taking out any single one will remove the appearance of spirals altogether.[3]

If these alien scientists happened to be extreme optimists they might spend a lifetime studying only the observable features of automobiles, hoping to unravel the whole story that way. In the process they would know a lot about the high-level behaviors of cars but very little else. They would be able to describe and classify all of the cars' behaviors in fine detail, but they would never be able to explain all of them, because that is simply impossible without an underlying model of how cars are operated, have owners, are made of metal, must stay on roads, collide as a consequence of operator and mechanical problems, etc. For example, predicting that more collisions happen when the sun sits low on the horizon and hits the cars from the front is quite easy, based on prior observations, but explaining *why* it happens requires nothing short of an understanding of drivers and their perceptual apparatuses. Or consider explaining why the cars move without the concept of an engine; or of how an engine operates without some idea of fossil fuels, electricity and flammability, density and strength of aluminum and iron, etc. In other words, a model of their components and all elements related to the automobiles, constitutes a complete understanding of automobiles; social convention and cognitive limitations are needed for understanding traffic – the behavior of groups of cars in cities. The high-level behaviors of automobiles *are an emergent property of the interactions between all the elements that matter to their behavior*, nothing more and nothing less.

2.5 Intermediate Conclusion

As we have argued above, multimodal natural realtime dialogue is likely to be most adequately described as a complex system. Figure 3 gives a list of many factors and phenomena that can affect the way observable features in a dialogue turn out. The enormous complexity involved in even a single item on this list makes it ever clearer that embodied, realtime face-to-face communication is a complex system involving a large number of functions,[4] the result of many interacting subsystems, none of which has clear domination over the system's characteristics – each element contributes to some part of the system's operation through its local operation and interactions with other elements. Evidence from evolution points in this direction too; in particular, evolution is likely to have come up with a tangled web of mental mechanisms that serve many purposes in many ways, because once one mechanism is in place it is more likely to be modified in subtle ways and reused than for another mechanism to evolve from scratch – a phenomenon called *exaption*. The result of such processes is systems with large amounts of structural dependencies – mixed heterogeneous systems.

---

[3] An interesting exception appears when removing Rule 3 – it makes the spirals somewhat less spirally but does not remove them completely.

[4] The term *function* is used here as in psychology, anatomy and biology, as *functioning, ability, role*, etc., akin to the concept of *structure* in anthropology (cf. [17]): The "family" is a structure encompassing more than its parts, but yet can only be pointed at by naming its constituents or from the exterior, by naming its connections to the tribe, as it exists at a different level of organization. This kind of metonymy shows in fact that it's beneficial to clearly separate the substrate and the emergent functions (i.e. to abstract based on *organizational levels*) when wanting to identify structuring feedback loops, to run them and validate (or dismiss) abstraction hypothesis.

1. Timespace
  1.1 Physical constraints
    1.1.1 Body can only be in one place at a particular time
    1.1.2 Sensory organs limited area coverage
    1.1.3 Manipulators of limited number (arms-hands 2, fingers 2x5, typically)
  1.2 Temporal constraints
    1.2.1 Body takes time to move (especially important for sensory apparatus)
    1.2.2 Body only exists a particular period in time (hence the need to communicate across time)
    1.2.3 Sensory uptake takes time
  1.3 Cognitive apparatus
    1.3.1 Variable time for processing different types of information from senses

2. Information-carrying capacity of our communicative apparatus (body)
  2.1 Arms and hands
    - Placement, speed, shape, manner of movement may all matter
  2.2 Face
    2.2.1 Gaze direction, fixations
    2.2.2 Head direction, movement
  2.3 Mouth
    - Speech, non-speech sounds/paraverbals
  2.4 Body
    - Stance, direction, shape

3. Cognitive capacity
  3.1 Perceptual integration: Hearing and vision are different types of data
  3.2 Attentional control
    - To understand well we have to focus our attention on a single individual's communicative acts; this is perhaps the single biggest reason for the existence of turntaking
    3.2.1 Visual attention
    3.2.2 Auditory attention
  3.3 Knowledge (this is big)
    3.3.1 Individual differences
    - Individuals have different amounts and types of knowledge, hence a need for grounding
    3.3.2 Knowledge of social convention
    - Various types of behavior may be inhibited or expected by social rules of conduct
    3.3.3 Situation recognition
    - A situation needs to be classified correctly in order to be acted upon with the intended effect
  3.4 Memory
    3.4.1 Memory types
    - We have different memory systems for events, words, concepts; these have various limitations
  3.5 Goals & Intentions
    - Various goals may come into play; this is a list in and of itself. These factors are closely related to and interact strongly with knowledge.
  3.6 Planning
    3.6.1 Planning of body movement
    3.6.2 Planning of words
    3.6.3 Synchronization of various bodyparts
    - For sensing (e.g. fixate on the right place) and for information production
  3.6 Learning

Fig. 3. These are only some of the constraints that a communicating system must take into account; most of them may influence, in one way or other, the way participants in dialogue behave

So how complex is natural multimodal communication? Is the complexity greater than that of an automobile (minus its human operator)? Surely. Is it more complex than the example cellular automata world depicted in Figure 1? Most certainly, as the preceding sections clearly hint at. How about an ecosystem? Probably not; besides being dependent on very complex energy transfers, many of the functional elements in a (human-less) ecosystem contain cognitive perceptuo-motor systems that rival human ones. Therefore we can assume that the complexity of multimodal communication, as a system of systems, lies somewhere between an automobile engine and an ecosystem. When trying to formalize systems with a large number of functions and inter-structural dependencies, the requirement for a high level of model detail is thus likely to be very strong, as no single factor explains a significant part of the whole system's operation, just as the rules in the spiral world example above.

We can now make the following summary about multimodal realtime dialogue:

(1) Observable behaviors of dialogue participants – glances, manual gestures, choice of words, intonation and prosody, etc. – are not any more sufficient for explaining the phenomena of communication than the movement of automobiles is sufficient to explain their operation.

(2) In order to be adequate, our human communication models may very likely have to encompass most (if not all) the components and couplings that make up the system; anything less is likely to be both incomplete and incorrect. Leaving out a large set of phenomena tightly integrated with, and observed to affect, dialogue behaviors, such as e.g. gesture, prosody and intonation – even breathing – is very likely to leave us with an incomplete model of dialogue, quite possibly a model that is also incorrect.

In face of this conclusion we need to answer several questions. The main one, the one we will address in the next section, is *What methods can be employ to build a model that can take the part of a human dialogue participant and thus explain sufficiently how embodied multimodal dialogue works?*

3   Models and Methods

If there is one thing clearer now than it was 50 years ago regarding natural language and dialogue, it would be that cognition related dialogue is more complex than had we dared to imagine. It has been said that biological research is difficult because in living systems everything is causally connected to everything else. Luckily this is unlikely to be true of cognitive mechanisms (and probably also biology), but we can be sure that any subsystem we may identify in multimodal dialogue is bound to have multiple connections to other subsystems in the human cognitive system.

Historically, an important tool for studying human behavior in psychology has been hypothesis refutation. Based on Popper's (in)famous argument that hypotheses can never be proven, only refuted [18], much psychological research today addressing cognitive architecture proceeds by experimentation based on fairly broad-stroke generalizations about its information structures. However, as eloquently argued by Newell [19], "you can't play 20 questions with nature and hope to win", meaning that a coarse-grain approach through hypothesis testing through human subject experimentation must be supported by other research methods.[5] The general idea behind the information processing view of intelligence, as introduced by Turing [21, 22] and others, has taken hold in many parts of psychological research. While strong versions of the thinking-as-computation stance have led to in-fights among researchers, modeling with structures does not imply isomorphism – that the modeled reality is modular – nor does it imply that the modeled object has to be computationally reducible.[6] We will come back to these issues shortly.

Simulation models vary widely depending on the phenomena under study. For example, the behavior of a homogenous system, e.g. a liquid consisting of one type of molecule in large numbers, behaving according to the laws of physics, can be described by relatively simple equations. Equations that take into consideration large-scale indicators of monetary inflation can be used to model large-scale movements of a market. But in neither case can these equations be used to describe individual molecules or currency transactions, respectively. Not so for many other systems. Consider the example of a car engine: trying to understand how it works by only looking at the carburetor and the battery is not likely to get us very far. The automotive engine is composed of a large number of heterogeneous components, each responsible for only a small part of its total operation, yet ignoring any one of them will likely leave us with an incorrect model. To take a hypothetical example from the brain, we might be able to model spatial hearing sufficiently abstractly for certain tasks that the human auditory system needs to perform, but typically that (limited) model will break down in many other contexts and for many other tasks. If we want to have a finer granularity of the spatial hearing faculty, the only solution would be to model it in more detail, because what defines it at those other tasks may very likely be its composition at lower levels of detail, which interact in complex ways with *other systems* needed for *other tasks*. As the list in Figure 3 shows, a model that can take the vast amount of relevant systems into account, and produce the kinds of patterns observed in multimodal dialogue, is not going to be simple. The architecture of such a system will have much more in common with the global telephone network and Internet than with the mathematical models of physics, that is, it will most likely be composed of heterogeneous interacting systems that are "nearly decomposable" but not quite, and it will be highly detailed. Furthermore, these models will be highly dynamic. The only (presently known) way to make such models is to implement them as information structures, in the form of programs, and run them on computers, monitoring their performance and comparing it to the natural systems they are supposed to represent. This has been the conclusion in many other fields studying complex systems and is recognized as a powerful

---

[5] Kosslyn [20] has taken this argument further and argued that binary decision making in researching complex systems can be done provided that the hypotheses are (a) anchored in detailed processing models and that (b) they are formulated from the viewpoint of multiple levels of analysis within a processing system. This is in accordance with the view argued here (see below).

[6] The computational stance is nevertheless an efficient framework for the construction of experimental (mathematical) models of the mind (cf. [23, 24, 25, 26]); it has advanced our understanding of the mind in several aspects, in many cases with superior results over other approaches, a good example being how neural impulses collect from the ears in the form of information that encodes position and orientation of sounds, directly in support of the survival of a species.

methodology for studying weather systems, evolution of galaxies, physical processes and more (cf. [27, 28, 29, 30, 31, 32]).

3.1 Large Heterogeneous Systems and Model Validity

Complex models with heterogeneous components call for a heightened need of thorough verification. One difficulty is that in such systems any subset of the observed behaviors can be mapped onto an infinitely large set of underlying hypothesized mechanisms, which are a challenge to verify. To take an analogy, uncovering the 8 rules of the spiral world (Figure 2) would be quite complicated simply by studying the emergent surface forms of the spirals. Numerous rule sets could undoubtedly be concocted that would generate similar, perhaps even identical spirals. But uncovering the *actual* rules would necessitate digging deeper, probably building a simulation of the world where one could try out different rule combinations running inside the logic believed to be responsible for their execution. Our human communication models might contain a high level of detail, but if it only addresses a limited level of detail it might be correct or it might be incorrect – in fact, there would be no way to tell.

Part of the problem thus lies in the fact that most current models, produced by the standard divide-and-conquer approach, only address a subset of a system's behaviors; yet for most complex systems, if we were to attempt to create a model that addresses *all* of the system's behaviors, the set of possible underlying mechanisms would be greatly reduced [33] – quite possibly reducing the probable mechanisms behind it to a small finite set. A way to address this problem is thus to take an interdisciplinary approach, employing results from various levels of abstraction to bear on the modeling efforts. Use of such hierarchical approaches is common in e.g. physics, as all physicists know, for example, that behind the science of optics lie the more detailed models of electromagentic waves [34]. Thus, when dealing with heterogeneous, large, densely-coupled systems (HeLDs) it is important that we try to constrain the search space for possible designs, and one powerful way to do this is to build multilevel representations (cf. [33, 35, 36, 37]); indeed, in understanding natural HeLDs this may be the only way to get our models right. Notice that the thrust of the argument is not that multiple levels are "valid" or even "important", as that is a commonly accepted view in science and philosophy, but rather, that to map correctly to the many ways subsystems interact in HeLDs they are a *critical necessity*, lest we chase variations on our altogether incorrect models ad infinitum.[7] Unless simulations are built at fairly high levels of fidelity it is not possible to experiment with changes and modifications to the architecture at various levels of detail. Without this ability we cannot differentiate between a large set of models that, on paper, look like they might all work. To quote Simon [32] on this subject, for much simpler phenomena: " Even a few particles, three or more, reacting in classical Newtonian fashion, create the notorious three-body problem, which is usually not solvable in closed form, and which, under many circumstances, leads to chaotic system behavior."

---

[7] A short overview of the importance, as well as pitfalls, of multiple levels of description in science is given by Bakker & Dulk [38].

So the solution to the problem of model validity, as well as the solution to increased model detail, is to attempt to anchor current models in a theory about phenomena at a higher or lower level of detail, assuming those theories have been experimentally grounded.

Another useful weapon in the fight for complete and accurate models is modular construction. Modular approaches, in contrast to monolithic designs, have been shown to speed up the development of large, complex robotic and simulation systems, and to facilitate the collaborations of large teams of researchers [39, 40, 41, 42]. To take some examples, Martinho et al. [43] created an architecture designed to facilitate modular, rapid development of theatrical agents for virtual worlds and modularity played a large role in the construction of Bischoff et al.'s HERMES robot [44]. Simmons et al's robot Grace [45], with over 20 collaborators from 5 institutions, is another great example of a project that has benefited from a modular approach. Of course, whether the mind/brain can be modeled in a modular fashion is still debated in the research community and not all are convinced of its merits. However, in the software engineering sense, this claim in its essence simply represents a practical solution to a highly challenging problem: it does not force us into – or even in the slightest sense imply – the view that the brain is literally a set of components. Rather, the claim of modular construction is that our understanding of the brain/mind can be fruitfully formalized that way when implemented as computer models. Of course, we'd like to incorporate as many faculties of the mind as possible when modeling cognition, but this is impossible to do all at once; unlike monolithic approaches, a modular approach enables us to do this incrementally and to capture many of its aspects in many ways, thus preserving their richness under various perspectives. The trick is to realize that a modular construction does not have to imply a *theory of modularity*. To see how this could be so, we need to look at some theoretical building blocks that can lead the way. And so the next question for our modeling efforts arises, *What kinds of modularity?*

3.2 Abstract Modules and Near-Decomposability

The concept of an *abstract module* builds on Simon's [3, 46, 47] concept of "near-decomposability" (ND): Systems that are divided into subsystems of interacting elements at multiple levels, where interactions between elements within a subsystem are an order of magnitude or two higher than interactions between subsystems. It can be found everywhere in nature, from the universe as a whole to biological to sub-atomic systems. A module in this sense is a theoretically motivated or practically motivated subcomponent or building block of a larger system, with causal relationships (couplings) to other such subcomponents (Figure 4). Together the subcomponents and their couplings define the system in question. We will look at examples of this in section 3.3 below, but first we will provide a general account of the idea and its benefits.

An abstract module represents *abstracted system functionality*. It has a goal or purpose g, an input i, an internal state S, a transformation process P, and an output o. In the tradition of many multi-agent systems, the goal can be a human-imputed justification for the module's existence – in other words the module's role in the architecture – and need not reflect an underlying theory (just like the existence of the module itself). The transformation process transforms the input to an output according to some rules; if i is a continuous physical force and P is a damping mechanism, o will be some derivative of i according to mechanical laws; if i is some discrete information packet and P a routing mechanism o may be i in unmodified form but with a new destination.

Figure 5-I shows causal relations between six physical (or hypothetical) entities with particular causal relationships. To model these using abstract modules, several approaches can be taken. In II, the relationships have been implemented as three simulation models, with messages taking the place of hypothesized (or real) causation; left-hand side in II represents transmitting modules and right-hand side receiving modules. In III, the structure in I has been implemented as two alternative modular models, X and Y. In X, two modules are used to represent all causal relationships of I. In Y some modules from II have been merged. Notice that even in

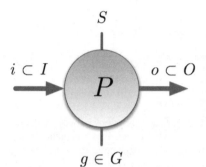

Fig. 4. An abstract module is composed of a process P, input i, output o, a state S and a goal g

this implementation, where e.g. each module is running on its own computer or as its own thread, the original physical/theoretical relationship between the causes and effects has not changed (except insofar as in this example their effects on each other may not have the same resolution as reality would have it). In both II and III the modules' internal state (see Figure 4) represents the state of the causes and effects in I. Looking at Figure 5-I as physical reality, or a theoretical model of physical reality, nothing in II or III has changed in our modularization of the physical or hypothetical systems in I.

Because the approach can be employed purely for the practical purposes of getting a handle on excess complexity, it follows that the cognitive modules proposed by Fodor [48], for example, can be modeled as a single abstract module in which the module's state and goal is not shared with other modules, only its input and output. But if the modular model is in this way completely independent of the theory, what then is the benefit of the modularization? Doesn't it get in the way? The short answer is *no* – even if the modules in our implementation are completely orthogonal to the actual theory the system implements they will allow for the construction of larger, more detailed models, and help relate the work to related fields. Additionally they will help anchor a given level of organization in tangible, physical structures wherever this is appropriate. There are significant benefits to modularization:

- *Modular systems are easier to expand than monolithic ones.* This is a well-known fact in software engineering and computer science.
- *A modular model of a complex system is easier to simulate, as modules can be moved between processors.* The primary reason why this is important in cognitive research is that so much of cognition has no serial dependencies and can

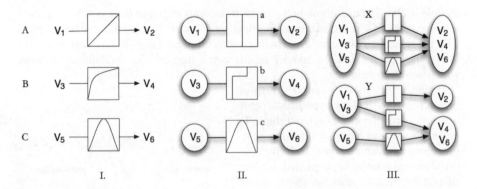

Fig. 5. Causal relations between variables [V_1, V_6]. I, II and III, left-hand side: Causes; right-hand side: Effects. Part I depicts physical causal relationships between variables (A – linear relation; B – logrithmic relation; C – hyperbolic relation). Alternatively, part I may represent theoretical models of physical or hypothetical constructs. In II, these relationships have been implemented as three modular simulation models, one module per causal factor and one per measured effect, with messages taking the place of physical relationships. The functions *a* and *b* connecting the modules have also been quantized from what they were in I. The left-hand side represents transmitting modules and the right-hand side receiving modules. In III, two modules are used to represent all causal relationships of I. In both II and III the modules' internal state (see Figure 4) represents the state of the causes and effects in I, respectively, and the modularization is thus independent of the theoretical model.

(and should) therefore be executed in parallel. In addition, computing power is becoming increasingly available prices continue to drop and advances keep being made. This point is less important for systems that are small enough to be run on single processors than more computationally intensive ones, but as the power of processors increases the benefits even there are becoming increasingly obvious.

• *Modular approaches facilitate collaborations between scientists, labs and universities.* This is extremely important, as HeLDs are difficult to build; sharing models and runnable code between scientists and even institutions may speed up the progress of cognitive research by orders of magnitude [49].

Even though modularization with abstract modules can be kept independent of the underlying model, this does not mean that modularization in a runnable model should never mirror modularization (whether hypothetical or real) in the system being modeled – quite the contrary: It may in fact sometimes be beneficial to make modules in a model directly mirror modules in the modeled system. To take the example of Fodor again, we could build a model where our abstract modules directly implement the way in which he intended his mind modularity to work.[8] It is important to keep in mind, however, that when such assumptions about actual modularity are made they must be made explicitly and clearly and not implicitly, as is often the case. This allows the validity of such a local hypothetical modularization to be further

---

[8] This would presumably require a significant amount of detail to be added "between the lines" in his theory, as it is a relatively high-level and coarse-grained.

investigated – and eventually decided – in the course of the model verification procedure.

The idea of abstract modules as presented here continues along the line of Marr's [50] three levels of analysis, theory, representation and implementation[9] – but abstract modules go further, dealing with complex system architectures, relationships between semi-independent entities, and abstractions at multiple levels of detail. Although to some extent compatible with Minsky's Society of Mind [51] (multiple interacting subcomponents), the idea of abstract modules differs significantly from it in its emphasis (a) the importance of gross architecture in complex systems, (b) hierarchical models, and (b) the practical benefits of modularity for building runnable models. As Simon [3, 46, 47] points out about ND systems, they can be described as a hierarchy at multiple levels of abstraction (detail) where mechanisms at each level interact more between each other than any other part of the system as a whole. This concept is illustrated in Figure 6. The decomposition into levels, and subsystems at each level, can be structural and/or functional. A functionally decomposable system will have functions that can be isolated and implemented computationally as abstract modules – independently of how or whether its functional decomposition mirrors its actual physical/structural instantiation.[10] As one descends down this scale, detail, i.e. physical and temporal granularity, increases – the model involves smaller objects operating at higher frequencies.

Figure 7 shows three canonical abstracted examples of systems resulting from applying this methodology. In Example I a target system is decomposed at two main levels, the highest and the lowest. An example is e.g. a goal-stack for topics to be discussed (the high level), and neural mechanisms coding for the speaker's representation of spatial relations so that he is able to look at the listener (low level). Alternatively, the lowest level could be a neural model of goal representation, with spatial relations simply modeled at the top level as Cartesian points in space. In Example II the system is decomposed into three levels; take our first model and add a middle level describing how neurally-encoded spatial information (lowest level) informs the control of neck and eye-muscle tension (mid-level) to bring head and eyes to the desired positions, relative to the speaker's and listener's bodies. Example III is an example of "the modeler's nightmare": Here a system has multiple valid decompositions at any level (there are no discernable levels), potentially all equally good (or bad).

Furthermore, some abstract modules at each level have causal connections to abstract modules at different levels of description. Encountering this situation may in fact point to a possibility that (a) the phenomena one is trying to model are in fact not causally connected or that (b) they are in essence atomic. Note though that this does not mean one cannot model the system in a modular fashion, only that the modules

---

[9] It is important to note that Marr's usage of "implementation" referred to the substrate – the hardware – that a model runs on, that is, how a system can be realized physically e.g. the brain or a CPU, while my use of the term "implementation" is used throughout in the sense of "software implementation", i.e. how a system is implemented as a software program. A key point here is that software implementations can approximate the hardware implementation to various degrees, along almost a continuous scale of fidelity.

[10] Of course any functional feature of an abstract runnable system must be implemented as causal chains at some physical level (not necessarily in a one-to-one relationship), lest we assume some sort of metaphysical causation – see Scheutz [52].

and their connections will have a high level of arbitrariness.

A key feature of ND heterogeneous systems is that the causal chains between their elements are a tangled web of different types of interactions, or couplings (Figure 8). We can classify these along at least two main dimensions, *den sity* and *tightness*. A dense coupling between two components makes them high ly-dependent on each other on many variables; a sparse coup ling means only one or a few variables on either side affect the other. A variable in component *A* is tightly coupled to a variable in component *B* if changes in it affect changes in the other in a (close to) 1:1 relationship. A loose coupling implies a statistical relationship or that e.g. only part of the range of one variable affects the other. Of course, any given HeLD may be composed of a combination of components that vary along both dimen-

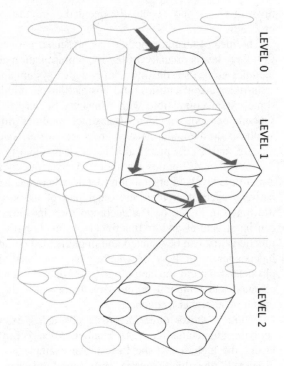

Fig. 6. Abstraction levels: Each level of description can be broken into smaller constituents that interact through rules different from the level above. A causal connection at Level 0 (top arrow) may in fact stand for a complex set of causal interactions at the next level below (small arrows).

sions; what makes a system a HeLD is its large number of components and the existence of a significant number of dense couplings. But what does it mean to implement a tightly coupled causal relationship (theoretical model) as loosely coupled modules (implementation model)? It means that the implementation model will probably represent the theoretical model incompletely (and the theoretical model may in turn implement the actual phenomenon incompletely), resulting in lower fidelity of simulation, and less predictive power. Depending on the questions asked of such a system, the answer may be wrong, or only correct to certain approximation.

3.3 Model Examples

Abstract modules can be used as building blocks for any sort of system; they can be used to turn architectural ideas into *runnable models* that can be put the scrutiny that only dynamic runnable models can (e.g. interaction with the real world). They have for example been used in one form or other for robotics [53, 54], models of market innovation [39], and neurocognitive modeling [55].

To exemplify the use of abstract modules in the context of multimodal communication, we will now take a brief look at two systems that use abstract modules, both implementing turntaking skills. The first system implements a new version of the Ymir Turntaking Model (YTTM [56]), a model based on a broad set of psychological research on human face-to-face communication. The model incorporates multiple modes and has been tested extensively in realtime dialogue with people. A recent implementation of the model is speech-only but has several new perception mechanisms and a new system for managing real-time decision-making and planning. The model is built using around 20 abstract modules that implement various functions such as managing architecture-wide semi-global (internal) states that concern realtime resource (CPU) allocation, decisions and perceptual tasks, as well as speech recognition and speech synthesis (one module each). To take an example, intonation is processed in a special prosody processing module, decisions when to take and give turn are managed by a group of decider modules and the decision to start speaking is managed by a relatively large, modular planner. Most of these modules take input from 2-3 other abstract modules in the system. None of the implemented modules are purported to map directly, or even indirectly, to brain or cognitive "modules". But they *are* assumed to implement functionalities that influence each other in the way that the system architecture implies.

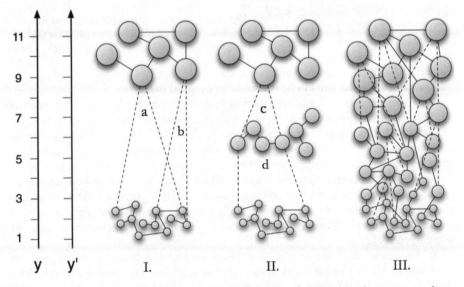

Fig. 7. All systems can be decomposed at multiple levels of abstraction; the more complete a theory is, the better such decompositions are theoretically connected. Here, circles represent decompositions of a system into abstract modules – each module containing an appropriate method for its function, e.g. an artificial neural net, rule set, fuzzy logic, etc.). The lowest level (bottom) represents the finest-grained grouping of functions and/or structure in the system; the highest level (top) represents the most abstract; lines represent coupling. Example I: Modularization at two scales; example II: modularization at three scales; example III: modularization and decomposition at multiple, overlapping scales. For number of neurons in the brain $y' \approx 10^y$ neurons.

In this system the density of the coupling between modules is moderate (averaging 5 connections per module), information transfer between modules is on the order of 6-12k bits per second per module, and the coupling tightness is relatively high, implying that the majority of the modules operate highly predictably based on their input, and thus embody relatively simple internal processes.

Although the YTTM so far seems a reasonable initial step in the direction of modeling complex multimodal realtime turntaking, significant additional research is needed, in particular regarding how the behavior produced by the model compares to real human data and whether the factors (causal chains) it proposes can be implemented by neural mechanisms – a necessity for any model claiming cognitive realism. Both of these are currently work in progress – the latter to be discussed in our next example.

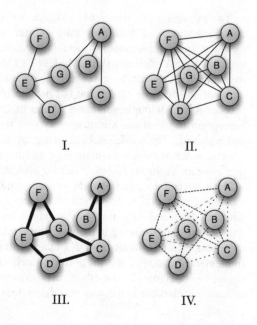

Fig. 8. Types of couplings between a set of hete-rogeneous abstract modules. I: Sparse coup- ling. II: Dense coupling. III: Tight coupling. IV: Loose coupling.

The second example of a system we will look at exemplifies how abstract modules can help connect theories at different levels of abstraction. In this system, selected parts of the YTTM, more specifically some of the abstract modules it proposes for handling decision and planning in multimodal turntaking [55], have been implemented as neural mechanisms. The neural planner is a modified version of the Augmented Competitive Queuing model (ACQ [57]), which was built to model Macaque brain mechanisms that control grasping [58, 59]. This new implementation of the YTTM gives it learning capabilities, but the key advance on other implementations of it is the increased level of detail in the implementation and its link to brain research.

At the neural level the model now proposes *motor schemas* that compete for execution in a way that produces emergent action sequencing. Motor schemas are a kind of abstract modules that map directly onto purported neural mechanisms. Albeit somewhat simpler than the original decision and motor control mechanisms in the YTTM, the replaced sections are now anchored to empirical brain modeling: rather than being purely motivated by data from gross-behavior analysis they are theoretically motivated at a much finer level of granularity. Because of the flexibility of abstract modules, some parts of this neural implementation of the YTTM still include abstract modules that have not yet been linked to models from other fields, including modules that control motivational levels and perception of speech and gesture: these have been implemented to handle particular functions without any claims that their existence is somehow based on existing modularity found in the real world. In accordance with the above account, however, the factors these modules control, e.g. motivational level, are assumed to represent real-world factors. Because abstract modules help isolate logical, as well as structural, parts of a system in its model, modeling can be done without necessarily representing the whole system at a single level of abstraction.

These two models of embodied multimodal turntaking together exemplify how levels of abstraction can be bridged with the help of abstract modules; the synthesis of the original cognitive turntaking model and a neural model of planning and motor control produced a mixed-level, mixed-abstraction approach, bridging cognitive and neural levels in a manageable way, and perhaps more importantly, in a way that can produce performance data that can be directly compared to the systems being studied.

4   Neurocognitive Architecture

One of the questions that arises when modeling cognitive phenomena as varied as those encountered in natural communication is whether we are likely to encounter the need to have our abstract modules represent actual modules. Put in a different way, is the brain/mind modular, and if so, to what extent? (That is, are there systems or mechanisms that clearly, or perhaps not so clearly, form spatial and/or structural groups?) One way to begin to answer this is to look at data produced by recent brain research, since neural structures is ultimately how all animal cognitive functionality must be implemented.

Modularity and hierarchy are known to exist in the human brain [60]. The smallest scale thought to matter to its computation is the neuron and the set of chemical compounds known to be able to alter the computational characteristics of these. There are about 500 major groupings of neurons in the human brain where the groups are composed of a selected set of neurons; each of the groups consists of 5 types of neurons, on average, each of which sometimes creates sub-groupings [61]. The human brain thus consists of a total 2500 different types of neurons. Each of the 500 groupings uses specific ways to compute, and each connects to other groups in specific ways. These groups then make up larger interconnected groups, many of which are dedicated to a particular part of mental processing such as vision, hearing, sight, motion control, speech generation, speech understanding, balance, emotions, etc. [61]. Of course these facts are not a proof that cognitive and brain architecture is isomorphic, but it hints strongly at modular organization on *some* levels of analysis. Further signs of modularity can be seen in the numerous gross anatomical areas identified in the last 30-40 years that have particular functional characteristics, including the several layers of visual processing in the back of the brain, neural nuclei for spatial hearing, learning (cf. [62, 63]), cognitive control and planning [64. 65], and more recently, strong evidence of *causal connections* between frontal lobes and decision making, obtained using transcranial magnetic stimulation [66]. These correspondences between mental-level phenomena and neural tissue, which is composed of heterogeneous types of neurons, give us some hope that a modeling methodology based on abstract modules will be relevant and successful in modeling mental phenomena computationally, including conversation skills. There exist, however, reasons to believe the opposite: Results from the complete mapping of all 302 brain cells of the nematode C. elegans, and their 7000 synaptic connections [67], have not resulted in any significant deepening of our understanding of how a brain operates, and even simple tasks such as the nematode's crawling seem as unexplained as ever, from the perspective of its brain and neural architecture (cf. [68]).

Elsewhere I have argued that AI researchers need to study intelligence in a larger context than they typically do, and that to do so they need new tools, methodologies and collaboration strategies to build larger models of the phenomena they are studying [49]. The same can be said about cognitive scientists and psychologists working on understanding human communication and cognition in general. Again, it is imperative that we build *runnable models* of these phenomena – it is the only (known) way to address the complexity explosion that happens when we try to understand larger parts of the human and animal minds. It is equally imperative that we aim at modeling these phenomena *in toto* – as completely and comprehensively as possible. [11] It is not enough for psychology to limit itself to (observable) behavior, or to a purely cognitive level – data, theories and methods from neurology, medicine, artificial intelligence and other fields must be used to help constrain the vastness of the possible explanations for the observable surface phenomena (even those produced in controlled experiments with large and repeatable results).

So to understand complex systems such as the human mind/brain system we are going to need models at various levels of detail, for various purposes. In employing this method, one can choose the level of abstraction in accordance with the desired model resolution, available data, and available measuring techniques – in essence employing numerous instances of the model in Figure 4 at various levels in Figure 6, and then expand as more information comes to light. Scientific theory thus becomes built up over time, incrementally covering and explaining more phenomena and excluding alternative explanations. Evidence from research based on these assumptions, including the use of various versions of hierarchies of abstract modules, points to significant benefits of the approach (cf. [33, 40, 53, 55, 64, 71]). Eventually we will want them to be interconnected enough to present the "mind atlas", with details of fine and gross anatomy and function equally represented in a runnable simulation. What that model will look like is an empirical question; however, the evidence so far indicates that it would be equally absurd to expect the human mind/brain to be exclusively built out of a huge number of uniform, specialized modules (what Bryson [69] calls "vertical modules"), as advocated – to different degrees – by e.g. some "massive modularity" hypothesis enthusiasts (see Carruthers [70] for a review), as it is to contend that the human mind/brain is a massive collection of undifferentiated neurons with no discernable low or high-level structures – neural spaghetti. Barrett and Kurzban [72] provide a thorough overview of arguments on both sides of the modularity debate.

---

[11] In particular, a direct result of the requirement for a detailed, comprehensive, runnable model is that our models will – for the most part – *never* be complete; we will be doomed to build models for various purposes, for answering various sets of questions. This can already be seen in modeling efforts for many natural phenomena such as ocean currents, weather systems, ecosystems, etc.

Clearly the human brain, and thus by extension the mind, is organized in many ways and on many levels, but both extremes on the organizational spectrum seem implausible. Assuming then that the substrate of the human mind lies somewhere along the spectrum from being perfectly hierarchically organized to being complete spaghetti, we need powerful tools to analyze and model it.

5 Conclusion

We have painted a picture of multimodal dialogue as a complex system composed of a large set of functions, produced by a multitude of systems and subsystems that interact in complex ways, producing emergent properties. With examples from cellular automata, cognitive modeling and brain research, I have argued that because of this, if we wish to obtain a comprehensive model of multimodal embodied communication, we cannot apply a divide-and-conquer approach exclusively, or only study the various (surface) dialogue phenomena or brain function in isolation – we have to take an integrative approach. Because of its complex-system nature, multimodal realtime dialogue calls for an approach that can model it at a high level granularity – a necessity for achieving correctness in models of complex systems.

The evolution of science rests on the power of the tools we have at our disposal; the need for more powerful tools and methodologies for extending – and especially for interconnecting – research in psychology, brain science and cognitive science is as calling today as the need for the microscope was in the early days of biology. Whether or not one takes to either of the extremes in the mind-brain debate (extreme modularity or "neurocogntive spaghetti"), hierarchies of abstract modules can be a powerful approach to modeling large systems with complex causal structure.

Abstract modules are an embodiment of abstracted functionality. They have been used in many systems to date, from humanoid robotics [40, 53, 54] to integrative cognitive models [55, 57, 58] to economic simulations [39], and shown to be a flexible and malleable methodology. Benefits of the approach are numerous, the main ones being (a) easier integration of models based on different theoretical foundations and originating in different disciplines, and (b) the ability to manage a greater amount of overall complexity. A third major benefit is (c) the ability to mix different levels of abstraction when building a model, to get increased levels of detail where needed. A fourth major benefit is that (d) isolated models built with the method can more easily be extended, can more easily be related to other models. Last but not least, (e) they can be run as simulations whose performance can be compared directly to the systems being modeled.

We have looked at some evidence from brain research in support of the idea that functional validity coincides with structural validity, i.e. evidence of brain modularity may in some cases result in certain levels of isomorphism between cognitive models and the brain. As we have seen, however, not only can abstract modules be used for understanding behavior and cognition independently of whether the phenomena modeled are modular or not – that theory and implementation at different levels of abstraction can coincide but need not do so – but that the approach is also independent of physical and functional modularity (or monolithicity); functional and structural validity can be completely disjoint or can overlap to differing degrees in models based on abstract modules. As long as causal relationships are correctly identified and represented by the theory, abstract module hierarchies can be used to implement any theory as a runnable computer model, with the necessary and appropriate abstractness, fidelity and predictive power. For complex systems such as multimodal dialogue skills, which calls for modeling a wide range of realtime cognitive skills ranging from the control of saccades to social interaction, abstract module hierarchies represent a powerful and proven approach to scientific research.

Acknowledgments. For insightful and illuminating discussions on numerous topics related to this paper I would like to thank Deepa Iyengar, Hannes Högni Vilhjálmsson, Eric Nivel and Hrafn Th. Thórisson, as well as my many colleagues at the ZiF in the summer of 2006, whose thoughts and ideas have influenced several parts of this chapter. Special thanks to Hrafn for the cellular automata simulation and to Eric, Hrafn, Hannes, Deepa and Ipke for numerous insightful and brilliant comments on the manuscript. Big thanks to Eric for important last-minute edits and suggestions. Thanks also to the anonymous reviewers for challenging questions. Big thanks to Ipke Wachsmuth and Günther Knoblich for conceiving and arranging the research year on Embodied Communication in Humans and Machines at ZiF in Bielefeld. Thanks to Jimmy Bonaiuto for our very fruitful and fun collaboration on the neurally-based turntaking model and to Gudny R. Jonsdottir for her work on the next generation of the YTTM. This work was supported in part by a Fellowship grant from Zentrum für interdisziplinäre Forschung, a research grant from RANNÍS, Iceland, and by a Marie Curie European Reintegration Grant within the 6th European Community Framework Programme.

References

[1] Gerver, D.: Simultaneous listening and speaking and retention of prose. Quart. J. Exp. Psych. 26(3), 337–341 (1974)
[2] Lee, T.: Simultaneous Listening and Speaking in English into Korean Simultaneous Interpretation. Meta 44(4) (1999), http://www.erudit.org/revue/meta/1999/v44/n4
[3] Simon, H.A.: Can there be a science of complex systems? In: Bar-Yam, Y. (ed.) Unifying themes in complex systems: Proceedings from the International Conference on Complex Systems, 1997, Cambridge, MA, vol. 1997, pp. 4–14. Perseus Press (1999)
[4] Magnusson, M.S.: Understanding Social Interaction: Discovering Hidden Structure with Model and Algorithms. In: Anolli, L., Duncan Jr, S., Magnusson, M.S., Riva, G. (eds.) The Hidden Structure of Interaction: From Neurons to Culture Patterns, IOS Press, Amsterdam (2005)
[5] Card, S.K., Moran, T.P., Newell, A.: The Model Human Processor: An Engineering Model of Human Performance. In: Boff, K.R., Kaufman, L., Thomas, J.P. (eds.) Handbook of Human Perception Vol. II, John Wiley and Sons, New York (1986)
[6] Chandrasekaran, B., Josephson, S.G.: Architecture of Intelligence: The Problems and Current Approaches to Solutions. In: Honavar, V., Uhr, L. (eds.) Artificial Intelligence and Neural Networks: Steps Toward Principled Integration, Academic Press, San Diego (1994)

[7] Lieberman, M.D.: Reflective and Reflexive Judgment Processes: A Social Cognitive Neuroscience Approach. In: Forgas, J.P., Williams, K.R., von Hippel, W. (eds.) Social judgments: Implicit and explicit processes, pp. 44–67. Cambridge University Press, New York (2003)

[8] Nanayakkara, T., Shadmehr, R.: Saccade Adaptation in Response to Altered Arm Dynamics. J. Neurophysiol 90, 4016–4021 (2003)

[9] Spivey, M.J., Tannenhaus, M.K., Eberhard, M.K., Sedivy, J.K.: Eye movements and spoken language comprehension: Effects of visual context on syntactic ambiguity resolution. Cogn. Psych. 45, 447–481 (2002)

[10] Thórisson, K.R.: Computational Characteristics of Multimodal Dialogue. In: AAAI Fall Symposium on Embodied Language and Action, Massachusetts Institute of Technology, Cambridge, MA, November 10-12, pp. 102–108 (1995)

[11] O'Connell, D.C., Kowal, S., Kaltenbacher, E.: Turn-Taking: A Critical Analysis of the Research Tradition. Journal of Psycholinguistic Research 19(6), 345–373 (1990)

[12] Sacks, H., Schegloff, E.A., Jefferson, G.A.: A Simplest Systematics for the Organization of Turn-Taking in Conversation. Language 50, 696–735 (1974)

[13] Wison, M., Wilson, T.P.: An oscillator model of the timing of turn-taking. Psychonomic Bulletin and Review 12(6), 957–968 (2005)

[14] Goodwin, C.: Conversational Organization: Interaction Between Speakers and Hearers. Academic Press, New York (1981)

[15] Duncan Jr, S.: Some Signals and Rules for Taking Speaking Turns in Conversations. J. of Personality and Soc. Psych. 23(2), 283–292 (1972)

[16] Wolfram, S.: A New Kind of Science. Wolfram Media (2002)

[17] Levi-Strauss, C.: The family. In: Shapiro, H. (ed.) Man, culture and society, Oxford University Press, Oxford (1956)

[18] Popper, C.: Conjectures and Refutations. In: The Growth of Scientific Knowledge, Routledge, London (1963)

[19] Newell, A.: You can't play 20 questions with nature and win. In: Chase, W.G. (ed.) Visual information processing, Academic Press, New York (1973)

[20] Kosslyn, S.M.: You can play 20 questions with nature and win: Categorical versus coordinate spatial relations as a case study. Neuropsychologia 44(9), 1519–1523 (2006)

[21] Turing, A.M.: Computing machinery and intelligence. Mind 59, 433–460 (1950)

[22] Turing, A.M.: On Computable Numbers, With an Application to the Entscheidungsproblem. Proceedings of the London Mathematical Society, Series 2 42 (1936)

[23] Laughlin, S.B.: The Implications of Metabolic Energy Requirements for the Representation of Information in Neurons. In: Gazzaniga, M.S. (ed.) The Cognitive Neurosciences III, pp. 187–196. M.I.T. Press, Massachusetts (2004)

[24] Thagard, P.: Mind: Introduction to Cognitive Science, 2nd edn. MIT Press, Cambridge (1996)

[25] Chalmers, D.: Does a Rock Implement a Finite State Automaton? Synthese 108, 310–333 (1996)

[26] Chalmers, D.J.: A Computational Foundation for the Study of Cognition. Philosophy-Neuroscience-Psychology Technical Report 94–03, Washington University (1994)

[27] Calabretta, R., Parisi, D.: Evolutionary Connectionism and Mind/Brain Modularity. In: Callebaut, W., Rasskin-Gutman, D. (eds.) Modularity: Understanding the Development and Evolution of Natural Complex Systems, pp. 309–330. MIT Press, Cambridge (2005)

[28] Takahashi, K.: Development of Holistic Climate Simulation Codes for a non-Hydrostatic Atmosphere-Ocean Coupled Systems. In: Annual Report of the Earth Simulator Cente, Japan, April 2004 – March 2005, pp. 52–67 (2005)

[29] Vlachos, D.G.: A review of multiscale analysis: Examples from systems biology, materials engineering, and other fluid-surface interacting systems. Adv. Chem. Eng. 30, 1–61 (2005)

[30] Abadi, M.G., Navarro, J.F., Steinmetz, M., Eke, V.R.: Simluations of Galaxy Formation in a Lambda CDM Universe II: The Fine Structure of Simulated Galactic Disks. Astrophys. J 597, 21–34 (2003)

[31] Wildberger, A.M.: A.I. and Simluation. Simulation, 1–2 (March 1999)

[32] Simon, H.A.: Complex systems: The interplay of organizations and markets in contemporary society. Computational & Mathematical Organization Theory 7(2), 79–85 (2001)

[33] Scwabacher, M., Gelsey, A.: Multi-Level Simulation and Numerical Optimization of Complex Engineering Designs. In: 6th AIAA/NASA/USAF Multidisciplinary Analysis & Optmization Symposium, Bellevue, WA. AIAA-1996-4021 (1996)

[34] Schaffner, K.F.: Reduction: the Cheshire cat problem and a return to roots. Synthese 151(3), 377–402 (2006)

[35] Gaud, N., Gechter, F., Galland, S., Koukam, A.: Holonic Multiagent Multilevel Simulation Application to Real-time Pedestrians Simulation in Urban Environment. In: Proceedings of IJCAI-2007, pp. 1275–1280 (2007)

[36] Dayan, P.: Levels of Analysis in Neural Modeling. In: Encyclopedia of Cognitive Science, MacMillan Press, London, England (2000)

[37] Arbib, M.A.: Levels of Modeling of Visually Guided Behavior (with peer commentary and author's response). Behavioral and Brain Sciences 10, 407–465 (1987)

[38] Bakker, B., den Dulk, P.: Causal Relationships and Relationships between Levels: The Modes of Description Perspective. In: Hahn, M., Stoness, S.C. (eds.) Proceedings of the Twenty-First Annual Conference of the Cognitive Science Society, pp. 43–48 (1999)

[39] Saemundsson, R., Thórisson, K.R., Jonsdottir, G.R., Arinbjarnar, M., Finnsson, H., Gudnason, H., Hafsteinsson, V., Hannesson, G., Ísleifsdóttir, J., Jóhannsson, Th., Kristjánsson, G., Sigmundarson, S.: Modular Simulation of Knowledge Development in Industry: A Multi-Level Framework. In: WEHIA – 1st International Conference on Economic Sciences with Heterogeneous Interacting Agents, University of Bologna, Italy, 15-17 June (2006)

[40] Thórisson, K.R., Benko, H., Arnold, A., Abramov, D., Maskey, S., Vaseekaran, A.: Constructionist Design Methodology for Interactive Intelligences. A.I. Magazine 25(4), 77–90 (2004); Menlo Park, CA: American Association for Artificial Intelligence.

[41] Fink, G.A., Jungclaus, N., Kummer, F., Ritter, H., Sagerer, G.: A Distributed System for Integrated Speech and Image Understanding. In: International Symposium on Artificial Intelligence, Cancun, Mexico, pp. 117–126 (1996)

[42] Fink, G.A., Jungclaus, N., Ritter, H., Saegerer, G.: A Communication Framework for Heterogeneous Distributed Pattern Analysis. In: International Conference on Algorithms and Architectures for Parallel Processing, Brisbane, Australia, pp. 881–890 (1995)

[43] Martinho, C., Paiva, A., Gomes, M.R.: Emotions for a Motion: Rapid Development of Believable Pathematic Agents in Intelligent Virtual Environments. Applied Artificial Intelligence 14(1), 33–68 (2000)

[44] Bischoff, R.: Towards the Development of 'Plug-and-Play' Personal Robots. In: 1st IEEE-RAS International Conference on Humanoid Robots, September 7–8, 2000, vol. 8, MIT, Cambridge (2000)

[45] Simmons, R., Goldberg, D., Goode, A., Montemerlo, M., Roy, N., Sellner, B., Urmson, C., Schultz, A., Abramson, M., Adams, W., Atrash, A., Bugajska, M., Coblenz, M., MacMahon, M., Perzanowski, D., Horswill, I., Zubek, R., Kortenkamp, D., Wolfe, B., Milam, T., Maxwell, B.: GRACE: An Autonomous Robot for the AAAI Robot Challenge. A.I. Magazine 24(2), 51–72 (2003)

[46] Simon, H.A.: Near decomposability and the speed of evolution. Industrial and Corporate Change 11(3), 587–599 (2002)

[47] Simon, H.A., Ando, A.: Aggregation of Variables in Dynamic Systems. Econometrica 29, 111–138 (1961)

[48] Fodor, J.: The Modularity of Mind. Bradford Books / MIT Press, Cambridge (1983)

[49] Thórisson, K.R.: Integrated A.I. Systems. Minds & Machines 17, 11–25 (2007); Invited paper at The Dartmouth Artificial Intelligence Conference: The Next 50 Years — Commemorating the 1956 Founding of AI as a Research Discipline, July 13-15, 2006, Dartmouth, New Hampshire, U.S.A. (2006)

[50] Marr, D.: Vision. W.H. Freeman, New York (1982)

[51] Minsky, M.: The Society of Mind. Simon & Schuster, New York (1986)

[52] Scheutz, M.: When physical systems realize functions... Minds and Machines 9, 161–196 (1999)

[53] Ng-Thow-Hing, V., List, T., Thórisson, K.R., Lim, J., Wormer, J.: Design and Evaluation of Communication Middleware in a Distributed Humanoid Robot Architecture. In: Accepted to IROS (2008)

[54] Thórisson, K.R., List, T., Pennock, C., DiPirro, J., Magnusson, F.: Scheduling Blackboards for Interactive Robots. Reykjavik University Department of Computer Science Technical Report, RUTR-CS05002 (2005)

[55] Bonaiuto, J., Thórisson, K.R.: Towards a Neurocognitive Model of Multimodal Turntaking. In: Wachsmuth, I., Knoblich, G., Lenzen, M. (eds.) Embodied Communication in Humans and Machines, forthcoming, Oxford University Press, London (2007)

[56] Thórisson, K.R.: Natural Turn-Taking Needs No Manual: A Computational Model, From Perception to Action. In: Granström, B., House, D., Karlsson, I. (eds.) Multimodality in Language and Speech Systems, pp. 173–207. Kluwer Academic Publishers, Dordrecht, the Netherlands (2002)

[57] Bonaiuto, J., Arbib, M.A.: What Did I Just Do? A New Role for Mirror Neurons (in preparation)

[58] Fagg, A., Arbib, M.A.: Modeling parietal-premotor interactions in primate control of grasping. Neural Netw. 7–8, 1277–1303 (1998)

[59] Alstermark, B., Lundberg, A., Norrsell, U., Sybirska, E.: Integration in descending motor pathways controlling the forelimb in the cat: 9. Differential behavioural defects after spinal cord lesions interrupting defined pathways from higher centres to motorneurones. Experimental Brain Research 42(3), 299–318 (1981)

[60] Garel, S., Rubenstein, J.L.R.: Patterning of the Cerebral Cortex. In: Gazzaniga, M.S. (ed.) The Cognitive Neurosciences III, pp. 69–84. M.I.T. Press, Massachusetts (2004)

[61] Swanson, L.W.: Interactive Brain Maps and Atlases. In: Arbib, M.A., Grethe, J.S. (eds.) Computing the Brain, pp. 167–177. Academic Press, San Diego (2001)

[62] Bryson, J.: Modular Representations of Cognitive Phenomena in AI, Psychology and Neuroscience. In: Davis, D. (ed.) Visions of Mind, pp. 66–89. Idea Group, London (2005)

[63] Bryson, J., Stein, L.A.: Modularity and Specialized Learning: Mapping Between Agent Architectures and Brain Organization. In: Wermter, S., Austin, J., Willshaw, D. (eds.) Emergent Neural Computational Architectures based on Neuroscience, Springer, Heidelberg, Germany (2001)

[64] Koechlin, E., Ody, C., Kouneiher, F.: The Architecture of Cognitive Control in Human Prefrontal Cortex. Science 302, 1181–1185 (2003)

[65] Miller, E.K., Cohen, J.D.: An Integrative Theory of Prefrontal Cortex Function. Annu. Rev. Neurosci. 24, 167–202 (2001)

[66] van 't Wouta, M., Kahn, R.S., Sanfeyd, A.G., Alemanc, A.: Repetitive transcranial magnetic stimulation over the right dorsolateral prefrontal cortex affects strategic decision-making. Cognitive Neuroscience and Neuropsychology 16(16), 1849–1952 (2005)

[67] Oshio, K., Morita, S., Osana, Y., Oka, K.: C. elegans synaptic connectivity data. Technical Report of CCeP, Keio Future, No.1, Keio University (1998)

[68] Zheng, Y., Brockie, P.J., Mellem, J.E., Madsen, D.M., Maricq, A.V.: Neuronal Control of Locomotion in C. elegans Is Modified by a Dominant Mutation in the GLR-1 Ionotropic Glutamate Receptor. Neuron 24, 347–361 (1999)

[69] Bryson, J.: Evidence of Modularity From Primate Errors During Task Learning. In: Cangelosi, A., Bugmann, G., Borisyuk, R. (eds.) Proceedings of The Ninth Neural Computation and Psychology Workshop (NCPW 9), World Scientific, Singapore (2005)

[70] Carruthers, P.: The case for massively modular models of mind. In: Stainton, R. (ed.) Contemporary Debates in Cognitive Science, pp. 205–225. Blackwell, Oxford, England (2005)

[71] List, T., Bins, J., Fisher, R.B., Tweed, D., Thórisson, K.R.: Two Approaches to a Plug-and-Play Vision Architecture - CAVIAR and Psyclone. In: Thórisson, K.R., Vilhjalmsson, H., Marsella, S. (eds.) AAAI-2005 Workshop on Modular Construction of Human-Like Intelligence, Pittsburgh, Pennsylvania, Menlo Park, CA, American Association for Artificial Intelligence, pp. 16–23 (July 10, 2005)

[72] Barrett, H.C., Kurzban, R.: Modularity in Cognition: Framing the Debate. Psych. Rev. 113(3), 628–647 (2006)

Con-tact – On the Problem of the Absence of
Eye Contact and Physical Contact in Virtual Interaction

Barbara Becker

Institut Medienwissenschaften, University of Paderborn
Warburger Str. 100, 33100 Paderborn, Germany
bbecker@uni-paderborn.de
http://wwwcs.uni-paderborn.de/~bbecker/

Abstract. The concrete face-to-face interaction can be regarded as a responsive process, characterized by the fact that – beyond our intentions – we always react to the implicit or explicit demands of the other. This form of responsivity is essentially determined by the corporal-sensual presence of the communication partner: the expression of the eyes, gestures and body posture, or the rhythm and sound of the voice. These aspects evocate an implicit horizon of meaning which always affects the intentions of the speaker. In responding to the explicit as well as implicit demands of the other, responsibility for the communication process and the other may arise, which is essential for the success and the continuity of the communication process. In this article I discuss whether this kind of responsibility exists in virtual communication when the nonverbal sphere of communication does not exist, and how it might be bbecplaced at least to some extent.

Keywords: face-to-face interaction, responsivity, responsibility.

1 Introductory Remarks

The manifold significance of physical contact in the context of interpersonal comm-unications is apparent in the everyday use of the term. Thus one speaks of looks meeting (touching) and of grasping (in the sense of understanding) the other in various contexts. Tactility in both the concrete and metaphorical sense is therefore the starting point for my examination of communication processes in "virtual space."[1]

Firstly I will specifically relate the increasingly broad concept of tactility to the phenomena of physical touch and being touched, leading secondly to interpersonal con-TACT, which, as already indicated above, contains the concept of touch in its root. Thirdly, and based on this, I will include comments on currently observable processes of communication in virtual spaces, concluding with preliminary reflections on possible socio-political consequences of the spread of "virtual contacts".

---

[1] The concept "virtual space" is used in a relatively broad sense here, as is quite common prac-tice; it refers here primarily to communication in and via the Internet.

I. Wachsmuth and G. Knoblich (Eds.): Modeling Communication, LNAI 4930, pp. 169–180, 2008.
© Springer-Verlag Berlin Heidelberg 2008

The following questions and issues form the background to this discussion:

- Is communication in the sense that the other's expectations and the unavailable character (*Unverfügbarkeit*) of his otherness can only be demonstrated in concrete interaction between persons who are physically present, possibly inherently bound up with the exchange of glances and/or physical encounters?
- To what extent is the absence of physical responsiveness a significant indicator in the search for reasons for the frequently reported lack of acceptance of mutual responsibility in "virtual" communication processes?[2]
- Are the fictional mutual attributions in cyberspace more a result of individual interpretations and projections than is the case in communication processes in the real world, because in the latter seeing and touching, body language and facial expression express more and different things than what is specifically said? And do virtual contacts underline the wish of the "EGO" to possess the other and make him into an object?

Some of these points will be discussed in the following, without making a claim to an exhaustive analysis.

2   On Touch / Contact

For quite some time, tactility has been a central point of interest for several disciplines. Interestingly, reference is made to a new form of tactility in the context of digital media – for example by De Kerkhove [6][3] –, whereby (oddly) the material-physical dimension of contact is often ignored. It is necessary to rethink what characterizes concrete contact and to relate this to man's physical existence.

Let us first look at concrete touching and feeling. In his approach to the complex phenomenon of tactility, the phenomenologist Bernhard Waldenfels [19] differentiates between a Gnostic and a pathic level of touch: he describes the Gnostic aspect as the conscious, intentional action of a physical individual who deliberately approaches a contact partner, be it a material object or another person. The tactile exploration of environment in early childhood in the course of which a small child "grasps" its surroundings can be seen as prototypical in this context. Here, tactility proves to be an essential modus of "being in the world."

Furthermore, in this childish grasping is to be found the second chief characteristic of contact: the pathic moment, characterized by the fact that one is always simultaneously touched by the person one touches. Because the touching person himself becomes the touched, he is both subject and object in one. This has two implications: firstly, a pervasive inner fissure or rupture is manifest here, because both levels, subject and object, cannot be made completely congruent, but are related to each other

---

[2] A number of studies point out the frequency of unexplained terminations of communication in the Internet, see also Döhring [7].

[3] The concept of tactility has become important in the field of media science where researchers are speaking more and more about visual tactility, referring here to film and television.

in a continual intersection. Furthermore, the de-centring of the actor is apparent in this doubling, because the intention of the toucher is refracted on the claims and implicit requirements of the other. Thus the child's intention when grasping a stone may be to pick it up, but the materiality of the stone may prove resistant to this intention in that the child's hand may slide off the slippery surface or the stone may be too unwieldy. The chiasmus (Merleau-Ponty [12]) of autonomy and heteronomy, of self-willed intention and simultaneous subjection to external control, is evident here in the specificity of the touched other, be it a concrete object whose materiality limits subjective intentions through its own materiality, or a touched person who in the act of being touched simultaneously becomes the toucher. The duality of "own" and "other" also becomes evident through touch.

The amalgamation of autonomy and heteronomy, which is inherent to the tactile exploration of the world, fundamentally determines "being in the world" for man. Action and passion are irrevocably connected in touching, as touching is both active doing and passive suffering. This duality reveals a split in the self, which is ruptured in the experience of touching. The touching actor, who is likewise touched by the person touched, cannot perceive himself as active and passive in absolute simultaneity, but is in an in-between situation that is not open to rational comprehension. In touching, a person experiences himself simultaneously as a self-aware individual who is at the same time a stranger to oneself – both levels cannot be made wholly congruent.

A further characteristic of touching is manifest here; the experience of another that is perceptible in every contact: Whether I touch myself or another, in every act of touching the strangeness and the limited availability (*Verfügbarkeit*) of the person or object touched becomes apparent. Touching thus always evokes fears, because the otherness of the person or object touched cannot be denied by imaginary visions of merging or unity. The other can neither be totally possessed not can his otherness be wholly denied by imaginary constructions or repressions. Thus the experience of unavailability (*Unverfügbarkeit*) when touching oneself or another is always associated with an irritation of the individual.

Normally a person is in continual con-tact with the world via touch, as he/she is always touching and being touched through and with his/her own body. Thus, through his physical-sensual integration in the world, man is in a permanent silent dialogue with his environment, which creates a "surplus du sens" (see also Merleau-Ponty [12]) beyond the concrete, explainable level. This silent dialogue contains continuous offers and invitations of which people are not generally conscious. Thus the self should be understood less as a self-determined entity than as a "responding ego" (cf. Meyer-Drawe [14]) that cannot be seen as an autonomous entity in accordance with earlier conceptions of the subject, although it makes an impact as a responding actor.[4]

---

[4] This de-centring of the subject operates not only through language, as Derrida and many others have shown, but also through the physical-sensual integration of the subject in the world, as Merleau-Ponty had already demonstrated before post-structuralist debates began. However, such a de-centring should not be equated with the frequently cited "death of the subject", as the latter always remains an "ego" even if it is a "responding ego".

3 Communication as Eye Con-tact

Transferring this idea to communicative processes, every interaction proves to be an ambiguous event: a person acts, but not in pure self-determination, but always in the context of the other's expectations, which are expressed in many different ways.[5] Responsibility in interpersonal communication therefore means becoming aware of the demands of the communication partner and answering to them. Furthermore, the strangeness and particularity of the other, which becomes apparent through his or her claims, has to be accepted without trying to integrate the other in the personal horizon of images and expectations.

Traditional sender-receiver models of communicative processes, according to which an actor sends a particular message, which the addressee receives in the way intended by the actor, have long been discredited. This is not only because a self-determined function that generates meaning is attributed to the recipient of the message, i.e. he/she interprets the message communicated in the context of his/her specific social embeddedness. Such one-sided models have been replaced by reciprocal concepts and the actor is interpreted as always already re-acting.

The following will relate this element of reciprocity to touch/contact in the sense of eye con-tact. Initially, the interaction of two physically present persons will serve as the starting point for my reflections. Contact can become virulent in different ways here: firstly, in concrete, physically realized and immediately perceptible contact; secondly, in a more metaphorical sense, e.g. when a glance (fleetingly) touches me. As well as concrete experience of touch and touching action, glances namely evoke the type of responsiveness typical of communication; see also Mersch [13]. The glance of another (and his/her voice) triggers something, before and alongside all explicit linguistic communication, to which a person reacts implicitly as a communicator. A glance can entice, pressurize, seduce, arouse feelings and be the spark kindling further interest in each other. Accordingly expressions are to be found in everyday speech such as "provoking", "challenging", "inflaming", "hurtful" looks or "touching", "alluring", "war" or "cold" glances – all attributes that point to the touching and challenging significance of eye contact. Thus eye contact frequently opens communicative dialogue, invites, makes demands, encourages or discourages. Glances attract and seduce, but can also establish boundaries and reject con-tact. Eye contact is always tied to the participation of the seer, even in apparently indifferent/ uninvolved seeing. "Looking and looking away mean more than mere seeing or not seeing", cf. Waldenfels [18], p. 125. Looks are also disturbing and disquieting; they attack us, strike us immediately, and call for re-actions.[6]

Thus a person's own glance, aroused by the person opposite, is always performed in the view of others, whereby glance and sight or "seeing and being seen" intersect[7] and in the course of this intersection create a gap which cannot be closed; see also

---

[5] This fundamental idea of the constitution of individuality in an intersubjective context was taken up by Mead [11] in a sociological context, but only peripherally related to physical embeddedness in the world.

[6] Again, see Mersch [13] on the significance of glances evoking dialogue in art, also Boehm [5].

[7] Merleau-Ponty [12] refers to this as chiasmus.

Waldenfels [18], p. 128. Being looked at[8] corresponds to the return of a look – both are inseparably interconnected and correspond to the amalgamation already described in the context of touch. As with the experience of touch, the exchange of looks as a communicative act clearly shows the moment of responsiveness that characterizes interpersonal communication: I look and am looked at to the same extent. I am constituted in the glance of the other just as he is configured in mine.

Thus meeting glances, in the same way as concrete touching, evoke a continual dialogism that cannot be made available to reflection. An affection that differentiates the visual from the discursive always plays a role in looks, because a look has an appellative character (see also Boehm [5]). It arises from mutual referentiality, which unfolds in an implicit way, beyond all linguistic exchange. This referentiality is multi-layered, as the other's glance not only calls for an answer but also places limits on occupative desire with a definite reminder of its own claims. Furthermore, a look demands recognition and respect: "respect has to do with attentiveness, consideration and respect, in the way that the French word 'regard' connects a look to something that affects us" (Waldenfels [18], p. 130). Thus as well as any explicit formulation, a claim is expressed in a look, to which we respond when we encounter the gaze of another (Waldenfels [18], p. 131).

In the following I will examine this moment of responsiveness in more detail, as the issue of responsibility can be made particularly clear here.

4 Responsiveness as Responsibility

Everyone is familiar with this situation: one is walking through town, a homeless person asks for money, glances do not usually meet, and at most one just throws some money into the receptacle held out. The situation is soon forgotten, any possible responsibility has been evaded.

How different is the situation when glances meet, when one person does not refuse to look at the other: the mutual gaze calls for a response, compels some sort of reaction, provokes a possible dialogue. If one returns the look, a responsive event occurs in the sense introduced above: ones take responsibility for the situation by responding to the look. This is intensified the moment hands are offered to be shaken.

Zygmunt Bauman [2] and Emanuel Levinas [9] similarly emphasize the relevance of the touching look for interpersonal relations. Their theory is that people acknowledge each other mutually with looks; by returning looks they enter into a reciprocal happening, as one reacts to the claims of the other manifest in the look and one first constitutes oneself as an individual by means of the resulting responsibility.

Touch and looks that touch thus create a form of responsive referentiality, from which a form of interpersonal responsibility can develop. Refusal to be touched by the other, in a concrete or metaphysical sense, can therefore be interpreted as a rejection of this responsibility. It is not without reason that one retreats from the demanding look of a person seeking help and avoids eye contact when making a donation, in order to avoid confrontation with the claims of the other and the acceptance of the

---

[8] This is true not only for the exchange of looks between people but also for things, for which Merlau-Ponty [12] assumes that one can feel looked at by them.

associated responsibility And this rejection is even more marked in the case of physical contact, as it breaks through the cognitive delineation of a boundary between the "ego" and others is an even more obvious manner.

This responsibility not only refers to the moment of reciprocity, which involves the recognition of the other as an equal counterpart, but also implies the acceptance of his otherness and unavailable character (*Unverfügbarkeit*). In touching the other and letting oneself be touched, the unavailable character (*Unverfügbarkeit*) of his otherness becomes apparent in a subtly subversive manner. This can neither be wholly "incorporated"[9] into one's own horizons of meaning through the production of hallucinations of symbiosis, nor can the otherness of the counterpart be ignored or glossed over – it is manifest in the touching glance as in the physical experience of touch. Thus touch breaks through imaginary unions and illusory understandings at the point where the difference of the other creates fissures and breaks in one's experience and exposes these illusions of symbiosis as occupation fantasies.

A similar argument is presented by Ouaknin [15], p. 129, who refers to an "ethics of delicate touch", following on from Levinas [9]. He means not only the physical act of touching, which in its potential delicacy should not have any possessive characteristics and can thus implicitly demonstrate recognition of the other.[10] Rather, it serves as a metaphor for a form of mutual referentiality based on mutual recognition of difference. Accordingly, Levinas describes love as a phenomenon in which the insurmountable otherness of the lovers is recognized and accepted. "The passion of desire consists in being together. Here, the other as someone different is not an object that becomes ours or that we become; in contrast, it retreats into its mystery" (Levinas [10], p. 57).

It cannot be denied that looks and tactile contacts may have a possessive nature: this is true both of the voyeuristic look and the occupative touch. Looks and touch are not infrequently accompanied by the wish to reduce the other to an object of one's own intentions and desires. But such attempts at incorporation[11] meet a limitation in interaction between physically present persons at the point where in touching and looking the unavailable character (*Unverfügbarkeit*) of the other ultimately becomes evident, stopped by the resistance of physical-material otherness. In returning or refusing to return a look and in the duality of touch, the claims of the other emerge in a subtly subversive manner, beyond the reach of any possessive intentions.

5 Meetings in Virtual Space

If we examine communication processes in virtual space in the light of the above discussion, the non-presence of the body is the first remarkable point, implying the absence of physical touch and eye contact. Tactility in virtual space, although sometimes conjured up as a new potential, has a different character there than in concrete contact. While the boundaries of tactile experience are immediately obvious in

---

[9] Again, see Baumann [3] on dealing with the other. Baumann differentiates between an emic and a phagic strategy.

[10] I use the word "potential" to indicate that I do not wish to deny the existence of violent forms of contact.

[11] See also Baumann [3] on the assimilating appropriation of the other.

touching material objects or physical bodies, because the resistance of the other's materiality is not perceptible in virtual space or is only created by elaborate artificial means, the issue of con-tacts via looks and touch is somewhat different for communication processes in the Internet.

In the following I will discuss the problem of responsiveness in Internet communication, emphasizing the question of mutual responsibility. Communication as a responsive event, where we react to the implicit and explicit claims of the other in the same way that we make our own claims, can be enacted in real-world contexts using physical and linguistic means of expression. In spite of multimedia aids (webcams, photographs, sound, video conferencing...), we are largely dependent on text as a communication medium in the Internet.

The claim to mutual respect that is manifest in mutual eye contact and reciprocal touch when shaking hands or hugging, is largely absent in the Internet. This poses the following question: does the feeling of responsibility for the other discussed above still develop when the challenging look is absent and reciprocal communication is not guaranteed by the physical presence of the communication partner?

It appears expedient here to look back briefly at traditional forms of communication that were also characterized by the non-presence of the participants. The romantic love letter serves as a link that was also characterized by the physical absence of the interaction partners as the lovers had to declare their feelings from a distance while simultaneously attempting to create closeness through letters and texts in order to evoke with language the dimension of touching and being touched[12] that was discussed above.

Usually the discourse of love is characterized by many non-verbal signs: seductive, enticing eye contact, gently caressing glances, different types of touch, gestures, small movements. In epistolary correspondence, this great variety of physical declarations of love has to be replaced by language, which clearly can hardly succeed. Thus it is not surprising that romantic love letters were permeated by a "myth of the unsayable": the descriptions of feelings often subsided into silence, with empty spaces in the text and a declaration of the impossibility of describing the writer's deeply felt emotions; for a more detailed discussion see Landfester [8].

The wise insight that language is too easily subject to conventions and cultural clichés and thereby likely to betray the uniqueness of one's own experience and the loving relationship which is experienced as being unique, is manifest in this refusal to describe feelings. Thus the silent subject retreated from the self-alienation that would automatically have set in if he/she had expressed him/herself in the normative language patterns of his/her epoch.

This myth of unsayability had another function as well as this very important one: it assumed a unity of the discourse partners, a form of successful communication. The resulting illusory fiction of consensus (see Landfester [8]) could be maintained so long as the partners did not have physical contact. In the moment of physical contact these imaginary constructs were often destroyed, because the other could no longer so easily serve as a surface onto which one's own fantasies could be projected, but made claims to recognition of his/her otherness through looks and touch. Through touch and

---

[12] Touch proves to be an essential moment of emotionality here, as is clear from the correspon--ding attributes (touched, to be moved).

looks the linguistically configured fiction of symbiosis was perforated, fissures appeared in the structure of the imaginary constellation of the relationship. Through reciprocal looks and touch the largely linguistically generated illusion of consensus is broken down, because the difference of the other is irrevocably stated by his/her physical presence.

This otherness/difference and unavailability (*Unverfügbarkeit*) of the beloved object is equally manifest in the challenging glance which seeks recognition and in physical, tactile experience; it leads to a disruption of the fictional picture and thus to irritation and fear. The human craving referred to by Ricoeur [16] to understand the other only from one's own point of view and thereby to reduce him to an object, comes up against limiting factors in concrete encounters. In an epistolary discourse of love, the other often merely serves/served as the object of the writer's own passion; the lover is more in love with his/her own passion than with the other person. Desire is projected back from the love object as a phenomenon and thus to one's own desire. Barthes [1] summarizes this phenomenon beautifully under the heading "loving love": "It suffices that I perceive the other in a flash as a type of inert, as it were stuffed object, in order to lead my desire for this devalued object back to my desire itself; it is my desire that I desire and the loved being is no more than its accomplice". If the loving subject is aware of this role of the imaginary in the discourse of love, he/she will avoid contact with the loved object if only because this desire will be thwarted by the independent claims of the other in a concrete encounter and reciprocal contact.

To what extent are these aspects described for epistolary discourses of love applicable to contacts in virtual space? An examination of studies of communication processes in the Internet shows highly varied scenarios. Whether people already know each other and maintain an existing connection through emails, or communicate anonymously in contact forums or "chat rooms" – these are very specific contexts with different conditions and problems. As at most one specific communication scenario can be analyzed in the framework of this brief essay, I will concentrate on so-called contact forums where people communicate who did not know each other initially. Communication in such forums is mostly text-based, although increasingly photographs are exchanged after the initial contact. These are, however, only relevant for a first impression and play almost no role in the actual communication process; see also Döhring's [7] detailed discussion. Let us look first as some characteristics of this type of communication scenario.

According to Döhring [7], p. 456, three types of contact forum can be identified:

- Thematically oriented on-topic online forums
- Sociable off-topic online forums (social networking)
- Online games involving several people

In the analysis of the contact forums, asynchronous and synchronous forms should be differentiated: the former take place with a time lag, the latter simultaneously. A differentiation can also be made with regard to the users' intentions: social networking sites are usually used to find a partner for communication, love or sex, while thematically oriented contact forums more usually facilitate the exchange of information and discussion of specific issues via the Internet, and contact is made by the participants with the aims of pursuing a thematically-oriented exchange. While communication on social networking sites is usually asynchronous (feedback relating to a personal ad can have a time lag), contact forums are usually synchronous (communication in flirting chats is simultaneous and is more like a meeting in a disco or a pub).

Let us look first the numerous social networking sites where people look openly for a partner, usually with a textual self-presentation. Although dramatic successes on these sites are frequently reported, the proportion of disappointments should not be underestimated. According to a study by Bühler-Ilieva and Geser (cited after Döhring [7]), 45% of the users of a Swiss dating site claim to have fallen in love on the basis of a first email contact. This "love at first click" (Döhring [7], p. 451) obviously has considerable potential for disappointment, as it is based to a considerable extent on projections and fantasies and its desire demonstrates characteristics of the state of being in love described above.

Overall, the number of lasting or reliable Internet contacts is surprisingly low in relation to the supposed level of Internet communication. Some surveys do indeed show that very active Internet users claim to have formed at least one or even more close social relationship in this way. This statement is relativized, however, when general Internet users are questioned. Here only 14% of those surveyed claimed to have made a friendship through Internet communication. Although the absence of a physical presence is often initially described as relaxing and liberating,[13] this absence involves fundamental problems that will be described later in more detail.

Internet contact processes, especially in contact forums, enable both active and passive participation. Thus it is possible to join in directly in an existing communication process or first to observe the communicative process from the "outside" and to join in at what appears to be a suitable point. Some Internet users concentrate on particular individuals in their attempts to make contact and address them specifically.[14] This form of initial contact, which is naturally mostly in written form, replaces the eye contact usual in a real world context, by means of which reciprocal interest is often primarily expressed.

One question that repeatedly emerges here concerns the degree of commitment in such communicative processes. Many Internet users describe the easy and relaxed nature of such communication processes, which are often more intensive and intimate as the participants' physical absence and anonymity makes them less shy and fearful. In this respect Internet communication is frequently described as particularly attractive for people who are socially excluded and disadvantaged. However, on the other hand this very anonymity and lack of physical presence are seen as the reasons why communication is often abruptly terminated, and the communicating persons apparently do not develop any real sense of responsibility for the other person or the relationship thus developed. Furthermore, partnerships and love stories via Internet are often characterized by unexpected break-offs which are not justified sufficiently; see also Döhring [7].

In this context the following observation is of interest: with regard to the question as to why people can express themselves more freely and in a less inhibited way in

---

[13] In this way shy or physically handicapped people in particular can express themselves all the more "freely" when they can deal competently and confidently with the vari ous possibilities for masquerading in the Internet.

[14] This corresponds with findings in studies by Turkle [17] and Becker and Mark [4].

the Internet, it has been said that in this case one does not have to look one's communication partner in the eye and that one therefore feels less pressure to evaluate or act (Döhring [7], p. 460). This statement is of considerable significance in the context of the issue central to this article and the facts described above. The physical presence of the communicators, in particular eye contact, is apparently a significant precondition for the development of a reciprocal sense of responsibility and prevents communication from being terminated without giving a reason. Although we discovered in a study of Internet communication and the conventions identifiable in this context (see Becker and Mark [4]) that there is an unspoken agreement among the participants, according to which the termination of contacts should always be explained, nevertheless in practice this only occurred when people had established a long-term contact, i.e. a certain degree of commitment had developed. Surveys showed that this usually occurred when the communicators had had personal contact through telephone conversations and/or reciprocal visits.

If this is not the case, the absence of challenging eye contact makes it possible to refuse to accept responsibility for the communicative relationship. Messages are written to a counterpart, but their implicit claims and demands such as are especially manifest in looks and touch, are not really perceived. This also means that the otherness and independence of the counterpart can be ignored in favour of one's own projections.

Accordingly, an illusory fiction of consensus, described above in the context of epistolary contact, frequently occurs in Internet communication (see also Turkle [17], Döhring [7]) and is a possible explanation for the regularly described disappointment of the communication partners when they meet in the real world.

Of particular relevance in this context is the degree of responsibility that the people in contact have for each other. The glance of the other, through which one feels touched beyond speech and which in this way calls for dialogue and evokes a responsive relationship between the communicating individuals, is absent in Internet communication. It is replaced by projective imaginations and fantasies: the other is thereby integrated in one's own scheme of things not as a specific other with his/her own ways of thinking and seeing, but rather as a product of one's own fantasies. Language, and especially the brief and rapidly produced language of the Internet, has a wide range of possibilities for projection that are also present in face-to-face communication but which are often contradicted by looks and gestures there. In the Internet the linguistic statements of the other are interpreted primarily from one's own perspective, whereby the absence of the physical presence of the other facilitates such projections.

Thus in the Internet a form of communication often seems to exist which Ricoeur [16] has described in another context as the "desire of the ego... to see the other primarily from one's own perspective", i.e. the desire to possess and make the other into an object. While looking and touching can break through the phantasmagorical impression of understanding and unity, as they create fissures in the linguistically configured unified space, the communicative reduction to language – as in the romantic letter – is always accompanied by the danger of succumbing to one's own idea of the other and ultimately supporting one's own perceptions and feelings instead of accepting the unavailable (*unverfügbar*) difference of the other.

However, responsibility in the sense discussed above would mean accepting the unavailable (*unverfügbar*) otherness of one's communication partner and sounding out and ultimately accepting the resulting boundaries to understanding. Firstly, responsibility in this sense means recognizing the illusory fictions of consensus that seem to develop more easily in virtual communication scenarios than in concrete, face-to-face interaction, as such and critically reflecting upon them. Secondly, responsibility means recognizing the difference of the other, who encounters one with his/her own claims and in the response to which one first constitutes oneself as a subject.

It could easily be supposed that Internet communication, seen from this point of view, becomes problematic where it is more a monologue than a dialogue, and responsibility for the other, through which the individual always also constitutes him/herself (cp. Bauman [2] and Levinas [10]), cannot develop.

Another aspect is worth to be mentioned here: More and more Internet communication takes place via ECAs (Embodied Conversational Agents), which simulate by their mimic and gestures a kind of personality. This illusion especially poses a problem if children are not aware of the fact that their communication counterparts in virtual spaces are artefacts.

Although the risk of a resulting irresponsibility cannot be denied, I would like to end with the observation that some of the problems discussed here can be offset by learning appropriate "media competence". If one is aware of the projective-illusory dimension of communication which accompanies every communicative act and is possible more pronounced in the Internet and is especially relevant when Internet contacts are not supplemented by concrete contacts involving the physical presence of the actors, then such contacts can indeed have the frequently described positive effects. However, in order to develop the sense of responsibility for each other which is ultimately the foundation for solidarity, the form of responsiveness that develops most often in concrete encounters,[15] where the challenging glance is reciprocated and one allows oneself to be touched by the other.

Even if there are a lot of open questions which cannot be answered in this context, I would like to end with a final remark: Learning to take responsibility for the other in interpersonal communication is the basis for democratic societies where the individuals are respecting each other and where their personal particularities are accepted. Internet communication takes the risk of ignoring this because it opens spaces of imagination where the communication partner can be constructed corresponding personal expectations more easily than in face-to-face interaction.

References

1. Barthes, R.: Fragmente einer Sprache der Liebe. Frankfurt: Suhrkamp (1984)
2. Bauman, Z.: Postmodern Ethics. Basil Blackwell, Cambridge (1993)
3. Bauman, Z.: Liquid Modernity. Polity Press, Cambridge (2000)
4. Becker, B., Mark, G.: Social Conventions in Computer-Mediated Communication. In: Schroeder, R. (ed.) The Social Life of Avatars, Springer, London (2001)

---

[15] Of course, responsibility can develop in other ways than in concrete interaction, but physical touching and being touched are a fundamental basis for its development.

5. Boehm, G.: Der stumme Logos. In: Metraux, A., Waldenfels, B. (eds.) Leibhaftige Vernunft. München, Wilhelm Fink Verlag (1986)
6. De Kerkhove, D.: Propriodezeption und Autonomation. In: Tasten, Schriftenreihe Forum der Kunst- und Ausstellungshalle der BRD, vol. 7, Bonn (1996)
7. Döhring, N.: Sozialpsychologie des Internet. Hogrefe Verlag, Göttingen (2003)
8. Landfester, U.: Von der Liebe zur Konsenshalluzination. In: Thiedeke, U. (ed.) Soziologie des Cyberspace, Verlag für Sozialwissenschaften, Wiesbaden (2004)
9. Levinas, E.: Die Spur des Anderen. Freiburg/Munich, Alber (1983)
10. Levinas, E.: Die Zeit und der Andere. Hamburg: Felix Meiner. [Engl.: Time and the Other. Trans. Richard A. Cohen, Pittsburgh, PA. Duquesne University Press (1989)
11. Mead, G.H.: Mind, Self, and Society. In: Morris, C.W. (ed.), University of Chicago Press, Chicago (1934)
12. Merleau-Ponty, M.: The Visible and the Invisible (trans. Lingis). Northwestern University Press, Evanston (1968)
13. Mersch, D.: Ereignis und Aura. Untersuchungen zur einer Ästhetik des Performativen. Suhrkamp, Frankfurt (2002)
14. Meyer-Drawe, K.: Illusionen von Autonomie. Kirchheim, Weinheim (1990)
15. Ouaknin, M.-A.: Meditations érotiques: essai sur Emmanuel Levinas. Balland, Paris (1992)
16. Ricoeur, P.: Oneself as Another (translated by Kathleen Blamey). The University of Chicago Press, Chicago (1992)
17. Turkle, S.: Life on the Screen: Identity in the Age of the Internet. Simon & Schuster, New York (1995)
18. Waldenfels, B.: Sinnesschwellen. Suhrkamp, Frankfurt (1999)
19. Waldenfels, B.: Bruchlinien der Erfahrung. Suhrkamp, Frankfurt (2002)

True Emotion vs. Social Intentions in Nonverbal Communication: Towards a Synthesis for Embodied Conversational Agents

Jonathan Gratch

University of Southern California
gratch@ict.usc.edu

Abstract. Does a facial expression convey privileged information about a person's mental state or is it a communicative act, divorced from "true" beliefs, desires and intentions? This question is often cast as a dichotomy between competing theoretical perspectives. Theorists like Ekman argue for the primacy of emotion as a determinant of nonverbal behavior: emotions "leak" and only indirectly serve social ends. In contrast, theorists such as Fridlund argue for the primacy of social ends in determining nonverbal displays. This dichotomy has worked to divide virtual character research. Whereas there have been advances in modeling emotion, this work is often seen as irrelevant to the generation of communicative behavior. In this chapter, I review current findings on the interpersonal function of emotion. I'll discuss recent developments in Social Appraisal theory as a way to bridge this dichotomy and our attempts to model these functions within the context of embodied conversational agents.

Keywords: emotion, nonverbal behavior, virtual humans, cognitive modeling.

1 Introduction

Do facial expressions convey privileged information about a person's mental state or are they communicative acts, independent of a person's actual beliefs, desires and intentions? This question is often cast as a dichotomy between competing theoretical accounts of nonverbal behavior. On the one hand, theorists such as Ekman [2] or Frank [3] argue for the primacy of emotion as a determinant of nonverbal behavior: emotions "leak" through our behaviors and convey true information about our current beliefs and feelings, which only indirectly serve social ends. On the other hand, *social intentions* theorists such as Fridlund [4] or Chovil [5] argue for the primacy of social ends as the determinant of nonverbal displays: organisms use displays strategically to satisfy their social intentions and any strong connections between displays and true feelings would unnecessarily restrict their flexibility in responding to life's demands.

This dichotomy between the emotional and communicative origins of nonverbal displays is reflected in virtual character research. Whereas there has been considerable advances in modeling emotions and giving virtual characters the ability to derive situationally appropriate emotions, this work is often seen as irrelevant to the

I. Wachsmuth and G. Knoblich (Eds.): Modeling Communication, LNAI 4930, pp. 181–197, 2008.
© Springer-Verlag Berlin Heidelberg 2008

generation of communicative nonverbal behavior [6][1]. Communicative agent research has focused almost exclusively on the role of nonverbal displays in conveying propositional content or in managing conversational flow. Behaviors are typically tied to a *conversational function model* [7, 8] that represents the specific communicative functions required to support effective face-to-face conversation. Functions, such as initiating a conversational turn or emphasizing a word, are associated with nonverbal behaviors, such as looking repeatedly at another person or raising one's eyebrows, respectively. When emotional behaviors are included in such models, they are typically associated with a specific communicative function divorced from any emotional state associated with the agent. For example, Poggi and Pelachaud [9] use emotional expressions to convey the performative of a speech act, showing "potential anger" to communicate that social consequences will ensue if a request is not fulfilled. Indeed, consistent with Fridlund's view, tying emotional behaviors to an agent's motivational state (such as one exists), could limit a system designer's ability to create effective interactions (see [6]). For example, a tutoring agent that displayed frustration at a student's repeated failures could work against the goal of promoting student engagement.[2] Disassociating emotional display from motivational state could, conceivably, create superhuman agents that strategically select nonverbal displays based purely on their communicative impact, unburdened by any "emotional baggage."

The trend to discount emotion models in communicative agent research has been reinforced by the intrapsychic focus of most computational emotion research. Motivated by findings on emotion's functional role in cognitive processes, research on computational models of emotion have explored emotion's function in decision-making [12, 13], learning [14] and coping with environmental stressors [15]. These models explore the relationship between emotion and goal directed behavior, often providing detailed models of how emotions arise from a calculation of the personal significance of external events in terms of an agent's beliefs, desires and intentions. To the extent that computational models of emotion have focused on social behavior, the focus has been on general notions such as believability or empathy [16], rather than on specific socially-strategic functions. When the social function of emotion is considered at all in this work, the (typically unspoken) assumption is that model-driven behaviors can convey important social information without an explicit need to deeply model the communicative function of these behaviors (i.e., conveying true emotional states serves social ends), though this argument is rarely developed in any detail.

In this chapter, I will review current findings on the interpersonal function of emotions and their potential role in communication. I will discuss some recent developments in *social appraisal theory* [17, 18] as a way to reconcile the true emotion and

---

[1] Also Justine Cassell and Matthew Stone, personal communication.

[2] Interestingly, the closest to an integration of communicative and emotional approaches comes in the area of tutoring. Lester's COSMO system associates pedagogical communicative acts with appraisals of student performance [10]. For example, COSMO responds with admiration when the student succeeds. In my view, this approach is best seen a purely strategic model that happens to exploit a model of the student's emotions in its strategic calculations. Elliott, Rickel and Lester [11] subsequently proposed a more ambitious synthesis that begins to address the themes I explore here. Unfortunately, this work was never developed further.

social intentions views of nonverbal behavior. I will then discuss our attempts to model these functions within the context of embodied conversational agents.

2 Social Emotions

Emotions are highly social. They can arise from our understanding of the social context, impact our behavior in ways that communicate our beliefs, desires and intentions to social partners, elicit social responses that alter the social context and, thus, transform our initial emotional response. In contrast to the view that emotions interfere with rational thought, recent scholarship has emphasized the adaptive nature of many emotional responses, including their role in social interactions [19-24].

The *social functional view* of emotion emphasizes the utilitarian role of emotions in social cognition and communication [19]. This view hypothesizes that humans evolved to survive through social relationships and emotions are a fundamental building block of effective social interactions. On the one hand, emotions inform and direct cognitive processes in ways that help us successfully navigate social interactions. On the other, emotional displays influence the behaviors of others by transmitting coordinating information and eliciting adaptive social responses. In contrast to Fridlund's social intentions view, the social functional view hypothesizes a tight coupling between emotional processes and emotional behavior – we display what we feel – and this rapid, involuntary and authentic nature of emotional displays is, in fact, necessary for facilitating coordination and group cohesion.

Several findings suggest that emotions help inform and motivate social decision making. It is generally accepted that emotions help inform the individual of personally significant events and recruit the cognitive and physical resources necessary to adaptively respond. Emotions such as love, guilt, shame or anger inform us about the quality of our social relationships [19]. For example, feelings of love signal our level of commitment to another, whereas anger informs us of threats to the righteousness of our own perspective [25]. Beyond informing us of the quality of the interaction, social emotions also prepare our minds and bodies to respond to the social environment. For example, anger alters our social perceptions, sensitizing us to the injustices of others [26], and triggers physiological changes, moving blood from the internal organs towards the hands and arms in preparation of physical confrontation [19]. Finally, emotions serve as rewards or punishments, reinforcing social behavior and promoting the formation of group bonds, loyalty and identity. Trusting others actually feels good: Studies by Zak [27] suggest that acts of trust, such as cooperating on simple social games such as the Prisoner's Dilemma, lead to the release of hormones implicated in the formation of social bonds – whereas harming others feels bad – anticipatory guilt and shame help enforce social norms [20, 28].

Whereas emotion may promote adaptive social decisions, displays of emotion often promote adaptive social responses in others. On the one hand, displays provide important coordinating information to other social partners [18, 21]. Our reactions to events convey important information about our interpretations of events – an undesired stimulus might result in a frown; an unexpected one might result in an expression of surprise – and thus indirectly convey information about how we are evaluating our situation vis-à-vis our current beliefs, desires, and intentions. They communicate our relationship with other social partners (e.g., through dominance or submission displays). On the other hand, displays of emotion seem to reflexively elicit adaptive social responses from others. Emotional behaviors are highly salient and, through affective priming [29], automatically alter perceptions and judgments. Emotional displays further trigger behavioral responses. Anger, for example, can elicit fear-related responses (even subliminal presentation) [30] or serve as a demand for someone to change the course of their interaction [31], distress can elicit sympathy [32], and joy seems to invite social interaction [33]. Many of these responses seem almost automatic and visceral and to have similar functions across a wide range of social animals [22].

Although the emotional and strategic views of emotional behavior agree that such displays help achieve social ends, they differ markedly in terms of their origins. The social functional view argues that there is considerable social utility in conveying our true feelings and that the social power of such displays, in fact, depends on their authenticity. Although there are certainly social circumstances that demand deception, arguably the vast majority of our social interactions are more mundane, where communication of true feelings and intentions is of mutual benefit. Whether you're a New Yorker navigating a busy sidewalk or a great ape finding your place in the social hierarchy, life presents us with numerous split-second decisions on how to respond to a continuously moving social landscape. In such situations, "reading" the minds of social partners can smooth interactions and avoid unnecessary "collisions." More substantial decisions, like our choice of friends, mates, or research collaborators, would yield greater mutual benefit if parties had privileged access to (at least some of) each other's beliefs and intentions. Indeed, game theorists have shown formally how so-called *commitment problems* -- where parties would receive higher utility by cooperating but choose not to based on concerns about deception (e.g., prisoner's dilemma) -- could be solved if true feelings and intentions could be divined from each other's observable behavior [3]. The social functional view of emotion argues that "authentic" emotional displays evolved because they give a selective advantage to social animals that could read each others thoughts and, thus, solve commitment problems to their mutual benefit. Consistent with this view, studies have shown that people that interact with each other before games like the prisoner's dilemma do a reasonable job at predicting the true intentions of their partners [34, 35]. This claim is further supported by findings suggesting that emotion displays play an important role in the development of mind-reading skills: discrepancies between felt emotion and other's responses to events draws attention to differences between self and other, stimulating the development of perspective taking [36], theory of mind [37] and sense of self [38]; moreover early deficits in the ability to produce or decode emotional displays may contribute to social deficits such as autism [39].

This tight, necessary, coupling between emotion and display posited by the social functional view of emotion is a major point of controversy in nonverbal behavior research and has stimulated a large body of research both supporting and contradicting this contention. Social intention theorists point to well-replicated findings illustrating how emotional displays change depending on the social context (i.e., depending on if one is alone or with friends or strangers), culture and ones social goals and intentions [40-42]. These theorists emphasize the primacy of social motives and intentions in determining facial expressions, downplaying or even discounting the role

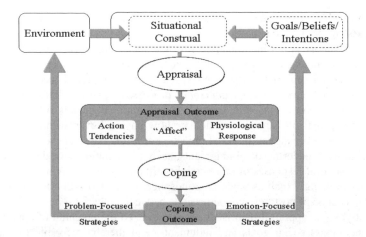

Fig. 1. Schematic view of appraisal theory, adapted from Smith and Lazarus [1]

of emotion. Emotion theorists explain away such findings by positing a separate downstream process that filters true emotion through a set of *display rules* that attenuate the expressions depending on contextual factors [2]. In the next section, I turn to social appraisal theories of emotion that attempt to reconcile these perspectives without appeal to two-process models. Social appraisal theories emphasize the importance of the social context, social goals and intentions in our experience of emotion, suggesting this controversy arises from a false dichotomy and holding the promise of a synthesis of emotional and communicative perspectives on nonverbal behavior.

3   Social Appraisal Theory

The (false) dichotomy between communicative and emotional views of nonverbal behavior in social agents has been reinforced by the apparent intrapsychic focus of emotion theories and the computation models they have inspired. Appraisal theory [e.g., 43], a dominant theoretical perspective on emotion and view most influential in the design of cognitive models involving emotional processes, treats emotion as largely an intrapersonal, self-centered process (see [17]). Appraisal theory has heavily influenced computational research on emotion as it treats emotion as a form of information processing, providing a concrete specification of how emotion both arises from and influences cognitive processes (see Figure 1). Appraisal theory emphasizes the role of individual judgments in the elicitation and differentiation of emotional responses, specifically judgments, deemed *appraisal variables or checks*, that characterize aspects of the personal significance of events (e.g., was this event expected in terms of my prior beliefs? is this event congruent with my goals; do I have the power to alter the consequences of this event?). Patterns of appraisal elicit emotional behavior, but they also trigger stereotypical cognitive responses formalized as qualitatively distinct *coping strategies* (e.g., planning, procrastination or resignation). These responses, in turn, alter the individual's subsequent judgments concerning their relationship to the environment, emphasizing a view of emotion as a dynamic, unfolding process closely tied to cognition.

Appraisal theory is not incompatible with the social functional view of emotion – individuals can hold social goals and appraise the social consequences of events – however, many appraisal theorists, and virtually all of appraisal theory's computational derivatives, emphasize *intrapersonal* processes and the relationship between individual goals and events. For example, computational models often incorporate complex reasoning mechanisms to calculate how physical events impact an individual's beliefs or desires about physical objects, but rarely consider the inferential machinery that must underlie social judgments, such as reputation. Nor do they consider how the behavioral responses of others might influence one's evolving understanding of a social exchange, such as when an atmosphere of antagonism arises from the reciprocal exchange of postures and expressions between potential rivals [18].

Recently, some appraisal theorists have emphasized the potential of appraisal theory to encompass social goals and judgments, and thereby reconcile the apparent contradictions between the emotional and social intentions views of nonverbal displays [17, 18, 44]. At the heart of this argument is the realization that many of the factors that social intention theorists point to as mediators of nonverbal displays (e.g., social motives, social goals, power, status, and cultural norms) are crucial for assessing the personal significance of events, should influence the appraisal process, and thus should play a central role in an organism's emotional response. Thus, social appraisal theorists do not deny the importance of social intentions in communicative behavior. Rather, they emphasize the centrality of these factors in producing an emotional response, and thereby influence external behavior.

Smith et al. [17] illustrate the social appraisal perspective by considering the problems raised by social emotions such as embarrassment. Appraisal theories have tended to downplay distinctions between certain social emotions such as guilt, shame and embarrassment. However, recent scholarship has emphasized important differences regarding when displays of shame and embarrassment are elicited and the social functions they seem to serve [45]. Guilt seems to involve transgressions that violate internal standards whereas shame and embarrassment seem to arise from the perceived negative evaluations of self by others. Shame and embarrassment seem further distinguished in that shame involves situations where both self and other agree that the transgression represents a fundamental character flaw, whereas embarrassment involves a temporary condition that might be (mis)perceived as a more fundamental flaw. For example, a shy individual might find it difficult to sing in public, and feel embarrassment that their poor performance might be viewed as an inherent defect in their singing ability. Consistent with the social intentions view, these displays seem to be strategically employed. For example Leary, Landel, and Patton [46] showed that participants exhibited less embarrassment and reported feeling less embarrassed after singing aloud in public when they believed that the experimenter already knew they were uncomfortable. Leary et al. [46] argue this result illustrates that embarrassment serves self-presentational ends and therefore ceases to be necessary once these ends are fulfilled.

Adopting a social appraisal perspective, Smith et al. [17] argue that distinctions between emotions such as shame and embarrassment can be handled within appraisal theory with some greater attention to social goals and social inferences. Embarrassment involves the appraisal of a social goal –i.e., reputation or self-presentation – which may or may not be threatened, depending on the inferences formed by others. Although requiring more complex inference than typically considered in computational models of appraisal, such social appraisals could be incorporated into computational appraisal models, facilitating a synthesis of communicative and emotional views of nonverbal behavior. I now consider the implications of this perspective within our own work on the EMA computational appraisal model.

4 Computational Models

EMA is a computational model of the cognitive antecedents and consequences of emotion as posited by appraisal theory [15, 47, 48]. As in many computational models based on appraisal theory, EMA emphasizes the role of individual goals and judgments in emotional processes.[3] Here I discuss the extent to which EMA supports social appraisal theory and suggest some straightforward extensions that can increase the relevance of such models to designers of communicative agents.

In translating appraisal theory into a concrete computational model of emotional processes, EMA draws extensively on common artificial intelligent methods of reasoning and representation. EMA must represent the agent's relationship to its environment and capture the dynamics of processes involved in interpretation (appraisal) and manipulation (coping) of this representation. To this end, EMA represents the relationship between events and an agent's internal beliefs desires and intentions by building on AI planning to represent the physical relationship between events and their consequences, and BDI frameworks to represent the epistemic factors that underlie human (particularly social) activities.

Appraisal processes characterize this representation in terms of individual appraisal judgments. These extend traditional AI concerns with utility and probability:

- Desirability: what is the utility (positive or negative) of the event if it comes to pass.
- Likelihood: how probable is the outcome of the event.
- Causal attribution: who deserves credit/blame.
- Controllability: can the outcome be altered by actions under control of the agent.
- Changeability: can the outcome change on its own.

Patterns of appraisal elicit emotional displays, but they also initiate coping processes to regulate the agent's cognitive response to the appraised emotion. Coping strategies work in the reverse direction of appraisal, identifying plans, beliefs, desires or intentions to maintain or alter. These include "problem focused" strategies (e.g. planning) directed towards improving the world (the traditional concern of AI techniques) but also encompasses "emotion-focused" strategies that impact an agent's epistemic and motivational state:

---

[3] EMA is an evolution of earlier computational models that anticipated some of the social appraisals discussed below (see [see 49]).

- Planning: form an intention to perform some act (the planner uses intentions to drive its plan generation)
- Seek instrumental support: ask someone that is in control of an outcome for help
- Procrastination: wait for an external event to change the current circumstances
- Denial: lower the perceived likelihood of an undesirable outcome
- Mental disengagement: lower utility of desired state
- Shift blame: shift responsibility for an action toward some other agent

Strategies give input to the cognitive processes that actually execute these directives. For example, planful coping generates an intention to act, leading the planning system to generate and execute a valid plan to accomplish this act. Alternatively, coping strategies might abandon the goal, lower the goal's importance, or re-assess who is to blame.

EMA uses an explicit representation of plans, beliefs, desires and intentions to capture output and intermediate results of processes that relate the agent to its physical and social environment. This represents the agent's current view of the agent-environment relationship, which changes with further observation or inference. EMA treats appraisal as a mapping from syntactic features of this representation to individual appraisal variables. Multiple appraisals are aggregated into an overall emotional state that influences behavior. Coping directs control signals to auxiliary reasoning modules (i.e., planning, or belief updates) to overturn or maintain features of the representation that lead to individual appraisals. For example, coping may abandon a cherished desire in response to an uncontrollable threat.

Even with its intrapsychic focus, EMA has a broad effect on behavior of the embodied conversational agents with which it has been integrated [50, 51]. Mentally, it impacts their communicative motives and biases their interpretation of ambiguous events, including the user's speech. Physically, it affects what agents say and the accompanying gestures, postures and facial expressions.

4.1 Social Appraisals

Certain appraisal checks identified by appraisal theory presuppose some form of social inference. Specifically, emotions such as anger involve an appraisal of *causal* attribution – i.e., which causal agent is responsible and blame/creditworthy for an action. Appraisal theories differ in the level of detail to which they consider causal attributions but researchers that have examined such appraisals closely emphasize that they involve complex social inferences and theory of mind. People rarely use simple causal interpretations when explaining social actions. In contrast to how causality is used in the physical sciences, the judgment of responsibility is a multi-step process involving judgments of causality, foreseeability, intention, coercion and excuse [52, 53]. As in other appraisal checks, social attributions involve evaluating consequences of events with personal significance to an agent. The evaluation is always from a perceiving agent's perspective and the significance of the consequences is based on an individual perceiver's preferences. The perceiver uses her own knowledge about the observed agents and her observations to form beliefs about others knowledge, beliefs and motives when forming an overall judgment.

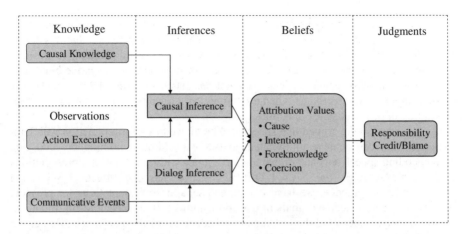

Fig. 2. Computational model of causal attribution

Although most computational appraisal models use simple criteria to assess causal attribution – and thereby sidestep the need for complex social judgments – Mao and Gratch have developed and empirically validated a detailed model of how people form such judgments (Figure 2), including not only causal factors, but also epistemic variables such as freedom of choice, intention and foreknowledge [54, 55]. As a result, an actor may physically cause an event, but be absolved of responsibility and blame, or conversely, blamed for what she did not physically cause.

Building on the causal representation used by EMA, which provides a concise description of the causal relationship between events and states and a clear structure for exploring alternative courses of actions, the model forms key inferences necessary to form attributions: recognizing the relevance of events to an agent's goals and plans (key for intention recognition), assessing an agent's freedom and choice in acting (key for assessing coercive situations) and detecting how an agent's plan facilitates or prevents the plan execution of other agents (key for detecting plan interventions).

The model derives attribution variables via inference over prior causal knowledge and observations, and uses beliefs of the variables to form an overall judgment. Two important sources of information contribute to the inference process. One source is the actions performed by the agents in social events (including physical acts and communicative acts). The other is the general causal knowledge about actions and world states. Causal inference reasons about beliefs from causal evidence. Dialogue inference derives beliefs from communicative evidence. Both inferences make use of commonsense knowledge and generate beliefs of attribution variables. These beliefs serve as inputs for the attribution process, which is described as an algorithm in our computational model. Finally, the algorithm forms an overall judgment and assigns proper credit or blame to the responsible agents.

4.2 Appraising Speech Acts and Communicative Goals

One limitation of EMA is its emphasis on physical actions and physical causality. EMA reasons about the relationship between physical actions and physical goals, allowing agents to appraise the individual and social consequence of past or future actions. For example, imagine that an EMA agent is about to defect against its cooperating partner in the Prisoner's Dilemma game. The model can reason that this action will achieve the agent's goal of maximizing monetary reward (leading to positive emotions) but harm the partner (leading the partner to experience negative emotions) and possibly involve negative personal emotions (such as guilt). User speech only impacts appraisal indirectly, as when a communication leads changes an agent's representation of physical states or actions.

Linguists have long argued that speech can be viewed as a form of action with consequences that can achieve or threaten goals [56]. Although nothing prevents one from encoding speech acts and communicative goals within the causal representations used by EMA (e.g., the SAY_I_DEFECT action has the effects I_WIN and YOU_LOSE), in practice, we have maintained separate representations for physical and communicative acts and goals in our applications [50, 51]. As a result, the agent doesn't directly understand the emotional consequences of its speech acts. Rather, an external dialogue manager produces the speech act and records its causal and epistemic consequences. Only then are these consequences made available to appraisal. In this sense, the agent doesn't anticipate and mitigate the emotional consequences of its speech, as posited, for example, by politeness theory [57].

Rather, appraisal models like EMA could use a uniform representation for physical and communicative acts. This will allow, for example, the agent to anticipate the social consequences of its speech and, for example, adopt mitigation strategies to deflect any negative effects for social partners (e.g., [58]).

4.3 Social Goals

EMA, like many appraisal models, reasons about the relationship between events and goals but doesn't make explicit distinctions between classes of goals. On the other hand, social appraisal theory argues that there are different classes of goals depending on the social considerations they involve. Some goals are purely individual and don't depend on other social actors for their satisfaction. Other goals are inherently social. For example, imagine an agent choosing whether to defect in a prisoner's dilemma game. This choice presumably impacts its individual goal of gaining material resources. It might threaten a social goal of acting fairly towards others. Finally, its choice might impact "second-order" goals such as "I want my partner to believe I'm fair." Social appraisal theories argue that threats to these goals lead to very different emotions: guilt or shame, respectively [17].

One place the connection between social goals and emotion has been explicitly considered is within the intelligent tutoring literature. For example, Elliott, Rickel and Lester [11] identify several goals a tutoring system should have including giving effective explanations about the subject domain, engaging the student, ensuring the student retains task knowledge, ensuring student exhibits proper caution towards hazardous situations. These goals are inherently social in that they cannot be achieved by the agent alone but requires cooperation by the student as well. Elliott et al propose specific emotional signals that might motivate the student to help achieve these goals.

In expanding such work, one organizing concept could be to map out how goals differ with respect to the social manipulations required to establish or repair them. For example, individual goals can be achieved by purely individual acts. Joint goals

(goals where both parties must contribute to its achievement) may require actions that impact the other party's motivational state. Second order goals (e.g., I want you to think I'm smart), can ignore the other party's motivations but must influence their belief state. Social appraisal theory argues that emotional displays of guilt, shame and embarrassment achieve these targeted social manipulations – though whether a communicative agent can implement and achieve these targeted effects is a fascination empirical question, as yet untested.

4.4 Social Perception and Reactivity

Most computational models of emotion de-emphasize the interactive nature of social emotions. Whether they are derived from an underlying appraisal model or arise from a communicative goal, computational systems typically follow a simple "transmission model" [59] in that a discrete emotion is calculated and transmitted faithfully to a human observer. In contrast, many contemporary theories emphasize that emotions can be dynamic and partial, reflecting the organism's transitory understanding of the physical and social context which continuously evolves from changes in the environment, inference, and social feedback. For example, feelings of antagonism may arise as facial expressions and postures are exchanged, as "one person's gradual leaning forward first leads to withdrawal until ground is held" [18]. In such a fashion, feelings may arise, not from each individual's understanding of how the interaction relates to their personal beliefs and desires, but is "co-constructed" from moment-to-moment feedback with a conversational partner [60]. This can be seen as analogous to arguments over deliberate vs. situated models of activity [61, 62]: as Herb Simon observed that the complexity of an ant's movements arise from the interaction of simple goal-directed behavior with a complex environment [63], complex emotional responses can arise from the interaction of social goals and the dynamic social environment.

Before an agent can "co-construct" emotional experiences with a human, it must perceive and respond to moment-to-moment changes in the social and physical environment. Unfortunately, most "embodied" conversational agents have a peculiar and unidirectional notion of embodiment. Although they have graphical eyes, they cannot see: most agents cannot detect the gaze, gestures, facial expressions or posture of their conversation partner. Though they have virtual ears, they cannot hear: most agents cannot detect the prosody or emotion in a human's voice. Rather, an agent receives a transcription of a speaker's words several hundred milliseconds after it was uttered. Thus, they are incapable of providing the rapid moment-to-moment emotional feedback seen in natural conversations [64]. When conversational agents do extract propositional and interactional (e.g., turn taking) meaning from the user's speech (after unnatural delay), rarely do they attempt to calculate the type of social appraisals discussed above, and which humans seem to perform effortlessly.

These limitations are beginning to change. Several technologies now support the real-time analysis of prosody [65], facial expressions [66], gaze and gestures [67]. In a few instances, these technologies have been integrated into complete agent systems that can rapidly respond to a user's nonverbal behaviors [68-71], although the integration is shallow when compared to the capabilities of most embodied conversational systems. For example, the RAPPORT AGENT [68] can appear to listen to user's

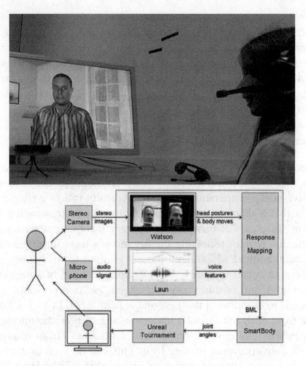

Fig. 3. A child telling a story to the RAPPORT AGENT

monolog by providing properly timed listening feedback triggered by the speaker's gestures and prosody. This has a demonstrable beneficial effect on speaker engagement and speech fluency even though the RAPPORT AGENT does not recognize or react to the content of user speech. For example, it uses the algorithm of Ward and Tsukahara (2000) to nod in response to certain prosodic contours. Such "tricks" can work in suitably constrained contexts but only scratch the surface of how to utilize multi-modal recognition technology.

I see two immediate ways to exploit perceptual information to improve the socio-emotional capabilities of agents. A "top-down" approach would be to incorporate incremental perceptual evidence into an agent's mechanisms for appraising the social context. Following the assumptions of the social functional view of emotion, such nonverbal signals should be diagnostic of the person's evaluation of events, and attending to them should improve the agent's understanding of the user's mental state. This could facilitate, for example, a sort of socio-emotional hypothesis testing: whenever an agent performs an act (physical or speech) that is relevant to another, the agent predicts how the other would appraise the act, then uses the observed response to confirm/disconfirm the agent's theory of the other's mind. More specifically, an agent might wish to provide helpful advice to a student. If the student scowls in response, this may indicate the agent's user model is incorrect or that it has failed to follow some social norm concerning politeness and autonomy [72].

A complementary approach would be to work "bottom-up" to extend the sophistication of the more reactive sensory-motor strategies such as the RAPPORT AGENT. Jondottir et al. [64] describe a preliminary attempt along these lines. They incorporated continuous speech recognition to provide emotional feedback when the user describes certain emotionally-salient events in sexual harassment video. The system was able to recognize these events with some accuracy, but couldn't come close to responding with the rapidity of human listeners. For example, when speakers describe a scene involving an inappropriate demand for a foot massage, most human listeners responded very rapidly with facial expressions indicating surprise (within 350msec on average). Although the system was able to recognize the term "foot massage," response times were on the order of 1 to 3 seconds, a highly noticeable delay. Nevertheless, it should be possible to extend the range of situations where a system can approximate "deep" feedback with shallow features by detecting shallow semantic and contextual features.

Though potentially powerful, such strategies must recognize the inherent complexity of emotional behavior. Whether nonverbal displays arise from social motives or true emotion, they depend on a myriad of unobservable factors including the individual's goals, beliefs, and understanding of the social context. Ultimately, systems that can integrate both cognitive and sensory-motor strategies will be needed to co-construct interactive emotional experiences.

5   Conclusion

I have argued that the conflicting views on the origins of nonverbal displays – that emotional displays either reflect true emotion or are tied to achieving specific social goals divorced from emotion – arise from a false dichotomy. Rather, both perspectives are largely correct: emotional displays convey social motives and social intentions, but such motives and intentions are key constituents of true emotion. Emotions help inform the organism how it is doing in the world and recruit the cognitive and physiological resources required to adaptively respond to threats and opportunities. As social animals, it should not be surprising that these threats and opportunities arise from our social needs and demand some form of communication and coordination with other social agents. Computational models of emotion have made considerable progress in allowing asocial agents to calculate the personal significance of events and adaptively respond. By suggesting how to extend these methods toward more social inferences, I hope to have, in some measure, bridged the gap between emotional and communicative methods to generate nonverbal behavior in embodied conversational agents.

Acknowledgements. The ideas expressed here grow out of discussions on the nature of nonverbal displays with Nicole Krämer and reflections on joint work on social attributions with Wenji Mao, and would not be possible without those collaborations. Wendy Treynor reviewed a version of the draft. This work was sponsored by the U. S. Army Research, Development, and Engineering Command (RDECOM), and the content does not necessarily reflect the position or the policy of the Government, and no official endorsement should be inferred.

References

1. Smith, C.A., Lazarus, R.: Emotion and Adaptation, in Handbook of Personality: theory & research. In: Pervin, L.A. (ed.), pp. 609–637. Guilford Press, New York (1990)
2. Ekman, P.: Universals and cultural differences in facial expressions of emotions. In: Cole, J. (ed.) Nebraska Symposium on Motivation, pp. 207–283. University of Nebraska Press, Lincoln, Nebraska (1972)
3. Frank, R.H.: Introducing Moral Emotions into Models of Rational Choice. In: Manstead, A., Frijda, N., Fischer, A. (eds.) Feelings and Emotions, pp. 422–440. Cambridge University Press, Cambridge (2004)
4. Fridlund, A.: Human facial expression: An evolutionary view. Academic Press, San Diego (1994)
5. Chovil, N.: Social determinants of facial displays. Journal of Nonverbal Behavior 15, 163–167 (1991)
6. Krämer, N.C., Iurgel, I., Bente, G.: Emotion and motivation in embodied conversational agents. In: Proceedings of the Symposium "Agents that Want and Like", Artificial Intelligence and the Simulation of Behavior (AISB). Hatfield, SSAISB (2005)
7. Cassell, J., et al.: Human conversation as a system framework: Designing embodied conversational agents. In: Cassell, J., et al. (eds.) Embodied Conversational Agents, pp. 29–63. MIT Press, Boston (2000)
8. Heylen, D.: Challenges Ahead. Head Movements and other social acts in conversation. In: AISB. 2005, Hertfordshire, UK (2005)
9. Poggi, I., Pelachaud, C.: Emotional Meaning and Expression in Performative Faces. In: Paiva, A. (ed.) Affective Interactions: Towards a New Generation of Computer Interfaces, pp. 182–195. Springer, Berlin (2000)
10. Lester, J.C., Towns, S.G., FitzGerald, P.J.: Achieving Affective Impact: Visual Emotive Communication in Lifelike Pedagogical Agents. International Journal of Artificial Intelligence in Education 10(3-4), 278–291 (1999)
11. Elliott, C., Rickel, J., Lester, J.: Lifelike Pedagogical Agents and Affective Computing: An Exploratory Synthesis. In: Wooldridge, M., Veloso, M. (eds.) Artificial Intelligence Today: Recent Trends and Developments, pp. 195–212. Springer, Berlin/Heidelberg (1999)
12. Lisetti, C., Gmytrasiewicz, P.: Can a rational agent afford to be affectless? A formal approach. Applied Artificial Intelligence 16, 577–609 (2002)
13. Scheutz, M., Sloman, A.: Affect and agent control: Experiments with simple affective states. In: IAT. 2001, World Scientific Publisher, Singapore (2001)
14. Blanchard, A., Cañamero, L.: Developing Affect-modulated behaviors: stability, exploration, exploitation, or imitation? in 6th International Workshop on Epigenetic Robotics, Paris (2006)
15. Marsella, S., Gratch, J.: Modeling coping behaviors in virtual humans: Don't worry, be happy. In: Second International Joint Conference on Autonomous Agents and Multi-agent Systems, Melbourne, Australia (2003)
16. Neal Reilly, W.S.: Believable Social and Emotional Agents, Carnegie Mellon University: Pittsburgh, PA (1996)
17. Smith, C.A., David, B., Kirby, L.D.: Emotion-Eliciting Appraisals of Social Situations. In: Forgas, J. (ed.) Affective Influences on Social Behavior, Psychology Press, New York (2006)
18. Parkinson, B.: Putting appraisal in context. In: Scherer, K., Schorr, A., Johnstone, T. (eds.) Appraisal processes in emotion: Theory, methods, research, pp. 173–186. Oxford University Press, London (2001)

19. Keltner, D., Haidt, J.: Social Functions of Emotions at Four Levels of Anysis. Cognition and Emotion 13(5), 505–521 (1999)
20. Barrett, K.C.: A functionalist approach to shame and guilt. In: Tangney, J.P., Fischer, K.W. (eds.) Self-conscious emotions: The psychology of shame, guilt, embarrassment, and pride, pp. 25–63. Guilford Publications, New York (1995)
21. Spoor, J.R., Kelly, J.R.: The evolutionary significance of affect in groups: communication and group bonding. Group Processes and Intergroup Prelations 7(4), 398–412 (2004)
22. de Waal, F.: Primates and Philosophers: How Morality Evolved. In: Macedo, S., Ober, J. (eds.), Princeton University Press, Princeton (2006)
23. Frank, R.: Passions with reason: the strategic role of the emotions. W. W. Norton, New York (1988)
24. Lutz, C., White, G.M.: The anthropology of emotions. Annual Review of Anthropology 15, 405–436 (1986)
25. Clore, G.L., Storbeck, J.: Affect as Information about Liking, Efficacy, and Importance. In: Forgas, J. (ed.) Affective Influences on Social Behavior, Psychology Press, New York (2006)
26. Tiedens, L.Z.: The Effect of Anger on the Hostile Inferences of Aggressive and Nonaggressive People: Specific Emotions. Cognitive Processing, and Chronic Accessibility Motivation and Emotion 25(3) (2001)
27. Zak, P.J.: Neuroeconomics. In: Philosophical Transactions of the Royal Society Biology, vol. 359, pp. 1737–1748 (2004)
28. Izard, C.: Human emotion. Plenum, New York (1977)
29. Klauer, K.C., Musch, J.: Affective priming: Findings and theories. In: Klauer, K.C., Musch, J., Mahwah, N.J. (eds.) The Psychology of Evaluation: Affective Processes in Cognition and Emotion, pp. 7–49. Lawrence Erlbaum, Mahwah (2003)
30. Dimberg, U., Öhman, A.: Beyond the wrath: Psychophysiological responses to facial stimuli. Motivation and Emotion 20, 149–182 (1996)
31. Emde, R.N., Gaensbauer, T.J., Harmon, R.J.: Emotional expression in infancy: A biobehavioral study. Psychological Issues 10 (1976) (1, Monograph No. 37)
32. Eisenberg, N., et al.: Sympathy and personal distress: Development, gender differences, and interrelations of indexes. In: Eisenberg, N. (ed.) Empathy and related emotional responses, pp. 107–126. Jossey-Bass, San Franciso (1989)
33. Haviland, J.M., Lelwica, M.: The induced affect response: 10-week-old infants' responses to three emotion expressions. Developmental Psychology 23, 97–104 (1987)
34. Brosig, J.: Identifying cooperative behavior: some experimental results in a prisoner's dilemma game. Journal of Economic Behavior and Organization 47, 275–290 (2002)
35. Frank, R.H., Gilovich, T., Regan, D.T.: The evolution of one-shot cooperation: an experiment. Ethology and Sociobiology 14, 247–256 (1993)
36. Dunn, J.: Children as psychologists: The later correlates of individual differences in understanding of emotions and other minds. Cognition and Emotion 9, 187–201 (1995)
37. Harris, P.L.: Children and Emotion. Blackwell, Oxford (1989)
38. Eder, R.A.: Uncovering young children's psychological selves: Individual and developmenal differences. Child Development 61, 849–863 (1990)
39. Phillips, M.L.: Facial processing deficits and social dysfunction: how are they related? Brain 127(8), 1691–1692 (2004)
40. Parkinson, B.: Do facial movements express emotion or communicate motives? Personality and Social Psychology Review 9(4), 278–311 (2005)

41. Manstead, A., Fischer, A.H., Jakobs, E.B.: The Social and Emotional Functions of Facial Displays. In: Philippot, P., Feldman, R.S., Coats, E.J. (eds.) The Social Context of Nonverbal Behavior (Studies in Emotion and Social Interaction), pp. 287–316. Cambridge Univ Press, Cambridge (1999)
42. Fernández Dols, J.M., Ruiz-Belda, M.-A.: Spontaneous facial behavior during intense emotional episodes: artistic truth and optical truth. In: Russell, J.A., Fernández Dols, J.M. (eds.) The Psychology of Facial Expression (1997)
43. Scherer, K.R., Schorr, A., Johnstone, T.: Appraisal Processes in Emotion. In: Davidson, R.J., Ekman, P., Scherer, K.R. (eds.) Affective Science, Oxford University Press, Oxford (2001)
44. Parkinson, B., Fischer, A.H., Manstead, A.S.R.: Emotion in social relations: Cultural, group, and interpersonal processes. Psychology Press, New York (2005)
45. Tangney, J.P.: Assessing individual differences in proneness to shame and guilt: development of the self-conscious affect and attribution inventory. Journal of Personality and Social Psychology 59, 102–111 (1990)
46. Leary, M.R., Landel, J.L., Patton, K.M.: The motivated expression of embarrassment following a self-presentational predicament. Journal of Personality and Social Psychology 64, 619–636 (1996)
47. Gratch, J., Marsella, S.: Tears and Fears: Modeling Emotions and Emotional Behaviors in Synthetic Agents. In: Fifth International Conference on Autonomous Agents, ACM Press, Montreal, Canada (2001)
48. Gratch, J., Marsella, S.: A domain independent framework for modeling emotion. Journal of Cognitive Systems Research 5(4), 269–306 (2004)
49. Marsella, S., Gratch, J., Rickel, J.: Expressive Behaviors for Virtual Worlds. In: Prendinger, H., Ishizuka, M. (eds.) Life-like Characters Tools, Affective Functions and Applications, pp. 317–360. Springer, Berlin (2003)
50. Swartout, W., et al.: Toward Virtual Humans. AI Magazine 27(1) (2006)
51. Rickel, J., et al.: Toward a New Generation of Virtual Humans for Interactive Experiences. In: IEEE Intelligent Systems, pp. 32–38 (2002)
52. Weiner, B.: Responsibility for Social Transgressions: An Attributional Analysis. In: Malle, B.F., Moses, L.J., Baldwin, D.A. (eds.) Intentions and Intentionality: Foundations of Social Cognition, The MIT Press, Cambridge (2001)
53. Shaver, K.G.: The attribution of blame: Causality, responsibility, and blameworthiness. Springer, Heidelberg (1985)
54. Mao, W., Gratch, J.: Evaluating a computational model of social causality and responsibility. In: 5th International Joint Conference on Autonomous Agents and Multiagent Systems, Hakodate, Japan (2006)
55. Mao, W., Gratch, J.: Social Judgment in Multiagent Interactions. In: Third International Joint Conference on Autonomous Agents and Multiagent Systems, New York (2004)
56. Austin, J.: How to Do Things with Words. Harvard University Press (1962)
57. Brown, P., Levenson, S.C.: Politeness: Some Universals in Language Usage. Cambridge University Press, New York (1987)
58. Martinovski, B., et al.: Mitigation Theory: An integrated approach. In: Cognitive Science (2005)
59. Shannon, C.E., Weaver, W.: A mathematical theory of communication. University of Illinois Press, Urbana (1948)
60. Fogel, A.: Developing through relationships: Origins of communication, self and culture. Harvester Wheatsheaf, New York (1993)

61. Agre, P., Chapman, D.: Pengi: An implementation of a theory of activity. In: National Conference on Artificial Intelligence (1987)
62. Suchman, L.A.: Plans and situated actions: The problem of human-machine communication. Cambridge University Press, New York (1987)
63. Simon, H.: The sciences of the Artificial. MIT Press, Cambridge (1969)
64. Jondottir, G.R., et al.: Fluid Semantic Back-Channel Feedback in Dialogue: Challenges and Progress. In: Intelligent Virtual Agents, Paris, France, Springer, Heidelberg (2007)
65. Ward, N., Tsukahara, W.: Prosodic features which cue back-channel responses in English and Japanese. Journal of Pragmatics 23, 1177–1207 (2000)
66. Bartlett, M.S., et al.: Fully automatic facial action recognition in spontaneous behavior. In: 7th International Conference on Automatic Face and Gesture Recognition, Southampton, UK (2006)
67. Morency, L.-P., et al.: Contextual Recognition of Head Gestures. In: 7th International Conference on Multimodal Interactions, Toronto, Italy (2005)
68. Gratch, J., et al.: Virtual Rapport. In: Gratch, J., et al. (eds.) IVA 2006. LNCS (LNAI), vol. 4133, Springer, Heidelberg (2006)
69. Breazeal, C., Aryananda, L.: Recognition of Affective Communicative Intent in Robot-Directed Speech. Autonomous Robots 12, 83–104 (2002)
70. Gratch, J., et al.: Creating Rapport with Virtual Agents. In: 7th International Conference on Intelligent Virtual Agents, Paris, France (2007)
71. Burleson, W.: Affective Learning Companions: Strategies for Empathetic Agents with Real-Time Multimodal Affective Sensing to Foster Meta-Cognitive and Meta-Affective Approaches to Learning, Motivation, and Perseverance, Unpublished PhD Thesis, MIT Media Lab: Boston (2006)
72. Wang, N., et al.: Experimental evaluation of polite interaction tactics for pedagogical agents. In: Intelligent User Interfaces (2005)

Facial Deception in Humans and ECAs

Isabella Poggi[1], Radoslaw Niewiadomski[2], and Catherine Pelachaud[2]

[1] Dipartimento di Scienze dell'Educazione,
Università Roma Tre, Italy
poggi@uniroma3.it
[2] IUT de Montreuil, Université Paris 8, France
{niewiadomski,pelachaud}@iut.univ-paris8.fr

Abstract. Deception is a relevant issue for the theories of cognition and social interaction. When we deceive, we influence others through manipulating their beliefs. This paper presents a definition of deception and of its functions in terms of a model of cognition and social action. We define as deceptive any act or omission aimed at making others believe something false or not believe something true about the invironment, our identity or our mental states. A typology of ways to deceive is outlined (omission, concealment, falsification, masking, negation, and false confirmation), and applied to deception in facial and bodily expression. An ECA is presented that can simulate, mask, or suppress facial expressions of emotions. The relationship of deception and politeness is investigated theoretically and through analysis of a video corpus. The results of the analysis are used to determine when an ECA masks, suppresses or simulates emotional expression.

Keywords: deception, social influence, ECA, politeness.

1 Introduction

The notion of Deception, traditionally studied since antiquity by moral philosophers ([1,6,36,39]) has been investigated in the fields of social psychology (see for example, [2,10]), nonverbal communication ([24,25,26,28,29,32]), ethology and evolution studies ([46,62]), mainly in connection with Machiavellanism and Theory of Mind ([11,12,20,37,38,63]).

Deception is an intriguing and relevant issue for the theory both of cognition and of social interaction, since by deceiving, we influence other people through manipulating their beliefs. Thus, studying deception is a good chance to investigate the mechanisms of knowledge and sociability, and just as observing Animals' deception can shed light on those device in Humans, their implementation in ECAs - Artificial Agents that exhibit intelligent motion and communicative multimodal behaviour driven by internal representations - is a way to test the cognitive and social mechanisms hypothesised.

An ECA is a socially aware autonomous entity with a humanoid aspect [14]. She is able to communicate verbally and nonverbally. She can manifest her emotional and intentional states through facial expression, voice, gaze direction, head

I. Wachsmuth and G. Knoblich (Eds.): Modeling Communication, LNAI 4930, pp. 198–221, 2008.
© Springer-Verlag Berlin Heidelberg 2008

movement, gesture, body movement, etc. Her model is based on studies from human communication, emotion and social behaviours (e.g. [7,19,28,27,40,51]). Thus, an ECA's behaviours are not drawn manually by animators but are automatically driven through algorithms [3,4,41,57]. Most ECAs embed models of emotions, communication skills, or personality. They are used mainly as interface in human-machine interaction. An ECA is viewed also as a *social* entity able to follow social norms when interacting with a user. She can be used on a web site to provide information (i.e. for short interaction only) but she can also be a companion, a friend, or even a virtual salesman.

In this paper we present a definition of deception and of its functions in terms of a model of cognition and social action [14], a typology of cases of deception, and we apply them to the construction of an Embodied Agent that exhibits deceptive facial expressions.

2   A General Model of Mind and Social Action

To define the notion of deception and to understand its functions in social interaction we present a model of mind, social action and communication in terms of goals and beliefs.

According to Conte and Castelfranchi [19], the life of an agent (be it a human, animal or a machine, an individual or collective entity) is regulated by goals. The notion of **goal** in this model is a very abstract one: a goal is a state that regulates the behaviour or the morphological features of the agent; when the perceived state of the world is discrepant with the goal, the agent performs actions or exhibits morphological features until the goal is achieved. So the notion of goal does not necessarily refer to an individual's conscious and deliberate intention, but applies as well to natural and artificial, individual and collective agents (persons, animals, machines, social organisations); and more specific notions such as need, motive, instinct, intention, social end, biological function can all be seen as sub-cases of goals. Actually, many goals are generally represented in an agent's mind, but some goals (e.g., biological functions) regulate the agent from outside; all the internal goals of the agent are in fact subgoals of these functions.

The structure of action is hierarchical; often a single action is not sufficient to achieve a goal, so the agent has to plan and perform more or less complex plans: sets of actions ordered according to a hierarchy of goals. An action is a means for Goal 1, and Goal 1 can in turn be a means for a further goal (Supergoal) G2. To pursue her goals the agent makes plans [45], that is, more or less complex hierarchies of goals, sub-goals, and super-goals, to be achieved by using external and internal **resources**; internal resources encompass actions of the agent's repertoire, and beliefs about the world and the agent itself, while external resources include the objects present in the environment and, more generally, world conditions; but they also include the "social resource", that is, other agents.

A **belief** is some assumption represented in the agent, whether consciously or not (that is, one that may be meta-believed or not). Beliefs are necessary to an agent since without them the agent could not achieve her goals. They are necessary at all the stages of goal pursuit: first, from the very decision whether to pursue some goal or not; then, to check if the conditions of pursuit are met; but also to assess what are the right actions to do, and to evaluate if they have been effective. The human animal, weaker and more clumsy than other animals, depends on the acquisition, elaboration and use of beliefs more than other animals do. This is why beliefs are a very important resource for Humans. Beliefs are relevant because (and inasmuch as) they are useful to goals, and so, among the most important goals of an agent's life are epistemic goals: the goals of knowing, of acquiring, checking, processing, elaborating beliefs. Moreover, beliefs are generally useful to the extent to which they are "true", that is, respondent to the world, an adequate and reliable map of reality.

Often an agent does not have all the resources or cannot perform all the actions she needs to achieve her goals. This gives rise to the need for cooperation among different agents. In fact, as an agent A has the internal or external resources needed to achieve his goals, he has power, but when he does not have those resources, he is in a situation of lack of power. And if another Agent B happens to have the resources that A needs, then A is dependent on B. According to the model presented [19], social exchange and interaction multiply the resources of people and their potential to reach more goals than they could by themselves. This is done through the device of goal **adoption** - the fact that people put their own resources to the service of other people's goals. An agent B adopts the goal of an agent A [16] when B comes to be regulated by a goal of A's (she pursues A's goal as her own goal): when B "helps" A to reach A's goals. Different kinds of adoption are possible: instrumental adoption (I lend you my car so I can avoid accompanying you), exploitation (I host you in the hut so you raise and care my cotton fields), social exchange (I lend you my car so you lend me your pied-à-terre), cooperative (I maintain the ladder while you pick the apples for both of us), altruistic (I dive into the sea to save you), affective (I take you to a movie I do not like just because I love you), and normative adoption (I let you cross the street because the light is red).

The device of adoption multiplies the agents' power, since it allows them to achieve many goals they could not achieve by themselves. But sometimes, in order to have other agents adopt our goals, we may have the sub-goal of **social influence**. An agent A has the goal to influence another agent B when she has the goal of raising or lowering the likeliness for B to pursue some goal: A influences B if A causes B to pursue some goal that B would have not pursued before, or not to pursue a goal B would have pursued. So influencing others is to induce goals in them.

Also social influence, like goal adoption, may be either selfish or altruistic. Selfish influence occurs when A influences B to pursue a goal that is an interest of A, for example if I order you to fetch me the newspaper, which is a goal of mine; altruistic influence occurs when A influences B to pursue a goal that is an interest of B; for example, if I am your doctor and I advice you not to eat fried food for the sake of your liver, which is an interest of yours.

3   The Two Faces of Communication

The notions of belief and social influence are a key to understand both communication and deception. In order to influence people you need to generate new goals in other people, or to activate goals they do not presently pursue. But since in the human animal goal generation and activation are generally cognitively determined, that is, they are triggered by beliefs [15], to influence a human's beliefs is a means to influence his or her goals. Both communication and, as we shall see, deception, are means to influence other people, either in our or in their own interest.

Let us first take communication. Communication is a two-face social behaviour: on the one side it is a gift that an agent gives to another, because by communicating we give beliefs to others, and beliefs are useful to achieve goals. But on the other side, communication is an act aimed at influencing other people. From the former point of view, communication is a case of reciprocal adoption of goals; in fact, it is ruled by a norm that Grice [35] calls the "Cooperation Principle". Castelfranchi and Poggi [17] agree with Grice [35] about the existence of such a principle and of the consequent Maxim of Quality "tell the truth", but they more generally propose the existence of a norm they call the "reciprocal altruism of knowledge", which sounds as follows:

> If A beliefs belief X,
> and X is relevant to a goal of B,
> A should communicate X to B.

This is but an instantiation, in the domain of knowledge and communication, of the general norm of "reciprocal altruism" stated by Trivers [60]. This is the bright face of communication, tending to rule out deception. But on the latter side, every act of communication is a request to my Addressee to do something for me; more precisely, with every communicative act we provide the other with information about our goals, relying on the principle that the very fact that we display our goals to the other is a good reason for him or her to adopt them [16]. So with requestive speech acts I tell my goal that the other perform some action, with interrogatives that he provide some belief, with informative acts, that he believe some belief.

To sum up, communication is on the one side an act of adoption of the other's goal to have beliefs, and on the other side a request for adoption, an act of influence, a way to have the other do what I want. And from this point of view, even the positive aspect we saw before - the fact that giving others beliefs is adopting their need for knowledge - can be turned into a means for influence. In fact, since, as we said, in humans the decision to pursue goals is triggered by beliefs, to influence a human's beliefs is a way to influence his or her goals.

The function of communication for social influence is based on the following device:

> If A has the goal for B to pursue goal G1,
> and if believing belief X causes B to pursue goal G1,
> then A will have the goal for B to come to believe X.

And conversely,

> If believing Y causes B to pursue goal G2,
> and A has the goal for B not to pursue goal G2,
> then A will have the goal for B not to believe Y.

This is the reason, for example, for the existence of persuasion. A Persuader has to convey some beliefs, and to convince the Persuadee of them, in order to have B decide to pursue some goals [51]. But if A is really concerned that B should pursue G1, and if letting B believe X is the best or the only way to do so, what matters that X be true or not? In principle, A's goal would be to have B believe X, whether true or false. So, here it comes the goal of deceiving.

To sum up, this is the relation between deception and the goal directedness of behaviour: to achieve one's goals an agent often needs to influence others, that is to induce them to pursue some goals; but when the beliefs apt to trigger those goals are different from true, the agent may have the goal to deceive.

4   The Default Rule of Telling the Truth

If the function of communicating is to influence others, and to influence we have to provide the information apt to trigger the goals we want, no matter the information is true or not, in principle either of the following rules could apply as default rule:

1. Deceive, except for when you have good reasons to tell the truth
2. Tell the truth, except for when you have good reasons to deceive.

Yet, in the human mind the latter seems to be implemented, as is affirmed not only by the Grician Maxim "tell the truth", but also by the very fact that we feel deception as a morally reproachable act. Actually, deceiving is by definition an aggressive act, since it thwarts a relevant goal of the other; more, a natural right: the right to knowledge. Since Grotius [36] on, the right to know the truth can be seen as a natural right of humans. So, the default rule is 2: to tell the truth. And it is possible to account for why this is so. The former rule would not be adaptive, mainly for two reasons. One is that if everybody always deceived, no one could trust the other [44,59], and so the great adaptive advantage of the reciprocal exchange of information would be lost. The second reason is that, just because communicating is a means to influence others, would we never tell the truth, the other would never know what we want of him; thus, again, the adaptive advantage of reciprocal influence and goal adoption would be lost [17].

Nonetheless, the rule has its exceptions: we generally feel we must tell the truth but sometimes we do not. This depends on our relationship to the Addressee and on the specific beliefs at issue. The former criterion here is that "you lie to your enemy". If the Addressee of my potential communication is someone whose goals I want to thwart, or not to adopt, then I will be likely to deceive him: if true beliefs are a gift, I will not give them to one I hate, one whose goals are in competition with mine. This is why, for example, war is the most typical habitat of lies and deception; as well as politics, commerce, criminal acts, love betrayal and so on. The latter criterion, that cuts across with the former, concerns the valence of the beliefs for the goals of the Addressee. So, "you withhold useful beliefs from your enemy, and harmful beliefs from your friend". Beliefs are usually good, because they are useful to plan for achieving goals; but some beliefs are very unpleasant to know and very hard to bear, they can cause you anxiety, confusion, pain; thus, it may be an altruistic act to withhold them from our friend, and a cruel action to reveal them.

5   What Is Deception?

According to Castelfranchi and Poggi [17], an agent A is deceiving an agent B when

- A has the **goal** for B to either have false beliefs or not to have true beliefs (hence, in any case, B should **not know the truth**) about some topic that is **relevant** for B
- The goal of A is a **non-communicative goal**, in that A also has the goal for B not to know of it
- in order to this goal A uses one of a number of means (e.g., A displays a morphological feature, or performs some behaviour, or omits to perform one).

Let us illustrate the elements of this definition.

- **Goal:** Necessary condition for deception is that A has the goal of not letting B have a true belief. But we can distinguish two types of it, finalistic versus functional (biological) deception. In finalistic deception, the goal of not letting B have true beliefs is a conscious goal of the agent, as it is in human deception. In functional deception, typical for other animals, the goal of not letting B have a true belief is a biological function: for example, in the aggressive mimicry of a chameleon, that changes its colour to hide and predate, or in the defensive mimicry of the shelduck, that pretends walking with a limp to distract a predator from its chicks.
- **Non–communicative goal:** The goal of not letting B believe true beliefs is noncommunicative, that is, for A not to communicate it is a necessary condition to achieve it. Obviously, if I tell you X and also tell you I want you not to believe something true, you will not believe X. This is where, for instance, deception differs from irony. In irony I tell you something I do not

believe is true, but I want you to know that I don't believe it true. In fact irony can be defined [17] as a case of "recitation", that is, a case in which one communicates something different from what one believes is true, but also communicates one does not believe it true. "Recitation", and therefore irony, are thus cases of "revealed" deception, hence not really deception.

- **Non-truth:** In deception A has the goal for B either to ignore relevant true beliefs or to have false beliefs: in both cases B does not really know the truth.
- **Truth:** But what is truth? In general, a belief is an agent's representation of the external or internal world, and it is a "true" belief when the agent believes, with a high level of certainty, that it is a reliable "model" of that world. But here again we can distinguish. For functional deception, the definition of truth is an objective one: true as a belief that an abstract omniscient agent sees as actually corresponding to the external world; truth as a responding, adequate representation of the world. For finalistic deception, instead, where the goal of not having the other believe something true is a conscious goal, a goal the individual does know he has, the definition of truth is a subjective one: true as *what the agent A believes is true* [17], after [1]. So, if one tells something that he believes is true, even if it is not true objectively, this does count as deception. For example, Ptolomaeus in saying that the earth was the centre of the universe was not deceiving, even if this was not objectively true. And conversely, if one tells something he believes is false, even if it is true in fact, he is deceiving.
- **Relevant:** Beliefs are means for goal pursuit and planning, so much that not to give beliefs is an aggressive act that obstructs the other's achievement of goals. But beliefs are relevant because - and inasmuch as - they are useful to our goals. So if I am paying at McDonald's, I ate a hot dog but I say a hamburger, if hamburger and hotdog cost the same, it is not deception. If I know I have AIDS and I do not tell my boyfriend, it is deception; but if I knew it about a friend of mine, and I do not tell my girlfriend, it is not.
- **Means:** Deception may be performed by a number of means: a speech act, like a sentence; a communicative nonverbal action, like a hypocrite handshake; a non-communicative action, like hiding your lover in the wardrobe; an omission, if I simply do not tell you anything; an object produced by the deceiving act, like a false banknote; an object used during an act of deception, like the mask used in a robbery; and for animal deception, generally for deception governed by a biological function, even a morphological feature, like the chameleon's colour [17].

6   Why Do We Deceive?

As mentioned above, the general reason why people deceive is that they want to influence others. But in everyday life, what are the specific reasons why we deceive others? According to Boffa et al. [5], we deceive either to cause or to prevent that an event occur, that someone assume a *belief* or an *evaluation*, feel an *emotion*, do some individual *action* or some *social action* toward someone else. Let us give some examples.

1. Deceiving to prevent an event:
   A's dad B suffers from heart disease. A does not tell him she failed her exam to prevent a heart attack to B.
2. To have someone assume a *belief*:
   In Stanley Milgram's experiment (as well as in innumerable studies in psychology) the subject believes that "pupils" are really striken by electrical shocks, while they are actors, confederates of the experimenter, that pretend suffering from the shocks. The whole experiment is carried on to obtain very important knowledge about obedience to authority.
3. To have someone assume an *evaluation*:
   The teacher asks a pupil if his dad is an alcoholic, and while he is in fact, the pupil denies to protect his father's image. A clerk tells his boss a false gossip about a colleague in order to induce a bad evaluation of him.
4. To have someone feel an *emotion*:
   Jago lets Othello believe that Desdemona is betraying him in order to arouse his jealousy.
5. To have someone do some *action*:
   B is a vegetarian, and he goes to dinner to his friend C. A, C's mother, is convinced that not to eat meat is unhealthy, so she makes vegetables stuffed with meat, but she tells him they are stuffed only with egg and bread, in order for him to eat them.
6. To have someone do some *social action*:
   The child lies to his mother to avoid being punished.

As one can see, the goals aimed at by acts of deception can be either good or bad, either selfish or altruistic. A case in which deception is not generally aimed at selfish goals is politeness. In politeness we care the goals of image and self-image of others [7]. This in some cases is at the service of selfish goals: for example in hypocrisy or adulation, where our true goal (the superordinate goal of our being polite) is not really complying with the other's goal of image, but influencing him to do something for us. Yet, in other cases politeness can simply be seen as a way not to hurt the other's feelings, not to wound his image or self-image. In some cases politeness could hardly be considered a case of deception, but it is rather one of "recitation". Yet, even though what I literally communicate is false, and both you and I know it is false, what I meta-communicate in doing so - that I respect your goal of image - is true [17].

7   What Do We Deceive about?

In communication we can provide beliefs about three domains: the world around us - we talk about objects, persons, events; our identity - our socio-cultural roots and personality; and finally about our own mind - our beliefs, goals and emotions. Also deception may concern the world, our identity and our mind. Take the pirate who hides his treasure; or a case of "tactical deception" like the rooster's call: the hen comes, thinking there is food here, while the rooster in fact only wants to copulate: in both cases deception is about the world. The chameleon's colour, as 'well as the false pretense of a cheater, are cases of deception about one's identity. And finally, an hypocritical smile to someone we hate, to mask our real feelings, is deception bout our mind.

Within states of our mind, in fact, sometimes we deceive about our emotions. An emotion is a complex subjective state that encompasses cognitive elements as beliefs, evaluations, causal attributions, images, as well as subjective feelings, physiological states, readiness to action, but also, typically, expressive traits of behaviour. So, emotions are mental states that naturally tend to expression: a goal of displaying them is embedded in their very neurophysiological program. Nonetheless, sometimes other goals suggest us to deceive about our emotions, and we may do so through all possible types of deception. Let us see some examples of the ways to deceive, about our emotions or other topics.

8   In How Many Ways Do We Deceive?

There are multiple ways to deceive, as witnessed by the huge number of words in a language that name acts of deception: to lie, to pretend, to cheat, to mislead... But all of these ways to deceive can be grouped in some basic ways in which a Deceiver manipulates the beliefs of the Dupe. The first important distinction is that between withholding true beliefs and providing false beliefs. But this main action over the Dupe's mind must be done in different ways depending on the previous condition of her mind before I give her that belief or not. Since any act of deception performs a manipulation of the Other's mind, the deceiver must be sophisticated in the Theory of Mind, and form an articulated representation of the other's beliefs. For example, it is not the same if I want you not to believe something that you already know vs. something you don't know anything about. So we can distinguish at least six different ways to deceive:

- **Omission.** A has the goal for B not to believe a belief K, but since B does not really know anything of K, for A it is sufficient not to do anything. *A is B's boyfriend, and he just discovered he has AIDS, but he is afraid of being forsaken by B. So he does not tell B.* As for emotions, we have a case of deceptive omission if one feels an emotion but does not display it at all. For example, *A is angry at B but he does not move any muscle of his face, nor does he become more tense in his movements.*
- **Concealment.** A does an action which is not communicative to prevent B from believing a true belief. For example, *A closes the door of the wardrobe to hide her lover from her husband.* A feels Emotion E1 but performs some non-communicative action to prevent B from perceiving his display. *B is ridiculous for A, so A is going to laugh, but not to offend B, he bites his lips to conceal his laughter.*
- **Falsification.** A provides B with a false belief, that is a belief different from what A believes is true. A pays B with false money. A does not feel Emotion E1 but displays a body expression of E1: *while meeting a colleague that she does not love particularly, she smiles at her very cordially.*

- **Masking:** A case of concealment brought about through falsification: providing a false belief in order to conceal a true belief. A mask is a prototypical example: *I conceal my true face with a fake one.* A feels Emotion E1, but pretends (falsifies) to be feeling an Emotion E2: so A conceals the expression of a true emotion by displaying the expression of a false emotion. *A is angry at B but conceals his angry expression with a friendly smile.*
- **Negation:** Denying a true belief. *Seeing your dirty face, I ask you if it is you who ate the jam, and you say: "No". Or: I ask you if you are disappointed, you are but you say "Not at all!".*
- **False confirmation:** The opposite of negation. You make a hypothesis that in fact is not true, but I let you believe it is.

These theoretical distinctions among the ways we deceive about our emotions partially correspond to the categories proposed by Ekman [28]. While analysing human facial expressions of emotions, Ekman distinguished between: modulating, falsifying, and qualifying an expression. In particular, falsifying a facial expression means to simulate it (to show a fake emotion), neutralize it (to show neutral face) or mask it (to hide an expression as much as possible by simulating another one). In our terms, simulating corresponds to what we call "falsifying": you display an emotion you really do not feel, but this is not aimed to hide a true one; masking as meant by Ekman is, like in our sense, producing a fake expression to conceal a true one; neutralizing may correspond either to concealing or to omitting; it depends how "active" you are in avoiding leakage of your spontaneous expression. If, say, you are quite an inexpressive person, you have not so much to do to have a neutral expression, this is your natural face; but if you are spontaneously expressive, having a neutral face requires some active inhibition of an expression that is ready to display.

9   Detecting Deception

Classical works by Ekman [24,25] and Ekman and Friesen [29,28] first revealed the work of facial, gestural and bodily expression in lying and deceiving, and hence also determined how one can detect deception from them. Cues to deception are typically borne by:

1. Concomitant signals of emotions caused by deception. When you deceive, you may feel specific positive or negative emotions [24]: embarrassment, shame or guilt of being deceiving (one more evidence of the default rule of telling the truth); fear of being caught; joy or amusement for being able to dupe the other. So, if the expressions of these emotions are superimposed onto those of the message to convey, this can be a cue that the Sender is lying: if for instance A is touching her own body often, B may understand that A is embarrassed and from this infer that A might be deceiving.
2. Detection from contradiction. In deceiving, our mind keeps both the deceptive and the true belief in memory, and thus, in communicating the false belief the expressions concerning the true one can leak along with the fake

ones. These expressions can leak either subsequently (immediately before or after), or in parallel, concomitant to the deceptive ones. In both cases, this is the route to deception detection:

A is displaying belief X
A is displaying belief Y
the two displays are contradictory
since
between two contrasting beliefs one must not be true
then
B infers that A must be deceiving

Let us see some examples of contradiction between subsequent expressions.

1. In a trial of high political import, the Italian politician Paolo Cirino Pomicino is being examined by the public accuser, Antonio Di Pietro, about his having taken money for his party by Italian industries. During the whole examination, Cirino Pomicino has a defying stare, sometimes an ironic smile, as if telling Di Pietro: *"I am not afraid of you, I have more power than you"*. But just for a moment, for a very short time, he stares off into space, and his ironic smile disappears from his mouth. His whole expression means: *"I am dismayed, I am very tired of still opposing him: I do not know how long I will still be able to resist him"*.
2. Upon hearing the Teacher's question, a Student pulls her head between her shoulders, as if trying to skip a hard blow. Immediately after, she takes on the typical posture and gaze of someone reflecting to find the right answer: she directs her eyes up in the sky, a type of gaze that communicates: *"I am trying to make inferences"*.

And now two examples of contradiction between concomitant expressions.

3. During an interview about racism, a subject tells he is very tolerant, but at the same time he *steps back*, with crossed arms.
4. A female politician, in commenting electoral defeat, displays sadness through her oblique eyebrows, but happiness through her smile.

10   Building an Embodied Conversational Agent That Deceives

In the previous sections we saw that many different skills and capacities from high level cognitive reasoning [13,18,22] to low level control of facial muscles can be involved in an act of deception. In following sections we describe an embodied conversational agent (ECA) that is able to deceive about her emotional state by using *deceptive facial expressions* instead of the "spontaneous" ones. That is the agent uses different types of strategies to display emotions: her true expressions of emotions are *inhibited, masked* by other expressions, or *fake expressions* are displayed instead. In particular our agent is able to modify her own facial expressions to take into account her relationship with her interlocutor. Thus, in certain situations, she will hide her true emotions covering them by socially appropriate facial expressions with the goal of being consistent with "the community", and thus will *deceive* interlocutors according to the definition of deception presented in section 5.

Now, one could wonder: is it useful, and possible, to build a Virtual Agent that can have, express, and deceive about emotions? As far as mere expression is concerned, the question finds a definitely positive answer in all research about Embodied Agents and Affective Computing [4,30,48,50,56]. This is both possible and useful for practical reasons, because the interaction with an ECA that expresses emotions may be more satisfying and motivating for the User than it is with a metallic voice or a motionless cold avatar [54]. But of course, that an Agent can even "feel" an emotion is a much more tricky issue ([17,31]). Here, one should first distinguish the question "is it possible?" from that "is it useful?", but second, independent on whether it is possible or not, also distinguish "useful for what?" As to the latter question, one should conclude that, even if to have Agents feel emotions is no good for practical purposes, yet, research aimed at this goal could still have relevant results for the advancement of human knowledge. In line with a traditional trend in AI, we think that simulation is an important test-bed for theories of human cognition. The same, in our view, could be said for deception. Simulating deception in a Virtual Human is in itself a valuable aim for theoretical purposes; moreover, doing so is also possible, as witnessed by previous research [22].

Moreover, we believe that ECAs should take different social roles related to the activities they carry out. For instance, when being a virtual salesman an ECA ought to be polite (e.g. she should respect the social distance with a new customer). When interacting with the user the ECA may, for example, display less negative emotions than it results from her virtual appraisal state. Thus an ECA ought to be aware of social rules and be able to control her behaviours. For example, an agent with nonverbal politeness knowledge will know which expressions to display and when; a deceiving agent can be used whenever displaying various social rules is desired (for example in pedagogical agents, virtual salesmen, virtual companions). The agent can cover emotional states (though the expressions of her true emotions can leak over the mask ones) and deceive about them by showing some expressions that are deceptive but adequate to the situation.

In this paper we imagine a Virtual Agent that does not really "feel" emotions but, 1. can express emotions, in that she can exhibit the facial expression that corresponds to a given emotion; 2. can "have" emotions in that, if not the internal feelings, she can trigger an internal representation of the cognitive structure of some emotions [49] or of their "mental ingredients" [52]; 3. can express emotions different from those she has - that is, she can deceive about her emotions. Since, according to the definition above, A deceives when it has the goal to let B assume something different from what A itself believes, a simple comparison between the structure of the emotion actually triggered in the agent with the structure of the emotion expressed in her face can tell if she is "deceiving" or not: if my internal representation tells me *I am now having the emotion X*, and my face expression, deliberately, either displays no emotion or an expression corresponding to emotion Y, I am deceiving.

In the following sections we introduce an ECA, that is able to display, in addition to spontaneous expressions of her emotional states, various deceptive expressions. Deceiving about emotions does not mean simply to "replace" one expression by another. People are able to recognize the real emotion from the face even if it is hidden or masked [23]. Similarly they distinguish between fake and felt expressions [32,34]. Thus a deceptive act of our agent also needs to be perceived by human interlocutors as such. Let us consider two different expressions: an expression of a true emotional state and a fake expression, that is one in which the displayer only pretends to be in an emotional state. A spontaneous smile informs the addressee that something positive happened to the displayer. A fake smile can have another (maybe even contrary) meaning. Thus, should the agent have the capacity to display these two facial expressions instead of only one, this would obviously increase her communicative skills. It is important to notice that the distinction between different types of facial expressions in the case of embodied agents makes sense only if these two facial expressions are distinguishable. Some recent experiments have indicated that using deceptive facial expressions in ECA systems is relevant. In a study on a deceiving agent, Rehm and André found that users were able to differentiate, even unconsciously, between the agent displaying an expression of felt emotion versus an expression of fake emotion [56].

In the next sections we present an ECA that is able to:

- express deceptive facial expressions,
- know which factors influence the display of facial behaviour,
- know how they influence facial behaviour.

Out of the deceptive strategies distinguished by Ekman [28], we first modelled cases of simulation (fake expression), inhibition (expression of emotion covered by a neutral face), and masking (superposition of a fake over a true expression). Our model embeds these varieties of deceptive facial expressions. To compute deceptive expressions (e.g. inhibited anger) we use the "spontaneous" expressions that is the expressions of the true emotion (e.g. expression of anger) and modify them. After presenting our computational model of deceptive expressions we propose a set of rules for facial behaviour management (see section 13). This set is based on the annotation of a video corpus, the results of experiments about facial expression management [8,42,43], and the theory of politeness [7]. Consequently our agent is not only able to display deceptive expressions but she "knows" in which situations she should use which facial expression management. At the moment we focused on interpersonal relations in which spontaneous facial behaviour should be altered. Although previous solutions of this problem exist in ECA's domain (see section 11), in our approach a variety of facial expressions (i.e. true expression, masking, inhibition, and fake expressions) is used for the first time. Knowing her own affective state and the type of relations between interlocutors our ECA automatically adapts the facial behaviour to the social context.

11   State of Art

Few animated agents implement the regulation of facial expressions. Prendinger et al. modelled "social role awareness" in animated agents [53]. They introduced a set of procedures called "social filter programs". These procedures are a kind of rules for facial expression management. Defining social filter programs Prendinger et al. considered both social conventions (politeness) and personalities of the interlocutors. The social filter program defines the intensity of an expression as the function of a social threat (power and distance), user personality (agreeableness, extroversion), and the intensity of emotion. As a result, it can either increase, decrease the intensity of facial expression, or even totally inhibit it.

The Reflexive Agent by De Carolis et al. [21] is also able to adapt her expressions of emotions according to the situational context. This agent analyses various factors in order to decide about whether displaying her emotional state or not. These factors are of two types: emotional nature factors (i.e. valence, social acceptance, emotion of the addressee) and scenario factors (i.e. personality, goals, type of relationship, type of interaction). In particular the Reflexive Agent uses *regulation rules* that define for which values of these factors the felt emotion should (or should not) be displayed [21]. Although many factors related to the management of facial displays are considered in this model, it uses only one type of deception, i.e. inhibition.

Different types of facial expressions were considered by Rehm and André [56]. For the purpose of the study on deceptive agents, they manually defined facial expressions of an agent according to Ekman's description (see section 9). They found that users were able to differentiate when the agent displays an expression of felt emotion versus a fake expression of emotion [56]. Moreover, a non-deceiving agent was perceived as more reliable, trustworthy, convincing, and credible [56].

Out of the models presented in this section, only the last one distinguishes between expression of a true and of a fake emotion. But the expressions of fake emotions were manually defined. In our work, we aim at building an agent that will modify her facial expressions depending on the relations she has with her interlocutors: our agent will deceive the interlocutor about her emotional state, but she will also (inadvertently) allow the human to perceive and interpret her behaviour. Our general aim is dual: build an agent able to know when and how to adapt her facial expression depending on the social context she is placed in. Moreover, the display of the modified expression should be interpreted perceptually as being different from the expression of felt emotion. Thus we introduce a diversification among facial expressions. Consequently our agent will be able to generate and use different types of deceptive displays.

12   Deceiving about Emotions in ECA

In this section we present an algorithm to compute the facial expression of the agent when she masks, fakes and inhibits her emotional expressions: e.g.,

expressing joy, masking anger, inhibiting sadness, expressing fake disappointment (see also [26,28,33,40]). Our model of facial expressions [4,47] is based on
Paul Ekman's studies [25,26,27,28]. We define facial expressions using a face par-
titioning approach. The face is divided in eight facial areas F_i, i= 1,..,8 (i.e., F_1
- brows, F_2 - upper eyelids, F_3 - eyes, F_4 - lower eyelids, F_5 - cheeks, F_6 - nose,
F_7 - lips movement, F_8 - lips tension). Each facial expression is a composition
of these facial areas, each of which could display signs of emotion. In the case of
deceptive facial expressions (as in an expression masking another one) different
emotions can be expressed on different areas of the face (e.g. anger is shown on
the eyebrows area while sadness is displayed on the mouth area). Recapitulating,
the main idea of our algorithm is to assign expressions of the emotions to the
different parts of the face. For this purpose we defined a set of rules that describe
the composition of facial areas in deceptive expressions.

12.1   Rules for Generating Deceptive Facial Expressions

Researchers have proposed a list of *deception cues* i.e. the features of expressions
that are useful in distinguishing between fake and felt expressions [28,24,25]. At
the moment, two of them are implemented in our model: *reliable features* and
the *inhibition hypothesis*.

First of all humans are not able to control all their facial muscles. Consequently
expressions of felt emotions may be associated with specific facial features like
sadness brows [28] or orbicularis oculi activity in the case of joy [25]. Such *reliable features* lack in fake expressions as they are difficult to do voluntarily. Fake
expressions are similar to the corresponding sincere - spontaneous - expressions,
but slightly differ from them for some subtle differences that are not easy to detect. For example, a false smile is distinguished from a true one as it lacks crow's
feet near the eyes that appear by the contraction of the *orbicularis oculi* [29].

On the other hand, people are not able to fully inhibit felt emotions. According
to the *inhibition hypothesis* [25], the same elements of facial expressions, which
are difficult to show voluntarily in the case of unfelt emotions, are also difficult
to inhibit in the case of felt emotions. Ekman enumerated all facial areas that
leak over the mask during the emotional displays management [28].

Deceptive facial expressions for six emotions - anger, disgust, fear, joy, sadness,
and surprise - are described in the literature [28,26]. Based on these studies, we
have defined a set of fuzzy rules that describe the characteristic features in terms
of facial areas for each type of deceptive expression. To each emotion corresponds
a rule. Thus we have defined six rules for each type of deceptive expression.

12.2   Algorithm

In our approach any facial expression is described by a set of fuzzy sets. The
main advantage of this approach is that slightly different expressions can be described by one label (like "joy" or "contempt"). For each of them we can find a
deceptive expression (masking, inhibition, fake expression) by applying suitable
rules. Let the *input expression* be an expression of emotion for which a deceptive

facial expression needs to be established. In case an input expression for which the deceptive facial expression is not defined explicitly by our rules (e.g. expressions of contempt or disappointment) a fuzzy similarity based algorithm is used in order to establish the degree of similarity between the input expression and expressions whose deceptive expressions are described by our rules (see [47] for details). Our fuzzy similarity algorithm compares any two facial expressions and outputs a value of similarity in the interval [0,1] (0 meaning "not similar at all" while 1 means identical expressions). Once the most similar expression (chosen among the 6 ones) is known we can apply corresponding rules to our input expression. For example, when we want to compute the deception face of contempt or of disappointment, we look to which expression of six-elements set mentioned above it is the most similar and we use the associated rule. For example, our fuzzy similarity algorithm outputs that the expression of disappointment is similar to the one of sadness. Thus masked, inhibited or fake facial expressions of two *similar* facial expressions are created using the same rules.

12.3 Example of Deceptive Expression

Figure 1 presents the agent displaying an expression of disappointment, that is masked by fake happiness. In Figure 1b the parts of expression copied from the expression of disappointment are marked with blue and those of happiness with red circles. We can notice that *orbicularis oculi* activity (characteristics of felt happiness) is not activated. This absence is an indicator of fake expression of happiness. Also the position of the brows can be observed (inner raised brows), which is characteristics of disappointment as the expression of disappointment is very similar (according to our fuzzy similarity based algorithm) to the expression of sadness. According to Ekman [26,28] the features of felt sadness that leak over the masking expression are: forehead, brows, and upper eyelids. In our model these elements of expression are represented by the facial areas F_1 (forehead and brows) and F_2 (upper eyelids). As a consequence, facial areas F_1 and F_2 can be observed in inhibited sadness, and thus, they can be also observed in masked disappointment (figure 1a). On the other hand the mouth area displays a smile (sign of happiness).

Similarly we can generate any cases of inhibited or fake facial expressions. Facial expressions generated with our model were evaluated in a study based on the "copy-synthesis" method (see [9] for details).

13 Facial Expression Management

Deceptive facial expressions are often used in given social context. Due to cultural, professional, and social rules we are often required not to show our felt emotions. With time we have learned to inhibit them, to mask them, to put on a fake one. An ECA being setup in an interaction i.e. a social context, ought to know when, where, and to whom she can show the expression of her emotion. That is she needs to know to manage the display of her facial expressions.

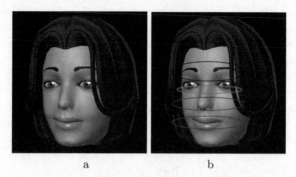

a   b

Fig. 1. a) Example of disappointment masked by happiness; b) decomposition of the expression in areas: blue areas correspond to the fake expression (happiness), while the red one to the felt one (disappointment).

In this section we present an ECA that uses a variety of deceptive facial expressions. Depending on her interpersonal relations with the interlocutor and her emotional state, the agent modifies her own "spontaneous" facial behaviour. That is in certain social contexts our agent will use some deceptive facial expressions instead of spontaneous ones. For that purpose we need to find rules that associate the factors (variables), which influence the display of facial behaviour with the occurrence of particular types of facial expressions. Our rules of facial behaviour management are mostly based on the results of the annotation of a video-corpus we have made for this purpose and the theory of politeness [7]. In the next subsection we briefly introduce the latter.

13.1 Politeness Strategies

Brown and Levinson proposed a computational model of politeness in language [7]. According to this theory, any linguistic act like request or promise can threaten the "face" of the speaker and/or hearer. Politeness consists in taking remedial actions to counterbalance the negative consequences of these face threatening acts.

Brown and Levinson proposed the classification of all actions that prevent face threatening. They defined five different strategies of politeness: bald, positive and negative politeness, off-record, and "don't do the action". The more antagonistic a given act is, the more likely a higher strategy is to be chosen. The decision about the strategy to be used depends on the level of threat of an action (FTA). Brown and Levinson proposed to estimate the FTA of an action by using three variables: social distance, power relation, and absolute ranking of imposition of an action. Finally, the FTA value is computed as a sum of these three values [7].

13.2 Annotation Scheme and Results

In order to define rules of facial behaviour management we decided to re-use the approach proposed by Rehm and André [55]. They analysed the relationship between different types of gestures and politeness strategies in verbal acts. They built a video-corpus called SEMMEL that contains various examples of verbal and nonverbal behaviour during face threatening interactions. Inspired by the encouraging results of Rehm and André's experiment, we decided to analyse the same video-corpus in order to find relations between politeness strategies and facial behaviour.

We used 21 videos of the SEMMEL video-corpus [55]. The overall duration of the analysed clips is 6 minutes and 28 seconds. In this study we used the original annotation of politeness strategies proposed by Rehm and André. They considered four of the politeness strategies from Brown and Levinson's model [7]: bald, positive politeness, negative politeness, and off-record strategy [55]. In our study the facial expressions (and corresponding emotional states) were annotated by a native speaker annotator. In our annotation scheme we considered four types of facial displays: expression of the true emotional state, inhibited, masked, and fake expression. Because of a relatively small number of examples analysed so far we decided to distinguish only between positive, negative emotions, and neutral state. Consequently, we did not consider distinctive emotional states and their corresponding expressions, but, instead, we consider *patterns* of facial behaviour. For example, a pattern called "positive masked" describes any facial expression that occurs in a situation in which a positive emotion is masked by another one. The following patterns of facial expression were considered in the annotation process: negative masked, negative inhibited, negative expressed, fake negative, neutral expression, fake positive, positive masked, positive inhibited, positive expressed.

We analysed the frequency of occurrence for each of them and we found that different types of facial expressions were not evenly distributed along the different strategies of politeness (see [47] for details). For example the "neutral expression" pattern was the most often observed (52% of all cases) while the "fake positive" pattern was observed in 26.5% cases. Some patterns were not observed at all. None of the "positive masked" expressions or "fake negative" expressions was annotated. We use this information to build our model of facial deceptive behaviour management in interpersonal relations.

13.3 Variables of Facial Expression Management

Different sources [7,8,42,61,64] show that two factors, social distance (SD) and social power (SP), are important to describe interpersonal relations. Social distance (SD) refers to the degree of intimacy and the strength of relation, while social power (SP) expresses the difference in status and the ability to influence others [58]. According to Wiggins *et al.*[64] all personality traits relevant to social interaction can be located in a two dimensional space defined by the orthogonal axes of dominance and affiliation. So two variables, dominance (corresponding to SP) and affiliation (corresponding to SD), are sufficient to describe interpersonal relations. Furthermore, Brown and Levinson include SD and SP in their theory of politeness (see section 13.1). Finally, power (SP) and social distance (SD) are two factors that influence human expressions according to various studies about facial behaviour ([8,42,61]).

Facial behaviour management is also conditioned by emotional factors. In particular, facial behaviour depends on the valence (Val) of an emotion [8,43]. Negative emotions are more often masked or inhibited, while positive emotions are often pretended.

Thus, in our model, we consider three variables to encompass the characteristics of the interaction and the emotional state of the displayer, namely: social distance (SD), social power (SP), and emotion valence (Val).

13.4 Facial Expression Management Model

In our model we consider three different emotional states: negative, positive, and neutral. For each of them we looked for the pattern of facial behaviour that best corresponds to each politeness strategy. The choice is based on the frequency of the co-occurrence of a strategy j and a pattern i in the annotated video clips (see section 13.2). When the data gathered in the annotation study were insufficient to make a choice, we also used the conclusions from other experiments [8,42,43]. Table 1 shows which pattern of facial expression i will be used for each type of emotion (positive, neutral, negative) and strategy of politeness.

Table 1. Facial behaviour and strategies of politeness

face threat	bald	positive	negative	off-record
positive emotion	positive expressed	positive expressed	positive inhibited	positive expressed
neutral state	neutral expressed	fake positive	neutral expressed	fake positive
negative emotion	negative expressed	negative expressed	negative inhibited	negative masked

In our model all three variables SD, SP, and Val take values in the interval [0,1]. In Table 1 different strategies of facial behaviour are ordered in columns according to the value of threat. We establish this value as the difference: $w = SD - SP$ which takes values in the interval [-1,1]. Then we split the interval of all possible values of w into four equal parts: $w \in$ [-1,-0.5] (very low) is associated with the bald strategy, $w \in$ (-0.5,0] with positive politeness, $w \in$ (0,0.5] with negative politeness, while $w \in$ (0.5,1] (very high) with the off-record strategy. Finally our facial management rules are of the type:

if Val(E_i) is {positive | negative | zero } and
w is {very low | low | high | very high}
then the expression of E_i is {expressed | fake | inhibited | masked}.

Using our set of rules we decide on the facial expression pattern of an emotion E_i. In the case of any "negative masked" expression or "fake positive" expression we use the expression of fake joy or masked joy. Finally, for any emotional state E_i, values of social distance SD and of social power SP, by using our rules, we can generate the corresponding facial expression (see [4] for details). Our model was evaluated in a study in which we analysed the perception of interpersonal relations from the facial behaviour of our agent [47].

The examples in Figure 2 illustrate the variety of facial reactions displayed by the agent at the same instant in different interpersonal relation settings. In particular, the first row includes the reactions of the agent when she discovers the dishonesty of her interlocutor, while in the second row we can see the agent's reactions for an unpleasant event.

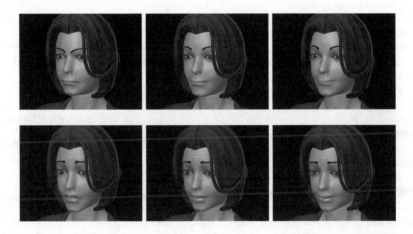

Fig. 2. Examples of different facial expressions displayed by the agent (in consecutive columns, interaction with: a friend, a stranger, a superior). Top row: the agent discovers the dishonesty of her interlocutor; lower row: the agent displays a reaction to an unpleasant event.

14   Conclusion

In the first part of this paper we presented a theoretical model of deception, its function, performance and detection, showing its relevance in terms of its cognitive mechanisms, its verbal and multimodal means, its specific goals and its impact over social interaction. As we deceive, we manipulate the other's mind in order to influence him, that is, to have him pursue the goals we want, be they in the other's or in our own interest. Therefore deception, as well as communication, may be either a selfish or an altruistic behaviour. In the second part of the paper, we described a model to generate facial expressions of an agent deceiving about her emotional state. Our model introduces the diversification of facial expressions for masked, inhibited and fake expressions. As a consequence, these different types of deceptive facial expressions can be distinguished by the user, because their appearance is different. Then we also presented how an ECA can deceive about her emotional state by adapting her facial behaviour to the social context. In particular we showed that different types of facial expressions used in the same situation can express interpersonal relations.

Acknowledgements. This work has been partially done while two of the authors were part of the "Embodied Communication" research group at ZIF. Part of the research is supported by the EU FP6 Network of Excellence HUMAINE and by the EU FP6 Integrated Project Callas.

References

1. Augustinus, A.: De Mendacio. In: Migne, J.P. (ed.) Patrologica Latina, tom. 40 S. Aurelii Augustini Opera Omnia 6, Turnolti: Brepols, pp. 488–518 (1968)
2. Bavelas, J.B., Black, A., Chovil, N., Mullett, J.: Truths, lies, and equivocations: The effects of conflicting goals on discourse. Journal of Language and Social Psychology 9, 129–155 (1990)
3. Becker, C., Kopp, S., Wachsmuth, I.: Simulating the Emotion Dynamics of a Multimodal Conversational Agent. In: André, E., Dybkjaer, L., Minker, W., Heisterkamp, P. (eds.) Affective Dialogue Systems, pp. 154–165. Springer, Heidelberg (2004)
4. Bevacqua, E., Mancini, M., Niewiadomski, R., Pelachaud, C.: An expressive ECA showing complex emotions. In: Proceedings of the AISB Annual Convention, Newcastle, UK, pp. 208–216 (2007)
5. Boffa, S., Pascucci, F., Poggi, I.: La banca delle bugie. In: Bonfantini, M., Castelfranchi, C., Martone, A., Poggi, I., Vincent, J. (eds.) Menzogna e simulazione. Edizioni Scientifiche Italiane, Napoli, pp. 227–240 (1997)
6. Bok, S.: Lying. Moral Choice in Public and Private Life. Pantheon, New York (1978)
7. Brown, P., Levinson, S.C.: Politeness: some universals on language usage. Cambridge University Press, Cambridge (1987)
8. Buck, R., Losow, J., Murphy, M., Costanzo, P.: Social facilitation and inhibition of emotional expression and communication. Journal of Personality and Social Psychology 63(6), 962–968 (1992)
9. Buisine, S., Abrilian, S., Niewiadomski, R., Martin, J.-C., Devillers, L., Pelachaud, C.: Perception of blended emotions: From video corpus to expressive agent. In: The 6th International Conference on Intelligent Virtual Agents, Marina del Rey, USA (2006)
10. Buller, D.B., Burgoon, J.K.: Interpersonal Deception Theory. Communication Theory 6(3), 203–242 (1996)
11. Byrne, R.W.: The Ape Legacy: The Evolution of Machiavellian Intelligence and Anticipatory Planning. In: Goody, E. (ed.) Social Intelligence and Interaction. Expressions and Implications of the Social Bias in Human Intelligence, Cambridge University Press, Cambridge (1995)
12. Byrne, R.W., Whiten, A.: Machiavellian Intelligence: Social Expertise and the Evolution of Intellect in Monkeys. In: Apes and Humans, Clarendon Press, Oxford (1997)

13. Carofiglio, V., de Rosis, F., Grassano, R.: An Interactive System for Generating Arguments in Deceptive Communication. In: Esposito, F. (ed.) AI*IA 2001. LNCS (LNAI), vol. 2175, Springer, Heidelberg (2001)
14. Cassell, J.: Nudge nudge wink wink: Elements of face-to-face conversation for embodied conversational agents. In: Cassell, J., Sullivan, J., Prevost, S., Churchill, E. (eds.) Embodied Conversational Characters, MITpress, Cambridge (2000)
15. Castelfranchi, C.: Reasons: Belief Support and Goal Dynamics. Mathware & Soft Computing 3, 233–247 (1996)
16. Castelfranchi, C., Parisi, D.: Linguaggio, conoscenze e scopi. Il Mulino, Bologna (1980)
17. Castelfranchi, C., Poggi, I.: Bugie, finzioni, sotterfugi. Per una scienza dell'inganno, Carocci, Roma (1998)
18. Castelfranchi, C., de Rosis, F.: Which User Model do we need, to relax the hypothesis of "Sincere Assertion" in HCI? In: UM99 Workshop on Attitudes, Personality and Emotions in User-Adapted Interaction, Banff, Canada (1999)
19. Conte, R., Castelfranchi, C.: Cognitive and social action, London, University College (1995)
20. Christie, R., Geis, F.L.: Studies in Machiavellianism. Academic Press, New York (1970)
21. De Carolis, B., Pelachaud, C., Poggi, I., De Rosis, F.: Behavior Planning for a Reflexive Agent. In: Proceedings of the Conference IJCAI 2001, Oporto, Portugal (2001)
22. de Rosis, F., Castelfranchi, C., Carofiglio, V.: On various sources of uncertainty in modeling suspicion and how to treat them. In: Workshop on Deception, Fraud and Trust in Agent Societies, Autonomous Agents, Barcelona (2000)
23. Devillers, L., Abrilian, S., Martin, J.-C.: Representing real life emotions in audiovisual data with non basic emotional patterns and context features. In: Proceedings of First International Conference on Affective Computing & Intelligent Interaction, Pekin, China, pp. 519–526 (2005)
24. Ekman, P.: Telling lies: Clues to Deceit in the Marketplace, Marriage, and Politics, New York, Norton (1985)
25. Ekman, P.: Darwin, deception, and facial expression. Annals of the New York Academy of Sciences 1000, 205–221 (2003a)
26. Ekman, P.: The Face Revealed. Weidenfeld & Nicolson, London (2003b)
27. Ekman, P., Friesen, W.V.: The repertoire of nonverbal behavior's: Categories, origins, usage and coding. Semiotica 1, 49–98 (1969)
28. Ekman, P., Friesen, W.V.: Unmasking the Face. A guide to recognizing emotions from facial clues. Prentice-Hall, Inc., Englewood Cliffs, New Jersey (1975)
29. Ekman, P., Friesen, W.V.: Felt, false, and miserable smiles. Journal of Nonverbal Behavior 6, 238–252 (1986)
30. Elliott, C.: The Affective Reasoner: A Process Model of Emotions in a Multi-agent System. PhD thesis, Institute for the Learning Sciences, Northwestern University (1992)
31. Fellous, J.M., Arbib, M.A. (eds.): Who needs Emotions? The brain Meets the Robot. Oxford University Press, New York (2005)
32. Frank, M.G., Ekman, P., Friesen, W.V.: Behavioral Markers and Recognizability of the Smile of Enjoyment. In: Ekman, P., Rosenberg, E.L. (eds.) What the Face Reveals: Basic and Applied Studies of Spontaneous Expression Using the Facial Action Coding System (FACS), Oxford University Press, Oxford (1995)

33. Gonzaga, G.C., Keltner, D., Londahl, E.A., Smith, M.D.: Love and commitment problem in romantic relation and friendship. Journal of Personality and Social Psychology 81(2), 247–262 (2001)
34. Gosselin, P., Kirouac, G., Doré, F.Y.: Components and Recognition of Facial Expression in the Communication of Emotion by Actors. In: Ekman, P., Rosenberg, E.L. (eds.) What the Face Reveals: Basic and Applied Studies of Spontaneous Expression Using the Facial Action Coding System (FACS), pp. 243–267. Oxford University Press, Oxford (1995)
35. Grice, H.P.: Logic and Conversation. In: Cole, P., Morgan, J.L. (eds.) Syntax and Semantics, Vol III, Speech Acts, Academic Press, New York (1975)
36. Grotius, H.: De iure belli ac pacis libri tres. Paris (1625)
37. Ivkovic, V., Grammer, K.: Communication, Deception, Indoctrination, Dogmatism and Memes - Neuroethology of Mind Control. Collegium Antropologicum 26 Suppl, 91 (2002)
38. Janovic, T., Ivkovic, V., Nazor, D., Grammer, K., Jovanovic, V.: Empathy, communication, deception. Collegium Antropologicum 27(2), 809–822 (2003)
39. Kant, I.: Grundlegung sur Metaphysik der Sitten, Leipzig, 1785. Engl. Tr. Groundwor of the Metaphysics of Morals. In: Gregor, M. (ed.) Introduction by Korsgaard, C., Cambridge University Press, Cambridge (1997)
40. Keltner, D.: Signs of appeasement: Evidence for the distinct displays of embarrassment, amusement, and shame. Journal of Personality and Social Psychology 68, 441–454 (1992)
41. Kopp, S., Wachsmuth, I.: Synthesizing Multimodal Utterances for Conversational Agents. The Journal Computer Animation and Virtual Worlds 15(1), 39–52 (2004)
42. La France, M., Hecht, M.: Option or Obligation to Smile: The Effects of Power and Gender and Facial Expression. In: Philippot, P., Feldman, R.S., Coats, E.J. (eds.) The Social Context of Nonverbal Behavior (Studies in Emotion and Social Interaction), pp. 45–70. Cambridge University Press, Cambridge (2005)
43. Manstead, A.S.R., Fischer, A.H., Jakobs, E.B.: The Social and Emotional Functions of Facial Displays. In: Philippot, P., Feldman, R.S., Coats, E.J. (eds.) The Social Context of Nonverbal Behavior (Studies in Emotion and Social Interaction), pp. 287–316. Cambridge University Press, Cambridge (2005)
44. Maynard Smith, J.: Do animals convey Information about Their Intentions. Journal of Theoretical Biology 97, 1–5 (1982)
45. Miller, M., Galanter, E., Pribram, K.H.: Plans and the structure of behavior. Rinehart and Winston, New York, Holt (1960)
46. Mitchell, R.W., Thompson, N.S. (eds.): Deception: Perspectives on Human and Nonhuman Deceit, Albany (NY), Suny (1986)
47. Niewiadomski, R.: A model of complex facial expressions in interpersonal relations for animated agents. Ph.D. Thesis. University of Perugia (2007)
48. Ochs, M., Niewiadomski, R., Pelachaud, C., Sadek, D.: Intelligent Expressions of Emotions. In: Tao, J., Tan, T., Picard, R.W. (eds.) ACII 2005. LNCS, vol. 3784, Springer, Heidelberg (2005)
49. Ortony, A., Clore, G.L., Collins, A.: The cognitive structure of emotions. Cambridge University Press, Cambridge (1998)
50. Picard, R.: Affective Computing. MIT Press, Cambridge (1997)
51. Poggi, I.: The goals of persuasion. Pragmatics and Cognition 13(2), 297–336 (2005)
52. Poggi, I.: Emozioni, credenze e scopi. Incognito (2007)
53. Prendinger, H., Ishizuka, M.: Social role awareness in animated agents. In: Proceedings of the fifth international conference on autonomous agents, Montreal, Quebec, Canada, pp. 270–277 (2001)

54. Reeves, B., Nass, C.: The media equation: how people treat computers, television, and new media like real people and places. Cambridge University Press, Cambridge (1996)
55. Rehm, M., André, E.: nforming the Design of Embodied Conversational Agents by Analysing Multimodal Politeness Behaviors in Human-Human Communication. In: Workshop on Conversational Informatics for Supporting Social Intelligence and Interaction (2005)
56. Rehm, M., André, E.: Catch Me If You Can - Exploring Lying Agents in Social Settings. In: Int. Conf. on Autonomous Agents and Multiagent Systems (AAMAS 2005), pp. 937–944 (2005)
57. Rickel, J., Marsella, S., Gratch, J., Hill, R., Traum, D., Swartout, B.: Towards a New Generation of Virtual Humans for Interactive Experiences. IEEE Intelligent Systems, 32–38 (2002)
58. Spencer-Oatey, H.: Reconsidering power and distance. Journal of pragmatics 26, 1–24 (1996)
59. Swift, J.: Gulliver's travels. Dublin, Faulkner (1726)
60. Trivers, R.L.: The evolution of reciprocal altruism. Quarterly Review of Biology 4, 35–37 (1971)
61. Wagner, H.L., Smith, J.: Facial expression in the presence of friends and strangers. Journal of Nonverbal Behavior 15(4), 201–214 (1991)
62. Whiten, A., Byrne, R.: Tactical Deception in Primates. Behavioral and Brain Sciences 11, 233–244 (1988)
63. Whiten, A., Perner, J.: Fundamental Issues in the Multidimensional Study of Mindreading. In: Whiten (ed.) Natural Theories of Mind, Basil Blackwell, Oxford (1991)
64. Wiggins, J.S., Trapnell, P., Phillips, N.: Psychometric and geometric characteristics of the Revised Interpersonal Adjective Scales (IAS-R). Multivariate Behavioral Research 23(3), 517–530 (1988)

Theory of Mind as a Theoretical Prerequisite to Model Communication with Virtual Humans

Nicole C. Krämer

University Duisburg-Essen, Forsthausweg 2, 47057 Duisburg, Germany
nicole.kraemer@uni-due.de

Abstract. Given the weaknesses that most current implementations of conversational virtual humans show, it is argued that future developments might benefit from the incorporation of a theory of mind. First, findings concerning the effects of current embodied agents´ communication will be presented. Then, basic principles of human communication are depicted. Drawing on models of perspective taking, common ground, imputing one´s knowledge to others and theory of mind, necessities for the human agent communication are derived. In the next step, recent implementations from various research groups are presented that take first steps into this direction. Finally, conclusions for future research are drawn.

Keywords: theory of mind, embodied conversational agents, human-computer-interaction, perspective taking, common ground.

1 Introduction

"It is the nature of the human condition that, try as we may, we cannot enter into the reality of another individual´s experiences, thoughts, or feelings. Imprisoned as we are within our own bodies, the fallible process of communication is the primary agent currently available for crossing the psychological expanse between two or more individuals" (Burgoon & Bacue, 2003).

Aiming at better acceptance and usability of modern technologies so-called embodied conversational agents (ECAs) gain increasing attention in interface design. Numerous research groups develop virtual agents that are capable of conducting human-like dialogues with the user. The shared goal and expectation is that by incorporating the ability of language and nonverbal communication, the interaction with computers and technologies will be facilitated and rendered more intuitive [1, 2]. The secret and complexity of human communication, that is aptly described in the statement by Burgoon and Bacue [3] cited above, is, however, difficult to capture and rebuild. In consequence, most of current implementations have to start out from partly oversimplistic assumptions. Thus, various currently implemented models of human-agent-interaction implicitly assume that the information that is sent by the agent is perceived and interpreted by the user in the intended way. This basically refers to the Shannon-Weaver model of communication [4] that in its classical form disregards the fact that the listener individually constructs meaning [5, 6]. The construction –

I. Wachsmuth and G. Knoblich (Eds.): Modeling Communication, LNAI 4930, pp. 222–240, 2008.

actually happening in every interaction – will usually lead to effects on the part of the receiver that have not been intended by the sender. Dialogue modeling thus can merely be successful when the fact that individual interpretations occur, is taken into account. Interactions can thus be expected to be most efficient and satisfying if at least some knowledge of the interlocutor´s cognitive (what does she know?) and emotional (how does she feel?) states is available – enabling the sender to more successfully predict the effect of his utterances or actions. In human-human-communication, several mechanisms have been proposed that guarantee at least basic understanding of interaction partners: Imputing one´s own knowledge on others [7, 8], the ability to build common ground [9, 10] and to take the other´s perspective [11]. One basic prerequisite for these abilities is the so called "theory of mind" [12, 13] every human has. "Theory of mind" is the knowledge that other humans wish, feel, know or believe something, and the ability to see other entities as intentional agents, whose behavior is influenced by states, beliefs, desires etc. This entails a direct understanding of what other people know or might feel in a specific situation. An agent or system, on the other hand, in most cases does not have this knowledge – neither implicit (since functioning the same way) nor explicit (e.g. as a set of rules). Therefore, human-agent-communication is even more prone to misunderstandings than e.g. human-human-communication. One simple example can be used to illustrate potential shortcomings: The system itself – certainly – does not have an idea that the user becomes confused if he made a request and does not receive any kind of answer or feedback for 10 seconds.

Within the chapter, it will be discussed whether the implementation of a user model that is equivalent to the human "theory of mind" could improve human-agent communication. The contribution of communication research and social psychology to this emerging research area seems crucial in two ways. Firstly, it would have to provide the basic knowledge on the mechanisms of human communication as a fundament for modelling a kind of "socio-emotional intelligence" in the virtual humans. Secondly, acceptance and evaluation studies can help to measure the psychological effects of ECAs in detail and provide hints for optimization and meaningful task-media fits [14]. Here, the focus will be on the former approach that might be termed "realisation research". To start with, current findings concerning the effects of agent communication will be presented in order to answer the question whether there is the need to improve current systems at all. In the next step, basic principles of human communication are depicted and subsequent necessities for the human agent communication are derived. Finally, recent implementations from various research groups are presented that take first steps into this direction.

2 Communicating with Virtual Humans

Although there are a considerable number of studies focussing on the evaluation of embodied agents [15,16,17], merely a few studies specifically target acceptance and efficiency of agents´ communicative abilities. What has been shown extensively, though, is that the social effects that agents evoke by their communication efforts are manifold and that the human users react with behaviour that is so far merely known from human-human-interaction. The following account summarizes the effects communicating interface agents as well as robots have on quantitative as well as qualitative aspects of the human´s communication behaviour.

Concerning quantitative aspects, several studies consistently show that human-like appearances on the screen may lead to a distinct increase of natural speech utterances on the part of the user: When a TV/VCR system is represented by an anthropomorphic figure instead of a merely text- or audio-based interface, human users are more inclined to use natural language (instead of e.g. a remote control) when interacting with the system [18]. Virtual faces thus seem to "invite intuitive interaction" [19]: A virtual person is perceived as social to at least a degree that potentially existing restraints to talk to a machine might be overcome. Within a further study, these results could be affirmed: Krämer, Bente, and Piesk [20] showed that a system is more likely to be addressed via natural speech when an embodied agent is present, whereas with a text interface users prefer to use the remote control to communicate their input. Additionally, within the GrandChair project empirical data indicate that elderly participants tell longer stories when they are confronted with an artificial child than when there was no addressee [21, 22]. But not only verbal activity might be triggered by embodied conversational agents: As Kaiser and Wehrle [23, 24] show, virtual agents within a computer game evoke nonverbal reactions that are related to specific behaviors of the agent. When the agent announces his oncoming departure, the user shows signs of disappointment and when the agent praises the user, a proud smile can be observed.

With regard to qualitative aspects of communication, early empirical data already showed that the availability of social cues does not only lead to enhanced communication attempts on the part of the human user but also to communication behavior that is similar to human-human-interaction. Moreover, this even holds when just basic social cues such as speech output are given. Nass, Steuer, and Tauber [25] prove that etiquettes - as they are used within human to human communication – might be applied within human-computer-interaction: criticism of a system is given only to another system, not the system being criticized. Also, within a study on "auditory embodiment" Oviatt, Darves, and Coulston [26] demonstrated that 7-10 year old children spontaneously adapt basic acoustic-prosodic features of their speech (amplitude, durational features) to the features of a speech output system they are interacting with. That this phenomenon - as hypothesized by the *communication accomodation* theory [26, 27] – holds also for human computer interaction, is proven by the analysis of 2200 utterances. Bell and Gustafson [28] demonstrate similar adaptations when people are interacting with the "August" system that is represented by an embodied agent. But not only structure but also contents of speech are subject to adaptations: qualitative content analyses of users´ utterances while interacting with the agent Max within the Heinz Nixdorf Museum in Paderborn, Germany, show that utterances resemble those of human to human communication [29]: 57% of users formally greeted the agent (probably since triggered to do so by the agent) and, more surprisingly, at least 30% bade farewell – the latter being especially astonishing as users simply had to step back from screen and keyboard. 4.2% of utterances were common phrases as used within human communication (such as "How are you?"). More than one third of questions addressed to the agent implied human-likeness ("Do you have a girlfriend?", "Can you dance?") or tested this very assumption. A more controlled experimental study, which by means of a between subjects design systematically compared a text based interface with a speech based and an agent based interface, supported and augmented these findings [16]: When a TV/VCR system was represented by a virtual face, the users showed more polite phrases ("thank you" or "please") and used personal pronouns such as "you" more often. Furthermore, orders were given in a more personalized way ("Could you record James Bond" instead of "James Bond should be recorded"). Other studies moreover show that self-disclosing utterances are more frequent when the system is represented by a talking head than compared to a merely speech-based system [26, 30].

Given these results one might feel inclined to conclude that the human user readily adapts to the technology and that further improvement might not be necessary. But although the user does already seem to communicate successfully with current virtual humans, additional research demonstrates that the behaviour of the agent matters and that even subtle aspects of the agent´s nonverbal behaviour bring about distinct effects: In this line, it has long been demonstrated and acknowledged that the nonverbal behavior of an embodied agent has sustainable effects [31, 32]. Rickenberg and Reeves [32] conclude that it is not sufficient "... to focus on whether or not an animated character is present. Rather the ultimate evaluation is similar to those for real people - it depends on what the character does, what it says, and how it presents itself" (p. 55). Several studies indeed give evidence for the impact of even subtle communicative cues, e.g., the importance of the agents´ gaze behavior. Rickenberg and Reeves [32] empirically show that participants experienced more anxiety and performed worse when the interface agent present appeared to observe the user. Heylen, van Es, Nijholt, and van Dijk [33] prove that human-like gaze behavior of a cartoon-like talking face is evaluated more positively with regard to usability, satisfaction, involvement and naturalness than when displaying a small amount of gaze movements or random movements. Cowell and Stanney [34] also demonstrate that larger amounts of gaze at the participant lead to the character being experienced as more trustworthy and positive.

The effects of gestures are also analyzed by various research groups: McBreen and Jack [35] show that agents exerting deictic, iconic, metaphoric and beat gestures are evaluated as more useful, more friendly and more natural than agents who merely show pointing gestures – although the amount of gestures is seen as overdoing. Still, a word of caution is in order since in the study gesture was confounded with presentation as 2D or 3D agent. Buisine, Abrilian, and Martin [36] analyze the relation of speech and gesture by testing whether redundancy (relevant information is given by speech AND iconic and deictic gesture) or complementarity (relevant information is given by speech OR iconic and deictic gestures) is rated more favourable. Merely with male participants the redundant strategy was superior and evaluated more positive. Cassell and Thórisson [37], on the other hand, show that especially process-oriented nonverbal behavior (e.g. turn taking and beat gestures) is evaluated positive while merely showing emotional aspects (showing confusion or smiling) led to less favourable evaluations with regard to speech comprehension, smoothness of interaction and usefulness. Krämer et al. [38] did not prove different evaluations depending on gestures: agents with gesture, with dissynchronized gestures and without gestures were rated similarly.

However, it could be documented that more subtle behavioral aspects such as head movement quality affect the evaluation of the embodied agent. In a study addressing the impact of head positions and head movement activity, it was shown that a virtual TV/VCR assistant is evaluated more positively when his head movement activity is increased [39]. In sum, these results point to a strong impact of even subtle nonverbal phenomena on the perception and evaluation of virtual characters.

In sum, it can be stated that results demonstrate that in most cases even very subtle nonverbal behavior does have an influence on the acceptance and even efficiency of an embodied agent. This gives rise to the assumption that it is necessary to carefully design the communicative behaviour of the agent since it has been shown to matter. But then the critical question of how human communication behaviour should be modelled arises. Are there any models that are sufficiently detailed to be implemented? What are the necessary fundamentals and what will help to decide what cues to choose in a given situation? In order to discuss this, the next paragraph will give an overview on basic aspects of and prerequisites for human communication.

3   Attributes and Prerequisites for Human Communication

It has long been acknowledged that human communication is not comparable to that of machine communication. The process of message transmission valid for machines that has been aptly described by Shannon and Weaver [4] falls short of human communication. Instead of merely comprising of message transmission (in the sense that the message that has been encoded by the sender has just to be decoded by the receiver and automatically conforms to what has been sent), human communication must be seen as determined by the receiver's abilities, attributes and current state. Especially communication models of systems theory provenience stress that the receiver's current "structure" affects the decoding of a message [5, 6]. Instead of decoding and "understanding" the message in exactly the way it was intended, the human receiver constructs and interprets the message. Since the fact that human perceivers construct their environment already holds for basic perceptions e.g. with regard to colour (e.g., physically identical objects are – depending on background, circumstance and context - seen as having different colours), it can be seen as all the more true for communication processes: "Far from being a physical property of objects, color is a mental property. ... What is true for color is true for everything in our experienced worlds: the warmth of a smile, the meaning of a glance, the heft of a book, the force of a glare" [40, p. XI]. The elemental conclusion that can be derived is of course that this renders human communication difficult because it entails that the sender has neither control nor direct knowledge about how the receiver will decode and interpret the message. The only resource the human sender has to predict the effects of her utterances – given that she does not know her interaction partner intimately – is the fact that she herself being a human being possesses basic knowledge of human nature. In fact, different disciplines have developed models to explain the fact that humans can communicate successfully although the messages are understood against the background of the receiver's attributes and states. These models all draw on the fact that sender and receiver have fundamental similarities since they share human processing with regard to needs, thoughts, emotions etc. This enables the speaker to design messages to be appropriate to what he assumes to be the knowledge of the recipient [audience design hypothesis, 41, 42; see 7]. In psychology, models on perspective taking [43], common ground [41], imputing one´s own knowledge in others [7, 8] have been proposed. Additionally, in ethology the basic ability of a "theory of mind" [13] has been described that might be seen as a meta-theory to unify the different approaches. In the following, the different models will be described separately.

3.1 Perspective Taking

Krauss and Fussell [43] describe the process of perspective taking in communication from a social psychological point of view: They start out from the statement that in communication, the fundamental role of knowing what others know is axiomatic and that this has been widely acknowledged [44, 45, 46, 47, 48]. The importance of perspective taking (or role taking, point-of-view appreciation, see [7]) has further been stressed by Baldwin [49], Kohlberg [50] and Rommeveit [51]. According to these views, the failure to take other´s perspective can be the basis for misunderstandings and dispute. A prerequisite for successful communication is that the message is tailored to the knowledge of the recipient: "Messages are formulated to be understood by a specific audience, and in order to be comprehensible they must take into account what that audience does and does not know" [43, p. 3]. Although this ability has been stressed as an important prerequisite for communication, Krauss and Fussell [43] state that remarkably little discussion of the process by which communicators take the perspective of others into account can be observed. They review several studies that indicate that speakers indeed take their addressee´s knowledge and perspectives into account when they formulate messages. They show that on the one hand, the accuracy of people´s assessments of others´ knowledge is fairly high but that they, on the other hand, seem to be biased in the direction of their own knowledge (see also [7], see below). Besides own knowledge, other sources of information are, for example, category membership or knowledge about the social distribution of knowledge (the latter leading, however, to the "false consensus effect", in which subjects assume that others are more similar to themselves than is actually the case, Ross, Greene, & House [52]). Krauss and Fussell [43] conclude that people´s assumptions about other´s knowledge are necessarily tentative and best thought of as hypotheses that need to be evaluated and modified over time. Perspective taking is thus not only characterized by theories on what others know; in face-to-face interactions one might additionally use conversational resources such as the possibility to receive feedback on the own assumptions with regard to other´s knowledge: "During the course of the interaction, each participant´s apparent understandings and failures to understand the partner´s messages provide feedback about the appropriateness of the assumptions on which these messages are based" [43, p. 21]. Burgoon and White [53] in their "interaction adaptation theory" that not only focuses on verbal interaction but also nonverbal mimicry and reciprocity stress the importance of this mutual "online" adaptation and joint construction of the other´s knowledge even more: "All message production, and especially that in interpersonal conversation, implicitly begins with an alignment toward the message recipient and the predisposition to calibrate one´s messages to the characteristics of the target (as well as the topic, occasion, and setting). Put differently, adaptation is an intrinsic feature of all communication, and, as such, carries with it the implication that to fully understand message production requires knowing the extent to which message content and form are influenced by, and jointly constructed with, cointeractants" (p. 282).

3.2 Common Ground

The theory of common ground has been proposed as one important aspect of using language. Drawing on Stalnaker [54] and Karttunen and Peters [55], Clark [41] describes common ground as the joint basis for communication: "Two people´s common ground is, in effect, the sum of their mutual, common, or joint knowledge, beliefs, and suppositions" (p. 93). He assumes common ground to be a sine qua non for everything humans do with others: to coordinate and communicate with others humans have to appeal to their current common ground. This implies that in case there is no common ground no communication or understanding, respectively, would take place: To illustrate this he aptly quotes Ludwig Wittgenstein who, in his philosophical investigations, stated: "If a lion could talk, we could not understand him".

Thus, it can be assumed that there should be an initial common ground in each conversation that can be broadened during the interaction. The most obvious starting point in terms of communal common ground is human nature: "whenever I meet other humans (…) I assume as common ground that they and I think in the same way about many things. … I possess a folk psychology about people in general – about human nature – and, right or wrong, this allows me to get started" [41, p. 106]. As an example he points out that if a sound is audible to someone, he will assume that it is also audible to the other, that people take the same facts of biology for granted, that everyone assumes certain social facts (people use language, live in groups, have names). In most cases, i.e. when interacting with people from the same cultural area, even cultural facts, norms and procedures can be taken as belonging to the common ground. Hence, Clark [41, p. 107] comes to the conclusion that "It is hard to exaggerate the number and variety of basic concepts we take as common ground for everyone". Moreover, humans use the knowledge of cultural communities (e.g. when categorizing people by nationality, profession etc.) to infer what information members of that community might have. Being a member of that community herself someone might use inside information on this, otherwise people usually possess outside information in the sense of the assumptions that outsiders possess about the knowledge the insiders might share. By basic grounding principles during the interaction humans try to assert the common ground by e.g. finding evidence of (joint) category membership.

During interactions, moreover, personal common ground is built on joint perceptual experiences and joint actions. Here, people try to ground what they do together. Similarly to the approach by Krauss and Fussell [43, see above] it is further assumed that the actual conversation can be used for preventing discrepancies. Humans have verbal and nonverbal strategies to discover and repair situations where the mutual knowledge is misinterpreted. "Contributors present signals to respondents, and then contributors and respondents work together to reach the mutual belief that the signals have been understood well enough for current purposes" [41, p. 252].

In fact, Clark [41] lists several grounding principles that permit the location of common ground as well as the establishment of mutual knowledge. One example is the linguistic copresence heuristic that entails that anything that has been said during the course of the conversation is known to both [46]. Another general principle that humans rely on is the principle of closure: human agents performing an action require evidence that they have succeeded in performing it. Within human-human-interaction this is relevant in the sense of joint closure: the participants of a joint action try to establish the mutual belief that they have succeeded well enough for current purposes (e.g. shake hands). This might be accomplished by providing each other with subtle feedback. Within human-computer-interaction this need for feedback and closure has also been described: here, telephone buttons that do not beep when pressed or a display that does not change when an action has been taken are confusing [56].

3.3 Imputing One's Knowledge to Others

Drawing on concepts like perspective taking [43], common ground [41] or emphatic accuracy ([57]; ability to accurately infer the specific content of another person's thought and feelings) Nickerson [7] forms a model of how humans build beliefs on the knowledge of their interlocutors that he sees as an important prerequisite for communication: "To communicate effectively, people must have a reasonably accurate idea about what specific other people know. An obvious starting point for building a model of what another knows is what oneself knows, or think one knows" (p. 737). He thus assumes the ability to impute one's own knowledge (including beliefs, opinions, suppositions, attitudes) to others to be vital for human-human communication. He likens the procedure to the assumptions of the simulation view of Theory of mind approaches [58, 59, see below].

The model he proposes is tailored to the case that one needs a model of what a specific individual knows (e.g. when directly communicating with him/her instead of writing a newspaper article). If nothing about the specific individual is known the group model may be the best one can do:

(a) One starts with a model of one's own knowledge. Additionally one applies to this reasons one has for believing one's knowledge to be unusual, and constructs from this basis a default model of a random other.

(b) One develops the default into an initial model of a specific other in accordance with any differentiating knowledge one may have on the individual.

(c) One modifies one's working model on an ongoing basis in accordance with new information obtained (similar to what Krauss & Fussell [43], propose when stating that a tentative hypothesis is formed that is adapted during the course of the interaction)

The utility of the heuristic to impute one's knowledge is aptly depicted in the following quote: "imputing one's knowledge to a specific other is a *default* measure; it is what one does in the absence of knowledge, or of a basis for inferring, that the other's knowledge is different from one's own. ... If one has no direct knowledge of what another, whom one is addressing, does or does not know, and little or no knowledge that would provide the basis for making inferences in this regard, the only thing left to do is to use one's own knowledge as a default assumption as to what the other know" [7, p. 745]. This is not only functional with unknown persons but also works with familiar people to fill in gaps (e.g., what does my friend Anne, who is a dentist, know on Buddhist religion?). In fact, the heuristic is the best basis for anticipating how other people will react. As many other scholars, Nickerson [7] also refers to the unifying aspect of human nature: "If this were not the case, how would people be able to understand other people´s reactions, to be happy with them when they have cause to celebrate, or to sympathize when they are in pain? This idea is captured in the principle of humanity, according to which, when trying to understand what someone has said, especially something ambiguous, one should impute to the speaker beliefs and desires similar to one´s own (Gordon, 1986; Grandy, 1973)." (p. 747). The conclusions drawn from this have indeed been shown to provide correct assumptions [60], but of course it is not sufficient to merely transfer one´s own knowledge or perspective (see Piaget´s [61], concept of egocentrism). Complications with knowledge imputation arise for example with the overestimation of the commonality of one´s own knowledge, the false consensus effect [see above, 52, 62] or the "curse of knowledge" (it is especially problematic when well-informed agents impute their knowledge to less informed agents). With regard to the utility of the heuristic it can hence be stated that - as with many psychological heuristics - it serves well in general, but that necessary adjustments are executed to an insufficient degree (see general reasoning heuristic of anchoring and adjustment, [63]). In consequence, people often erroneously assume that other people have the same knowledge. The model eventually predicts that "one is likely to overestimate the extent to which a random other person´s knowledge corresponds to one´s own" (p. 740) and that this can contribute to communication difficulties.

In order to adjust the initial default model one can use various clues to what specific others know: Here, *shared immediate context* (see common ground theory, [64, 65]), *shared past experiences, category membership* (e.g. gender may provide a clue to the likelihood that one will have certain types of knowledge [66]), *implicit models of knowledge structures* ("If one knows A, one probably knows B") and *levels of knowledge* (people who understand concepts at a given level are also likely to understand concepts of a less deep level) might be helpful.

3.4 Theory of Mind

The term "theory of mind" was coined by Premack and Woodruff [13] as they referred to the "ability – which may or may not be unique to human beings – to explain and predict the actions, both of oneself, and of other intelligent agents" [67, p. 1]. Theory of mind (ToM) is the ability to see other entities as intentional agents, whose behavior is influenced by states, believes, desires etc. and the knowledge that other humans wish, feel, know or believe something [12, 13, 68]. In recent years, ToM has been discussed as a basic prerequisite for human-human interaction and various terms have been established: Mentalising (take another person´s mental perspective and predict what they can know [69]), mindreading [70] and intentional stance [71] all basically refer to the same ability. Dennett [71] for example states that attributing mental states to a complex system (such as a human being) is by far the easiest way of understanding it, i.e. coming up with an explanation of the complex system´s behaviour and predicting what it will do next. The ability is seen as an important and innate part of human nature that is crucial for all aspects of our everyday social life and our natural way of understanding the social environment:

In this line, Sperber [72] states that "attribution of mental states is to humans as echolocation is to the bat" [cf. 70, p. 4]. Also, Toby and Cosmides [40] stress the function and innateness of the ability: "We are "mindreaders" by nature, building interpretations of the mental events of others and feeling our constructions as sharply as the physical objects we touch. Humans evolved this ability because, as members of an intensely social, cooperative, and competitive species, our ancestors´ lives depended on how well they could infer what was on one another´s minds" [40, p. XIII].

Indeed, theory of mind has been discussed as a prerequisite for communication between human interactants: Although "mindreading" does of course not allow for a 100% correct prediction of mental states but provides a general orientation on other people´s processes and a prediction of the effects of communication. Baron-Cohen [70] thus sums up: "A ...reason why mindreading is useful, and thus why it may have evolved, is the way in which it allows us to make sense of communication. ... A range of theorists – Grice (1967), Sperber and Wilson (1986), Austin (1962) – have argued that when we hear someone say something ...., aside from decoding the referent of each word (computing its semantics and syntax), the key thing we do as we search for the meaning of the words is to imagine what the speaker´s communicative intention might be. That is, we ask ourselves "What does he mean? " Here the word "mean" essentially boils down to "intend me to understand"" (p. 27). Hence, in decoding speech humans go beyond the words we hear or read and hypothesize about the speaker´s mental states. Similarly, Frith and Frith [69] refer to Grice [73] and his idea that a successful understanding of an utterance depends upon perceiving the intention of the speaker as well as to Sperber and Wilson´s [74] theory of relevance. They conclude that pragmatics of speech rely on mentalising and that in many real-life cases the understanding of an utterance cannot be based solely on the meanings of the individual words (semantics) or upon the grammar by which they are connected (syntax).

The functioning of a theory of mind module has so far been merely described on a global level. While during the first years it was mainly analyzed whether the ToM ability is unique to humans and when it develops in children, recently the neurological bases of ToM have drawn interest [75, 76, 77, 78]. In parallel, models become more elaborated. Recently, cognitive based ToM (assumption concerning cognitive states) and affective based ToM (assumption concerning the other person´s emotion) have been differentiated [77, 78, 79]. Another distinction has been made between theory-theory and simulation-theory [67] that basically disagree on the basis of a theory of mind. 'Theory-theorists´ suggest that the ability to explain and predict behaviour is based on a folk psychological theory of the structure and functioning of the mind that might either be innate, learned individually, or acquired through a process of enculturation [80, 81; see 67]. The simulationist view [82, 83, 84] on the other hand holds that "what lies at the root of our mature mind-reading abilities is not any sort of theory, but rather an ability to project ourselves imaginatively into another person´s perspective, *simulating* their mental activity with our own" [67, p. 3]. Thus, Humphrey [85] argues that humans mindread by using the own experience of introspection as a simulation of another´s mental states. Gordon [86] also holds a radical simulationism view stating that human´s concepts of mental states are acquired through a process of simulation, without subjects needing to have introspective access to their own mental states as such.

Similarly, Grammer [87] proposes that communication can work without involving direct cognitive processing. His analogue communication view suggests that if there is something like a theory of mind it might operate without consciously ascribing own or other´s mental states. With regard to the origin of the ToM ability, the different theoretical perspectives also hold diverging views: While theory-theorists partly propose that the theory is learned on the basis of experience [88, 89, see also 69] and partly assume that folk-psychology is embodied in an innate theory of mind module, the ability to simulate is always conceptualized as an innate genetic endowment. But not all authors see the different views as mutually exclusive: Heal [90] and Perner [91] try to close the gap between the different approaches and argue for a simulation/theory mix.

One of the most sophisticated models of ToM is presented by Baron-Cohen [70] who explains the child´s development of mindreading. He proposes an eye-direction-detector and an intentionality detector that provide input to a shared-attention mechanism. While these allow to read behaviours in terms of volitional mental states and to read eye direction in term of perceptual mental states, the ToM-module is needed as a way of representing the set of epistemic mental states and in order to tie together the volitional, perceptual and epistemic mental state into a coherent understanding of how mental states and actions are related.

In sum, it might be stated that the different models on common ground, perspective taking, imputing one´s knowledge and ToM show major similarities with regard to the fact that all propose that humans possess a direct but implicit knowledge on other humans (be it via simulation or via a learned or innate theory on fellow humans) that form a starting point for mutual comprehension. Building on this, the dialogue can be used to clarify and broaden mutual knowledge by means of grounding processes.

4   Lacking Aspects in Human-Agent Communication

As was already depicted in the introduction and as will be affirmed by everyone who tried to converse with an embodied agent, current dialogue and agent systems are prone for misunderstandings and failed comprehension attempts. Although the reasons for this are certainly manifold, one of the most important causes is the fact that basic needs and customs of the human users are neglected. One of the examples from our own research might exemplify the problems. In one of our studies on the human reactions towards an embodied television guide the participants showed a striking tendency to more often repeat sentences in exactly the same or slightly altered way – that did not occur when interacting with merely text- or speech-based systems [14, 16]. This might be attributed to the fact that the virtual face was not able to give immediate feedback as to whether the utterance had been understood (see "need for closure" described above). People thus seemed to come to the conclusion that no immediate reaction from the face meant that the system did not understand, while they patiently waited for an answer when no face was displayed. This suggests that the statement "One cannot not communicate" [6] might also be true for agents: as soon as a face is displayed on the screen, humans will take every behavior – even a blank face – as communication. The latter is a tendency that every human in a communication will naturally be aware of and will avoid misunderstandings by, for example, a cogitation display. The agent will not "know" or sense the necessity for this kind of behaviour because of his disability to anticipate the user´s states.

The Wittgenstein statement "If a lion could talk, we would not understand him" is thus probably not only true for lions but also for agents – in their current forms. Also, because of the lack of a human theory of mind the agent might be likened to a human with autism – given the failure to ascribe mental states to himself and others [70].

But what exactly is lacking? As described by all the models summarized above, humanness enables to directly infer states and thereby communication effects in other people – either by simulating and imputing one´s own knowledge or by an in-built or learnt theory on other humans. The agent has neither: If he has a mind at all he has no theory of its own mind and thus no possibility to simulate or impute his knowledge on others. Also, no agent so far has a complete user module that can be compared to a theory of mind in the sense of the theory-theory approach. Thus, a large amount of small aspects that are taken for granted within human-human communication and would thus never be made explicit (e.g. feedback rules in turn taking) are not present in human-agent communication. Especially Clark´s [41] statement that it is hard to exaggerate the number and variety of basic concepts we take as common ground for everyone (see above) shows that it will be difficult to compile the knowledge on human nature that we rely on in everyday communication – even if we tried. Also, to simply implement rules or knowledge will probably not be sufficient: As Frith and Frith [92] aptly state mere knowledge will not be enough to successfully mentalize: "The bottom line of the idea of mentalising is that we predict what other individuals will do in a given situation from their desires, their knowledge and their beliefs, and not from the actual state of the world" [92, p. 6]. The obvious consequence of these considerations is thus to try to implement theory-of-mind-like abilities. In fact, this has been proposed in several recent approaches as will be depicted in the next paragraph.

5   Current Implementations of a Theory of Mind

The attempt to model how people commonly react in specific situations is not new in technological implementation. Early artificial intelligence software already used default or prototypical models of people as points of departure for anticipating how individuals will react in those situations [93, 94, see 7]. Also, more recent multi-agent systems integrate aspects that mimic theory of mind abilities. Within PsychSim, a multiagent-based simulation that models interactions and influence among groups or individuals, a theory of mind in terms of a recursive model of other agents is implemented [95]. Based on the assumption that the action an agent takes should – like in real life – be influenced by how he believes others will react, the agents are enabled to form complex attributions about others. Further, their messages are enriched to include the beliefs and goals of other agents. Thus, each agent itself has a state as well as actions and goals and, moreover, each agent's beliefs consist of models of all of the agents (including itself), representing their state, beliefs, goals, and policy of behaviour. The overarching goal is to develop a better understanding of the causes and remedies of school bullying, a theory of mind is incorporated to simulate and study classroom social interactions. Peters [96] on his way to build a memory system for embodied agents implements the ToM-Module by Baron-Cohen [70]. In order to be able to store perceived attention levels of each agent in his multi-agent system over time, Peters [96] simulates the main components of Baron-Cohen´s model: the intentionality detector for detecting objects in the environment that move under their own volition; the eye-direction-detector that searches for eyes and determines their direction and the theory of mind module for storing higher-level theories about the intention of the other based on interpretation of their behaviour. In the latter, multiple attention levels over time are integrated into a single metric called level of interest. As within Baron-Cohen´s [70] model, here, several previous entries are amalgamated into one new entry, that is, the higher-level representation "attention level". The agents are thus provided with a social memory of gaze direction and attention of other agents in the environment in order to interpret their interest. This again might be decisive with regard to the decision of whether to start an interaction with another agent. When comparing these approaches to the models and suggestions described above, it is apparent that these implementations indeed consider the mechanism of mentalising about another entity. But being a theory of mind of fellow agents, they certainly lack the richness that an adequate model of a theory of mind for humans (compared to less complex agents) would need to have.

In consequence, the theory of mind-like modules that have been developed for human-technology-interaction should be more advanced in this respect. Here, as early as 1994 Traum [97] implemented the concept of grounding within the TRAINS-93 NL dialogue system [98, 99]. The goal was to determine, for any given state of the conversation, whether material has been grounded or what it would take to ground the material. As a prerequisite all mental states of the participating agents had to be considered and the model was augmented with social attitudes (including mutual belief, shared plans, and obligations). Miscommunication was seen as a non-alignment of the mental states of agents that can be overcome by grounding acts. In a more recent approach from the application area of human-robot-interaction, Breazeal et al. [100, 101] implemented the joint attention theory [102, 103] that includes possibility to establish common ground [10]. As a prerequisite, a theory of mind is built: the robot has to have the ability to infer the mental states of other people. This is seen as the basic requirement for cooperation: "For collaboration, it is important that Leonardo be able to establish mutual beliefs between itself and its human partner. This entails that the robot be able to represent beliefs for itself as well as model the beliefs of others" [100]. The ability to infer mental states is, however, not implemented directly but the ability for social learning based on the AIM model on the early imitation of faces is simulated [104; see also the discussion on mirror neurons [105, 106]). Although explicitly built for human-technology-interaction, these latter models all the same will have to be enriched by knowledge on human minds. Currently, the systems would be not successful to predict or interpret any given human´s mental state and would probably not be able to pass the most basic theory of mind tests that have been developed for humans.

6   Suggestion with Regard to a Research Approach Based on ToM

The approaches depicted above are promising but will have to be broadened. In order to, in future, anticipate the effects of its dialogue moves and behaviours, the agent has to possess not only a knowledge on its own abilities (e.g. that it will take two minutes to retrieve a specific information) but, more importantly, knowledge on the human interaction partner (e.g. on the fact that the human will be confused if she does not receive immediate feedback). A first step into this direction might be the development of a user model that is endowed with global knowledge on human needs and states – equalizing a ToM module as modelled in the theory-theory approach. The contents of this module will have to be developed via a research program that will have to make implicit knowledge on human nature that every human being possesses explicit. Here, the everyday interaction abilities we take for granted in human communication have to be taken into account. To accomplish this, an iterative research program starting out from detailed analyses of human-human- and human-machine dialogue will have to be conducted. The latter might help to uncover abilities as well as needs of the human user that can be implemented and, in a next step, evaluated. As to be found in the models depicted above, the resulting implementations should incorporate two aspects: a ToM module with basic knowledge on human abilities, knowledge, states, etc. and interaction abilities that enable the agent to verify the knowledge, beliefs, needs and emotions of the user and to progressively build common ground with the user. In parallel, computer vision techniques, as they are advanced, will provide an important prerequisite by enabling the system to take more information on the user into account (e.g. gesture, facial expressions).

That the task ahead is not an easy one has long been acknowledged during the course of AI research. Already (or especially?) the seemingly most simple abilities – the ones we take for granted in humans - prove to be very difficult to implement: "Cognitive scientists were awakened by a series of encounters with alien minds, whose starkly contrasting designs and surprising incapacities drew attention to previously overlooked natural human competences and to the computational problems they routinely solve. They encountered artificial mentalities in the computer lab that had obstinate difficulties in seeing, speaking, handling objects, understanding, or doing almost anything that humans do effortlessly" [40, p. XIII]. To this end, the implementation of theory-of-mind like abilities in virtual humans will further promote basic research on human abilities and yield findings on human nature.

References

1. Cassell, J., Sullivan, J., Prevost, S., Churchill, E. (eds.): Embodied conversational agents. MIT Press, Cambridge (2000)
2. Takeuchi, A., Naito, T.: Situated facial displays: towards social interaction. In: Katz, I., Mack, R., Marks, L., Rosson, M.B., Nielsen, J. (eds.) Human factors in computing Systems: CHI 1995 Conference Proceedings, pp. 450–455. ACM Press, New York (1995)
3. Burgoon, J.K., Bacue, A.E.: Nonverbal communication skills. In: Greene, J.O., Burleson, B.R. (eds.) Handbook of communication and social interaction skills, pp. 179–220. Lawrence Erlbaum Associates, Mahwah (2003)
4. Shannon, C., Weaver, W.: A Mathematical theory of communication. Univ. of Illinois Press (1948)
5. Maturana, H.R., Varela, F.J.: Autopoiesis and cognition. Reidel, Dordrecht (1980)
6. Watzlawick, P., Beavin, J.H., Jackson, D.: Pragmatics of Human Communication. Norton, New York (1967)
7. Nickerson, R.S.: How we know – and sometimes misjudge – what others know: Imputing one´s knowledge to others. Psychological Bulletin 125, 737–759 (1999)

8. Nickerson, R.S.: The projective way of knowing: A useful heuristic that sometimes misleads. Current Directions in Psychological Science 10, 168–172 (2001)
9. Clark, H.H.: Using language. Cambridge University Press, Cambridge (1996)
10. Clark, H.H., Brennan, S.A.: Grounding in communication. In: Resnick, L.B., Levine, J.M., Teasley, S.D. (eds.) Perspectives on socially shared cognition, pp. 127–149. APA Books, Washington (1991)
11. Eisenberg, N., Murphy, B.C., Shepard, S.: The development of empathic accuracy. In: Ickes, W. (ed.) Empathic accuracy, pp. 73–116. Guilford Press, New York (1997)
12. Premack, D., Premack, A.J.: Origins of human social competence. In: Gazzaniga, M.S. (ed.) The cognitive neurosciences, pp. 205–218. MIT Press, Cambridge (1995)
13. Premack, D., Woodruff, G.: Does the chimpanzee have a theory of mind? The Behavioral and Brain Sciences 4, 512–526 (1978)
14. Krämer, N.C.: Soziale Wirkungen virtueller Helfer. Gestaltung und Evaluation von Mensch-Computer-Interaktionen, Kohlhammer, Stuttgart (in press)
15. Dehn, D.M., van Mulken, S.: The impact of animated interface agents: a review of empirical research. International Journal of Human-Computer Studies 52, 1–22 (2000)
16. Krämer, N.C.: Social communicative effects of a virtual program guide. In: Panayiotopoulos, T., et al. (eds.) Intelligent Virtual Agents 2005, pp. 442–543. Springer, Hamburg (2005)
17. Ruttkay, Zs., Pelachaud, C.: From Brows to Trust: Evaluating Embodied Conversational Agents. Kluwer, Dordrecht (2004)
18. Krämer, N.C., Nitschke, J.: Ausgabemodalitäten im Vergleich: Verändern sie das Eingabeverhalten der Benutzer? In: Marzi, R., Karavezyris, V., Erbe, H.-H., Timpe, K.-P. (Hrsg.) (eds.) (Hrsg.) Bedienen und Verstehen. 4. Berliner Werkstatt Mensch-Maschine-Systeme, pp. 231–248. VDI-Verlag, Düsseldorf (2002)
19. Krämer, N.C., Bente, G.: Virtuelle Helfer: Embodied Conversational Agents in der Mensch-Computer-Interaktion. In: Bente, G., Krämer, N.C., Petersen, A. (Hrsg.) (eds.) Virtuelle Realitäten, pp. 203–225. Hogrefe, Göttingen (2002)
20. Krämer, N.C., Bente, G., Piesk, J.: The ghost in the machine. The influence of Embodied Conversational Agents on user expectations and user behaviour in a TV/VCR application. In: Bieber, G., Kirste, T. (eds.) IMC Workshop 2003, Assistance, Mobility, Applications, Rostock, pp. 121–128 (2003)
21. Smith, J.: GrandChair: Conversational Collection of Family Stories. Media Lab. MIT, Cambridge (2000)
22. Cassell, J., Bickmore, T.: External manifestations of trustworthiness in the interface. Communications of the ACM 43(12), 50–56 (2000)
23. Kaiser, S., Wehrle, T.: Animating and analyzing facial expressions in human-computer interactions: An appraisal based approach. Paper presented at the ISRE General Meeting, Bari (July 2005)
24. Kaiser, S., Wehrle, T., Schmidt, S.: Emotional episodes, facial expression, and reported feelings in human-computer interactions. In: Fischer, A.H. (ed.) Proceedings of the Xth Conference of the International Society for Research on Emotions, pp. 82–86. ISRE Publications Würzburg (1998)
25. Nass, C., Steuer, J., Tauber, E.R.: Computers are Social Actors. In: Adelson, B., Dumais, S., Olson, J. (eds.) Human Factors in Computing Systems: CHI 1994 Conference Proceedings, pp. 72–78. ACM Press, New York (1994)
26. Oviatt, S.L., Darves, C., Coulston, R.: Toward adaptive Conversational interfaces: Modeling speech convergence with animated personas. ACM Transactions on Computer-Human Interaction 3, 300–328 (2004)

27. Burgoon, J., Stern, L., Dillman, L.: Interpersonal Adaptation: Dyadic Interaction Patterns. Cambridge Univ. Press, Cambridge (1995)
28. Bell, L., Gustafson, J.: Repetition and its phonetic realizations: Investigating a Swedish database of spontaneous computer-directed speech. Proceedings of the International Conference on Phonetic Sciences 2, 1221–1224 (1999)
29. Kopp, S., Gesellensetter, L., Krämer, N.C., Wachsmuth, I.: A conversational agent as a museum guide. Design and evaluation of a real-world application. In: Panayiotopoulos, T., et al. (eds.) Intelligent Virtual Agents 2005, pp. 329–343. Springer, Heidelberg (2005)
30. Gong, L., Nass, C., Simard, C., Takhteyev, Y.: When non-human is better than semihuman: Consistency in speech interfaces. In: Smith, M., Salvendy, G., Harris, D., Koubek, R. (eds.) Usability Evaluation and Interface Design: Cognitive Engineering, Intelligent Agents and Virtual Reality, LEA, Mahwah, N.J, vol. 1, pp. 390–394 (2001)
31. Krämer, N.C., Simons, N., Kopp, S.: The effects of an embodied conversational agent´s nonverbal behavior on user´s evaluation and behavioral mimicry. In: Pelachaud, C., et al. (eds.) Intelligent Virtual Agents 2007, pp. 238–251. Springer, Hamburg (2007)
32. Rickenberg, R., Reeves, B.: The effects of animated characters on anxiety, task performance, and evaluations of user interfaces. In: Letters of CHI 2000, pp. 49–56 (April 2000)
33. Heylen, D., Es, I., van, N.A., Dijk, B.: Experimenting with the gaze of a conversational agent. In: van Kuppevelt, J., Dybkjaer, L., Bernsen, N. (eds.) Proceedings of the International CLASS Workshop on Natural, Intelligent and Effective Interaction with Multimodal Dialogue Systems, Kluwer Academic, New York (2002)
34. Cowell, A.J., Stanney, K.M.: Embodiment and interaction guidelines for designing credible, trustworthy embodied conversational agents. In: Rist, T., Aylett, R.S., Ballin, D., Rickel, J. (eds.) IVA 2003. LNCS (LNAI), vol. 2792, pp. 301–309. Springer, Heidelberg (2003)
35. McBreen, H., Jack, M.: Empirical evaluation of animated agents in a multi-modal e-retail application. In: Proceedings of the AAAI Fall Symposium on socially intelligent agents (2000)
36. Buisine, S., Abrilian, S., Martin, J.-C.: Evaluation of multimodal behaviour of agents. Cooperation between speech and gestures in ECAs. In: Ruttkay, Z., Pelachaud, C. (eds.) From Brows to trust. Evaluating Embodied Conversational Agents, pp. 217–238. Kluwer, Dordrecht (2004)
37. Cassell, J., Thorisson, K.R.: The Power of a Nod and a Glance: Envelope vs. Emotional Feedback in Animated Conversational Agents. Applied Artificial Intelligence 13, 519–538 (1999)
38. Krämer, N.C., Tietz, B., Bente, G.: Effects of embodied interface agents and their gestural activity. In: Aylett, R., Ballin, D., Rist, T., Rickel, J. (eds.) 4th International Working Conference on Intelligent Virtual Agents, pp. 292–300. Springer, Hamburg (2003)
39. Krämer, N.C.: Bewegende Bewegung. Sozio-emotionale Wirkungen nonverbalen Verhaltens und deren experimentelle Untersuchung mittels Computeranimation, Pabst, Lengerich (2001)
40. Toby, J., Cosmides, L.: Foreword. In: Baron-Cohen, S. (ed.) Mindblindness. An essay on autism and theory of mind, MIT Press, Cambridge (1995)
41. Clark, H.H.: Arenas of language use. University of Chicago Press, Chicago (1992)
42. Fussell, S.R., Krauss, R.M.: Coordination of knowledge in communication: Effects of audience design on message comprehension: Reference in a common ground framework. Journal of Experimental Social Psychology 25, 203–219 (1992)
43. Krauss, R.M., Fussell, S.R.: Perspective taking in communication: Representation of others´ knowledge in reference. Social Cognition 9, 2–24 (1991)

44. Bakhtin, M.M.: Discourse in the novel. In: Holquist, M. (ed.) The dialog imagination, University of Texas Press, Austin (1981)
45. Clark, H.H.: Language use and language users. In: Lindzey, G., Aronson, E. (eds.) Handbook of Social Psychology, pp. 179–231. Random House, New York (1985)
46. Clark, H.H., Marshall, C.E.: Definite reference and mutual knowledge. In: Joshi, A.K., Sag, I., Webber, B. (eds.) Elements of discourse understanding, pp. 10–63. Cambridge University Press, Cambridge (1981)
47. Graumann, C.F., Herrmann, T.: Speakers: The role of the listener, Multilingual Matters, Ltd. Clevedon, UK (1989)
48. Mead, G.H.: Mind, Self and Society. University of Chicago Press, Chicago (1934)
49. Baldwin, J.M.: Social and ethical interpretations of mental development. Macmillan, New York (1906)
50. Kohlberg, L.: Stage and sequence: The cognitive-developmental approach to socialization. In: Goslin, D.A. (ed.) Handbook of socialization theory and research, pp. 347–480. Rand McNally, Chicago (1969)
51. Rommeveit, R.: On message structure: A framework for the study of language and communication. Wiley, New York (1974)
52. Ross, L., Greene, D., House, P.: The false consensus phenomenon: An attributional bias in self-perception and social perception processes. Journal of Experimental Social Psychology 13, 279–301 (1977)
53. Burgoon, J.K., White, C.H.: Researching Nonverbal Message Production: A View from Interaction Adaptation Theory. In: Greene, J.O. (ed.) Message Production, pp. 280–312. Lawrence Erlbaum Ass., Mahwah (1997)
54. Stalnaker, R.C.: Assertion. In: Cole, P. (ed.) Syntax and semantics 9: Pragmatics, pp. 315–332. Academic Press, New York (1978)
55. Karttunen, L., Peters, S.: Conventional implicature of Montague grammar, Paper presented at the Berkeley Linguistics Society, Berkeley, CA (1975)
56. Norman, D.A.: The design of everyday things. Doubleday, New York (1988)
57. Ickes, W.: Empathic accuracy. Journal of Personality 61, 587–610 (1993)
58. Gordon, R.: Folk psychology as simulation. In: Davies, M., Stone, T. (eds.) Folk psychology, vol. 3, pp. 60–73. Blackwell, Oxford, England (1995)
59. Lillard, A.: Ethnopsychologies: Cultural variations in theories of mind. Psychological Bulletin 123, 3–32 (1998)
60. Shantz, C.U.: Social cognition. In: Mussen, P. (ed.) Handbook of child psychology, vol. 3, pp. 495–555. Wiley, New York (1983)
61. Piaget, J.: The language and thought of the child. Harcourt, New York (1921)
62. Goethals, G.F., Allison, S.J., Frost, M.: Perception of the magnitude and diversity of social support. Journal of Experimental Social Psychology 15, 570–581 (1979)
63. Tversky, A., Kahnemann, D.: Judgment under uncertainty: Heuristics and biases. Science 185, 1124–1131 (1974)
64. Clark, H.H., Carlson, T.B.: Context for comprehension. In: Long, J., Baddeley, A. (eds.) Attention and performance IX, pp. 313–330. Lawrence Erlbaum Ass, Hillsdale (1981)
65. Clark, H.H., Haviland, S.E.: Comprehension and the given-new contract. In: Freedle, R.O. (ed.) Discourse production and comprehension, pp. 1–40. Ablex, Norwwod (1977)
66. Ross, M., Holmberg, D.: Recounting the past: Gender differences in the recall of events in the history of a close relationship. In: Olson, J.M., Zanna, M.P. (eds.) Self-inferences processes: The Ontario Symposium, vol. 6, pp. 135–152. Lawrence Erlbaum Ass., Hillsdale (1988)

67. Carruthers, P., Smith, P.K. (eds.): Theories of theories of mind. Cambridge University Press, Cambridge (1996)
68. Whiten, A.: Natural theories of mind: Evolution, development and simulation of everyday mindreading. Basil Blackwell, Oxford (1991)
69. Frith, U., Frith, C.D.: Development of neurophysiology of mentalizing. Phil. Trans. R. Soc. Lond 358, 459–473 (2003)
70. Baron-Cohen, S.: Mindblindness. An essay on autism and theory of mind. MIT Press, Cambridge (1995)
71. Dennett, D.C.: The intentional stance. MIT Press, Cambridge (1987)
72. Sperber, D.: Paper presented at conference on Darwin and the Human Sciences, London School of Economics (1993)
73. Grice, H.P.: Meaning. Philosophical Review 66, 377–388 (1957)
74. Sperber, D., Wilson, D.: Relevance: Communication and Cognition. Blackwell, Malden (1995)
75. David, N., Bewernick, B., Cohen, M.X., Newen, A., Lux, S., Fink, G.R., Shah, N.J., Vogeley, K.: Neural Representations of Self versus Other: Visual-Spatial Perspective-Taking and Agency in a Virtual Ball-Tossing Game. Journal of Cognitive Neuroscience 18, 898–910 (2006)
76. Vogeley, K., Bussfeld, P., Newen, A., Herrmann, S., Happé, F., Falkai, P., Maier, W., Shah, N.J., Fink, G.R., Zilles, K.: Mind Reading: Neural Mechanisms of Theory of Mind and Self-Perspective. NeuroImage 14, 170–181 (2001)
77. Shamay-Tsoory, S.G., Tibi-Elhanany, Y., Aharon-Peretz, J.: The ventromedial prefrontal cortex is involved in understanding affective but not cognitive theory of mind stories. Social Neuroscience 1, 149–166 (2006)
78. Shamay-Tsoory, S.G., Tomer, R., Berger, B.D., Goldsher, D., Aharon-Peretz, J.: Impaired affective theory of mind is associated with right ventromedial prefrontal damage. Cognitive Behavioral Neurology 18, 55–67 (2005)
79. Kalbe, E., Grabenhorst, F., Brand, M., Kessler, J., Hilker, R., Markowitsch, H.J.: Elevated emotional reactivity in affective but not cognitive components of theory of mind: A psychophysiological study. Journal of Neuropsychology 1, 27–38 (2007)
80. Gopnik, A.: How we know our minds: The illusion of first-person knowledge of intentionality. Behavioral and Brain Sciences 16, 1–14 (1993)
81. Wellman, H.M.: The child's theory of mind. MIT Press, Cambridge (1990)
82. Heal, J.: Replication and functionalism. In: Butterfield, J. (ed.) Language, Mind, and Logic, pp. 135–150. Cambridge University Press, Cambridge (1986)
83. Harris, P.L.: Children and emotion: The development of Psychological understanding. Basil Blackwell, Oxford (1989)
84. Gordon, R.M.: Folk psychology as simulation. Mind and Language 1, 158–171 (1986)
85. Humphrey, N.: Consciousness regained. Oxford University Press, Oxford (1984)
86. Gordon, R.M.: "Radical" simulationism. In: Carruthers, P., Smith, P.K. (eds.) Theories of theories of mind, pp. 11–21. Cambridge University Press, Cambridge (1996)
87. Grammer, K., Filova, V., Fieder, M.: The communication paradox and a possible solution: Toward a radical empiricism. In: Schmitt, A., Atzwanger, K., Grammer, K., Schäfer, K. (eds.) New aspects of human ethology, pp. 91–120. Plenum, New York (1997)
88. Gopnik, A.: Theories and modules: creation myths, developmental realities and Neurath's boat. In: Carruthers, P., Smith, P.K. (eds.) Theories of theories of mind, pp. 169–183. Cambridge University Press, Cambridge (1996)

89. Astington, J.: What is theoretical about the child's theory of mind? A Vygotskian view of its development. In: Carruthers, P., Smith, P.K. (eds.) Theories of theories of mind, pp. 184–199. Cambridge University Press, Cambridge (1996)
90. Heal, J.: Simulation, theory, and content. In: Carruthers, P., Smith, P.K. (eds.) Theories of theories of mind, pp. 75–89. Cambridge University Press, Cambridge (1996)
91. Perner, J.: Simulation as explicitation of predication-implicit knowledge about the mind: arguments for a simulation-theory mix. In: Carruthers, P., Smith, P.K. (eds.) Theories of theories of mind, pp. 90–104. Cambridge University Press, Cambridge (1996)
92. Frith, C.D., Frith, U.: How we predict what other people are going to do. Brain Research 1079, 36–46 (2006)
93. Minsky, M.L.: A framework for representing knowledge. In: Winston, P.H. (ed.) The psychology of computer vision, McGraw-Hill, New York (1975)
94. Schank, R.C., Abelson, R.P.: Scripts, plans, goals, and understanding: An inquiry into human knowledge structures. Lawrence Erlbaum Ass., Hillsdale (1977)
95. Marsella, S.C., Pynadath, D.V.: Modeling influence and theory of mind. Artificial Intelligence and the Simulation of Behavior.In: Joint Symposium on Virtual Social Agents, pp. 199–206 (2005)
96. Peters, C.: Designing Synthetic Memory Systems for Supporting Autonomous Embodied Agent Behaviour. In: 15th IEEE International Symposium on Robot and Human Interactive Communication (ROMAN) (2006)
97. Traum, D.A.: Computational Theory of Grounding in Natural Language Conversation. Ph.D. Thesis, Computer Science Dept., U. Rochester (1994)
98. Traum, D.: Conversational Agency: The Trains-93 Dialogue Manager. In: Proceedings of the Twente Workshop on Language Technology 11: Dialogue Management in Natural Language Systems, pp. 1–11 (1996)
99. Traum, D., Dillenbourg, P.: Miscommunication in Multi-modal Collaboration. In: Working notes of the AAAI Workshop on Detecting, Repairing, and Preventing Human-Machine Miscommunication, pp. 37–46 (1996)
100. Breazeal, C., Buchsbaum, D., Gray, J., Gatenby, D., Blumberg, B.: Learning from and about Others: Towards Using Imitation to Bootstrap the Social Understanding of Others by Robots. In: Rocha, L., Almedia e Costa, F. (eds.) Artificial Life, pp. 31–62. MIT Press, Cambridge (2004a)
101. Breazeal, C., Brooks, A., Gray, J., Hoffman, G., Kidd, C., Lee, H., Lieberman, J., Lockerd, A., Mulanda, D.: Humanoid Robots as Cooperative Partners for People. IJHR [24.7.2005] (2004b), Available: http://web. media.mit. edu/ ~cynthiab/ NewFiles/pubs.html
102. Cohen, P., Levesque, H.: Teamwork. Nous 25, 487–512 (1991)
103. Cohen, P., Levesque, H.: Persistence, Intention, and Commitment. In: Cohen, P.R., Morgan, J., Pollack, M.E. (eds.) Intentions in Communication, pp. 33–69. MIT Press, Cambridge (1990)
104. Meltzoff, A., Moore, M.K.: Explaining facial imitation: A theoretical model. Early Development and Parenting 6, 179–192 (1997)
105. Rizzolatti, G., Fadiga, L., Matelli, M., Bettinardi, V., Paulesu, E., Perani, D., Fazio, F.: Localization of grasp representations in humans by PET: 1. Observation vs. execution. Experimental Brain Research 111, 246–252 (1996)
106. Williams, J.H., Whiten, A., Suddendorf, T., Perrett, D.: Imitation, mirror neurons and autism. Neuroscience and Biobehavioral Reviews 25, 287–295 (2001)

Listening Heads

Dirk Heylen

University of Twente
The Netherlands
d.k.j.heylen@ewi.utwente.nl

Abstract. In [1] we discussed functions of head movements and gaze. In this paper, we will go into more depth in the classification of various head movements: how they are distinguished in both formal and functional terms. We look at the distribution of a selection of primitive head movements and their related meanings and the way they are composed out of smaller units. This catalogue is not intended to be exhaustive and does not take into account the component items from other modalities such as speech, facial expressions, gestures and posture. The research is motivated by our desire to build systems that can interpret and mimick expressive human behaviour.

Keywords: head movements, corpus analysis, embodied agents.

1 Introduction

The way people move their head when they talk and listen to each other is one of the most fascinating forms of nonverbal communication to study because the apparent restriction in parametric variation does not seem to put a bound on the number of different expressive gestures that can be made and the diversity of functions that are served by them. The repertoire of behaviours is defined by only a few parameters but movements can be combined into one or can differ in velocity and amplitude. Movements may also be concatenated in different ways giving rise to configurations with different meanings. Depending on the context the meanings of a movement may change as well. There are clearly more head movements than simple nods or shakes. Also the meanings conveyed may be complex. Even if all the shakes in every context investigated by [2] share a core meaning of *negativity*, this is not to say, that this core is the only meaningful component to them nor that various forms of shaking can be exchanged from one context to the other. As Kendon writes:

> The head shake is used in many different discourse contexts where [...] it yet comes to have a very different force, depending upon how this theme of negation combines with the other semantic themes that are also being expressed. [p. 148]

In this paper, Kendon goes to some effort to argue that the general theme of negation is present in each of his examples, while at the same time showing the subtle variations in meanings that the contexts gives rise to.

I. Wachsmuth and G. Knoblich (Eds.): Modeling Communication, LNAI 4930, pp. 241–259, 2008.
© Springer-Verlag Berlin Heidelberg 2008

There is no doubt that these variations in performance intersect with and modify the meaning of the gesture. Furthermore, the head shake may be combined in various ways with other movements, such as movements of the eyelids, mouth expressions, and gestures of the shoulders, such as the raising of the shoulder in a 'shrug' or with manual gestures of various kinds. [p. 149]

But this analysis only scratches the surface, as Kendon points out himself. In general, research into the 'morphology', 'syntax', 'semantics', and 'pragmatics' of head movements is very incomplete. Compared to the analysis of other communicative signals such as spoken language, facial expressions and gestures, the interest in head movements has been marginal. Our aim is to give these humble movements the attention that they deserve as we believe they are of interest in both applications that analyse and interpret human behaviours as well as in applications of virtual humans where they need to be generated. They may be easier to recognize by computer vision techniques than facial expressions, but are still highly informative. This means that the ratio between detection and interpretation quality and thus the knowledge gain might be much higher than with other verbal and nonverbal cues.

With respect to the generation side, the proper selection and execution of head movements is important as they carry different kinds of information both while an agent is talking and listening. While talking, head movements play an important role in providing cues as to the information structure of the sentence. They are used to put emphasis on important parts of the utterance and can thereby signal higher or lower attitudinal involvement of speakers with the things they are saying. Besides their information-bearing impact, head movements play an important role in visual prosody improving the auditory speech perception ([3]). We will discuss the functions and determinants of head movements in Section 4.

Nodding and shaking are typical actions that listeners are commonly known to engage in. Head movements are part of a small feedback loop between speakers and listeners. They provide on-line, real-time feedback to speakers on all kinds of matters related to the speech: showing recognition of perception, understanding, agreement, attitude and engagement in general. They are also known to enter in behaviours of listeners that fall under the heading of interactional synchrony. Hadar and colleagues [4] report that approximately a quarter of all the head movements of the listeners in the conversations they looked at occurred in sync with the speech of the interlocutor.

Because of the way head movements function in interaction, we have decided to pay special attention to them in the Sensitive Artificial Listener project [5]. In the next section we will outline the goals and challenges of this project. We summarise the results of a typical experiment that we have carried out. This is to motivate the kind of research on head movements we present in the rest of the paper. This concerns ongoing work on the classification and interpretation of head movements. We first describe the data that we have used for this paper (Section 3). Next, in Section 4, we review the literature on head movements and their functional determinants. This leads to the presentation of some types of head movements that we distinguish and of their distributional properties (Section 5).

By the end of this paper, we hope to have shown the richness of head movements in face-to-face conversations and the importance of studying them for developing responsive embodied conversational agents.

2 The Sensitive Artificial Listener

Gumpertz [6] points out the reciprocal nature of the actions of speakers and listeners as a defining characteristic of communication.

> Communication is a social activity requiring the coordinated efforts of two or more individuals. Mere talk to produce sentences, no matter how well formed or elegant the outcome, does not by itself consitute communication. Only when a move has elicited a response can we say communication is taking place.

Responses to talk by recipients can take the form of a subsequent move in the next turn, but also the behaviors of the non-talking participant in the conversation displayed during the turn of the speaker can count as some kind of "response". They provide the speaker with feedback on whether and how the listener perceives, attends to, or understands the speaker's utterance and on the way in which the message is received in general, i.e. how the beliefs, attitudes and the affective state of the recipient is changed. These cues and signals enable communicators to synchronize the communicative actions of turn-taking. They are also involved in grounding processes and in the building of rapport.

The bulk of work on the generation of communicative behaviors of embodied conversational agents is on generating the appropriate non-verbal behaviors that accompany the speech of the embodied agent. The generation of the verbal and non-verbal behaviors to display during the production of speech by another actor, that is the behavior of a listening agent, has received less attention. A major reason for this neglect may be the inability of the interpretation modules to construct representations of meaning incrementally and in real-time, that is contingent with the production of the speech of the interlocutor. Another reason may be that the production of language and speech by speakers seems more important than the way it is perceived, which can be seen as a rather passive and reactive kind of behavior.

When one takes a look at the various modalities through which embodied agents can communicate, it appears that language, facial expressions, gestures and gaze are the main kinds of expressive behaviors that have been studied so far. Posture and head movements form another group of nonverbal behaviours, that are very informative about the intentions, attitudes, emotions and the mental state of interlocutors, in particular, "auditors", but these have been less widely studied. In the Sensitive Artificial Listener project we specifically focus on these behaviours.

A peculiarity of the SAL project is that a person can talk to four different characters with individual personality profiles. The character Poppy, for instance, is cheerful and optimistic and will try to cheer up the interlocutors when they are in a negative state and be happy for them when they are in a positive state. Obadiah, on the other hand, is gloomy and passive and will say things with the opposite effect. The voices, created by (amateur) actors are also quite expressive. The choice of talking head should match this, as should their nonverbal behaviors. In order to build up a repertoire of feedback and other expressions that match the personalities, we have carried out several tests in which we have asked participants to judge small video clips of an embodied conversational agent displaying various kinds of feedback behaviour ([5]).

In one of the studies ([7]) we varied the gaze behaviour and the head movements of a character to create differences in the judgment of personality. Earlier experiments carried out by Fukayama et al. [8] for gaze and Mignault and Chauduri [9] for head movements formed the basis for this study, complemented by many other works on gaze[1] and head movements.

Similar to the study in [8], a probabilistic model of the behaviours was implemented that determined the gaze of the RUTH talking head ([14]). We limited the variation in movements by fixing the head tilt. We tried to combine some of the results of the studies by Fukayama et al. and Mignault & Chauduri in order to model the behaviours for a happy, friendly, unobtrusive, extrovert agent (A) and for an unhappy, unfriendly and rather dominant agent (B).

The head tilt for A was set to +10° (raised). According to the study by Mignault and Chauduri a head tilted upwards can be perceived as more dominant which is not exactly what we wanted, but it also has an effect on the impression of happiness, which is what we aimed for. The amount of gaze was set at 75% and the mean gaze duration was kept short (500ms). We expected this would create the impression of engagement, friendliness and liking. In the [8] experiment short gaze durations were associated with friendly characters. Gaze aversion for A was downwards, which is associated with submissive rather than dominant personalities.

For B the head tilt was 0°. According to Mignault and Chauduri this may lead to low scores on happiness. With respect to gaze, the amount of gaze was kept at 75% just as with A, but the mean gaze duration was set at 2000ms, resulting in longer periods of gaze. We expected that this would create a rather dominant, unfriendly impression. Gaze aversion for B was to the right.

For both A and B two animations were created, one with smaller (A1, B1) and one with larger movements (A2, B2). Each animation lasted 40 seconds. The four movies were shown to 21 participants, divided into three groups that were each shown all the movies but in a different order: (A1 B1 A2 B2; B1 A1 B2 A2; A2 B2 A1 B1). The ordering did not have an effect. To rate the impressions we had the participants fill out a questionnaire for each movie consisting of a rating on a 7-point scale for 39 dutch adjective pairs with the following translations.

---

[1] In particular, [10],[11], [12], and our own work [13].

extrovert - introvert, stiff - smooth, static - dynamic, agitated - calm, closed - open, tense - relaxed, sensitive - insensitive, polite - rude, suspicious - trusting, interersted - uninterested, credbile - incredible, sympathetic - unsympathetic, self-confident - uncertain, cold - warm, weak - strong, selfish - compassionate, formal - informal, winner - loser, thougthful - reckless, unattractive - attractive, organized - disorganized, unfriendly - friendly, reliable - unreliable, refined - rude, involved - distant, flexible - linear, amusing - boring, attentive - absent, lazy - industrious, inactivy - lively, optimistic - pessimistic, happy - depressed, loving - unloving, empathetic - unempathetic, dominant - submissive, aggressive - timid, stubborn - willing, enterprising - passive, realistic - artificial.

Factor analysis reduced the number of dimensions to the following 8 factors.

1 absence, unfriendliness, rudeness
2 submissive, weak, sensitive
3 warm, energetic
4 dull, drained
5 unreliable
6 rigid, static, linear
7 informal
8 attractive

A scores higher on Factors 2 (submissiveness) and 5 (unreliable). B scores significantly higher on Factors 1 (absence, unfriendliness...) and 4 (dullness). Large movements create a more unfriendly impression (Factor 1) whereas small movements score significantly higher on Factor 2 and 8, that is, the smaller movement animations are considered more submissive, but are also more attractive.

All in all the differences in the generated behaviours resulted in several impression values that fitted the intended personality of the agents. However, this way of designing behaviours by combining functions associated with behaviours as mentioned in the literature poses many problems. If one tries to achieve an effect on various impression variables, a particular behaviour may be very well suited for yielding good scores on one variable but mediocre scores on another Also the combination of two behaviours may yield a combined effect that is different from what might be expected from the descriptions of the behaviours considered independently. Adding yet more behaviours - such as speech, for instance - may change the results again. Context plays an important role as well. The literature reports on functions and impressions, derived from data in a particular context which can be very different from the context of use that we are considering. Furthermore, the precise set of impression categories that one is aiming for may not correspond exactly to the categories used in the studies in the literature. Expressions are ambiguous and fit more than one category.

In a study related to the one described in the previous section, we looked at how people would interpret a combination of facial expressions, gaze shifts and head movements by an embodied agent ([15]). We asked people to think of the small video clips that were shown as the behaviour of an agent that was listening to someone speaking. In some cases there was a clear tendency to associate a label with a particular head movement across the various contexts in which it was put. For instance, the nods were associated with *agree, understand*, labels, in various constellations. However, when combined with a smile it was mostly associated with *like* and *accept*. In this case the smile added a nuance. The case of shakes was similar, with dislike popping up when the nods combined with a frown. With the head tilt we found mostly associations with *disbelief* or *not understand* labels, which might be combined with *interest, surprised*, and *bored* depending on the way the tilt was executed and the other expressions it combined with. These judgement studies are one way to study the contribution of head movements to the communicative repertoire. Another way to get more insight is by looking at real data of real people as we will do here.

3   Head Movements in Context

To study why people move their heads in conversations the way they do, we are gathering together a video corpus of dyadic and multi-party conversations. The corpus consists of available material from the Humaine and AMI data sets, both EU projects, complemented by new recordings. For the presentation in this paper, the examples are limited to a Dutch television program[2].

A central problem with head movements, just as with many other movements it is not a priori clear how to segment the continuous stream into meaningful segments. It is possible that two meaningfull stretches overlap (partially). To take an example from our data set, there is a moment where a person turns his head to the left to look from one person to another and while turning also displays tiny shakes. This combines two kinds of movements with different functions that will often occur on their own.

One way to characterise units of analysis is by following Birdwhistell who analysed body movement into different hierarchically organized units analogous to the way in which in speech and language phonemes combine into syllables or morphemes, morphemes combine into words and words into phrases.

> [K]inemes combine to form *kinemorphs*, which are further analyzable into *kinemorphemic* classes which behave like linguistic morphemes. These, analyzed, abstracted, and combined in the full body behavioral stream, prove to form *complex kinemorphs* which may be analogically related to words. Finally, these are combined by syntactic arrangements, still only partially understood, into extended linked behavioral organizations, the *complex kinemorphic constructions*, which have many of the properties of the spoken syntactic sentence. [16, p. 101]

---

[2] The talkshow B&W that was broadcasted October 3, 2002.

Fig. 1. B nose-tracked

Birdwhistell distinghuishes three kinemes of head nod (the "one nod", the "two nod", and the "three nod"), two kinemes of lateral head sweeps "one" and "two" sweep), one kineme of head cock and one of head tilt. Furthermore, he distinguishes several connective kinemes that use the entire head. Kinemes such as these have allokines that differ in intensity, extent and duration. In Section 5 we distinguish some further kinemes.

Several movements may combine to form complex units. A head nod, typically consists of multiple repeated up and down movements. But there are other cases as well. Let us consider a specific example and determine some options to cut up the movement stream in meaningful units.

In the picture above we see a frame of a video in which the person's nose has been tracked. The white line shows the trace of the tip of the nose as it moved from the start of the line (now just left from his mouth) to the position the nose is currently in. This complex movement was executed in about 3 seconds.

The snapshot of the annotation window in Figure 3 shows some of the annotations for this episode(the darker shaded part in the picture). It shows four levels of annotation. The top level indicates the camera position. It shows the start of the camera position on the restaurant chef BLAAUW just before the 23th second of this fragment. The video continues to show BLAAUW beyond the segment shown here. The second line ("ja maar er zij(n)" // "yes but there are") is part of the transcription for the host of the show. The third line shows the annotations for the head movements that we have visualised in the picture. These are presented in the table below. Finally, the line below this provides the annotations of what the chef is saying. The text is not completely shown. What he says is the following, with each line starting a new (possibly incomplete) sentence.

en, ik ben restaurant (sic)	and, I am restaurant (sic)
ik werk met smaken	I work with flavours
ik werk met	I work with
mijn gerechten	my dishes

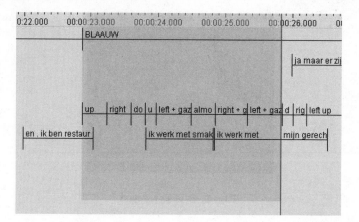

Fig. 2. Annotation of nose-tracked fragment

As one can see, the head movement in this analysis is annotated in 8 parts. We present the same information in tabular form below with the timing information (start time, end time and duration) given in milliseconds .

44 up	22.882	23.240	.358
45 right + gaze (towards person opposite)	23.240	23.600	.360
46 down right	23.600	23.810	.210
47 up	23.810	23.970	.160
48 left + gaze (towards host)	23.970	24.490	.520
49 almost stationary	24.490	24.850	.360
50 right + gaze (towards person opposite)	24.850	25.330	.480
51 left + gaze (towards host)	25.330	25.850	.520

The mean duration of an annotation is .371 seconds; the shortest movement lasts .160 and the longest .520 seconds. The general guideline for these segmentations was that a new unit starts as soon as the head movement changes direction or the movement stops. We call this an *elementary movement.* The way the movement is segmented by elementary movements in this case is mechanical and does not necessarily identify the meaning-bearing segments.

The labels given for the movements are simple and quite straightforward. First the head moves upwards (44) than sideways to the right if we take the perspective of the viewer (45). This is followed by a small movement further to the right (46) which is slightly more downwards. Next the head moves up again a little bit (47) and then it turns to the left (48). For about 360 milliseconds the head remains almost stationary followed by a turn right (50) and a turn to the left (51). At the start of this last movement the head moves up first for a couple of frames before it turns left. This pattern of movements occurs several times in the video, both by the same speaker but also by others.

There are gaze shifts associated with movements 45, 48, 50, 51. These are all either right or left movements in which BLAAUW alternates between looking at the host and the person sitting opposite. The lateral movements may thus be explained by the desire to alternate the gaze between these two persons indicating that they are intended addressees of the utterance and possibly also to elicit feedback from them. The first movement to the right follows the end of the first sentence. The movement back is accompanied by the second utterance, after which there is a small pause in the speech and the head remains almost stationary (49) with the gaze fixated on the host of the show. There is thus a close correspondence between the head movements and the production of the utterances that we can explain by mechanisms of addressing and requests for feedback.

In Section 5 we will identify more typical head movement patterns and the functions with which they are associated. We will introduce the functional specifications in the next section.

4   Functional Schemes

What explains all the head movements that people make when they are in a conversation? Of course there is not one single function that underlies all the kinds of movements that are made. On the functional level we combined a number of information sources in order to arrive at a list of determinants that was as exhaustive as possible. The most important sources of inspiration that we will refer to in the following sections were [2], [17], and [18]. Other works that we have relied on are amongst others [4] and [19], [20] and [21]. In the next section we introduce the kinds of labels that have been introduced in the literature to describe the functions and meanings of head movements. We conclude by the taxonomy we are using in most of our annotations.

When one looks at classifications of determinants of head movements during conversations, there are three general classes one can distinguish. The first involves determinants that are related to other kinetic behaviours, mostly induced by the rhythm of the speech. The second, and probably major determinant of head movements involves movements made in order to properly attend to an object or a person. The third class tells something about the way the movement might perceived by others or is intended to be perceived by others: the signalling function of a movement. Movements can tell something about stress (prominence, attitude, the structure of the interaction (turn taking, for instance), etc.

These classes are not mutually exclusive. Any behaviour can function as a signal when it is perceived by another observer, of course. Also the way in which the signal works can be different. If someone turns his head to look at someone the intention behind it may be caught by an observer and the movement thus works as a signal. But the way the head is turned may also have an expressive value. Through its form of exceution it may reveal anxiety, desire, or anger. Other movements may act as symbols, conventionally agreed upon signals.

It is important to note that a single movement may be determined by a combination of functions from different types and also that there are some systematic relations between the various functions. For instance, a movement with the head and a shift in eye gaze to pay attention to a particular person or object may - by conventional signalling procedures - also have the effect of a deictic pointing gesture.

As a first way to get an idea of what kinds of functions a head movement can serve we can turn to Kendon ([2]) whose study focusses on the function and placement of head shakes. He distinguishes various types of elements to which they may be related.

1. *Semantic*: The referential content of the utterance. A shake may be equivalent to a statement ("no"), or to some kind of modifier: expressing negation or intensification
2. *Pragmatic*: Its illocutionary force. A shake may express denial, for instance.
3. *Stance*: The speaker's own stance with respect to what is spoken. In the case of shakes these can be attitudes such as lack of knowledge, uncertainty, doubt, or disapproval.
4. *Role*: The dialogic role of the utterance within the interactional sequence in which it is occurring.

These functions are all largely equivalent to linguistic functions. Similar and other functions are also presented in the paper by McClave ([17]), which we now turn to to get a more complete picture of the functions. In discussing the literature on head movements McClave mentions the following functions:

a. Head nods function as stress markers ([16])
b. Turning the head can have a deictic function ([16])
c. Head movement characteristics (speed and amplitude) correlate with the speech characteristics and can be said to serve a motoric functions ([19]); including the movements made at dysfluencies in the speech.
d. Postural shifts of the head mark boundaries: phonological, syntactic, semantic and interactional like turns ([2], [20]); listeners can signal the start of a response ([20])
e. Head movements can control interpersonal interaction (approach, withdrawal) ([22])
f. Particular patterns of movements can vary according to the discourse function of an utterance ([23])
g. Listeners can use head movements to provide feedback ([24], [21])

Again, these classes are not mutually exclusive. Furthermore, in the study she reports on in the paper she elaborates on the following functions of head movements, which partly overlap with the functions described before in the literature.

h. Shakes and sweeps can signal *semantic concepts* such as negation, inclusivity, intensification, and uncertainty.
i. Head movements can have *narrative functions*:
   1. marking the switch from indirect to direct discourse
   2. expressing mental images of the characters

3. for deixis and the referential use of space
4. marking alternatives or elements from a list

j. Small lateral shakes occur when doing a lexical repair as if erasing or wiping away something are related to *cognitive processing*

k. Head nods of speakers may serve the *interactional function* to elicit feedback from listeners.

McClave notes that head movements can play a role in interpersonal interaction ([e.]). This effect that different movements or positions of the head on the person who perceives them has been taken into account in several studies on perception of facial displays and other forms of body movement ([25], [26], [27], [28], [29], [30], [31], [9]). Head positions and movements can give the impression of shyness, dominance, approachability or distance. Some of these variables we used in the study reported on in the previous section.

In our annotations we group the various functions as follows (with a reference to the list of functions above). Note that we do not provide an exhaustive list of all the possible meanings but indicate what we mean by giving a few examples.

1. Motoric / speech [c.]
   (a) movements resulting from speech production
   (b) movements resulting from acts like sneezing
2. Markers (linguistic, conversational) [d.]
   (a) Information structure
       i. given/new, topic/comment...
       ii. stress, prominence [a.]
   (b) Discourse structure [f.]
       i. punctuation: question markers, end of sentence
       ii. discourse relations: direct/indirect speech, listing of alternatives... [i.]
   (c) Interaction structure [g.], [k.]
       i. grounding: backchannel requests, backchannels
       ii. turn-taking
       iii. addressing
3. Symbolic, semantic, pragmatic
   (a) Semantic: propositional, adjectival, adverbial [h.]
   (b) Pragmatic: illocutionary force, deixis [b.]
4. Cognitive processes [j.]
   (a) thinking, memory search
   (b) attention (focus of)
5. Stance, attitude, emotion [e.]
   (a) epistemic markers (doubt, certainty...)
   (b) emotion related states: nervousness, anxiety
   (c) interpersonal attitudes: dominance, shyness

In the example of the lateral movements we gave in the previous section, the major determinant of the head movement seems to lie in the interactive function: turning the head from one participant to the other to indicate they are considered addressees of the utterance and to elicit a grounding act. This builds on the focus of attention function. Its relation with speech indicates also the boundaries of segments. More illustrations of this classification scheme will be presented in the section to come where we identify some typical head movements. One of the questions we address is whether functions are articulated through different forms of movements. To a certain extent this is obvious: nods signal yes, shakes signal no; but for other movements and functions the relation may be more subtle.

5   Form and Function

Several researchers have observed that sometimes differences in the formal execution of a head movement may distinguish different functions. In [4], an attempt to relate form and function has been made for a limited number of head movements. They show that kinematic properties such as amplitude, frequency and cyclicity distinguish between signals of 'yes and no' (symmetrical, cyclic movements), anticipated claims for speaking (linear, wide movements), synchrony movements occurring in phase with stressed syllables in the other's speech (narrow, linear) and movements during pauses (wide, linear). Kendon notes somethings similar.

> Head shakes vary in terms of the amplitude of the head rotations employed, in the number of rotations and in the speed with which these are performed. There is no doubt that these variations in performance intersect with and modify the meaning of the gesture. ([2, p. 149])

In the following section we will analyse the data from the B&W corpus and discuss some of the mappings of head movement forms with functions; not just head shakes but also other kinds of movements. We hope this adds to a better understanding of how the variations in form give rise to variations in meaning.

5.1   Basic Movements

Our analysis of the nose-tracked data in the B&W corpus allowed us to identify some seven classes of basic movements that differ in form and function[3].

1. Tiny nods
2. Tiny shakes
3. Lateral sweeps (medium sized)
4. Moves lateral or horizontal (medium sized)
5. Waggle
6. Various head repositionings
7. No motion

These basic movements can occur in different contexts with different functions. They can also combine into larger meaningful composite movements. We will now provide some details about form and functions for each of them.

---

[3] Not surprisingly, such a classification resembles classifications by others, at least with respect to form, rather closely [32]. Here we provide some more details on execution and function. A more detailed comparison between the various classifications made in the literature and the one made here is important as this might reveal subtle but important differences.

Fig. 3. Fragment showing a downward segment of a nod

Nods. Almost all nods in the corpus are tiny movements only a few are slightly bigger but these also remain small. The elementary movements that make up nods like these typically last about one to three frames and cover about 15 pixels. To get an idea about the size and duration, the picture below shows the first elementary downward movement from a nod made by Witteman (the host of the show). This movement took 220 milliseconds.

A couple of times the size of one nod movement down was twice this length. Typically nods occur as a kind of beats, in synchrony with the speech and they express some kind of insistence. The small up and down movements often repeat a couple of times, as one would expect.

(Tiny) Shakes. The next snapshot from the annotation window shows a segment with several shakes.

The fragment first shows some longer movements (the first three movements annotated) followed by many small movements left and right. At first they correspond with a hesitation in the speech, but also the semantic context of the utterance before and after is negative "there is no alternative".

What we call shakes are similar in size and number of repetitions to the nods but instead of vertical movements these are horizontal. Other lateral movements, with different formal properties, also occur in the corpus but they will be called differently; see sweeps and moves below. Shakes occur in a number of contexts (with explicit or implicit negations or at hesitation points) and express several of the semantic functions mentioned in the literature: negation, inclusivity, intensification and uncertainty. Besides this semantic dimension the context in which they occur in our corpus is often one in which the speaker is agitated or insistent. The corpus also showed one or two instances of listeners displaying their head in synchrony with the nods and shakes of the speaker.

Sweeps. The head shake forms a particular kind of excursionary, horizontal movement to the left or the right and back again, after perhaps several cycles to the initial position. Kendon ([2]) points out that there are different kinds of lateral movements.

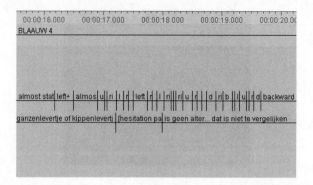

Fig. 4. Annotation of several movements including several shakes

Head shakes can be distinguished from head turns of various other kinds (such as turning the head momentarily to the left or to the right to glance at something, or to accomplish the 'look-away' that is common as a speaker initiates a turn at talk or initiates a new unit of discourse within a turn) because they are always performed within the 'frame' of the orientation the person is using, which may be either the orientation in use for a current turn at talk, or the orientation that a person is using as a recipient of another's utterance.

What is not mentioned in this characterisation is that in what are classically called shakes the head typically moves as a pendulum from the starting position to the side and then back *beyond* the original position and then back again.

Lateral movements that are not counted as shakes not only differ in their configuration but also in their amplitude and speed. A relatively fast movement of medium size, we call a sweep. Sometimes there is a pause at the end of the sweep or a small repositioning of the head before the retraction takes place. A sweep often marks stress in argumentative discourse. The start and end positions of the sweep or retraction movement may also be adorned with tiny shakes. Besides the movement of the head the gaze position changes alongside (often the eyes blink at transition points). The head and eyes are directed towards the addresse at the start of the sweep and are turned away (mostly downwards) at the end of the sweep. Retraction of the head also restores the gaze. This makes them different from the lateral movements by BLAAUW described in Section 3, because they are faster.

Most sweeps combine a movement left or right with a downward movement. They function as *underliners*.

A snapshot from the annotation window makes the difference in size between sweeps and the (tiny) shakes immediately clear.

Moves (downwards or lateral). In the definition by Kendon above, the head shake is distinguished from head turns of other kinds. There are lateral movements that are not part of shakes and which we will not classify as sweeps either but which

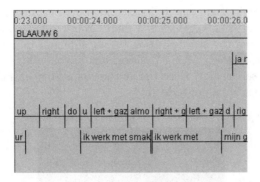

Fig. 5. Annotation illustrating sweeps

we call a move. An example of what we call a move is the turn away while listening depicted in the following picture by BLAAUW.

Here the picture shows a fairly slow movement where BLAAUW was looking at the speaker at first and then turned his head (and gaze) away. During this movement the speaker is finishing his question. Immediately after this the listener retracts to the initial position with a fast movement and after a slight motionless phase starts speaking.

Most of the movements categorized as 'moves' involve a turning away from looking at a person towards looking in front and downwards. Depending on the position of the other person this can be a movement sideways and down or simply a movement down. They can also involve a movement directing the head from one person to another. They can be faster or slower depending on the agitation of the person.

Deictic move. A special kind of move is where a speaker moves his head and gaze from one person (mostly) the addressee of the utterance to another person (or an object) and back typically when making reference to the person (or object) in the utterance. This can be accompanied by a pointing gesture with the hand.

Fig. 6. BLAAUW displaying a lateral move

Waggles. The waggle is similar to a shake. The main direction of movement is horizontal. However, the waggle has a more arch-like form. As with the shake the head moves from the start position to one side and then to the other side, but not just back to the starting position but beyond this. This is illustrated by the following screenshot. Here the speaker is *listing* all kinds of examples. Gradually, the waggle's amplitude grows.

Fig. 7. C displaying a waggle

The waggle is typically found when a speaker is making a list or when alternatives are being considered, which can occur without speech.

Head repositionings. When speakers return from a deictic move excursion to looking back at the addressee, we label this as a repositioning. The label is also applied at movements that position the head differently just prior to the onset of speech.

No motion. Episodes where a person in view does not show any movement occur mostly when they are not speaking. But there are occassions where speakers hold their head stationary as well for a shorter period of time.

These classes do not, of course, exhaust all possible movements, nor do they constitute the definitive classification of basic head movements. Some of the movements, or the way they are executed may be typical for the context and setting (for instance the table arrangement) We do believe though that similar constructs can be found in other contexts as well.

These basic movements combine in several ways, some of which have been mentioned before. There are various ways in which the basic movements combine to form more complex movements both by concatenation and by layering. In the case of nods, shakes, sweeps and waggles, the movement episode typically consist of repetitions of a two movements back and forth (left/right or up/down). As we mentioned above, in the case of sweeps and waggles, the start and end phase of each elementary movement may be adorned by either a stationary moment or some tiny nods or shakes. A typical case of layering occurs when somebody is speaking, producing tiny shakes along side and meanwhile turns his complete head and gaze from one addressee to another. Again these cases do not exhaust all the noteworthy combinations.

6   Conclusion

The data described and analysed above is only one of the set of contexts that we are looking at. These preliminary investigations of which only a part is presented above, shows us in some detail how we can segment and label head movements of both speakers and listeners. The interpretation and the context shows a lot of overlap with previous findings in the literature with respect to the functions. One of the functions that has not been paid much attention to but which is a dimension that we are particularly investigating is what the head movements tell us about the mental state of the speaker or listener and the interpersonal attitudes. In particular, we find the level of excitement and the positive versus negative attitude (argumentative, defensive, etc.) towards the other important variables to work with in future work.

For the purpose of our investigations we use this data analysis in several ways. On the one hand we use the data to design and implement algorithms that can track, segment and label movements to be used as input for our sensitive artificial agent system. On the other hand we use this to establish a kind of lexicon of movements and contexts that we use in the generation of ECA behaviour because these simple movements can be highly expressive, as we hope to have shown.

Acknowledgements. Thanks are due to Justine Cassell for valuable comments and the Humaine Network of Excellence for partly supporting this work.

References

1. Heylen, D.: Head gestures, gaze and the principles of conversational structure. International Journal of Humanoid Robotics 3, 241–267 (2006)
2. Kendon, A.: Some uses of head shake. Gesture 2, 147–182 (2003)
3. Munhall, K., Jones, J.A., Callan, D.E., Kuratate, T., Vatikiotis-Bateson, E.: Visual prosody and speech intelligibility. Psychological Science 15, 133–137 (2004)
4. Hadar, U., Steiner, T., Rose, C.F.: Head movement during listening turns in conversation. Journal of Nonverbal Behavior 9, 214–228 (1985)
5. Heylen, D., Bevacqua, E., Tellier, M., Pelachaud, C.: Searching for prototypical facial feedback signals. In: Pelachaud, C., Martin, J.C., André, E., Chollet, G., Karpouzis, K., Pelé, D. (eds.) Intelligent Virtual Agents, pp. 147–153. Springer, Berlin, Heidelberg (2007)
6. Gumpertz, J.: Discourse Strategies. Cambridge University Press, Cambridge (1982)
7. Heylen, D.: Multimodal backchannel generation for conversational agents. In: van der Sluis, I., Theune, M., Reiter, E., Krahmer, E. (eds.) Workshop on Multimodal Output Generation, Aberdeen, Scotland (2007)
8. Fukayama, A., Ohno, T., Mukawa, N., Sawaki, M., Hagita, N.: Messages embedded in gaze of interface agents - impression management with agent's gaze. In: Proceedings of CHI 2002, pp. 41–48. ACM, New York (2002)

258   D. Heylen

9. Mignault, A., Chauduri, A.: The many faces of a neutral face: Heat tilt and perception of dominance and emotion. Journal of Nonverbal Behavior 27, 111–132 (2003)
10. Argyle, M., Cook, M.: Gaze and Mutual gaze. Cambridge University Press, Cambridge (1976)
11. Cassell, J., Thórisson, K.R.: The power of a nod and a glance: Envelope vs. emotional feedback in animated conversational agents. Applied Artificial Intelligence 13, 519–538 (1999)
12. Kendon, A.: Some functions of gaze direction in social interaction. Acta Psychologica 26, 22–63 (1967)
13. Heylen, D., van Es, I., van Dijk, B., Nijholt, A.: Experimenting with the gaze of a conversational agent. In: van Kuppevelt, J., Dybkjaer, L., Bernsen, N.O. (eds.) Natural, Intelligent and Effective Interaction in Multimodal Dialogue Systems, Kluwer Academic Publishers, Dordrecht (2005)
14. Reuderink, B.: The influence of gaze and head tilt on the impression of listening agents (2006)
15. Bevacqua, E., Heylen, D., Pelachaud, C., Tellier, M.: Facial feedback signals for ecas. In: Proceedings of AISB 2007: Artificial and Ambient Intelligence, Newcastle University, Newcastle upon Tyne, UK (2007)
16. Birdwhistell, R.L.: Kinesics and Context. Essays on Body Motion Communication. University of Pennsylvania Press, Philadelphia (1970)
17. McClave, E.Z.: Linguistic functions of head movements in the context of speech. Journal of Pragmatics 32, 855–878 (2000)
18. Chovil, N.: Social determinants of facial displays. Journal of Nonverbal Behavior 15, 141–154 (1991)
19. Hadar, U., Steiner, T., Grant, E., Rose, C.F.: Kinematics of head movements accompanying speech during conversation. Human Movement Science 2, 35–46 (1983)
20. Duncan, S.: Language, paralanguage, and body motion in the structure of conversations. In: McCormack, W., Wurm, S. (eds.) Language and Man. Anthropological Issues, pp. 239–268. Mouton, The Hague (1976)
21. Duncan, S.: On the structure of speaker-auditor interaction during speaking turns. Language in Society 2, 161–180 (1974)
22. Kendon, A.: Some functions of the face in the kissing round. In: Conducting Interaction. Editions de la Maison des Sciences de l'Homme, pp. 117–152. Cambridge University Press (1990)
23. Kendon, A.: Movement coordination in social interaction: some examples described. Acta Psychologica 32, 100–125 (1970)
24. Yngve, V.: On getting a word in edgewise. In: Papers from the sixth regional meeting of the Chicago Linguistic Society, Chicago: Chicago Linguistic Society, pp. 567–577 (1970)
25. Krumhuber, E., Manstead, A.S., Kappas, A.: Temporal aspects of facial displays in person and expression perception: the effects of smile dynamics, head-tilt, and gender. Journal of Nonverbal Behavior 31, 39–56 (2007)
26. Costa, M., Menzani, M., Bitti, P.E.R.: Head canting in paintings: An historical study. Journal of Nonverbal Behavior 25, 62–73 (2001)
27. Pendlton, K.L., Snyder, S.S.: Young children's perception of nonverbally expressed "preference": the effects of nonverbal cue, viewer age, and sex of actor. Journal of Nonverbal Behavior 6, 220–237 (1982)
28. O'Leary, M.J., Gallois, C.: The last ten turns: behavior and sequencing in friends' and stranger's conversational findings. Journal of nonverbabl behavior 9, 8–27 (1985)

29. Costa, M., Dinsback, W., Manstead, A.S., Bitti, P.E.R.: Social presence, embarrass-
    ment, and nonverbal behavior. Journal of nonverbal communication 25, 225–240
    (2001)
30. Harrigan, J.A., Oxman, T.E., Rosenthal, R.: Rapport expressed through nonverbal
    behavior. Journal of Nonverbal Behavior 9, 95–110 (1985)
31. Bente, G., Feist, A., Elder, S.: Person perception effects of computer-simulated male
    and female head movement. Journal of Nonverbal Behavior 20, 213–228 (1996)
32. Cerrato, L., Skhiri, M.: Analysis and measurement of head movements signalling
    feedback in face-to-face human dialogues. In: Paggio, P., Jokinen, K., Jönsson, A.
    (eds.) First Nordic Symposium on Multimodal Communication, Copenhagen, pp.
    43–52 (2003)

Dynamic Field Theory and Embodied Communication

Yulia Sandamirskaya and Gregor Schöner

Institut für Neuroinformatik,
Universitätstr. 150, Bochum, Germany
yulia.sandamirskaya@neuroinformatik.rub.de
gregor.schoner@neuroinformatik.rub.de
http://www.neuroinformatik.rub.de

Abstract. Dynamical Field Theory is a neurally based approach to embodied and situated cognition, in which information is represented in continuous activation fields defined over metric spaces. The temporal evolution of activation patterns under the influence of inputs and neuronal interaction is described by a dynamical system, whose stable states, localized peaks of activation, are the units of representation. This approach has been successfully used to capture many elementary forms of cognition. Communication poses the new challenge of understanding how different modalities can be integrated in a continuously unfolding communicative process. In this chapter we give a brief introduction to Dynamical Field Theory in embodied cognition, and discuss extensions of its ideas to embodied communication. We sketch a highly simplified example of how sequence generation may occur in dynamical fields. We apply these concepts to a specific exemplary problem in embodied communication, turn taking, the temporal structure of which we capture in a simple model.

Keywords: Neural dynamics, embodied cognition, modelling, turn taking.

1 Embodied Cognition and Embodied Communication

Over the last decade or so, a reexamination of our understanding of cognition and cognitive processes has begun which emphasizes that cognition takes place in organisms who act in complex, structured environments [1,2,3]. Cognition, in this view, unfolds in real time, continuously linked to sensory information and continuously coupled to motor systems, which impact on the sensed world [4]. People bring to any cognitive act a history of prior experience both in the sense of the immediate behavioral and sensory context, in which the cognitive act takes place, as well as in the sense of the longer personal history of learning and development, on which cognition builds. The embodied perspective on cognition calls into doubt the postulate of universal representations of knowledge, on which cognition can operate by processing information. Instead, this perspective demands that an understanding of cognition be based on principles of neuronal

I. Wachsmuth and G. Knoblich (Eds.): Modeling Communication, LNAI 4930, pp. 260–278, 2008.

function, in particular, on the temporally and spatially continuous evolution of neuronal representations, which may be updated at any time by sensory signals and which remain linked to motor surfaces at all times [5].

Communication involves, of course, a particularly high level of cognition. Are the insights from the embodied and situated perspective on cognition relevant to understanding communication? As this books argues in the most varied ways, communication is embodied in the obvious sense that natural communication occurs between people with physical and physiological bodies, and their cognitive abilities originate from processes in their nervous systems. Each individual brings his or her particular history of behavior, memories, intellectual capabilities to a communicative situation. Communication is situated in the similarly obvious sense that it is acted out in a specific, structured environment, in which the interaction between communicating people or agents occurs. For each actor, the actions of other actors shape the environment, in which communicative processes are embedded. Communication is multimodal, including verbal but also many non-verbal sensory and motor dimensions such as gesture, mimic, and bodily pose. Communication happens at different level of awareness.

The most saliently embodied aspect of communication may be turn-taking [6]. In conversation between two or more actors, almost all time is taken up by explicit verbal communication. Speaker and listeners switch roles very quickly. Typical durations of the silences between such switches are of the order of 100 to 300 ms, often faster than even a simple reaction time [7]. Such smooth transitions may be viewed as evidence for anticipatory planning [8]. They require time-continuous monitoring of the speaker's behavior, picking up potentially subtle, graded cues as to when the turn will be yielded. Such cues include changes of prosody, gestures, gaze shifts toward the listener, implicit verbal cues such as filler utterances, or explicit verbal cues such as asking a question.

We will use turn-taking as an exemplary problem in embodied communication, around which we will highlight how concepts from embodied cognition may be useful to understand embodied communication. Our mission is to examine conceptual convergence and interchange between these two areas from the perspective of Dynamic Field Theory (DFT), a particular mathematically explicit theoretical framework within which concepts of embodied cognition can be made precise [9,5,4]. DFT and its neuronal basis will be briefly reviewed in the next section.

Three aspects of DFT seem to us potentially relevant to understanding embodied communication. The first is *autonomy*. In cognition, autonomy refers to the fact that cognitive processes unfold continuously in time on the basis of the current and past behavior and influenced by current and past sensory information. Dynamical systems thinking emphasizes autonomy, which may be contrasted with the input-compute-output perspective on which the framework of information processing is based. That acts of communication such as a lecture, a group discussion, or a dialog, unfold in real time is obvious. Such acts are not appropriately described as series of input-output mappings. Instead, the state of the complete system containing communicating partners and the environment impacts on how the communicative process unfolds. For instance, the inner state of the participants (their arousal, mood, knowledge, willingness to contribute to the discussion or to express an opinion), the nature of the interaction (e.g., eye contact, gesture, prosody), the environmental conditions (e.g., noise level, people in the background), as well as the behavioral and cognitive context (e.g., nature of the relationship, recent experiences) all may modulate the multidimensional behavior of the participants. Turn-taking might be the most accessible signature of autonomy.

The second aspect is *gradedness*. In Dynamic Field Theory (DFT), the state of a neuronal system may be varying along continuous dimensions, which include an "intensity" dimension that measures the potential impact of each factor. In communication, the states of the participants and of the environment may vary in graded fashion as well. For instance, gestures may differ in their extent and expressiveness, voices in volume and timbre, the strength of emotions and their expression through various channels may vary. Those graded factors may influence the time course of communication by shifting, for instance, points of turn taking, and the level or tone of the response. Graded variations like these may potentially lead to qualitative change, switching the overall shape of a communicative act, say from neutral to hostile.

Such a switch would be an incident of loss of stability. *Stability* is the property of states in an autonomous dynamical system of resisting change. In a stable state, small changes in conditions lead to small changes in the state of a system. Given the amazing flexibility of nervous system, any state that persists long enough to be observable must have some degree of stability, so that it resists the myriad influences that push the system in other directions. Stability plays a crucial role in cognitive systems that are situated within time varying real-world environments. In fact, autonomy, the continuous evolution of a system in contact with such environments, cannot lead to macroscopically coherent behaviors if mechanisms of stability do not protect the current state of the system from the ensemble of perturbations coming from within a system as well as from its environment. Stability is also a prerequisite for the coherence of higher levels of behavior to be preserved under processes of development, learning and adaptation. In Dynamic Field Theory (DFT), stability is shown to emerge from the underlying neuronal dynamics [10].

Stability is clearly a relevant concept to understand how processes of embodied communication may unfold continuously in time under the influence of multiple graded variables. States with a higher degree of stability may persist of larger periods of time and resist competing influences. In turn taking, for instance, very stable states of the communication system may prevent a transition to a new state, while less stable or even unstable states may be both the prerequisite to change as well as the mechanism through which change comes about.

A challenge for understanding embodied communication under the constraints of autonomy, gradedness and stability is sequence generation. Much of cognition, but certainly all communication involves sequential changes of state, whose serial order is typically relevant. Generating sequential shifts of states require that the states are released from stability. On the other hand, a sequence as a whole must resist perturbations and thus have some sort of stability. Understanding sequence generation from a neuro-dynamical perspective is not a solved problem, although a number of efforts exist [11,12,13,14,15,16] After reviewing the main concepts of Dynamic Field Theory (DFT), we will therefore provide a sketch of how sequence generation can be conceived of within DFT.

We will then explore how theoretical concepts from Dynamical Systems thinking may impact on our understanding of embodied communication. This we will done by providing an explicit mathematical model of turn taking, with which we attempt to account for some of the qualities and one quantitative feature of the phenomenon. The model is, however, largely metaphorical in nature. It is meant to illustrate, how the time structure of communicative processes may emerge from time-continuous processes, how categorical change in continuous representations may emerge from multiple possible causes and how all kinds of contributions to the system's dynamics may matter, not only contributions that are specifically linked to a particular contents. The dynamical systems metaphor, we thus aim to illustrate, promotes thinking about underlying forces and regularities, from which the complex, multi-facetted patterns of communicative behavior may emerge.

2   Dynamic Field Theory (DFT)

The following is a brief survey over DFT, which has been reviewed more extensively elsewhere [9,17,4]. The mathematics of DFT come from the field of dynamical neuronal networks, pioneered by [18], [19] and [20] and currently the preferred route of many computational neuroscientists to function (e.g., [21], [22]). On this basis, DFT is an approach that emphasizes concepts that align closely with the needs of experimenters in human embodied cognition. In DFT, the basis concepts are inspired by principles of neuronal function in the central nervous system, but behavioral experiments provide the major constraints for both modelling and theoretical thinking.

At the core of DFT is the notion of continuous activation fields. While these have been historically derived as an approximate description of cortical neurophysiology [19], they arise in DFT our of more abstract arguments linked to an analysis of embodied cognition. This will be our first concern. Next we will discuss the dynamics of activation fields based on inputs and interactions, emphasizing peaks as units of representation. Finally, we will take the reader through three instabilities of the dynamics of activation fields which are critical to understanding how sequences can be generated from attractor states that turn unstable.

In order to represent metric information in terms of dynamical state variables, we need two dimensions (Fig. 1). One is the metric dimension along which information is specified. To model communication, metric dimensions that may play a role include the direction of an deictic gesture, a range of visual expressions, a range of prosodic speech patterns, etc. Seemingly categorical aspects of communication such as the contents of a verbal message may likewise be thought of as embedded in an underlying continuum, which reflects relationships of

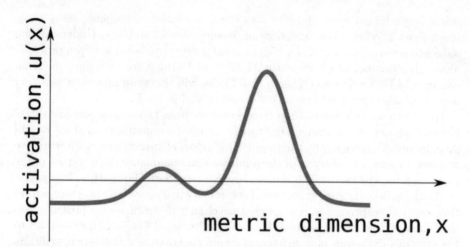

Fig. 1. A dynamical field is an activation pattern, $u(x, t)$, defined over metric dimension, x, at any moment in time, t. Peaks of positive activation represent a decision that the field has a well-defined state along the dimension, x, specified by the location of the peak in the field. Patterns of non-positive activation, by contrast, represent graded information typically derived from input.

semantic similarity [23,24]. In general, the multi-dimensional metric space spans the range of possible communicative intentions as a whole, comprising all aspects of mental state that impact on the communicative process. For now, we shall be visualizing dynamic fields over a single dimension, however.

The second dimension is the extent to which any given value along the metric dimension is currently active. This is the activation concept of cognitive science, known in this form also as the principle of space coding in neuroscience, according to which the location in the neural network determines what is encoded, while neuronal activation signals the absence or presence of information [25,26]. The activation dimension may also represent graded values such as the strength of a particular dimension, confidence in an estimate, or how close a particular representation is to impact on the further evolution of a communicative process.

Activation fields evolve continuously in time under the influence of inputs and internal interactions. This evolution is described by a dynamical system. The mathematical description is motivated by the dynamic properties of neurons in the central nervous system [19,20,27,10]. The fundamental property of the field dynamics, the stability of activation patterns, emerges from the biophysics of neurons irrespective of the specific neuronal model and its implementation details (see [10] for an argument).

In the absence of any inputs, the resting level of the dynamic field is therefore a stable state. Inputs may arise from sensory information or from other dynamic fields. Within the setting of communication, input is expected to reflect the impact of the other communicative partner, sensed in various ways. Additional inputs may reflect the influence of memory, knowledge, and the sensed environment. Inputs may be focused on particular field locations and thus specify a particular value of the metric dimension. Alternatively, inputs may be global (homogeneous), affecting the whole field and impacting on the dynamic regime in which the field operates.

Neuronal interaction is the dependence of the time course of activation at one field location on the current activation at other field locations. Neuronal interaction may stabilize localized peaks of activation, which are the stable objects that form the elementary units of representation in DFT. Nearby field locations are assumed to mutually excite each other, driving up activation, while distant locations are assumed to mutually inhibit, driving down activation. Only sufficiently activated locations contribute to interaction. This is modelled mathematically by applying a sigmoid nonlinearity to all activation variables contributing to interaction. This pattern of neuronal interaction is generic in the cerebral cortex, but can also be observed in many subcortical structures.

Two types of attractor solutions emerge from the interaction pattern in neural fields. Input-driven attractors are largely subthreshold patterns of activation in which the contribution of the neuronal interaction is negligible. In such states, the field merely filters external input, but does not make any selection or detection decisions. One may visualize these solutions as representing a passive, information processing mode, in which cognition is not yet engaged.

Self-stabilized attractors, by contrast, are localized patterns of activation with levels sufficient to engage interaction by exceeding the threshold of the sigmoid nonlinearity. Local excitatory interaction thus lifts activation within the peak beyond levels induced by input, while global inhibitory interaction suppresses levels elsewhere below the levels justified by the resting level or by inputs. Such peaks of activation are stable against small variations in local input as well as against weak competing inputs at other field locations. Such localized peaks of activation are the units of representation, their location encoding metric information about the underlying dimension while their level of activation indicates something like the strength, certainty, or intensity of the represented value.

In fact, self-stabilized peaks represent the outcome of various forms of decision making. This can be seen by noting that an instability connects the subthreshold, input-driven patterns of activation to self-stabilized peaks. The simplest form is the *detection*-instability, in which a localized external input is increased in strength (see [4] for a review of this and the following instabilities). At a critical input strength, the subthreshold pattern of activation becomes unstable and a localized peak forms. That peak remains stable, even if input strength drops again (within limits, see below). This provides a process model of the detection decisions central to most early psychophysics and often conceived of in terms of signal detection theory [4].

Another form of this instability is, at first, more surprising (Fig. 2). It arises starting from a subthreshold pattern of activation. If activation is now boosted by a homogeneous form of input (modelled, for example, by increasing the resting level of the field), the field location with highest subthreshold level of activation first pierces the threshold. This makes the subthreshold solution unstable, and a self-stabilized localized peak grows out of this event. Because the location of

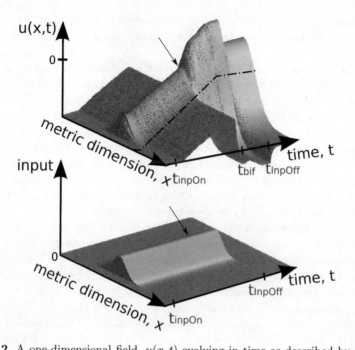

Fig. 2. A one-dimensional field, $u(x,t)$ evolving in time as described by the field dynamics. When localized external input arrives at time $t = t_{inpOn}$ (bottom plot), the field relaxes to the subthreshold pattern of activation defined by the input (top plot). At the same time the homogeneous resting level begins to be lifted gradually (the resting level of the field is marked with a dotted line). This induces an instability at time $t = t_{bif}$ (marked with an arrow on both plots) and the field relaxes to a new attractor, a self-stabilized peak dominated by interaction. Even later, at $t = t_{inpOff}$, when the external input is removed, the localized peak of activation is sustained by interaction.

the peak is determined by preexisting inhomogeneities in the field, this type of instability could be viewed as a form of categorization [28,4].

Another way of looking at this instability is that it amplifies small, subthreshold patterns of activation into macroscopic decisions, which can be acted out. Thus, if small traces of previous patterns of activation can be left by a simple learning mechanism, then this instability can activate such prior experience into units of representation. This opens the fields to generate long-term memory of their own behavioral history. In the context of communication such a mechanism can be used to model endogenous factors determining the course of an interchange, beyond a processing of only the incoming information.

If the general level of activation in the field is sufficiently high, interaction may enable the dynamic field to sustain a localized peak of activation even after the original localized input has been removed. Such sustained patterns of activation represent a form of metric working memory [5]. Thus information about past stimulation can be preserved over much longer time scales than the dynamic time scale of individual neurons.

Localized peaks may arise from yet another form of decision making, the *selection* among multiple localized inputs. Selection is also an elementary cognitive function that can be modelled with dynamic fields. This function too emerges from an instability. When two metrically close inputs are presented to the field, the detection instability will lead to a broader peak centered around an averaged location between the two peaks. When the metric distance between two localized inputs is larger, however, the dynamic field is bistable and has the potential to build a peak at either of the two locations. A single peak of activation, which emerges due to the detection instability, will be centered around one of the two locations specified by the inputs. The sites which pass the threshold and participate in interaction are too distant in this case in order to support each other due to the local excitation. Asymmetries in input, fluctuations, or prior activation history may favor one over the other states, but the far-reaching inhibition prevents simultaneous activation of both locations.

3   Sequence Generation within DFT

Generating sequences of states or actions is central to cognition. A train of thought could be viewed of as a sequence of mental states. Language is sequential at many levels — sequences of articulatory gestures, of sounds, of words or larger syntactical elements, of ideas or arguments. Goal-directed action is another important form of sequence generation within (embodied) cognition. Think of the actions needed to make coffee or to fetch an object from a cup-board [29]. In communication too we observe sequences of mental states, utterances, gestures, and other communicative acts.

Sequence generation is conceptually cheap in classical information processing approaches such as those based on the analogy with the digital computer. In fact, those approaches are essentially based on the concept of processing by moving from one step in a sequence to the next. This processing is, in a sense, atemporal, because it doesn't matter, how much real time elapses while such a step is made. The advance of information through the processing system itself marks time. In contrast, in an embodied vision of cognition, all processes are temporally autonomous, may at any time be linked to new sensory information or to ongoing motor behaviors or even to other processes running concurrently. Stability is critical for such highly interlinked processes to stay on track. Because stable states resist change, they are capable of persisting under time-varying conditions. But there is a dilemma. The very resistance to change makes it difficult to conceive of the generation of a sequence of states. After all, moving from one state to the next requires that the previous state be released from stability, that is, become unstable, so that the system is driven toward the next state.

That it is not impossible to reconcile this need for stability and instability in a dynamic approach to embodied cognition is illustrated by the simple model that will be briefly sketched now [30]. It is not in the nature of this chapter (and of the volume in which it appears) to provide a detailed mathematical description of this model (nor of next section's turn taking model). Therefore, we focus on sketching the main ideas of the model, explaining the overall architecture, variables, and dynamical principles. The equations are listed in the appendix in enough detail to be implementable by the mathematically skilled reader, but are probably not accessible to the typical reader.

The model consists of an ensemble of activation fields (Fig.3). All fields represent metric or categorical information relevant for what happens at any stage within a sequence of actions (e.g., feature values, movement parameters, descriptors of utterances or gestures). A set of fields (arranged in a stack in Figure 3) represents the ordinal position within the sequence. Each field in the stack is responsible for one step in the sequence. This encoding comes about through a coupling among the fields that guarantees their sequential activation: Each field provides spatially homogeneous, excitatory input to its "successor" field, that is, the field that represents the next ordinal position in the sequence. In addition, each field inhibits its predecessor. As a result, only one field in the ordinal stack can be activated at a time.

Beyond the stack of ordinal fields, one additional output or "motor" field represents the currently activated action plan (Fig. 3). This field receives localized (one-to-one) input from all ordinal fields. The motor field activates the sensori-motor action system that brings about the planned action. That sensori-motor system is modelled for now only by assuming that sensory feedback about the successful termination of an action is provided at a variable time after initiation of the action (a more specific model will be provided in the next section). This signal represents the "condition of satisfaction" [31] of the planned action and generates spatially homogenous excitatory input into all fields in the ordinal stack. This input triggers an instability through which the currently activated ordinal field becomes deactivated and its successor becomes activated. This is the elementary transition in sequence generation from step in a sequence to the next.

All activation fields are endowed with the neuronal interaction that leads to the selection of a single peak even when multiple localized inputs are present. As a result, except for the brief moment of transition from one step to the next, there is always a peak present in one field of the stack of ordinal fields and one matching peak in the motor field. Where the peaks are located within the fields and thus, what action is planned and triggered at any particular point in a sequence is determined by localized inputs into the fields. There are two potential sources of such localized input that determine the "contents" of the sequence: external input from sensory systems or internal input from a memory trace that represents earlier experience, when the sequence was first learned or imitated. In summary, localized input determines *what* is done at each step. Sensory feedback representing the "condition of satisfaction" determines *when* the transition to the next step is made.

The notion of a neural representation of the ordinal position of an item in a sequence is consistent with the neurophysiology of frontal cortex, in which neurons tuned to ordinal position have been found and lesions of which affect

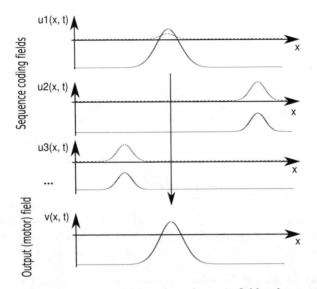

Fig. 3. A sequence generation model based on dynamic fields whose stable states are single localized peaks. A stack of such activation fields, $u_i(x, t)$ (solid lines), encodes the ordinal position of steps, $i = 1, 2, 3$, in the sequence. All fields are defined over a shared metrical dimension, x. The fields may be preactivated by localized input (dotted lines) representing information about what action is expected at each step in the sequence. Each field excites its successor and inhibits its predecessor, so that only a single field can be active at a time ($u_1(x, t)$ at the depicted instant). The output or "motor" field, $v(x, t)$ (bottom of stack) receives localized input from all ordinal fields and thus carries a peak matching the currently active ordinal field.

the capacity to generate sequential action [32,33]. The proposed dynamical architecture addresses the fact that the "acting out" in time of action sequences is flexible, so that the system is capable of remembering where in a sequence it is even as variable amounts of time elapse while each individual action is realized.

4   A Dynamic Field Model of Turn Taking

Generating the amazingly smooth and fast transitions between turns requires that inherently time-variant events, the individual speaking turns, be coordinated with good temporal precision. Some authors have postulated that turns are governed by oscillators, so that their durations are multiples of a base unit [7]. This does not seem to capture the full level of temporal flexibility of embodied communication as reflected, in fact, by the distributions of silent intervals at turn switches observed experimentally by these very authors (Fig. 4, left). These distributions have a lot of counts at surprisingly short times (of the order of 100 milliseconds!) but are still broad relative to their means.

Another view is that turn taking requires anticipation, that is, predicting when a chance to switch may occur [8]. Here we present a dynamical field model

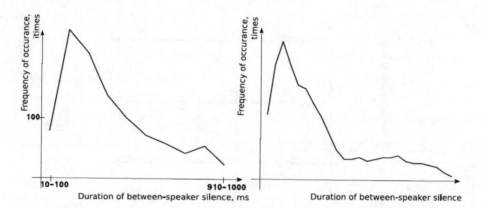

Fig. 4. Left: A histogram of the durations of silences between turns observed experimentally in actual human conversation is drawn from the data provided in (M. Wilson & Wilson, 2005). Right: A corresponding histogram generated from the dynamic turn taking model. As the time scale in our model is arbitrary, we compare only the overall form of the distributions of the silent periods' durations. See Fig. 6 for how silences are measured in the model.

that is primarily a metaphor for how the timing properties of turn taking may arise. Within this picture, there is no fixed underlying oscillator, although the duration of each act is timed and may thus be predictable. The model does not have an explicit mechanism for anticipation, but turn switching is based on receiving a graded signal from the communication partner. This may, in effect, generate anticipation. The model does not address the rich inner structure of dialog, nor the multi-modality of its embodiment, and thus remains at a much more metaphorical level than has typically been the case for DFT based models. Hopefully, the model can provide a perspective for how the framework of dynamical systems thinking may help understand the autonomous, graded, and real-time structure of embodied communication.

We sketch the conceptual structure of the model. The mathematical equations are listed in the Appendix. Consider two partners, "A" and "B", communicating with each other (Fig. 5). Each actor is modelled as a sequence generation system defined over a metric dimension, x, that represents a feature value that characterizes each communicative act. For our simple toy model, this feature dimension was simply the planned duration of each communicative act.

There are two contributions to the contents of the sequence. One represents a prior plan of a series of communicative acts, modelled by localized inputs associated with each step in the sequence. The other is a reactive component, represented by localized input generated at each turn by the action of the other partner. Presently, this is merely a random mapping from the feature value of that other partner's action onto a feature value of the present partner's sequence plan.

Assume, for now, that communicator "A" has generated the beginning of a planned sequence, so that a peak in ordinal field number 1 is located over the

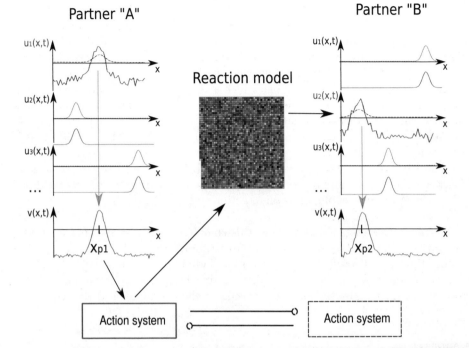

Fig. 5. The dynamic field model of turn taking consists of a dynamic sequence generation model for each of two communication partners "A" and "B" (stacks of fields on the left and the right). The action system itself, which generates communicative acts, is modelled by a neuronal oscillator, which generates a single timed event when activated and then deactivates itself. The action systems of the two partners compete so that only is active at a time. Another channel of interaction is the reaction model which provides localized input into the sequence generation system of one partner (at the depicted instant: "B") based on the current action of the other partner (at the depicted instant: "A").

associated input (left panel of Fig. 5). This leads to a matching peak at location, x_{p1}, in that actor's motor field (bottom of the stack). Communication partner "B" might be in another state. This communicator may have no peak at all (no communicative intention). More typically, however, this partner may have some communicative intention represented by a peak at a particular location in a particular ordinal position of a prior communicative plan. In the figure, partner "B" is at the second ordinal position in an ongoing sequence having generated a peak in the second ordinal field together with the matching peak at location, x_{p2}, in the motor field. Thus, communicator "B" faces the action of "A" already with some communicative intention, a prepared communicative act.

We model turn taking by providing a caricature of the action system that each communicator uses to "act out" communicative intentions. These systems generate single "actions" with a well-defined duration by starting a limit cycle oscillator with a specific frequency. In fact, the frequency of the oscillator and thus the duration of its "action" is encoded along the metric dimension of the sequence generation systems. Thus, different actions take different amounts of time. Each oscillator has two inner state variables (excitation and inhibition). Excitation arises from zero, reaches a maximum, and falls back to zero for each cycle of the oscillator. After a single cycle, the oscillator turns itself off. This is controlled by an activation variable, which is either in an "on" state or an 'off" state. Input from the motor field and absence of competition from the other actor turns the activation variable "on". When the associated oscillator reaches the end of a cycle, then the activation variable is switched to an "off" state through a dynamic instability.

The level of the activation variables controlling each oscillator is exchanged between the two communicators as a signal for how close they are to yielding the turn. A large level of activation of action system "A" inhibits action system "B" and vice versa.

Figure 6 illustrates simulations of this complete model by showing for both actors the time courses of a state variable characterizing the respective oscillator. Episodes of oscillator activation are individual communicative actions. These episodes vary in duration as dictated by the frequency of the limit cycle oscillators encoded by the location of peaks in the neural fields of the sequence

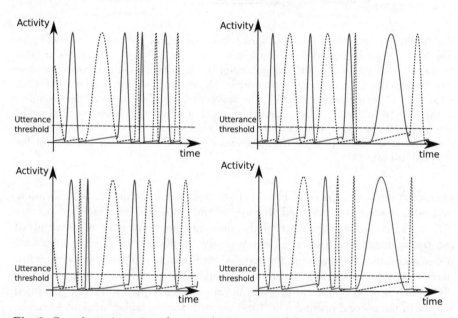

Fig. 6. Sample trajectories of turn taking generated by the model. The activity of each of the oscillators modelling the action systems of actor "A" (solid lines) and "B" (dotted lines) is shown by plotting one of two oscillator state functions. Positive values beyond a threshold (solid horizontal lines) signal that the oscillator is in the "on" state and a communicative act is ongoing. When the state variables of both actors are below the threshold, then this is interpreted as a silence interval the duration of which contributes to the histogram shown in Fig. 4.

generation systems. An action system, whose state variable is below a threshold, is in the off state waiting its turn. When the state variables of both action systems are below threshold, then both action systems are in the off state and a period of silence between turns is observed. The amount of silence at each turn switch varies because the state variables change at variable rates due to the variable durations of actions. Moreover, turn switches involve instabilities in the dynamics of the action systems. This gives noise a sizeable influence on the exact time at which a transition is realized. As a result, the histogram of the durations of silent intervals obtained from an ensemble of simulation runs shown in Fig. 4 is quite broad, although centered on a most frequent interval. This characteristic of a small mode and long tail matches the shape of the distributions obtained from human data shown in the same figure on the left.

5   Discussion

We presented a simple mathematical model of turn taking as a metaphor for how the time structure of embodied communication could be understood within the neuronally based theoretical framework of Dynamic Field Theory. The dynamic activation fields and dynamic action systems in the model generate their time courses *autonomously*, based on continuous time. They are not paced by a rigid input-compute-output cycle, but are open to sensory input at any time. Because the systems are almost always in a *stable* state, such continuous coupling does not prevent the systems from performing their assigned function. The systems are sensitive to input only while near an instability, which leads to a switch of turn.

These instabilities start at the level of the action system, which turn on and off in response to graded signals received internally as well as from the communication partner. The instabilities amplify small graded changes of signals into macroscopic changes. This is how dynamical systems can make sense of and depend on *graded* variables while at the same time being able to make categorical decisions and to discard graded information as they set on the course of a new action step.

The simplistic models of the action systems as self-controlled, one-shot oscillators stands in for the much richer action systems engaged when people communicate. These include the speech articulatory system, systems controlling the prosody of their utterances, gesturing, controlling facial expression and body posture. All these systems may have graded components, from which communication patterns may derive signals for how close the actor is to yielding the turn. That we model such complex systems as stable limit cycle oscillators is a deliberate scientific move. The coupling among stable oscillators is the basis for coordination of timed actions [34,35]. Thus, it is easy to imagine how the multiple action involved in generating communicative acts maybe coordinated with each other as well as across two communication patterns through couplings of the kinds modelled in simplified form here. This metaphor may provide an avenue toward an account for the remarkable temporal regularity and order observed in embodied communication [36].

The meaning transmitted in and expressed through communicative acts has been modelled only minimally here. In DFT, meaning is encoded through continuous metric dimensions. The location of peaks along such dimensions signifies specific instances of such metric information. In principle, coupled networks of dynamic fields may generate distributed representations of perceptual objects (see [37] for an example). The multiple modalities and perceptual dimensions that are relevant to embodied communication could easily be cast in dynamic field terms. Within the toy model presented here, the field dimension represented the duration of a planned communicative act and in that respect acted merely as a place holder for more substantive communicative meaning.

The field dynamics provides a framework for integrating different sources of specification of meaning. For instance, a memory trace of previously activated or stimulated patterns of activation may bias the ordinal fields to particular locations. On the other hand, current input from the other actor's communicative act may be overlaid and fused with such a prior plan. This may lead to the selection of activation patterns that in some way match the received message. The metrics of patterns of activation within continuous activation fields forms the basis for determining such matches. This metrics can be exploited by conceiving of structured forward mappings, like those of connectionist networks, to replace the random world matrix of our toy model.

Thus, much of the machinery needed to enrich the processing exists within connectionist and dynamical systems approaches. The challenge will be to translate insights obtained from substantive models of the information processing involved in embodied cognition [8] into dynamic terms. What is needed for this to happen is that aspects of embodied communication that provide entry points into dynamical systems thinking are identified and collaboratively explored in both theory and experiment. During the research year, from which this book emerged, first steps in such a direction were made. We are looking forward to the new and exciting ideas that may emerge from this ongoing research effort.

A   Mathematical Description of the Models

The sequence generation model. The dynamic fields, $u_i^A(x, t)$, represent the ordinal position, $i = 1, \ldots, N$, of items in the sequence of communication partner, A, along the feature dimension, x, and evolve in time, t, according to:

$$
\tau_o \, \dot{u}_i^A(x, t) = -u_i^A(x, t) + h_o^A + \int f\big(u_i^A(x', t)\big) w_{oo}(x, x') dx'
$$

$$
+ C_+ F_{\text{env}} \int f\big(v^A(x', t)\big) f\big(u_{i-1}^A(x', t)\big) dx'
$$

$$
- C_- \int f\big(u_{i+1}^A(x', t)\big) dx' + P_i^A(x, t)
$$

$$
+ \int \text{WorldModel}(x, x') f\big(v^B(x', t)\big) dx'. \tag{1}
$$

The analogous equation for communication partner, B, is obtained by switching upper indices A and B. The symbols represent the following:

- τ_o: the time constant of the field dynamics;
- h_o^A: constant resting level of the field;
- $f(u) = 1/(1+\exp(-\beta(u-u_o)))$: a sigmoidal function, where β is a parameter and u_0 a threshold;
- $w_{oo}(x,x') = -w_{\text{inhib}} + w_{\text{excite}}\exp(-(x-x')^2/2\sigma^2)$: the "mexican-hat" interaction kernel with parameters w_{inhib}, and w_{excite};
- C_+F_{env}: models sensori-motor feedback about accomplishment of the current action, defined below;
- C_-: strength of backward inhibition along the stack;
- $P_i(x,t)$: localized preactivation of the ordinal field number i encoding what is represented or planned at that ordinal position in the sequence;
- WorldModel(x,x'): a $N \times N$ matrix models communication by associating an output of partner B within an input to partner A's ordinal stack. Here a random matrix.

The motor field, $v^A(x,t)$, of partner A is governed by:

$$\tau_M \dot{v}^A(x,t) = -v^A(x,t) + h_m^A + \int f\big(v^A(x',t)\big)w_{mm}(x,x')dx'$$
$$+ \Sigma_{i=0}^{N}\Big[\int f\big(u_i^A(x',t)\big)w_{mo}(x,x')dx' + C_+\int f\big(u_i^A(x',t)\big)dx'\Big] \quad (2)$$

Again, the analogous equation applies to communication partner, B. The new symbols represent the following:

- h_m^A: resting level;
- $w_{mm}(x,x')$: interaction kernel analogous to $w_{oo}(x,x')$;
- $w_{mo}(x,x')$: a gaussian projection kernel from the ordinal position stack to the motor field.

The turn taking model. The sensori-motor system that generates a communicative act is described by two action variables, x_A, and y_A. In the present model the only significance of these action variable is to signal that an action is ongoing. This happens when the associated dynamics has a limit cycle solution. The Hopf normal form generates such a limit cycle:

$$\tau_h \dot{x}_A = g_A\left[\gamma(\mu - x_A^2 - y_A^2)x_A - \omega_A y_A\right] - (1-g_A)x_A$$
$$\tau_h \dot{y}_A = g_A\left[\gamma(\mu - x_A^2 - y_A^2)y_A + \omega_A x_A\right] - (1-g_A)(y_A - 1) \quad (3)$$

This is the equation for partner A. The analogous equation applies to partner B. The symbols mean the following:

- τ_h: time scale of the oscillator dynamics;
- γ: parameter determining the relaxation rate of the limit cycle;
- μ: parameter determining the amplitude ($= 2\sqrt{\mu}$) of the limit cycle;

- g_A (and the analogous g_B): dynamic neuronal activation variables described below that turn on ($g_A = 1$) and off ($g_A = 0$) the stable limit cycle solution. When they are off ($1 - g_A = 1$), the dynamics has a fixed point at ($x_A = 0, y_A = 1$).
- ω_A determines the frequency of the limit cycle and is determined from the motor field by

$$\omega_A = C \int x f(v^A(x,t)) dx \tag{4}$$

where the constant C is a normalization factor.

The neuronal activation variables g_A and g_B evolve according to a competitive dynamics that is built from two normal forms of the degenerate pitchfork bifurcation, coupled competitively:

$$\tau_g \dot{g}_A = \alpha_A g_A - |\alpha_A| g_A^3 - g_B^2 g_A + \xi \tag{5}$$
$$\tau_g \dot{g}_B = \alpha_B g_B - |\alpha_B| g_B^3 - g_A^2 g_B + \xi \tag{6}$$

The coupling makes that only one neuron may be activated at a time, e.g., $g_A = 1$ and $g_B = 0$ (see [38] for mathematical analysis). The factors α_A or α_B determine which of the two neurons is activated. These factors are designed to be positive (enabling the associated neuron to be turned on) only if there is a peak in the motor field of the corresponding communication partner. They become very small when the associated oscillator is near one end of its limit cycle (e.g., $x_A \approx -\sqrt{\mu}$), generating a tendency for the associated oscillator to be turned off. These factors α_A and α_B also serve to generate the signal, F_{env}, that provides the "condition of satisfaction" to the stack of ordinal fields. Because the competitive dynamics go through a degenerate pitchfork bifurcation each time an oscillator is turned on or off, noise ξ is essential to push the neurons away from unstable states.

References

1. Thelen, E.: Time-scale dynamics and the development of an embodied cognition. In: Port, R.F., van Gelder, T. (eds.) Mind as motion: Explorations in the dynamics of cognition, pp. 69–100. MIT Press, Cambridge (1996)
2. Clark, A.: An embodied cognitive science. Trends in Cognitive Sciences 3(9), 345–351 (1999)
3. Anderson, M.L.: Embodied cognition: A field guide. Artificial Intelligence 149, 91–130 (2003)
4. Schöner, G.: Dynamical systems approaches to cognition. In: Sun, R. (ed.) Cambridge Handbook of Computational Cognitive Modeling, Cambridge University Press, Cambridge (2007)
5. Spencer, J.P., Schöner, G.: Bridging the representational gap in the dynamical systems approach to development. Developmental Science 6, 392–412 (2003)
6. Sacks, H., Schegloff, E.A., Jefferson, G.: A Simplest Systematics for the Organization of Turn-Taking for Conversation. Language 50(4), 696–735 (1974)

7. Wilson, M., Wilson, T.P.: An oscillator model of the timing of turn-taking. Psychonomic Bulletin and Review 12(6), 957–968 (2005)
8. Thórisson, K.R.: Natural turn-taking needs no manual: Computational theory and model, from perception to action. In: Granström, B., House, D., Karlsson, I. (eds.) Multimodality in Language and Speech Systems, pp. 173–207. Kluwer Academic Publishers, Dordrecht, The Netherlands (2002)
9. Thelen, E., Schöner, G., Scheier, C., Smith, L.: The dynamics of embodiment: A field theory of infant perseverative reaching. Brain and Behavioral Sciences 24, 1–33 (2001)
10. Hock, H.S., Schöner, G., Giese, M.A.: The dynamical foundations of motion pattern formation: Stability, selective adaptation, and perceptual continuity. Perception & Psychophysics 65, 429–457 (2003)
11. Rumelhart, D.E., Norman, D.A.: Simulating a skilled typist: A study of the skilled motor performance. Cognitive Science 6, 1–36 (1982)
12. Houghton, G.: The problem of serial order: a neural network model of sequence learning and recall. In: Dale, R., Mellish, C., Zock, M. (eds.) Current research in natural language generation, pp. 287–319. Academic Press Professional, Inc., London (1990)
13. Boardman, I., Bullock, D.: A neural network model of serial order recall from short-term memory. In: Proceedings of the 1991 International Joint Conference on Neural Networks, Seattle WA, July 8-12. International Neural Network Society, pp. II–879–884 (1991)
14. Beiser, D.G., Houk, J.C.: Model of cortical-basal ganglionic processing: encoding the serial order of sensory events. Journal of Neurophysiology 79(6), 3168–3188 (1998)
15. Farrell, S., Lewandowsky, S.: An endogenous distributed model of ordering in serial recall. Psychonomic Bulletin and Review 9(1), 59–79 (2002)
16. Deco, G., Rolls, E.T.: Sequential memory: A putative neural and synaptic dynamical mechanism. Journal of Cognitive Neuroscience 17(2), 294–307 (2005)
17. Erlhagen, W., Schöner, G.: Dynamic field theory of movement preparation. Psychological Review 109, 545–572 (2002)
18. Grossberg, S.: Biological competition: Decision rules, pattern formation, and oscillations. Proceedings of the National Academy of Sciences (USA) 77, 2338–2342 (1980)
19. Wilson, H.R., Cowan, J.D.: A mathematical theory of the functional dynamics of cortical and thalamic nervous tissue. Kybernetik 13, 55–80 (1973)
20. Amari, S.: Dynamics of pattern formation in lateral-inhibition type neural fields. Biological Cybernetics 27, 77–87 (1977)
21. Wilson, H.R.: Spikes, Decisions, and Actions: Dynamical Foundations of Neurosciences. Oxford University Press, Oxford (1999)
22. Deco, G., Schürmann, B.: Information Dynamics: Foundations and Applications. Springer, New York (2000)
23. Goldstone, R.L.: Similarity, interactive activation, and mapping. Journal of Experimental Psychology: Learning, Memory, and Cognition 20, 3–28 (1994)
24. McClelland, J.L., Rogers, T.T.: The parallel distributed processing approach to semantic cognition. Nature Reviews Neuroscience 4(4), 310–322 (2003)
25. Churchland, P.S., Sejnowski, T.J.: The computational brain. Bradford Book/The MIT Press, Cambridge (1992)
26. Williams, R.J.: The logic of activation functions. In: Rumelhart, D.E., McClelland, J.L., the PDP research group (eds.) Parallel distributed processing, vol. 1, pp. 423–443 (1986)

27. Grossberg, S.: The quantized geometry of visual space: The coherent computation of depth, form, and lightness. Behavioral and Brain Sciences 6, 625–692 (1983)
28. Wilimzig, C., Schöner, G.: How categorical behavior emerges from continuous neural representations: Dynamic field theory (in preparation)
29. Humphreys, G.W., Forde, E.M.E., Francis, D.: The organization of sequential actions. In: Monsell, S., Driver, J. (eds.) Control of Cognitive Processes — Attention and Performance XVIII, pp. 427–442. MIT Press, Cambridge (2000)
30. Sandamirskaya, Y., Schöner, G.: Dynamical field theory of sequence generation (in preparation)
31. Searle, J.R.: Intentionality — An essay in the philosophy of mind. Cambridge University Press, Cambridge (1983)
32. Aldridge, J.W., Berridge, K.C.: Coding of serial order by neostriatal neurons: A "natural action" approach to movement sequence. Journal of Neuroscience 18(7), 2777–2787 (1998)
33. Procyk, E., Tanaka, Y.L., Joseph, J.P.: Anterior cingulate activity during routine and non-routine sequential behaviors in macaques. Nature Neuroscience 3, 502–508 (2000)
34. Schöner, G., Kelso, J.A.S.: Dynamic pattern generation in behavioral and neural systems. Science 239, 1513–1520 (1988)
35. Schöner, G.: Timing, clocks, and dynamical systems. Brain and Cognition 48, 31–51 (2002)
36. Streek, J.: Gesture as communication i: Its coordination with gaze and speech. Communication Monographs 60(4), 275–299 (1993)
37. Johnson, J.S., Spencer, J.P., Schöner, G.: A dynamic neural field theory of multi-item visual working memory and change detection. In: Proceedings of the 28th Annual Conference of the Cognitive Science Society (CogSci 2006), Vancouver, Canada, pp. 399–404 (2006)
38. Schöner, G., Dose, M.: A dynamical systems approach to task-level system integration used to plan and control autonomous vehicle motion. Robotics and Autonomous Systems 10, 253–267 (1992)

'I, Max' – Communicating with an Artificial Agent

Ipke Wachsmuth

Artificial Intelligence Group, Faculty of Technology, University of Bielefeld
33594 Bielefeld, Germany
ipke@techfak.uni-bielefeld.de

Abstract. With the advent of communicating machines in the form of embodied agents the question gets ever more interesting under which circumstances
such systems could be attributed some sort of consciousness and self-identity.
We are likely to ascribe to an agent with human appearance and conducting
reasonable natural language dialog that it has desires, goals, and intentions.
Taking the example of 'Max', a humanoid agent embodied in virtual reality,
this contribution examines under which circumstances an artificial agent could
be said to have intentional states and perceive others as intentional agents. We
will link our examination to the question of how such a system could have self-
awareness and how this is grounded in its (virtual) physis and its social context.
We shall discuss how Max could be equipped with the capacity to differentiate
between his own and a partner's mental states and under which conditions Max
could reasonably speak of himself as 'I'.

Keywords: embodied agents, intentional states, machine consciousness, self-
knowledge, emotion, memory.

1 Preliminaries

A lot of people talk to their computer – mostly if it doesn't work as desired. This is
certainly by no means true communication with the machine, which need not be
explained further. Research into artificial intelligence aims, among other things, at enabling machines (or even machine 'beings') to communicate with people as genuinely
and naturally as possible. This requires, first of all, machines that are able to perceive
and represent their environment, draw conclusions and act accordingly.

Evaluating whether communication between a human being and a machine may
actually be possible depends on what is to be understood precisely by 'communication'. If it is supposed to be transferring information that makes the receiver change
its behavior, then even pushing the button that releases the copying machine from
stand-by to action may be considered human-machine communication. In this sense
the term is, in fact, used in the engineering sciences. If, however, both communicating
partners are required to be systems acting autonomously and making use of a common
repertoire of signs in order to inform each other or to negotiate deals, this seemed,
first of all, rather limited to humans. The communicating partners might even be
expected to perceive themselves – as well as each other – as intentional agents, and to
be conscious of themselves and the other.

I. Wachsmuth and G. Knoblich (Eds.): Modeling Communication, LNAI 4930, pp. 279–295, 2008.

With the advent of communicating machines in the form of embodied agents the question gets ever more interesting whether such systems could have some sort of consciousness and self-identity in a foreseeable future. It is tempting to ascribe an agent which has human appearance and which can conduct reasonable natural language dialog that it has certain beliefs and desires, pursues certain goals, and behaves rationally in the sense that it will act to further its goals in the light of its beliefs. That is, we are likely to conduct such a dialog from the intentional stance [10]. But still, even when our artificial opposite had a name to which it attends and called itself 'I', we would assume that attributing the agent consciousness is inadequate at the given time.

In the case of human beings, the term consciousness describes the fact that we are aware of our thoughts and sensations. Our thinking, feeling and will are – more or less well – available to us and, by way of language, we are even able to communicate this (more or less well) to others. At a closer look, the somewhat colorful concept of consciousness is differentiated into quite different forms[1]. *Firstly*, there is a consciousness of sensations: human beings are aware of the quality of what they experience, e.g. how it feels to touch something or feel pain. *Secondly*, there is a consciousness as being aware of oneself: people know of their physical existence and identity, e.g. they recognize themselves in a mirror. This knowledge is rooted in the perception of one's own body, which we can touch to confirm that we exist and which establishes ourselves in the environment.

And *thirdly*, perception of our physical self, our body and its position in the environment is presumably the basis for our self-perception as an acting being that employs means to pursue goals, even if these are shifted to abstract realms (how to reach my goal = how to get there). This includes being conscious of oneself as a subject of experience, relating one's feelings and thoughts to one's own body and mind and knowing that oneself has caused the effects of actions. This still does not mean, though, that one has to refer to oneself as 'I' or must even have the ability to talk, as will be shown later.

The action perspective, however, is essential to this view, for actions cause changes in the world, whether intentional or unintentional. Actions may have success or fail depending on whether goals aimed at are achieved or not. If an action is successful we are happy, if it isn't we may feel angry. In particular this also applies to communicative actions that constitute the special topic of this contribution. If I tell someone else that 'my knee hurts' this is – different from an involuntary 'ouch' – intentional communicative acting. It is intended to inform the other person about my condition, and I am convinced that he (or she) is able to understand me and my feelings and it is my desire that he should feel sorry for me. I might even expect the other one to offer help.

When communicating with each other, human beings assign each other such 'inner life' (intentional states). Analogous to ourselves, we assume that the other person has intentions, beliefs, desires and goals, which we cannot identify directly, however. We imply that they are there, though, since the other person is a being equally thinking and feeling. And we communicate with the aim of influencing the internal states and thus the actions of the other person. This may be successful or fail. The other person

---

[1] We shall relate these ideas, put forward here for motivation, to research literature in Section 3.

may stick to her opinion that I am feeling well – although I am telling her that my knee hurts – if she doesn't actually see me limp. Or she believes that my knee hurts although I have only pretended pain, i.e., beliefs may be false.

Human beings possess the ability to recognize in others not only an object of the environment but an acting subject, an image of ourselves, but with its own perspective and intentions. We can even develop a mental model of our communication partner, making assumptions – possibly false ones – about the other's beliefs, desires, and intentions ('Theory of Mind'; see also Krämer [16]). Developing such representation of the other – a 'partner model' – is only possible due to the fact that intentional states have contents that can be expressed in the form of statements (she knows I am very busy, she wants me to come home earlier today, she wants me to go with her to the movies tonight, etc.). Such representation requires symbols of some kind as 'thought signs', which carry contents that form the basis of our logical thinking and rational acting.

Being able to not only understand others as intentional agents but also to reason about their thoughts and goals requires a high degree of consciousness, which – as many researchers believe – is coupled to symbolic representations of the world (but see [2] for discussion). We shall in the following firstly investigate whether and under what circumstances artificial systems can be justifiably attributed intentional states, i.e. can *have* intentional states. Secondly, given certain cognitive conditions, are machines able to *know* about themselves, and are they capable of understanding intentions and perspectives of a dialog partner? Before discussing this, two additional aspects shall be addressed that are closely linked to consciousness, namely, emotion and memory.

As already mentioned above, our feelings play a decisive role when evaluating the success of an action. Even more, emotions are considered to be a basic condition for organized action in modern theories of cognition. Among other things, emotion is understood to be a control medium of the cognitive system to regulate attention directed to incoming stimuli in order to differentiate between important and unimportant matters. The fact that one becomes aware of something is apparently in major parts connected to affective experiencing. Moreover, emotions are of essential importance to the ability of differentiating between various options for actions (see Damasio [9]), as well as for the significance of experiences that affect our memories more permanently. In the case of human beings, storing information is closely connected with the affective appraisal but also, on the other hand, with the realization that the event concerned is very special or rare. This observation indicates that not only emotion but also memory constitutes an important aspect of consciousness.

Our experiencing would be incomplete and the awareness we have of ourselves would not be very profound, if our mind were not equipped to store memories – in particular those that concern ourselves, something we have experienced just before, or experienced yesterday or a long time ago. Generally, we are able to access our personal past, an ability that has been called autobiographical memory; cf. Conway and Pleydell-Pearce [8]. This is the basis of a form of consciousness called 'autonoetic' (knowing of oneself) allowing us to imagine our identity – uncoupled from current experiences – in the past and the future. Studies of patients with impaired consciousness and impaired memory suggest a connection between autonoetic consciousness and memory, in particular episodic memory; cf. Markowitsch [18].

In the section to follow we will introduce 'Max' [14], an artificial humanoid agent embodied in virtual reality (see also [13]). To examine the questions raised above, we will then turn to current research discussions of how an artificial system could have consciousness and self-awareness. Finally, we will discuss the conditions under which Max could reasonably speak of himself as 'I'. As we go along, we shall sketch starting points for the technical realization of such conditions and also discuss the roles of emotion and memory.

2 Who Is Max?

"Could you imagine Max being conscious of himself one day?", I was asked on a conference some time ago. Earlier in the meeting, I had presented our Bielefeld works on a 'situated artificial communicator' called Max. Max is an artificial agent (a 'virtual human') communicating with his human opposite verbally and through body language, with gestures and mimic. Resembling human appearance he can be met in our laboratory in the setting of a three-dimensional computer graphics projection. Max helps us investigate in detail the basics of communicative intelligence and how it is possible to describe it – in parts – so precisely that a machine can be made to simulate it (the virtual human Max is a program-controlled software-machine). This means that collecting insights about the functioning of human communication is an important focus of our work. A technical goal is also the construction of a system as functional and convincing as possible that may be applied in different ways.[2]

Our research scenario deals with the cooperative construction of objects, such as an airplane from a *Baufix* wooden toykit. This is to test whether Max shows a kind of 'understanding' in changing situations that enables him to perform a dialog with a human being. Even if he may not be taken for a human being, Max is intended to show forms of communication that are familiar to us, look into our face when talking or listening, gesticulate naturally, look enquiringly if he does not understand us and – before talking himself – he should wait till we have finished.

The human and Max are opposing each other, for instance at a table (see Figure 1). With the exception of the person shown left, the pictured scene is projected virtual reality. On the table, there are different building bricks, three- and five-hole bars, several screws with colored caps, a cube with holes on all sides etc., all items will be assembled in the course of the dialog. The human sees Max and the entire setting three-dimensionally by means of stereo glasses and hears the synthetic voice of Max due to surround sound from hidden speakers. Max 'sees' the human, his gaze direction as well as hand and arm movements by means of an infrared tracking system and cordless data gloves, and – via a radio microphone – he 'hears' him speak which he processes with a speech recognizer. Both the human and Max are able to have individual parts assembled by natural language instructions and gestures, carried out in simulation with realistic sounds added. This is done, for example, as follows:

[2] Since January 2004, Max has been performing at the Heinz Nixdorf Museums-Forum in Paderborn where he informs visitors – in a dialog situation – on all things to know about one of the exhibition areas and the computer museum. It is the first time Max came into real-life application.

Fig. 1. Cooperative dialog with Max   **Fig. 2.** Max, unpleasantly touched

Max: Hello, I'm Max. How can I help you? [*smiling*].
Human: Explain the assembly of a propeller.
Max: Let's do it together. First, a screw has to be inserted into the middle of a three-hole-bar.
Human: Insert the yellow screw into the bar [*points to a three-hole-bar, the first screw is inserted into the first hole*].
Max: No, that was the wrong hole [*screw slips out*].
Max: I'll explain it to you again. A screw has to be inserted into the middle of a three-hole-bar.
Human: Insert the screw into the middle of the three-hole-bar [*screw is inserted into the middle of the three-hole-bar chosen before*].
Max: Okay, that's correct. Now insert this into the three-hole-bar [*points to the bar with the screw*].
Human: You do it.
Max: Okay, I will perform the action [*the objects are connected as instructed*].
Max: And now the bars need to be turned crosswise to each other [*shows the rotation using a gesture*] etc.

The cognitive architecture the virtual human Max is based on will be explained in a later section. Just this much: Max knows some grammatical rules and makes use of a semantic lexicon for translating the meaning of words in order to represent the meaning of his opposite's utterances in the form of symbolic descriptions using compositional and reference semantics. Within a limited vocabulary, Max is able to talk and coordinate his gestures due to his flexible body. Simulated facial muscles enable him to express 'emotional conditions' (see Figure 2), which – among other things – are influenced by achieving or failing communicative goals. Max's verbal utterances are produced from a repertoire of stereotype expressions by adapting their parameters to the current situation – including the generation of appropriate gestures. This also includes the term 'I', without Max having a notion of himself (at the current time).

In the theory of communicative action, these dialog expressions could be seen as actions in the proper sense only against the background of attributing intentional states. This means, e.g., Max ought to have a mental state of some kind such as 'wants to have an answer', to make his initial question 'genuine' communication. First of all,

Max's body movements, too, are (simulated) physical events. Only in connection with an intended communicative function (as represented in the form of goals) would they gain importance as gestural actions, i.e., only by the fact that a sequence of individual movements is projected and carried out in line with a currently represented mental state of a communicative goal. Seen from the philosophical angle, they would be attributed the status of actions only if Max were able to perform his dialog from the first-person perspective. Would it thus be possible for Max to have that kind of consciousness of his self? Before trying an answer, a brief overview of the state of research into 'machine consciousness' will be given.

3   Consciousness in Artificial Systems?

The question as to whether machines are able to develop forms of consciousness has been a topical subject within artificial intelligence, the neurosciences and, not least, in the philosophy of mind. Research into 'machine consciousness' is expected to yield also further insights on human consciousness. In particular we might find it somewhat strange to attribute a human-like opposite a profound ability to communicate, if he were not able to reasonably speak of himself as 'I'. This would require, however, to configurate the artificial agent accordingly, so as to enable him to adopt a first-person perspective. After outlining a few research approaches towards this subject, different forms of 'self-knowledge' will be discussed in particular.

3.1 Machine Consciousness

Machine consciousness projects can be placed along a spectrum, one of its poles represented by modeling physical brain processes. The digital neuromodels by Igor Aleksander, for instance, are based on the theory that brain cells balance sensory input in a way that allows them to consistently represent real-world objects, in other words, they encode a neuronal depiction of the exterior world; cf. Aleksander, Morton, and Dumall [1]. The other pole is the embedding of preprogrammed rules for controlling the behavior of an artificial agent; e.g., Sloman [26]. Roughly in the middle between both extremes, there is the Global Workspace theory of Baars [3], [4] positing that consciousness emerges if multiple sensory inputs trigger neural mechanisms, which compete to ascertain the most logical response to the inputs. The "Intelligent Distribution Agent (IDA)" model by Franklin and Graesser [12], for instance, is based on this hypothesis.

Research approaches towards modeling mental states and practical reasoning are frequently based on functional models of planning and choosing actions by means-ends analysis, mainly in versions of the *belief-desire-intention* paradigm (BDI); cf. Rao and Georgeff [22]. The BDI approach comes from Michael Bratman [7]; one of its fundamentals can be traced back to the work of Daniel Dennett [10] on the behavior of intentional systems. The basic idea is the description of the internal working state of an agent by means of intentional states (beliefs, desires, intentions) as well as the layout of a control architecture that allows the agent to choose rationally a sequence of actions on the basis of their representations. By recursively elaborating a hierarchical plan structure, specific intentions are generated until, eventually, executable actions are obtained; cf. Wooldridge [29]. Identification and representation of beliefs, desires and intentions are also useful for analyzing the behavior of artificial agents that communicate with humans or other artificial agents; see Rao and Georgeff [23].

Modeling intentional states is based on their symbolic representation. One of its assets is the flexibility it provides for planning and reasoning. In beliefs, for instance, facts concerning the world may be stored that an agent is not (or no longer) able to perceive at the moment, which, however, are to affect his further planning. An agent being able to pursue his goals not only in the light of currently perceived information but also with reference to world knowledge, remembered past and anticipated future will be superior to other agents that do not possess this ability. Even in view of the continuing debate on the significance of symbolic representations for human intelligence it is reasonable to assume that humans represent intentional states symbolically and draw their conclusions on this basis.

It is a difference, though, whether an agent draws conclusions simply on the basis of his beliefs and desires or whether he makes use of them – with a corresponding description – for drawing conclusions, recognizing them to be his own. In many cases such differentiation may not have functional advantages. An agent should be expected, however, to represent his intentional states explicitly as being his own ones, if he must also record and deal specifically with other agents' intentional states. Agents are going to communicate with the intention of changing the inner states of other agents, i.e. their beliefs and intentions. Given a favourable situation, an agent being 'conscious' of his goals may realize them in an opportunistic way.

3.2 Physically Grounded Self-knowledge (Anderson and Perlis)

From the philosophical point of view, consciousness develops if an agent constructs a model of himself and integrates it into his model of the world [11], [19]. It is a frequently discussed question whether this requires a certain linguistic competence and, in particular, the capacity of using in self-representations an indexical symbol ('I') that refers to oneself. According to Anderson and Perlis [2], usage of an indexical symbol is not imperative for an agent – whether human or artificial – for being able to recognize oneself as the origin of actions. Rather, they argue, it would suffice if the agent had a basal concept of himself rooted in his bodily self-perception which they term *essential prehension* – in opposition to John Perry's [20] well-known problem of the *essential indexical*.

In their initial argument, Anderson and Perlis use the example of the fictitious robotic agent JP-B4 that accumulates information about himself on a self-token[3] 'JP-B4' (he is thus expected to recognize, for instance, that he himself caused an oil stain). This self-token is a self-representation for JP-B4, if especially any physical action performed by JP-B4 which keeps his self-token as a direct object in the description of the action, is directed towards himself within the world. To this end they need the assumption that JP-B4 has proprioceptive sensors reporting the spatial position of his limbs and his movable sensors. With this, JP-B4 is able to represent his body as an object (one of many) which, however, is made special due to the fact that

---

[3] The authors speak of self-referring (mental) token or self-representing (mental) token which is to be understood as a 'marker' of some kind, indicating self-related information.

the positions of perceived objects (such as the oil stain) can be determined relative to the agent.

In the case of humans, too, Anderson and Perlis go on to argue, perception of one's own body (somatoception) through the tactile sense, proprioception, etc. constitutes the basis of a *physical* self-representation fixed in the environment that is even required for actions as simple as reaching for an object and that is rooted in self-identification. Analogous to JP-B4 they postulate as the only basis for this a special mental self-representing token ('SR*') that is to mark automatically somatoceptive information and that must also be present in mental representations of (initially physical) self-directed actions. This self-token may also serve to relate to oneself externally perceived informations and align those with body perception without the thinking of a self-symbol (indexical thoughts) being required.[4] Finally, Anderson and Perlis argue that intentional and reflexive self-representations are the result of the cognitive system using the same token 'SR*' when representing intentional states,[5] and that a more comprehensive *self-awareness* is rooted herein.

3.3 Implicit and Explicit Self-knowledge (Beckermann)

Beckermann [6] deals with the problem under what conditions cognitive systems (also artificial ones) – or 'agents', a term that is preferred here – may obtain an explicit form of self-awareness based on reflexive self-knowledge. He supports the thesis that cognitive agents[6] may possess reflexive self-knowledge exactly when they make use of (meta)-representations concerning themselves and that are, in addition, coordinated with 'agent-relative' representations.

Agent-relative knowledge is knowledge represented from the perspective of a particular agent. As long as the agent perceives the world and himself from his own perspective only, he does not need an explicit reference to himself (and, accordingly, no self-symbol) in his representations. Rather, he is able to generate representations on the basis of an implicit reference system in the center of which the agent himself is located. An example: 'The apple nearby that can be reached for' which he is able to grab without thinking 'I'. Neither do sensations such as 'the knee hurts' require the reference to the 'I'. Agent-relative representations thus only include knowledge about the way in which the perceived environment – including the bodily self-perception – is related to the agent. Since they are solely set up from his own perspective, such a representation does not require a self-symbol.

Now, under what conditions would an agent be forced to introduce an explicit representation of himself? This is discussed by Beckermann as follows, a fictitious agent called 'AL' serving as an example: When representing the perceived environment, AL introduces an internal name for each object – such as 'object-6', 'object-7', etc. – thus representing information about the objects, i.e., their type, properties and relations to other objects. This procedure does not require AL to introduce a name *for*

---

[4] To put it simply: The fact that one sees externally what one feels internally – for instance when touching one's own body – leads to a connection of actions and effects of actions and, thus, to self-identification.

[5] If necessary, they allow the self-token also to be translated as 'I'.

[6] Here, cognitive agents are understood as systems that represent their environment in an internal mental model in order to better cope with their environment.

himself – he does not see himself as an object. This becomes inevitable only when AL encounters an object in his environment that he identifies as another cognitive agent. For AL this other agent also constitutes an object for which AL introduces a name – for instance, 'object-111'– whose behavior, however, actually depends on how the other one, for his part, represents the environment.

To be able to predict the behavior of his fellow being, AL has to set up representations of the other's (assumed) representations, i.e. meta-representations – a mental model of the other's mental model. If, for instance, AL believes that the agent he calls 'object-111' considers an item of the environment to be green – e.g., a sofa that AL calls 'object-7' –, or if AL believes that agent 'object-111' desires to sit down on 'object-7' – the green sofa – he sets up agent-relative meta-representations as follows ('believes' and 'wants' in this case concern the intentional states the other agent is assumed to have):

(believes object-111 (color object-7 green))
(wants object-111 (sitting-on object-7))

To be capable of representing which (assumed) representations the other one keeps about him, AL is forced to introduce an internal name for himself – such as 'object-100'. Only by means of this name for himself is he able, for instance, to represent adequately the other's desire to obtain food from AL or the other's belief that AL suffers from a hurting knee:

(wants object-111 (gives-food object-100 object-111))
(believes object-111 (pain-in-the-knee object-100))

The crucial factor is that AL would now be able to establish a systematic relation between explicit representations that contain this new name (for himself) and his former agent-relative representations with implicit self-reference; i.e. (sitting-on object-7) refers to (sits-on object-100 object-7), meaning: if AL knows he is sitting on the green sofa AL realizes that the agent who is *he himself* is sitting on the sofa. In the same way, AL's body perception could be represented not only in an agent-relative way but also explicitly, i.e. (pain-in-the-knee object-100), etc. And since AL's agent-relative representations correspond solely with his respective 'object-100' representations, the special role of the name 'object-100' as a self-symbol is resulting.

As a further effect, AL would also be able to generate meta-representations *about himself*, thus seeing himself from an external perspective, e.g. (desires object 100 (sitting on object 7)). Only then would he know his own beliefs and desires, could develop explicit self-knowledge and, hence, self-awareness. Only then is it conceivable that AL – together with his fellow beings – develops a language which includes word symbols like 'I' and 'you'. He would have learned the meaning of the word 'I', when he used it to express only such representations that are related to himself, i.e., he says 'I' only if he talks about himself.

Hence, explicit self-knowledge (i.e. representations with a name for oneself) develops only in the social context: if a cognitive agent meets other cognitive agents and he realizes that – just as he does – they represent their environment and thus him, too.[7] If the agent desires to represent for himself such representations of his fellow

---

[7] A bit trenchant: Hermits would be able to manage with agent-relative representations, i.e. implicit self-reference.

beings of which he is the object, he is forced to introduce his own internal name and make himself explicity an object of his representations. If he finally takes the step to bring his agent-relative representations in alignment with their explicitly self-related counterparts, he has got reflexive self-knowledge.

4 Max as a Cognitive Agent

Let us turn back to Max. Max is no fictitious robot but a fully implemented system that designs a humanoid agent in virtual reality. He is equipped with an articulate flexible body which – among other things – allows him to access parameters of his physis in order to enable him, e.g., to call up his position in the environment and his joint angles when planning his gestures; cf. Kopp and Wachsmuth [15]. As already mentioned above, our scenario deals with dialogs between a human and Max in the course of which a model airplane will be constructed.

Beliefs:	Behaviors:	Goals
position L5_LEISTE-natur-0 -0.0700	beh0 beh0	☐ Goals
type L5_LEISTE-natur-0 L5_LEISTE	linkDelibBehavior beh0 connected	☐ keepThinking
position L3_LEISTE-natur-1 0.2353	linkDelibBehavior beh14 connected	☐ constructTogether
type L3_LEISTE-natur-1 L3_LEISTE		☐ utter
position W_SCH_SCHRAUBE-gelb-0		☐ explainActionStep
type W_SCH_SCHRAUBE-gelb-0 SCH		☐ utter
position W_SCH_SCHRAUBE-rot-1 0		☐ constructOneStep
type W_SCH_SCHRAUBE-rot-1 SCHR		☐ evaluateAction
position GEWINDEBLOCK-gruen-0 -		☐ giveFeedback
type GEWINDEBLOCK-gruen-0 BLOC		☐ utter
position L3_LEISTE-natur-0 -0.2610		☐ havingTurn
type L3_LEISTE-natur-0 L3_LEISTE		☐ explainActionStep
userAction connect L3_LEISTE-natur		☐ utter
position W_SCH_SCHRAUBE-gelb-0		☐ constructOneStep
havingTurn max true		☐ utter
wantTurn max true		☐ determineActionStep
		☐ assemble
		☐ utter

Fig. 3. Present beliefs, behaviors, and goals of the Max system (from Kopp et al. [14])

As a cognitive agent, Max represents his (virtual) world in parts to be able to cope with the tasks when assisting the (virtual) construction of Baufix objects. For each Baufix object – either existing from the beginning or implemented later, e.g. aggregated ones – he introduces a formal internal name such as 'object-1', 'object-2', etc. (It is not relevant here that within the system actually a symbol generator provides somewhat more differentiated 'talking names', see Figure 3). Furthermore, he records beliefs about the type of the parts and their position giving the vectors of a reference point of an object within the world coordinate system, for example as follows:

> (type object-1 THREEHOLEBAR)
> (position object-1 (2,3,5))
> (type object-2 THREEHOLEBAR)
> (position object-2 (x,y,z))

(type object-3 SLOTHEADSCREW-yellow)
(position object-3 (x',y',z'))

Changes of the scene are represented by Max real-time, for instance, by asserting (connected object-26 object-27) when the according parts are connected. Intentional states of his dialog partner have so far not been represented by Max. He represents, however, whose turn it is to speak. Various routines enable Max to identify turn signals of his dialog partner (turn-taking) and to know whether it is his turn or whether he wants to have it (having-turn Max true, want-turn Max true; see Figure 3).

To organize the complex interplay of sensory, cognitive and actoric abilities, a cognitive architecture has been developed for Max [17], aiming at making his behavior appear believable, intelligent, and emotional. Here, 'cognitive' refers to the conception of structures and processes underlying mental activities. Fitted to his trial scenario, Max is equipped with limited knowledge of the world and is capable of planning and reasoning so that he may act as an intelligent assistant. Moreover he is equipped with reactive behaviors that enable him cope with disruptions and sudden changes.

In a hybrid system architecture the *Max* system integrates symbol-processing and behavior-based approaches concerning perception, reactive behavior, higher mental processes such as reasoning and planned action, up to and including focused attention and action appraisal. The central part is a *belief-desire-intention (BDI)* interpreter. Due to the hybrid architecture Max is both able to conduct a dialog with planned utterances and to produce spontaneous utterances, e.g. in the form of turn-taking and feedback signals. Additionally, specialized planners – e.g., for constructing Baufix objects – and specialized memory stores – e.g., with dynamically updated representations for the state of constructed objects have been integrated.

Explicitly represented goals (*desires*), which may be introduced through internal processing and through external influences as well, are serving as inner motivation that is triggering behavior. Intentions are generated by means of the BDI interpreter, which determines the current intention on the basis of existing beliefs, current desires and goals as well as the options for actions. Max can have several desires, the highest-rated of which is selected by a utility function to become the current intention. Options for actions are available in the form of abstract plans that are described by preconditions, context conditions, consequences that may be accomplished, and a priority function. If a concrete plan drawn up on the basis of these facts has been executed successfully, the related goal will become defunct.

The conduct of the dialog is based on an explicit modeling of communicative competences that are related to multimodal communicative acts [21] generalizing the speech act theory by Searle and Vanderveken [25]. Communicative acts are modeled as action-plan operators. The dialog is performed in accordance with the mixed initiative-principle, this means, for instance, that in case the human fails to answer, Max himself takes the initiative and acts as the speaker. The plan structure of the BDI module makes it possible to implement new goals during the performance of an intention that may replace the current intention, provided it has a higher priority. If the previous intention is not specifically abandoned in this process and its context conditions are still valid, it will become active again after the interruption.

Max's behavior is further influenced by (simulated) emotions, which determine as system parameters in which way Max performs actions. The emotive system is, on the one hand, fed by external stimuli (Max's virtual physis, e.g., has touch-sensitive areas), and, on the other, by the cognitive system: reaching or failing to reach main goals generates positive or negative emotions, respectively, that affect the valences of mood of the emotional system, which, in turn, control Max's unintentional external behavior. The emotional expression in Max's face and voice caused thereby may convey feedback-signals to his opposite. In parallel action, mood valences occurring continuously in a three-dimensional abstract space are categorized and symbolically represented as explicit beliefs; so they may take effect when choosing between options for actions; cf. Becker et al. [5]. Max is also able to utter verbally symbolically represented emotional states ('I am angry now'); in this sense, Max *seems* to be 'conscious' of them.

Now, what about the consciousness Max might actually have of himself as a subject? Insofar as his cognitive abilities are based on a BDI architecture, Max can be justifiably ascribed mentalistic attributes that may be characterized by terms such as knowledge, belief, intention. We may thus state, as an intermediate result, that Max not only represents his environment, he has also – in the discourse of the cooperative situation (constructing with Baufix) – intentional states (beliefs, desires/goals, and intentions), which constitutes him as being an intentional agent. But can – or could – he *know* about his intentional states and those of his dialog partners (more precisely, those he assumes his dialog partners to have)? A model enabling Max to make use of the corresponding meta-representations has so far been rudimentarily realized. Up to now it is only concerned with following up the role of the speaker as well as turn-taking. This is an example, however, which can already serve to indicate to what extent Max requires reflexive knowledge.

As already mentioned above, Max is able to identify turn signals of his dialog partner, i.e. that the other wants to take the role of the speaker (e.g., if the human interrupts him directly, says 'Max!' or raises his hand). Max actually represents his role as the speaker already with a self-symbol (having-turn Max true), even if this is unnecessary in a dyadic setting; an agent-relative representation would be entirely sufficient: (having-turn true) – or (having-turn false) if it is the other's – the human's – turn. Our next plans include to enable Max to have a reasonable conversation with more than one partner, thus he should be able to keep an account of who of those participating is speaking or wants to do so. It could be expected that for this he uses symbol names for his partners (having-turn Other-1, having-turn Other-2, etc.). But does this actually require him to have a self-symbol, as in (having-turn Max)? Even if this social situation suggests recording the turn-holder by name, Max may still manage without a self-symbol, namely, by representing (having-turn true/false) whether he or someone else is speaking and by differentiating the others by name. To know explicitly 'It's my turn', however, Max ought to have a self-symbol.

Let's look at the (as yet fictitious) situation where three agents – Other-1, Other-2, and Max – are having a conversation and are taking turns. As long as Max 'wants' to have his turn only to say something (want-turn true) he will just have to wait for a suitable opportunity. However, the conversational situation of explicitly passing the speaker-role also may occur (turn-giving), signalling to a direct addressee and to be understood as a call for action, i.e. taking the turn; cf. Sacks et al. [24]. In this case, however, Max should be in a position to recognize that he himself is the addressee and, for instance, represent (wants Other-2 (give-turn Other-2 Max)), etc. In other words, Max would then have – or require – some form of explicit self-awareness that allows him to differentiate between his own and a partner's mental states.

5 Criteria for a 'Human' Non-human Consciousness

In this paper we examined under what conditions an artifical agent may be able to communicate with some sort of consciousness of being an intentional agent, the agent Max embodied in virtual reality serving as an example. In particular, we asked what kind of cognitive conditions are required to enable Max to know of himself and understand intentions and perspectives of a dialog partner. May – some day – Max justifiably talk about himself as 'I, Max'? But also: being a 'virtual human', might Max constitute a communication partner acceptable for humans?[8]

Let's return to the forms of consciousness first differentiated in the introduction, i.e. (1) consciousness of sensations, of the phenomenal quality of experiencing, (2) consciousness as knowledge of the physical identity, and (3) consciousness in the form of self-perception as an acting being, up to the self-perception as causing actions (here in particular: communicative actions). Let's now consider to what extent that may seem attainable for the artificial agent Max.

1. Qualia. Max can certainly not be ascribed sensations of the kind human beings have, since – due to his virtual body – he does not possess a neurophysiological basis required for qualitative experiencing. In this sense, the simulated emotional states can, for instance, not be experienced subjectively, this means that Max *does not* have feelings. Their functional role in the sense of behavior controlling appraisal, however, can be and has been modeled, at least to some extent – a mechanism of appraisal analogous to feelings, which, for instance, allows a differentiation between options for actions; see Stephan [27]. By means of such appraisal achieved through simulated emotions, Max might be able to develop preferences and directed attention. A positive or negative appraisal in achieving or failing communicative goals could to some extent be compared with emotional experiences.

2. Self-identification. Regarding a consciousness as knowledge of the physical identity, the situation is quite different. This concerns the question as to whether Max can have a basal concept of himself that is rooted in the self-perception of his (virtual) physis (*essential prehension* in the sense of Anderson and Perlis [2], see Section 3.1). Let's imagine the following experiment: In virtual reality, Max perceives his simulated – but not yet recognized – mirror image that moves exactly as Max does, e.g., when he places his hand on his left cheek (in our experimental system, touching Max's left cheek gives Max's emotive system a pleasant 'feeling'). It appears technically possible that Max can align the action observed externally and perceived internally by means of a self-token as outlined in Section 3.2. This *physically grounded* self-token mediates an essential awareness of location that is important for acting in space, it is reference point for agent-relative representations and may be the starting point for references a self-symbol makes to the own 'person'.

---

[8] An indication that this question is not entirely odd is the fact that Max is frequently asked by visitors of the Heinz Nixdorf Museums-Forum 'Are you a human being?'.

3. Self-perception as an acting being, even including self-perception of having caused actions (here, in particular, communicative actions): For this, it is mandatory that Max has symbolic representations of his environment and knowledge about how to represent planned actions as goals. Max should in particular be able to represent those as being his goals for which, according to Anderson and Perlis [2], a self-token would suffice. This makes only sense altogether, however, if it can be interlinked. Only through self-identification of his own physis would Max be able to relate agent-relative knowledge *to himself*, by coupling it to a self-token (which is hence grounded in his physis). Only then could he perceive himself as the origin of actions. Only by introducing a self-token into the representations of actions could he perceive himself as causing actions, i.e. establish causal relations between his actions and the effects they trigger.

On the basis of the ideas explained in Section 4, Max *can* be understood as a system perceiving and representing his environment and drawing conclusions in order to cope with the situation. It seems, in fact, relatively easy to construct the *Max* system in a way that all his agent-relative representations are automatically marked *as his own* by means of a self-token. According to the above thoughts, however, conscious self-awareness is coupled to *explicit* self-knowledge, that is, Max would require explicit self-representations incorporating a symbol name for himself, which express Max's view onto himself from an external perspective. To reach this, first of all representational states of the agent on their part must be made the object of representations, i.e. meta-representations need to be set up:

4. Meta-representations. Clearly, by means of the conditions created by a BDI architecture (see Section 4) it appears possible to configure Max in a way that enables him to set up meta-representations. A more difficult question is how to create an experimental situation that allows Max to set up a *reflexive* meta-representation. According to Beckermann (see Section 3.3), a social situation may be a suitable basis on which Max sets up assumed representations of a communication partner that deal with himself and that he would have to coordinate with corresponding Max-relative representations just as described. As a first step, a turn-taking situation as explained above appears suitable. In this context, Max must be able to set up also expressions in symbolic representations that allow him to make propositions on propositions, even including propositions on himself, such as 'the other wants me, Max, to take the turn'. Max should then be able to derive an according intention that makes him take the turn.

Let's suppose we succeeded in fulfilling such conditions (at least 2-4) for Max altogether. Then we would have to admit Max to be able to communicate as an intentional agent that has self-perception as an acting being. Just as Max would have representational states bearing his intentions, desires and goals, he would be able to ascribe such states to humans. And vice versa, it would then be entirely justified if a human being ascribed him, too, intentions, desires and goals that Max relates to himself, i.e., that are his own.

Yet, the fact that Max's knowledge of his own states would be limited to the moment only would remain rather unsatisfactory; this could still not be considered profound knowledge of himself (autonoetic consciousness). If Max did not know what he did yesterday or what he could be doing tomorrow, he would not have an 'I' persisting across time. A further important criterion thus is:

5. Memory. Max should not only be able to remember who (or whether he) triggered an action, he should also be able to recognize if an event is absolutely new to him, that he cannot remember having experienced before. In order to be aware of being confronted with a new event for the first time, Max should be able to have access to his personal history. He would need an autobiographical memory that enables him, – with reference to his communication partners – to ascertain, 'Yesterday I constructed a plane with you for the first time' or 'I have often (or never) constructed a plane with you'. This requires him, however, to be able to store memories of such an event in appropriate form. If it happened to him a repeated time, it should be possible to revise the uniqueness of the memory, up to daily experience.

How to realize such an autobiographical memory in the case of Max? As described above (Section 4) the behavior-triggering impetus of Max is based on explicitly represented goals. As a starting point for an autobiographical memory, Max may set up a record in appropriate form (marked with a time stamp and his self-token), when one of his goals has been achieved, or failed. It would probably not be helpful if Max stored a record for any processed (sub)goal; there would be far too many marginal ones that are of only temporary importance. Rather, the goals should be evaluated with respect to their significance. Such can be done by the emotive system, by coupling any goal reached and any goal failed with a positive or negative emotion (pleasure or anger), with 'higher' goals triggering stronger and sub-goals less emotional reactions. Permanency of storing memories can be made dependent on the strength of the emotional reaction, thus assuring that memories of main goals remain more pronounced. An adjustment of new and recorded former goals could, in turn, be evaluated emotionally. A goal that frequently failed and has now been achieved for the first time could give rise to Max's 'joyful excitement' and lead to a lasting, 'I'- related memory.

We now see the following picture of artificial consciousness developing: criteria required are self-identification, self-perception as an acting being, meta-representations and memories related to emotional appraisal. Given these conditions, it appears possible that Max approaches forms of 'human' (comparable to a human being's) consciousness and self-identity. The higher the degree of similarity, the more justifiably Max could talk of himself as 'I, Max', and the better Max might be acceptable as a social partner, as a 'human machine' for human beings.

Acknowledgments. This paper is a slightly polished version of an article originally published in German [28]. Assistance by Marion Kämper in providing the English translation and helpful comments by two reviewers and by Manuela Lenzen are gratefully acknowledged.

References

1. Aleksander, I., Morton, H., Dunmall, B.: Seeing is Believing: Depictive Neuromodelling of Visual Awareness. In: Mira, J., Prieto, A.G. (eds.) IWANN 2001. LNCS, vol. 2084, pp. 765–771. Springer, Heidelberg (2001)
2. Anderson, M.L., Perlis, D.: The Roots of Self-Awareness. Phenomenology and the Cognitive Sciences 4, 297–333 (2005)
3. Baars, B.J.: In the Theater of Consciousness. Oxford University Press, Oxford (1997)

4. Baars, B.J., Franklin, S.: How Conscious Experience and Working Memory Interact. Trends in Cognitive Science 7, 166–172 (2003)
5. Becker, C., Kopp, S., Wachsmuth, I.: Simulating the Emotion Dynamics of a Multimodal Conversational Agent. In: André, E., Dybkjær, L., Minker, W., Heisterkamp, P. (eds.) ADS 2004. LNCS (LNAI), vol. 3068, pp. 154–165. Springer, Heidelberg (2004)
6. Beckermann, A.: Self-Consciousness in Cognitive Systems. In: Kanzian, Ch., Quitterer, J., Runggaldier, E. (eds.) Persons. An Interdisciplinary Approach. ÖBV & HPT, Wien, pp. 174–188 (2003)
7. Bratman, M.: Intention, Plans, and Practical Reason. Havard University Press, Harvard (1987)
8. Conway, M.A., Pleydell-Pearce, C.W.: The Construction of Autobiographical Memories in the Self-Memory System. Psychological Review 107, 261–288 (2000)
9. Damasio, A.R.: Descartes' Error. Emotion, Reason, and the Human Brain. Putnam, New York (1994)
10. Dennett, D.C.: The Intentional Stance. MIT Press, Cambridge (1987)
11. Dennett, D.C.: Consciousness Explained. Little Brown, London (1991)
12. Franklin, S., Graesser, A.: A Software Agent Model of Consciousness. Consciousness and Cognition 8, 285–305 (1999)
13. Kopp, S., Allwood, J., Grammer, K., Ahlsén, E., Stocksmeier, T.: Modeling Embodied Feedback with Virtual Humans (same volume)
14. Kopp, S., Jung, B., Leßmann, N., Wachsmuth, I.: Max – A Multimodal Assistant in Virtual Reality Construction. KI – Künstliche Intelligenz 4/03, 11–17 (2003)
15. Kopp, S., Wachsmuth, I.: Synthesizing Multimodal Utterances for Conversational Agents. Journal Computer Animation and Virtual Worlds 15, 39–52 (2004)
16. Krämer, N.C.: Theory of Mind as a Theoretical Prerequisite to Model Communication with Virtual Humans (same volume)
17. Leßmann, N., Kopp, S., Wachsmuth, I.: Situated Interaction with a Virtual Human – Perception, Action, and Cognition. In: Rickheit, G., Wachsmuth, I. (eds.) Situated Communication, pp. 287–323. Mouton de Gruyter, Berlin (2006)
18. Markowitsch, H.J.: Autonoetic Consciousness. In: Kircher, T., David, A. (eds.) The Self in Neuroscience and Psychiatry, pp. 180–196. Cambridge University Press, Cambridge (2003)
19. Metzinger, T.: The Subjectivity of Subjective Experience: A Representationalist Analysis of the First-Person Perspective. In: Neural Correlates of Consciousness – Empirical and Conceptual Questions, pp. 285–306. MIT Press, Cambridge (2000)
20. Perry, J.: The Problem of the Essential Indexical. In: The Problem of the Essential Indexical and Other Essays, pp. 33–52. Oxford University Press, Oxford (1993)
21. Poggi, I., Pelachaud, C.: Performative Facial Expression in Animated Faces. In: Cassell, J., Sullivan, J., Prevost, S., Churchill, E. (eds.) Embodied Conversational Agents, pp. 155–188. The MIT Press, Cambridge (2000)
22. Rao, A.S., Georgeff, M.P.: Modeling Rational Agents within a BDI-Architecture. In: Allen, J., Fikes, R., Sandewall, E. (eds.) Principles of Knowledge Representation and Reasoning, pp. 473–484. Morgan Kaufmann, San Mateo (1991)
23. Rao, A.S., Georgeff, M.P.: BDI agents: From Theory to Practice. In: Proceedings of the First International Congress on Multi-Agent Systems (ICMAS-1995), San Francisco, pp. 312–319 (1995)
24. Sacks, H., Schegloff, E.A., Jefferson, G.: A Simplest Systematics for the Organization of Turn-taking for Conversation. Language 50, 696–735 (1974)

25. Searle, J.R., Vanderveken, D.: Foundations of Illocutionary Logic. Cambridge University Press, Cambridge (1985)
26. Sloman, A.: What Sort of Control System is Able to have a Personality? In: Trappl, R., Petta, P. (eds.) Creating Personalities for Synthetic Actors, pp. 166–208. Springer, Berlin Heidelberg New York (1997)
27. Stephan, A.: Zur Natur künstlicher Gefühle. In: Stephan, A., Walter, H. (eds.) Natur und Theorie der Emotion. Mentis, Paderborn, pp. 309–324 (2003)
28. Wachsmuth, I.: "Ich, Max" – Kommunikation mit künstlicher Intelligenz. In: Herrmann, Ch.S., Pauen, M., Rieger, J.W., Schicktanz, S. (eds.) Bewusstsein: Philosophie, Neurowissenschaften, Ethik, pp. 329–354. Wilhelm Fink Verlag (UTB), München (2005)
29. Wooldridge, M.: Intelligent Agents. In: Weiss, G. (ed.) Multiagent Systems – A Modern Approach to Distributed Artificial Intelligence, pp. 27–77. The MIT Press, Cambridge (1999)

Talking to Virtual Humans: Dialogue Models and Methodologies for Embodied Conversational Agents

David Traum

Institute for Creative Technologies, University of Southern California
traum@ict.usc.edu

Abstract. Virtual Humans are artificial characters who look and act like humans, but inhabit a simulated environment. One important aspect of many virtual humans is their communicative dialogue ability. In this paper we outline a methodology for study of dialogue behavior and construction of virtual humans. We also consider three architectures for different types of virtual humans that have been built at the Institute for Creative Technologies.

Keywords: Spoken dialogue, methodology, virtual humans, embodied conversational agents.

1 Introduction

Virtual Humans are artificial characters who look and act like humans but inhabit a simulated environment [1]. Virtual Humans can be built for a variety of purposes, including serving as role players in training applications, and non-player characters or artificial players in games. Since Virtual humans are built with explicit computational models of behavior, they can also be used to study how well these models work as models of human behavior. As with other aspects of artificial intelligence, one might focus on just the performance in a task (engineering approach) or the fidelity in modelling human behavior (cognitive science approach). These two goals converge more than for most AI applications, however, because for many purposes one wants a virtual human with human-like behavior rather than efficient behavior which may not be human-like.

We focus here on the dialogue aspect of virtual humans, though the same remarks could also be applied to other aspects. While it is still beyond the state of the art to build virtual humans with all the same capabilities as real people, there are a range of applications for which virtual humans can be useful. Many advantages can also be made by tailoring the virtual human to a specific domain and task rather than trying to attempt general coverage. First, some aspects of human behavior can be elided, as they are not relevant to the given domain. Secondly, one may also be able to take short-cuts in terms of how behavior in that domain is understood and generated, given a smaller set of relevant options. One must be careful, though, to not cut too deep, depending on the purposes. E.g., a more general theory can make it easier to extend the capabilities or move to a new domain.

In the next section, we outline a methodology for the study of interactive dialogue behavior and construction of virtual humans. Key is the use of several different types of scientific activities, applied in a spiral approach to increasing knowledge and virtual

I. Wachsmuth and G. Knoblich (Eds.): Modeling Communication, LNAI 4930, pp. 296–309, 2008.

human capabilities. In section 3, we describe the approach to dialogue modelling and three different virtual human dialogue architectures we have used at the Institute for Creative Technologies.

2 General Methodology

At the current state of practice in building virtual human characters, each one is a different, given it's specific domain and personalized knowledge, but also characteristics of the domain and genre of dialogue it is to engage in. While a lot can be re-used from character to character, we also use fairly different architectures and components for different classes of characters. However, we follow the same broad methodology for development of these architectures and characters. We endorse a cyclical approach, in which multiple passes are made at improving the virtual human, including building a full system fairly early in the process. Figure 1 shows several aspects of the complete process. One may start anywhere for which there are sufficient resources. This process combines a number of different scientific and engineering skills, including observation of behavior, annotation and analysis, theory formation and formalization, and computational modelling and implementation. In many cases, one may start from prior work on some of these aspects and not go through all the steps directly in one project. In other cases, however, the requisite data and understanding of the domain does not exist, and one must spend time developing a corpus of relevant dialogue and/theoretical or notions suitable for formalization of the domain.

On the empirical side, one may start with observation of the communicative behavior of the type of people that virtual humans are to emulate. The kind of behavior performed will depend on a number of factors, including some internal to the people involved, and some based on external aspects of the situation in which they find themselves. There are several issues with respect to which kind of data to collect. First, one needs to collect data from the same sort of activity. Allwood defines social activities as having the following parameters: [2]

1. type, purpose, function: procedures
2. Roles: competence/obligations/rights
3. Instruments: machines/media
4. Other physical environment

We will see very different kinds of language interaction depending on the number and nature of the participants and the activities, e.g., between a formal presentation, a travel agency booking, a courtroom trial, an auction, a press conference, and an informal negotiation. While broad investigation is still needed to be able to recognize the commonalities and differences such activities have on interaction, there have been a few efforts to try to explicitly capture some of this range of interaction. These include the Swedish Spoken Language Corpus [3] and the Dialogue Diversity Corpus collected by William Mann[1]. We may also distinguish activities as to whether they are fully natural (happening on their own, for their own purposes, without regard to experimenter collection), or

---

[1] http://www-rcf.usc.edu/ billmann/diversity/DDivers-site.htm

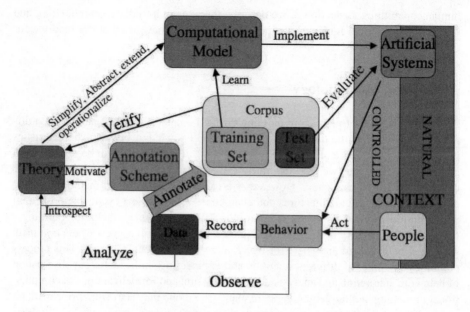

Fig. 1. Methodology for Virtual Human Creation

controlled in some way. The nature of control can also vary quite a bit. At one extreme
are situations in which experimenters bring subjects in to participate in laboratory interactions which the participants would never engage in on their own. These include
wholly artificial tasks meant to test specific theories, such as minimal pair differences
based on different conditions. There might also be naturalistic tasks which participants
are asked to role play at for the purposes of the experiment rather than engaging in
for their own reasons. Or the tasks may be completely natural except for the presence
of experimental observers and/or recording devices. All of these artificial interventions
can change the nature of the activity and the interactions which take place. This data
can still be of much interest however, as many of the most important characteristics of
dialogue will remain, despite the artificial elements.

Observation and analysis of this data can provide insight on some of the common
and important aspects, including theories about what kinds of behaviors are produced
and the patterns and relationships of behaviors to other behaviors and other aspects of
the context. In some cases these can be quite elaborate accounts of specific mechanisms
and types of behaviors. In other cases, these might be accounts of possibly significant
features that might predict certain types of behaviors.

Theories can also be used to calculate the effects of behavior on the participants,
context and future interaction. Some theories will have very broad applicability across a
range of participant types, activities, cultures, and specific contexts. Others will be more
limited to the specific situation under observation. Without broad observation or detailed
generative accounts of the mechanisms causing the behaviors, it can be difficult to tell
how widely applicable a theory is. At the current state of the art, both broad and narrow
theories are very important: narrow theories can more easily lead to empirical validation

and computational models. On the other hand, broad theories will generally be more useful for adapting to new domains with (slightly) changed activities and context.

There are generally two routes to computational models. One is to formalize the theory using human-constructed rules. Often this is not a straightforward process, as the theory is constructed at a very different level than is directly suitable for computational modelling. In some cases, one may need to extend the theory since it depends on commonsense concepts which are not amenable to formalization or have no good extant theory. In other cases, one may need to simplify some aspects that are important for the theory but inaccessible to the computational model. The question then arises as to how much to simplify. Here are several, guidelines for which phenomena in a theory to represent in a computational model for a virtual human in a specific domain. They are ordered from least to most stringent.

1. Represent phenomenon if there is general evidence of its presence in a cognitive model in some domains.
2. Represent phenomenon only if there is evidence from data that it occurs in this domain.
3. Represent phenomenon only if it leads to a functional consequence in agent behavior.
4. Represent phenomenon only if it is the simplest (not necessarily most faithful to the theory) way to achieve the consequence.
5. Represent phenomenon only if it leads to a necessary function for the domain tasks the character must perform.

Each of these guidelines may be appropriate for some modelling tasks, yet inappropriate for others, depending on whether one is most focused on getting a specific character built quickly, or on more extensible and generalizable principles that could be used to model more general behavior or re-use across characters and domains.

In the second approach to forming computational models, one uses theory only to pick out some of the most relevant types of features for analysis rather than a complete algorithmic process for recognizing, processing and producing behaviors. Here one also relies on a corpus of collected interactions with annotations of both the relevant features and the behaviors of interest, and uses machine learning techniques to learn decision procedures. These learning techniques could be of two types. One type includes explicit rules that can be inspected and compared to theoretical constructs, the other type has numerical representations that can be used to compute recognition of categories and behaviors, but does not directly lead to comparison with theories.

It is also possible to combine both the theoretical/algorithmic and machine learning approaches, so that theoretically derived models are used for some aspects and machine learning for others. For example, one might use a data-driven classifier to recognize some aspects of inputs, and a logical or rule-based system to calculate the effects in context, as is done in the MRE and SASO systems described below. One can also apply both types of processing methods to the same phenomena and arbitrate the results when they differ. These hybrid models hold great promise for allowing both robustness to noisy or unseen input while still having broad capability and generative capacity across various content topics.

However the computational model is derived, it can be used as a foundation for an implementation of a virtual human, or component of a virtual human. The implementation is not the end point, however, as the system can now be used to interact with people (and/or other systems) to generate behavior to study. One can evaluate the system from multiple perspectives, including:

– Is it a valid implementation of the computational model?
– Does it faithfully encode a theory?
– Does it have acceptable performance on a "test set"?
– Can it behave appropriately in interaction with people?

Unless virtual humans behave exactly like people, there may also be some reciprocal differences in the way people interact with the virtual human. Human-virtual human interaction thus represents a new type of context that must be analyzed. Purely human data can be used both as a starting point for analysis and implementation of virtual humans, and also as an ultimate performance goal, however it may not be the most adequate direct data, especially for machine learning. For this reason a cyclical approach allows study of how people react to the (previous generation) system, and produces more and more relevant data. In the case where data is needed before it is feasible to build a system, a Wizard of Oz approach [4] is often used, in which a person plays the role of the system, and is limited in some respects to the kinds of interaction that the system will have, while using human-level cognition for other tasks.

Thus, building a virtual human potentially requires all of the following skills:

– Minimally invasive observation and recording of natural human interaction
– experimental design, for controlled data collection
– data recording and organization
– behavior annotation
– theory-formation
– computational modelling
– machine learning algorithms
– programming and system design
– role-playing for specific domains
– wizard abilities
– dialogue evaluation

Not every project will include all of these tasks. Sometimes one can make do with prior work in some areas (e.g., a large extant corpus of recorded and annotated behavior, or a well-developed theory of human behavior). A number of these tasks are required, however, for proper spiral methodology.

Iterations of this process can be used to produce better and better virtual humans. There are several scales on which performance can be increased, including: accuracy of the phenomenon model, complexity of behavior modelled, robustness with respect to types of user, and complexity of tasks that are engaged in. We will look at some of these in more detail.

In terms of complexity of behavior, probably the simplest type of virtual human would be one that focuses on just some aspect of behavior, such as gaze, or backchannels. Here the system is not really engaging in a task with the user, but just displaying this behavior rather than all the other behaviors that would be needed for task performance. This kind of system can be very useful for exploring in detail how that phenomenon works, but does not address the interactions of multiple phenomena within a task. One can also build virtual humans for artificial "toy" domains, which illustrate multiple phenomena interacting in full task behavior, but are not tasks that anyone would naturally do. Examples include games, such as simple matching tasks. These kinds of domains allow progress on some very important phenomena and their integration, while abstracting from the complexities of more realistic tasks. There are also some real-world tasks that are relatively simple, such as information-seeking and direction-giving. More complex tasks, such as negotiation, tutoring, and collaborative construction often involve more complex reasoning, longer interaction, and multiple phases. Finally, one could design a virtual human for integration in a long-range virtual interaction, spanning many interactions with different people and engaging in different tasks.

Robustness of the system interaction can be measured in several ways. One important factor is the type of user involved. Many have remarked on the difference in performance of naive vs expert users of complex systems and user interfaces (e.g., [5]). In many cases this can be overcome by training a user to a system. In other cases, however, it is not practical to train users before interaction. There are, however more degrees of differences in the user population. The easiest type of user to achieve robust behavior with is a demonstrator. This user knows how to follow a "script" to show off the high points of the system while avoiding the weak points. Showing that at least a single reasonable interaction path works can be important in both verifying the integration of the system and fidelity to expected behavior. However, if one needs to do something other than the demonstration, it is not clear that the system will be as robust. The next level of user is a trained expert user. These people will know what works and what doesn't work and how to perform a range of useful tasks even with a system that has some serious flaws. Even novice users fall into multiple categories with respect to robustness. A *motivated* user, who really wants to get the task done with the system, will be willing to try multiple approaches until something works. This user is thus easier to achieve robustness with than a more general population user, who may be using the system only because they are told to (e.g., as part of an experiment) or because it is available (e.g., in a museum) without a specific need. These unmotivated users may quickly give up or move on to other items if the system does not quickly produce desired or interesting results. Finally, there is the *malicious user*, whose main goal is to "break" the system. Here the system must be much more robust to achieve the same levels of performance as with easier users.

This methodology is broadly similar to that employed by other designers of dialogue models for virtual humans, disembodied dialogue systems, and robots. For instance, in the TRAINS project (University of Rochester, 1990-1996), there were several cycles of data collection, theory formation, system building, and evaluation [6,7]. The current exposition is strongly influenced by the methodology used by Cassell and colleagues at MIT and Northwestern [8]. One difference in presentation, at least, is that the model presented in this chapter does not require an initial starting point of collection of human-human data, and the model can be influenced directly by human-computer testing, without explicit re-collection of human data. Li also discusses the use of multiple

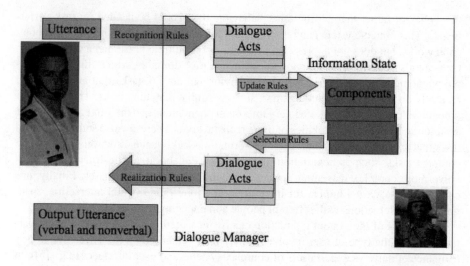

Fig. 2. Information State Approach to Dialogue

implementation-evaluation cycles as the method for design of the dialogue manager of a robot companion [9].

3   Aspects of Dialogue Theory for Virtual Humans

Dialogue interaction, whether in virtual humans or disembodied dialogue systems, can be built using many computational paradigms, from stimulus-response pairs, to finite state machines, to full agents including attitudes such as beliefs, desires, intentions, and complex reasoning. The information state approach [10,11] allows more direct comparisons between these mechanisms and different theories of dialogue. Following this approach, we conceptualize dialogue as a static part, consisting of a set of information state components and current values, and a dynamic part, consisting of dialogue acts that change the information state. These dialogue acts are abstractions of communicative behaviors (including speech non-verbal communicative behaviors) that would achieve the same effect. A dialogue manager for a virtual human consists of at least four processes, as shown in Figure 2. For each dialogue agent architecture (and perhaps even for each domain), there will be a different set of dialogue acts, and different processes. Different architectures may also assign different sets of these functions to different software components.

These processes mediate between observations, internal state, and actions that the agents perform. *Interpretation* is the process of recognizing important actions as having communicative function. From each observation, the interpretation process produces hypotheses about a set of dialogue acts that have been performed. The interpretation process could be formalized as a set of *recognition rules* in a rule-based system. *Update* changes the information state to be in accord with the performance of dialogue acts, given the previous context. This can include adding, deleting, or modifying some aspects of the information state. A theory of information state update can also be organized as a rule-based system, with specific effects for the performance of dialogue acts as well as other update rules. *Selection* is the process of deciding what to do given the current information state. It can be formalized as a choice of dialogue acts to perform, and could be implemented as a set of selection rules in a rule-based system. Finally, *realization* is in some sense the inverse of interpretation, deciding on an ordered set of physical behaviors that can be used to perform the selected dialogue acts give the current context.

Dialogue managers can differ in terms of several features, including the nature of components and dialogue acts, processing mechanisms for each of these processes, and how these processes are apportioned into multiple software modules. In the rest of this chapter, we outline three different architectures for virtual humans that have been built at ICT and their information states.

3.1   Question Answering Characters

Question answering characters have a set of knowledge they can impart when asked and goals for the presentation of this information subject to appropriate conditions. Question-answering characters must remain in character when deciding how to react to questions. Unlike question-answering systems [12] (which slavishly try to find the desired answer), question-answering characters should react to questions the way a person in that situation would, which may include lying, misleading, or finding excuses or other ways to avoid answering questions that they don't want to or are unable to answer. Question answering characters can be used for training, education, and entertainment. At the Institute for Creative Technologies we have recently built several question answering characters, including Sgt Blackwell – a simulated Army soldier who can be interviewed about ICT, the army and virtual human technology, a set of characters a reporter can interview to piece together a news story, and more recently characters who can be interviewed for training tactical questioning. These characters have a limited dialogue model of the character and focus on retrieval of appropriate answers given a question.

Sgt Blackwell, shown in Figure 3, is described more fully in [13,14]. Sgt Blackwell was designed as a technology demo exhibit for a conference. His speech model was designed for limited domain and three specific demonstrators. Sgt Blackwell's dialogue model includes a set of answers constructed ahead of time. These answers are in three categories, (1) "in domain answers", which are simple answers to questions, (2) "off-topic" answers, which are a set of responses to give when there is no appropriate in-domain answer, such as "I don't know" or "why don't you ask someone else", and (3) "prompts", to direct questioners back to the proper domain. The information state is very simple, and consists only of the local history of the last few utterances, and two thresholds: one for avoiding duplication of in domain answers (when possible), and a second threshold for avoiding repetition of off-topic answers. There is also a translation model mapping a language model for questions to a language model for answers, use to score each answer as to how well it addresses a new input question. This allows both high confidence on known questions as well as robustness to speech recognition errors and other small differences in asking the question.

Fig. 3. Sergeant Blackwell Question Answering Character

As described in [14], Sgt Blackwell is indeed robust to speech recognition errors. For known questions, accuracy does not decrease significantly until the word error rate is more than 50%. For novel questions, speech recognition does not significantly impact performance even at higher levels. While further study is required to fully understand the relationship, our hypothesis for at least part of the explanation is that this is so because the same language model is used to train the speech recognizer and the question answer classifier.

3.2   Group Conversation Characters

We have also been working on Group conversation characters, to serve as background characters for larger virtual simulations. These characters are not meant for direct interaction with users, but to serve as a middle level of detail [15]. Their behavior should be natural for a crowd, engaged in conversational interactions, and allow for natural variation for extended durations. We based this work on the conversation simulation of [16].

We have built several models of group conversation, with some examples shown in Figure 4. In [17], we extended the simulation of [16], and used this to animate bodies to drive the minor characters in the Mission Rehearsal Exercise (the left of Figure 4, also seen in the upper right corner of Figure 5). This model was extended in [18], with a new animation system, and including the ability to have members enter and

Fig. 4. Examples of Simulated Group Conversation

leave conversations and have conversation groups separate into subgroups. In [19] we extended the model to include locomotion and positioning.

For these characters, the information state consists of the set of characters and conversations. Each conversation has a set of participants, a turn-holder, a (forcasted) transition relevance place (TRP), and sequences of utterances, consisting of speaker, addressee, and whether it is main content or feedback.

Agents can perform a number of actions, including two types: Speech - which is not directly observable by humans, and non-verbal actions, which are. Speech actions include: beginning to speak, ending speech, TRP signals (that signal a possible end of turn), Pre-TRP signals (that signal that a possible end of turn is coming soon), Addressee selection, and positive and negative feedback. Non-verbal acts include position shifts (movement), orientation shifts, posture shifts, nodding, speaking gestures, and gaze.

Agents also have a set of adjustable parameters that govern their behavior in a probabilistic way. The main parameters are:

talkativeness: the likelihood of wanting to talk

transparency: the likelihood of producing explicit positive and negative feedback, and turn-claiming signals

confidence: the likelihood of interrupting and continuing to speak during simultaneous talk

interactivity: the mean length of turn segments between TRPs

verbosity: the likelihood of continuing the turn after a TRP at which no one is self selected

proxemic distance: the ideal distance between speakers of different familiarity

gaze distribution: the amount of time spent looking at different types of conversational participant (e.g., speaker, addressee, bystander)

overlap offset: the average point at which one will tend to start speaking at an oncoming TRP (before, at, or after) - leading to either small overlaps in speech, exact transitions, or pauses between turns.

These values of these parameters are used to influence behavior according to a probabilistic algorithm that will test against parameter values given configurations of the information state.

Fig. 5. An interactive peacekeeping scenario featuring (left to right in foreground) a sergeant, a mother, and a medic

So far we have evaluated these characters with respect to believability, fidelity of inferences from observed behavior to guiding parameter.

3.3 Advanced Virtual Humans

For deep interaction with humans, we need a richer model of information state. We have developed dialogue models for virtual humans that need to engage in multiparty teamwork and non-team negotiation. In the mission rehearsal exercise project [20] a human user (Army lieutenant) cohabits a 3D graphical virtual environment with animated virtual humans (a sergeant, a medic, a squad of soldiers, and some civilians) and interacts with them through face-to-face spoken dialogue to deal with an unanticipated dilemma (Figure 5) involving a traffic accident causing potentially serious injuries, and a weapons inspection where another unit may require urgent assistance.

Aspects of the information state and dialogue moves are described in [21], and the teamwork model is described in [22]. Figure 6 shows some of the conversational layers. We have evaluated several aspects of the mission rehearsal system, including a number of components of the language understanding capabilities, the system responsiveness and initiative, task success, and user satisfaction. This work is summarized in [23]. The original version of the system was one that was suitable for demonstrators but performed poorly for other classes of users. The final version had suitable performance for motivated users who were familiar with military protocol, but who were not necessarily familiar with interacting with virtual humans.

In the SASO-ST project [24,25], we go beyond team collaboration and negotiation to look at negotiation in a context where collaboration must be achieved rather than taken as a given. The virtual human model was thus extended to include representations of trust and explicit negotiation strategies in addition to the other aspects of information state.

For our first testbed domain, we developed a training scenario in which a local military commander (who has the rank of captain) must negotiate with a medical relief organization. A virtual human plays the role of a doctor running a clinic. A human trainee plays the role of the captain, and is supposed to negotiate with the doctor to

- contact – are individuals available accessible for interaction
- attention – what are individuals attending to
- conversation – what conversations are currently active
  - participants – who are the participants in the conversation
  - turn – who has the right to currently speak in the conversation
  - initiative – who is leading the progression of the conversation
  - grounding – how is information added to the common ground
  - topic – what is the conversation about
  - rhetorical – how is content in the conversation related
- social commitments (obligations)
- social roles – how are individuals related to each other
- negotiation – how do groups converge on shared plans
- individual model (beliefs, desires, intentions)

Fig. 6. Multi-party, Multi-conversation Dialogue Layers

Fig. 7. SASO-ST VR clinic and virtual human doctor

get him to move the clinic, which could be damaged by a planned military operation. Ideally, the captain will convince the doctor without resorting to force or threats and without revealing information about the planned operation. Figure 7 shows the trainee's view of the doctor in his office inside the clinic. The success of the negotiation will depend on the trainee's ability to follow good negotiating techniques, when confronted with different types of behavior from the virtual doctor.

As in the MRE project, we started with a simple version of the character that was suitable for demo users. The initial version was built very quickly, reusing over 80% of the programming of the MRE characters. By using this version to collect data with test subjects, as well as conducting additional role-play and wizard of oz data, we were able to more than double performance of the recognition components and reach a level where users have satisfactory experiences in which their success or failure has more to do with their negotiating tactics than ability to use the system.

4 Conclusions

In this article we have discussed general methodologies for building dialogue components for virtual humans, as well as several examples of different types of such dialogue models. For each of the architectures and domains, a spiral methodology involving all of study of human dialogue behavior, building computational models, implementation of systems, and evaluation of human interaction with systems has led to improved performance along multiple dimensions. This included both allowing a broader class of users to robustly interact with the systems as well as covering more aspects of the phenomena of multi-party multi-modal dialogue.

Acknowledgments

The author would like to thank the many others who have worked on the virtual humans described here and helped form the authors ideas, including Anton Leuski, Bilyana Martinovski, Susan Robinson, Jens Stephan, Ashish Vaswani, Sudeep Gandhe, Dusan Jan, Ronak Patel, Ed Hovy, Shri Narayanan, Rahul Bhagat, Dagen Wang, Jigish Patel, Michael Fleischman, Yosuke Matsusaka, Jeff Rickel, Jon Gratch, Stacy Marsella, Bill Swartout, Lewis Johnson, Patrick Kenny, Jarrell Pair, Pete McNerney, Ed Fast, Arno Hartholt, Andrew Marshall Marcus Thiebaux, Diane Piepol, Ernie Eastland, Justine Cassell, Matthew Stone and Staffan Larsson.

The effort described here has been sponsored by the U.S. Army Research, Development, and Engineering Command (RDECOM). Statements and opinions expressed do not necessarily reflect the position or the policy of the United States Government, and no official endorsement should be inferred.

References

1. Gratch, J., Rickel, J., Andre, E., Cassell, J., Petajan, E., Badler, N.: Creating interactive virtual humans: Some assembly required. IEEE Intelligent Systems, 54–63 (2002)
2. Allwood, J.: An activity based approach to pragmatics. Technical Report (GPTL) 75, Gothenburg Papers in Theoretical Linguistics, University of Göteborg (1995)
3. Allwood, J.: The Swedish Spoken Language Corpus at Göteborg University. In: Andersson, R., Abelin, Allwood, J., Lindblad, P. (eds.) Fonetik 1999: Proceedings from the Twelfth Swedish Phonetics Conference. Gothenburg Papers in Theoretical Linguistics, Department of Linguistics, Göteborg University, vol. 81, pp. 5–9 (1999)
4. Dahlbäck, N., Jönsson, A., Ahrenberg, L.: Wizard of oz studies – why and how. Knowledge-Based Systems 6(4), 258–266 (1993)
5. Paris, C.: Description strategies for naive and expert users. In: Proceedings of the 1985 Annual Meeting of the Association for Computational Linguistics (ACL-1986), pp. 238–245 (1985)
6. Allen, J.F., Schubert, L.K., Ferguson, G., Heeman, P., Hwang, C.H., Kato, T., Light, M., Martin, N., Miller, B., Poesio, M., Traum, D.R.: The TRAINS project: a case study in building a conversational planning agent. Journal of Experimental and Theoretical AI (to appear, 1995)

7. Allen, J.F., Miller, B.W., Ringger, E.K., Sikorski, T.: A robust system for natural spoken dialogue. In: Proceedings of the 1996 Annual Meeting of the Association for Computational Linguistics (ACL-1996), pp. 62–70 (1996)
8. Cassell, J.: Sistine gap: Essays in the history and philosophy of artificial life. In: Riskin, J. (ed.) Body Language: Lessons from the Near-Human, University of Chicago Press, Chicago (2007)
9. Li, S.: Multi-modal Interaction Management for a Robot Companion. PhD thesis, Bielefeld University (2007)
10. Larsson, S., Traum, D.: Information state and dialogue management in the TRINDI dialogue move engine toolkit. Natural Language Engineering. Special Issue on Spoken Language Dialogue System Engineering 6, 323–340 (2000)
11. Traum, D., Larsson, S.: The information state approach to dialogue management. In: van Kuppevelt, J., Smith, R. (eds.) Current and New Directions in Discourse and Dialogue, pp. 325–353. Kluwer, Dordrecht (2003)
12. Voorhees, E.M.: Overview of the trec 2003 question answering track. In: Proceedings of The Twelfth Text Retrieval Conference, pp. 54–69 (2003)
13. Leuski, A., Pair, J., Traum, D., McNerney, P.J., Georgiou, P., Patel, R.: How to talk to a hologram. In Edmonds. In: Edmonds, E., Riecken, D., Paris, C.L., Sidner, C.L. (eds.) Proceedings of the 11th international conference on Intelligent user interfaces (IUI 2006), Sydney, Australia, pp. 360–362. ACM Press, New York (2006)
14. Leuski, A., Patel, R., Traum, D., Kennedy, B.: Building effective question answering characters. In: Proceedings of the 7th SIGdial Workshop on Discourse and Dialogue, pp. 18–27 (2006)
15. O'Sullivan, C., Cassell, J., Vilhjalmsson, H., Dingaliana, J., Dobbyn, S., McNamee, B., Peters, C., Giang, T.: Levels of detail for crowds and groups. Computer Graphics Forum 21(4) (2002)
16. Padilha, E., Carletta, J.: A simulation of small group discussion. In: Proceedings of EDILOG 2002: Sixth Workshop on the Semantics and Pragmatics of Dialogue, pp. 117–124 (2002)
17. Patel, J., Parker, R., Traum, D.: Simulation of small group discussions for middle level of detail crowds. In: Proceedings of the Army Science Conference (2004)
18. Jan, D., Traum, D.R.: Dialog simulation for background characters. LNCS, pp. 65–74 (2005)
19. Jan, D., Traum, D.: Dynamic movement and positioning of embodied agents in multiparty conversations. In: proceedings of AAMAS 2007: Sixth International Joint Conference on Autonomous Agents and Multi-Agent Systems, pp. 59–66 (2007)
20. Rickel, J., Marsella, S., Gratch, J., Hill, R., Traum, D., Swartout, W.: Toward a new generation of virtual humans for interactive experiences. IEEE Intelligent Systems 17, 32–38 (2002)
21. Traum, D.R., Rickel, J.: Embodied agents for multi-party dialogue in immersive virtual worlds. In: Proceedings of the first International Joint conference on Autonomous Agents and Multiagent systems, pp. 766–773 (2002)
22. Traum, D., Rickel, J., Marsella, S., Gratch, J.: Negotiation over tasks in hybrid human-agent teams for simulation-based training. In: proceedings of AAMAS 2003: Second International Joint Conference on Autonomous Agents and Multi-Agent Systems, pp. 441–448 (July 2003)
23. Traum, D.R., Robinson, S., Stephan, J.: Evaluation of multi-party virtual reality dialogue interaction. In: Proceedings of Fourth International Conference on Language Resources and Evaluation (LREC 2004), pp. 1699–1702 (2004)
24. Traum, D., Swartout, W., Marsella, S., Gratch, J.: Virtual humans for non-team interaction training. In: proceedings of the AAMAS Workshop on Creating Bonds with Embodied Conversational Agents (July 2005)
25. Traum, D., et al.: Fight, flight, or negotiate: Believable strategies for conversing under crisis. In: Panayiotopoulos, T., et al. (eds.) IVA 2005. LNCS (LNAI), vol. 3661, pp. 52–64. Springer, Heidelberg (2005)

Can't Get You Out of My Head: A Connectionist Model of Cyclic Rehearsal

Herbert Jaeger[1] and Douglas Eck[2]

[1] Jacobs University Bremen
h.jaeger@jacobs-university.de,
http://www.faculty.jacobs-university.de/hjaeger/
[2] University of Montreal, Department of Computer Science, Canada
douglas.eck@umontreal.ca,
http://www.iro.umontreal.ca/~eckdoug

Abstract. Humans are able to perform a large variety of periodic activities in different modes, for instance cyclic rehearsal of phone numbers, humming a melody sniplet over and over again. These performances are, to a certain degree, robust against perturbations, and it often suffices to present a new pattern a few times only until it can be "picked up". From an abstract mathematical perspective, this implies that the brain, as a dynamical system, (1) hosts a very large number of cyclic attractors, such that (2) if the system is driven by external input with a cyclic motif, it can entrain to a closely corresponding attractor in a very short time. This chapter proposes a simple recurrent neural network architecture which displays these dynamical phenomena. The model builds on echo state networks (ESNs), which have recently become popular in machine learning and computational neuroscience.

Keywords: neural dynamics, periodic attractors, music processing, Echo State Networks.

1   Introduction

One scientific metaphor for the brain is to see it as a nonlinear dynamical system. This view has become popular in cognitive (neuro)science since about a decade [34] [33] and is particularly inviting when it comes to rhythmic or periodic phenomena. However, one should be aware that dynamical systems modeling still has narrow limitations. The mathematical tools of nonlinear dynamcal systems have been developed – mainly by mathematicians and theoretical physicists – for systems which are low-dimensional or structurally or dynamically homogeneous. In contrast, the (human) brain is high-dimensional, and its neural state variables are coupled in complex network structures with few symmetries, and are governed by local dynamical laws which differ greatly between locations and neuron types. Mathematical tools to capture the behaviour of high-dimensional, heterogeneous dynamical systems are in their infancy. The contribution of this chapter is to expand the power of the nonlinear dynamcial systems metaphor a small but definite step further toward structural and dynamical complexity.

I. Wachsmuth and G. Knoblich (Eds.): Modeling Communication, LNAI 4930, pp. 310–335, 2008.

To set the stage, we remark that many everyday human behaviours are periodic, and to a certain degree stable against perturbation. Familiar examples include

- repeating a phone number in one's mind;
- picking up a beat or ostinato motif from a piece of music and keep on tapping or humming it even when the instruments take a pause or after the piece has finished;
- in some children's games, the players are challenged to repeat arbitrary gestures.

For the amusement of the reader, and as a further example, we have put a few audiofiles online[1], which start with some random tone sequence, then repeat a short motif two to four times, then stop. The reader will find it more or less easy, on first hearing, to identify the periodic motif and continue reproducing it (covertly or overtly, to varying degrees of muscial precision). Figure 1 gives a graphical impression.

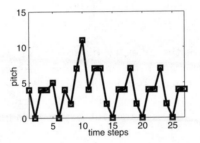

Fig. 1. A periodic pattern that sets in after a non-periodic preceding context can easily be recognized visually and acoustically (if one is instructed to watch out for repetitions). The figure depicts a little melody with discrete time steps and 12 half-tone pitches; its notes (marked by squares) are connected by lines.

Intriguingly, these phenomena combine dynamical and discrete-combinatorial aspects. From the dynamics angle, one will see periodic attractors at work, and would naturally investigate issues like stability, period length, and entrainment. From the combinatorial angle, one will remark that at least some of these examples can be seen as periodic symbol sequences (this is natural e.g. for the phone number rehearsal or muscial motifs), with an essentially arbitrary chaining of symbols from a finite "alphabet". In this perspective, one might find the descriptive tools from computer science and discrete mathematics appropriate, and might wish to investigate how many periodic sequences are combinatorially possible, what is the information of observing or generating one of them, etc.

---

[1] A zip file with ten demo files (.wav format) can be fetched from, http://www.faculty.jacobs-university.de/hjaeger/pubs/melodyPickDemos.zip

Here we present an entirely "dynamical" model, fleshed out as a recurrent neural network (RNN), which can simultaneously account for the dynamical sides of stable periodic pattern generation, as well as for the combinatorial side. Specifically, we describe an RNN architecture with the following properties:

1. the system can generate many periodic patterns which can be seen as symbol sequences;
2. the generation of such a pattern is robust against perturbations, i.e. it can be understood as a periodic attractor;
3. the number of different periodic attractors that the RNN can generate is exponential in the size of the RNN – this is the "combinatorial" aspect;
4. the RNN can be locked into each of its periodic attractors by driving it with a few (two to three) repeated external presentations of a corresponding cue pattern, from a random previous context (as in the demo examples illustrated in Fig. 1).

To preclude a likely misunderstanding, we emphasize that our system does not include an aspect of long-term storage, learning or recall. The periodic attractors hosted by the system have not been learnt, and they are not "stored". Our system realizes a purely dynamical, transient phenomenon, where a motif is picked up and kept "alive" in what one might call a dynamic short-term memory for a while – and that is all.

In order to facilitate the following discussion, we want to give a name to systems with the properties listed above, and call any such system a "cue-addressable periodic attractor system" (CAPAS).

CAPAS' have been variously considered in the cognitive and neurosciences. A well-known case is the cyclic rehearsal subsystem in Baddeley's influential model of acoustic/linguistic STM [1], where in the *phonological loop* cyclic rehearsal prevents memory traces from decaying. Baddeley's model of short-term memory includes a number of further modules and can explain intricate effects observed in human auditory short-term recall, which add important additional structure and functionality beyond go beyond the CAPAS phenomenon.

Instances of short-term imitation of a periodic pattern have been addressed in robotics (e.g., [38] [29]). As a basis for technical realization, coupled oscillator systems are typcially invoked, which become entrained to the external periodic cue signal (but compare [6] for an approach which rests on a chaotic neural network). The phenomena modeled in this kind of research are, on the one hand, simpler than CAPAS' insofar as either the external driving signal persists, reducing the phenomenon to pure entrainment (without the need for autonomous continuation); on the other hand they are more complex, because the imitation/entrainment often includes a mode or coordinate transformation of the driving signal, for instance from external visual 2-D input to motor control signals.

CAPAS are also related to some basic aspects of music cognition. Specifically, they relate to empirical and theoretical research on a listener's entrainment to the rhythmical patterns in a piece of music (overview in [11]). A particular challenge for modelling lies in the fact that the rhythmical patterns in real-life music are complicated, non-stationary, and replete with exceptions. A seemingly easy recognition task such as detecting the dominant beat can become arbitrarily challenging for cognitive modeling. Apart from symbolic/rule-based approaches, which we will ignore here, there are two major types of "dynamical" approaches. The first builds on neural oscillators which become entrained by the music signal (e.g. [22] [7]). The second type of approach calls methods and mechanisms from linear signal processing (such as delay line memory, coincidence detectors, correlation detectors) which are used to build up a representation of the rhythmic patterns in terms of autocorrelation measures as the stimulus music evolves (e.g. [4] [8]). A general problem for oscillator-based explanations is that the time it takes for the oscillators to synchronize with the driving signal is longer than what is observed in humans (but see [29] where in a motion control domain oscillators become entrained very quickly by adjusting their time constants). A possible problem for autocorrelation-based models is that these do not lend themselves directly (as do oscillator-based models) to be run in a generative mode; however, this is typically outside the scope of investigation.

Periodic (and non-periodic) motor behaviour, linguistic STM and music understanding and generation are phenomenologically and neurally connected in many ways. They are subserved by numerous coupled subsystems in the human cerebrum (see e.g. [12] for fMRI studies of multi-modal brain responses or [31] for therapeutic exploits of these interactions). In ecologically plausible settings, different sensory modes are active simultaneously and interact, as do perception vs. production modes.

Furthermore, we want to point out that much previous work on periodic attractors in recurrent neural networks exists, but it is of a different nature than CAPAS. Previous work almost invariably concerned the training of a network to stably reproduce a periodic teacher signal – in the early days of neural network research this was a frequently used challenge to demonstrate the performance of learning algorithms. Another important venue of research concerns the mathematical analysis of the (bifurcation) dynamics of small recurrent neural networks, where the typical finding is that even very small networks (2 neurons) exhibit a host of periodic and other attractors *across different weight settings*, see, for instance, [28]. Our present study aims at something quite different and has, as far as we can perceive, no precedent. Namely, we wish to set up (and analyze) a recurrent neural network which hosts a large (even huge) number of periodic attractors *with one given, fixed setting of weights*, such that the network can be driven into any of these attractors by a suitable cue input. The network is not previously trained to any of these attractors in particular, but acts as a kind of "periodic attractor reservoir".

The concrete model which we are going to develop here is based on Echo State Networks (ESNs, [14] [18]). The reason for choosing ESNs as a core component is that we need a delay line memory with certain additional stability properties; these are offered by ESNs, and the delay line / dynamical STM properties of ESNs are rather well understood [15].

The chapter is organized as follows. First we provide a more detailed motivation for exploring periodic motif reproducing systems, by discussing related phenoma that occur in music processing (Section 2). We proceed through the technical part of our contribution, by explicating the naive CAPAS intuition in the terms of nonlinear dynamical systems (Section 3), giving a short introduction to ESNs (Section 4), and explaining how we encode temporal data (Section 5). After describing our connectionist architecture (Section 6), we report the findings from two simulation studies, which highlight two complementary aspects of the architecture: its behaviour under limitations of resources (the biologically and cognitively relevant situation), and its behaviour when virtually unlimited resources are available (interesting from a theoretical nonlinear dynamics perspective).

All computations were done with Matlab on a notebook PC. The basic code is available online at `http://www.faculty.iu-bremen.de/hjaeger/pubs/MelodyMatlab.zip`. This chapter is an adaptation of a technical report [17], where the theoretically inclined reader can find the mathematical analyses behind this chapter.

2 Repetition and Content-Addressability in Melody Generation

We have noted that our model is capable of hosting a large number of periodic attractors, which can be activated by driving the system with the desired periodic trajectory for a few repetitions. In this sense, the host of attractors can be called *content addressable*. Note that this behavior is very different from that of a traditional recurrent neural network, which is capable of learning to repeat only patterns similar to those on which it has been trained. This property of content-addressable repetition turns out to be crucial for modeling melody production and perception. The vast majority of Western music is metrical, that is, built on a temporal framework of hierarchically-nested periodicities [5]. For example, part of what makes a waltz stylistically identifiable is its metrical structure of three events per measure ("3/4"). Meter lends stability to music in the sense that it provides a temporal framework around which a piece of music is organized. The impact of meter is seen, for example, in how musical repetition is carried out in Western music: when long segments of music are repeated in a piece of music, the repeated segments almost always fit neatly at some level of the metrical hierarchy. For example, in the nursery rhyme "Mary Had a Little Lamb", the melody repeats after exactly four measures (16 quarter notes).

The framework of meter gives rise to the perhaps unexpected side effect of content-addressability in music. Once a temporal framework has been established via meter, *almost any* sequence of notes can fit the style provide that sequence (a) obeys local stylistic constraints, e.g. what key and what scale is used and (b) repeats at the appropriate times. Musically-experienced readers will realize that we are simplifying things greatly. Our goal here is to highlight the fact that almost any sequence of notes (even a random one!) becomes melodic as soon as it is repeated at appropriate intervals. This suggests that a model able to discern melodies from non-melodies must at least be able to recognize that such repetition of arbitrary patterns is taking place. This amounts to recognizing that sequence $S = s_0, s_1, ..., s_k$ has been repeated, regardless of the actual combination of symbols s_k (here representing musical notes). We invite the listener to compare randomly-generated music to random music repeated at metrically-aligned intervals. To our ears, the random music sounds drifting and meaningless while the repeated music is strongly melodic[2].

Given that music has this content-addressable quality it is perhaps not surprising that previous attempts to learn melodies using dynamical systems (in all cases mentioned here, recurrent neural networks) have not worked very well. Mozer [26] introduced a model called "CONCERT" which used a recurrent neural network trained with Back-Propagation Through Time (BPTT) [37]) to learn a musical style by listening to examples (a task very similar to PPMM). Mozer trained the model on melodic sequences and then sampled from the trained model to see whether model-generated melodies were stylistically similar. Though CONCERT regularly outperformed (in terms of likelihood) third-order transition table approaches, it failed in all cases to find global musical structure and was unable to generate new waltzes when trained on examples from Strauss[3]. Similar results were had in other attempts early attempts to use neural networks to learn melody [32,30]. In short: local interactions between events are easy to learn; global structure is hard.

One reason that dynamical neural networks have difficulty with musical melody is that long-range dependencies are difficult to learn using gradient descent. Specifically, for a wide class of dynamical systems, error gradients flowing "backwards in time" either decay exponentially or explode, yielding the so-called "vanishing gradient problem"[2]. In previous work by the second author [10] this problem was addressed (to some extent at least) using the Long Short-Term Memory (LSTM) hybrid recurrent network [13]. Because LSTM can learn to bridge appropriate long-timescale lags it was able to learn to improvise blues music. However it was *not* able to respond effectively or generate music that was much different from what it had heard. That is, LSTM was able to bridge long time-lags and thus learn the global regularities that make up a musical style, but it was unable to deal with content addressability, having learned a set of recurrent weights specific to the examples on which it was trained.

Thus we argue that two qualities are valuable for addressing CAPAS with a dynamical system. First the system must discover repeated sequences (content-addressability; periodicity). Second the system must have a short-term memory capable of bridging long timespans. In following sections we will show that these qualities are met by an ESN-based CAPAS architecture.

---

[2] For the review versions of this manuscript, reviewers may find these audio files at http://www.iro.umontreal.ca/~eckdoug/repetition/

[3] In his interesting and well-argued paper, Mozer cannot be faulted for making inflated claims. He described the output of CONCERT as "music only its mother could love".

3   CAPAS Spelled Out as Dynamical Systems

In this section we give a more formal account of the particular version of CA-PAS which will subsequently be realized as an RNN, and introduce some basic notation.

The CAPAS's that we consider operate in discrete time and generate (and are driven by) discrete-valued signals which assume only a finite (and small) number of different values. To aid intuition, we employ a music-inspired terminology and refer to the possible different values as "pitches". We assume that there are p different pitches which are coded as equidistant values $i/(p-1)$ between 0 and 1 (where $i = 0, 1, ..., p-1$).

We furthermore assume that a CAPAS is initially driven by an external *cue* signal $m(n)$ (think of it as a "melody"), which itself has two phases. The first phase establishes a "distractor" context through a random sequence of length M_0 of pitch values, which is followed by r repetitions of a periodic motif of length k. All in all, the cue signals will have length $M_0 + rk$.

Our CAPAS's are driven by the cue $m(n)$ for times $n = 1, \ldots, N_0 + rk$; after which point the cue signal stops. The CAPAS's generate an open-ended output $y(n)$ for times $n = 1, 2, \ldots$.

Working in discrete time, we will thus be designing a model of the general type $\mathbf{x}(\mathbf{n}+1) = f(\mathbf{x}(\mathbf{n}), m(n))$, $y(n+1) = h(\mathbf{x}(\mathbf{n}+\mathbf{1}))$, where $\mathbf{x}(\mathbf{n}+1)$ is the system state, f, h are some nonlinear functions. This scheme only captures the cueing phase. When it ends, the system gets the input signal $m(n)$ no longer. It is then replaced by the output signal $y(n)$ to yield a system of type $\mathbf{x}(\mathbf{n}+1) = f(\mathbf{x}(\mathbf{n}), y(n))$, $y(n+1) = h(\mathbf{x}(\mathbf{n}+\mathbf{1}))$. In short, the driving input to the system can either be $m(n))$ or the fed-back own productions $y(n)$:

$$\mathbf{x}(\mathbf{n}+\mathbf{1}) = f(\mathbf{x}(\mathbf{n}), \{m(n)|y(n)\}) \tag{1}$$

$$y(n+1) = h(\mathbf{x}(\mathbf{n}+\mathbf{1})) \tag{2}$$

Having decided on the basic mathematical format, we can now express the basic dynamical properties desired from our system:

1. After the system has been driven with a two-phase cue signal, it should continue to run autonomously after time $M_0 + rk$ (with its own output fed back to its input channels). The output generated should be periodic of period length k, and this periodic pattern should be stable against perturbations. In other words, after the cueing the system should be locked into a periodic attractor. The output signal of this attractor should be close to the periodic motif of the cue.

2. The system (1) must be able to lock into a combinatorially large number of different attractors. By "combinatorially large" we mean that each attractor (modulo cyclic shift) corresponds to a sequence of length k, where each element may be one out of p possible elements. There exist in the order of p^k such sequences (due to shift symmetries the exact number is smaller and hard to calculate, but still at least exponential in a factor of k).

3. The system (1), when driven by an eventually periodic cue $m(n)$, should become entrained to this driving signal quickly. Concretely, we desire that the locking occurs within 2 to 4 repetitions.

We are not aware of a previous connectionist model or abstract nonlinear dynamical system which could satisfy these requirements. Specifically, the combination of noise robustness with fast entrainment appears hard to realize. As pointed out in Section 1, existing models for related periodic entrainment phenomena typically build on coupled oscillators – which do not synchronize with the driving cue quickly enough – or on linear operators (synchrony detection, delay line memory) which lack the desired stability in the free production phase.

4   Basic ESN Concepts and Notation

One component of the model proposed in this chapter is a delay-line memory, that is a subsystem whose input signal $u(n)$ is available on the output side in delayed versions $u(n-1), u(n-2), ..., u(n-k)$. Such delay lines are elementary filters in linear signal processing, but a neurally plausible realization is not to be immediately found. In the context of precise short-term timing tasks, a number of short-term neural timing mechanisms have been proposed [25]. One of these models [3] explains cerebellar timing by assuming that the input signal elicits transient nonlinear responses in an essentially randomly connected neural subsystem (the granule cells); from this complex network state the timing outputs are obtained by adaptive readout-neurons (Purkinje cells). The basis of temporal processing, in the view of this model, is a combination of the temporal evolution of a high-dimensional nonlinear input response in a large random network, with task-specific readout neurons that compute the desired output from the information implicit in this apparently random state.

This idea is also constitutive for the twin approaches of *Echo State Networks (ESNs)* [14] [16] [18] and *Liquid State Machines (LSMs)* [24] [19] [23]. Developed simultaneously and independently, these approaches devise a generic neuro-computational architecture which is based on two components. First, a *dynamical reservoir* (or *liquid*). This is a large, randomly connected, recurrent neural network which is dynamically excited by input signals entering the reservoir through, again, essentially random input connections. Second, adaptive *readout* mechanisms compute the desired overall system response signals from the dynamical reservoir states. This happens typically by a linear combination which can be learned by solving a linear regression problem (for which the Widrow-Hoff learning rule [36] provides a biologically realizable implementation). While this basic idea is shared between ESNs and LSMs, they differ in their background motivation and the type of neurons that are typically used. ESNs originated from an engineering perspective of nonlinear signal processing and use simple sigmoid or leaky integrator neurons for computational efficiency and precision; LSMs arose in computational neuroscience, aim at the biological modeling of cortical microcircuits and typically use spiking neuron models.

Here we use ESNs because we are not claiming neurophysiological adequacy, and because ESNs are easier to analyze. Specifically, we can benefit from the analysis of their dynamic short-term memory properties given in [15].

For a comprehensive introduction to Echo State Networks the reader is referred to the cited literature. The remainder of this section only serves to fix the notation. We consider discrete-time ESN networks with K input units, N internal network units and L output units. The activations of input units at time step n are $\mathbf{u}(n) = (u_1(n), \ldots, u_K(n))^\mathsf{T}$, of internal units are $\mathbf{x}(n) = (x_1(n), \ldots, x_N(n))^\mathsf{T}$, and of output units $\mathbf{y}(n) = (y_1(n), \ldots, y_L(n))^\mathsf{T}$, where $\cdot^\mathsf{T}$ denotes transpose. Real-valued connection weights are collected in a $N \times K$ weight matrix $\mathbf{W}^{\text{in}} = (w_{ij}^{\text{in}})$ for the input weights, in an $N \times N$ matrix $\mathbf{W} = (w_{ij})$ for the internal connections, and in an $L \times (K + N)$ matrix $\mathbf{W}^{\text{out}} = (w_{ij}^{\text{out}})$ for the connections to the output units. Here we do not use backprojections from the output units to the internal units or connections between output units. Note that connections directly from the input to the output units are allowed.

The activation of internal units is updated according to

$$\mathbf{x}(n + 1) = \mathbf{f}(\mathbf{W}\mathbf{x}(n) + \mathbf{W}^{\text{in}}\mathbf{u}(n + 1)), \tag{3}$$

where $\mathbf{f}$ are the internal unit's output functions – here we use the identity, applied element-wise to the network state vector. The ESN thus becomes a linear network, as far as the reservoir activations are concerned. The output is computed according to

$$\mathbf{y}(n) = \mathbf{f}^{\text{out}}(\mathbf{W}^{\text{out}}(\mathbf{x}(n); \mathbf{u}(n)), \tag{4}$$

where $(\mathbf{x}(n); \mathbf{u}(n))$ is the concatenation of vectors $\mathbf{x}(n)$ and $\mathbf{u}(n)$, and $\mathbf{f}^{\text{out}}$ is the output activation function – here we use $1/2 + \tanh/2$, which is a sigmoid ranging strictly between 0 to 1 with a value of $1/2$ for a zero argument. Introducing a sigmoid-shaped nonlinearity here is crucial for achieving a *stable* reproduction of the motif.

5   Signal Coding

To recall, the input signals which we will use are sequences $m(n)$, where $n = 1, 2, \ldots$ and $m(n)$ can take p equidistant values $i/(p-1)$ between 0 and 1 (where $i = 0, 1, \ldots, p-1$). In order to feed such a signal to the ESN, it is space-coded by mapping $m(n)$ on a p-dimensional binary vector $\mathbf{b}(n)$. Specifically, the space coding transforms $m(n) = i/(p-1)$ to a binary vector $\mathbf{b}(n)$ whose i-th component is one.

The ESN will be trained to function as a delay line memory, generating various time-delayed versions of such space-coding vectors $\mathbf{b}(n)$ as its output signals. Because we use a $(0, 1)$-ranging sigmoid $\mathbf{f}^{\text{out}}$ for the output activation function, this would make it impossible for the network to produce zero or unit values in

$\mathbf{b}(n)$ output vectors. To accommodate for this circumstance, we shift and scale the vectors $\mathbf{b}(n)$ to vectors $\mathbf{u}(n)$ whose components range in $(\nu, \mu) = (0.1, 0.9)$:

$$\mathbf{u}(n)[i] = (\mu - \nu)\,\mathbf{b}(n)[i] + \nu = 0.8\,\mathbf{b}(n)[i] + 0.1. \tag{5}$$

Such code vectors $\mathbf{u}(n)$ have components $\nu = 0.1$ and $\mu = 0.9$ where $\mathbf{b}(n)$ have 0 and 1. They provide the data format which the network finally receives as inputs, and which it should produce as outputs.

6   Architecture

The core of the CAPAS proposed here is a delay line memory. We realized this as a nonlinear recurrent neural network of the "Echo State Network" type. A number of reasons invited us to use such a network to implement the delay line, and not a linear tapped delay line made from concatenated unit delay filters, which would appear as the most standard implementation:

- We wish to create *stable* periodic dynamics, i.e., periodic *attractors*. Linear systems cannot generate stable perdiodic patterns. Nonlinear dynamics are needed, and ESNs have proven in the past to sustain periodic attractors [15].
- Theoretical results on the delay-line memory capacity of ESNs are available [15] [35].
- Ultimately we aim at connectionist models of cognitive and neural phenomena. The central mechanism of ESNs, an excitable random nonlinear dynamical medium (the "reservoir"), has been suggested as a neurobiological explanation for cerebellar timing [25], which adds further to our motivation to use these models.

The ESN delay line memory is the only trainable part of our CAPAS architecture. We first describe how this subsystem is set up and trained, and then proceed to describe the surrounding control architecture, likewise implemented in a connectionist fashion, which provides the CAPAS functionality.

The delay line subsystem is a standard ESN, as specified in eqns. (3), (4), with p input units, a linear reservoir of size N, and $p\,d$ sigmoid output units which for clarity are arranged in a $p \times d$ grid (see figure 2). For each delay j, we assign a separate output weight matrix $\mathbf{W}_j^{\mathrm{out}}$ of size $p \times (K + N)$, whose elements are determined by the training procedure.

The delay line memory task solved by this network is to replicate, in the jth column of output units, the p-dimensional input signal $\mathbf{u}(n)$ with a delay of j, that is, the signal vector $\mathbf{u}(n-j)$. The ESN is trained on the delay-line memory task in the standard fashion described, for instance, in [15]. Details are reported in the appendices.

This (trained and operative) delay line memory is embedded in a larger feedback cycle which is outlined in figure 3. The working principle can be outlined, as follows.

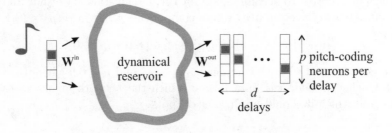

Fig. 2. The core ESN delay line memory setup

- The network's output (that is, d delayed versions of the current input) are monitored for how well they predict the current input. In the presence of an input which is periodic with period k, the k-delay block of outputs will be in consistent good agreement with the input. The prediction agreement for each of the d delayed output vectors is integrated over time and the "winner" output block is allowed to feed its signal back into the input channel.
- Technically, this requires (i) measuring and integrating the prediction error for the d output blocks, (ii) using the accumulated error as a basis for a competitive vote among the d outputs to determine one (or several) winners, (iii) feed the winning output(s) back into the input.
- In our simulations we operate the systems in two distinct phases. First, in the cueing phase, an external cue input (consisting in a transient random initial melody followed by two repetitions of a motif) is used as input. After that, the external input is replaced by the fed-back output(s) which are linearly combined according to the strength of their respective votes.

The details of our implementation are documented in Appendix A.

7   Simulations Studies

We ran two suites of numerical experiments to demonstrate two complementary aspects of our CAPAS architecture.

The first series of simulations used a small ESN of $N = 100$ throughout and explored a number of dynamical phenomena, of potential relevance for cognitive modelling, that arise from resource limitations.

The second suite served to demonstrate that the proposed architecture is fit to host a number of periodic attractors which is exponential in network size. To this end, a series of CAPAS architectures of increasing size was shown to host periodic attractors whose number grew exponentially with the size.

7.1   Study 1: CAPAS with Limited Resources

All details of this study can be found in Appendix B. Here we present an intuitive overview of the setup and the findings.

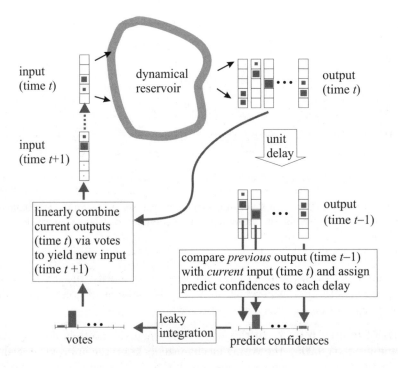

Fig. 3. The overall CAPAS architecture

An relatively small ($N = 100$) ESN was trained as a delay line memory in a setup with $p = 10$ input units and $d = 10$ delays. In the light of findings reported in [15], an ESN capable of perfect performance on this delay line memory task would need a memory capacity of $p\,d = 100$, the theoretical maximum for a 100-unit ESN. Because this theoretical maximum will not be reached, we can expect suboptimal learning performance especially on longer delays. In fact, a plot of the normalized mean root square errors (NRMSE) on training data shows that the NRMSE of recalling inputs with a longer delay is rather poor (see figure 4). The difficulties the ESN has with larger delays are also reflected in the large output weights earned on larger delays (figure 4, right panel). A detrimental consequence of large output weights is high sensitivity to noise. We can expect that if the trained network is used and noise is added to its operation, the produced outputs on the larger-delay channels will strongly deteriorate.

While we could have easily achieved a more accurate and more noise-resistant performance for the larger delays by using a larger reservoir (as we did in the second suite of experiments), we did not do so in order to investigate how the CAPAS performance deteriorates when the length of the motif ranges into the limits of the underlying short-term memory.

The trained ESN delay line memory was then employed as a module within the complete CAPAS architecture shown in figure 3, which was submitted to various tests involving motifs of different length k and amounts of noise added

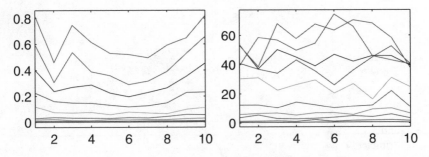

Fig. 4. Left: Delay learning test error (NRMSE) for the ten pitches (x-axis). Each plot line corresponds to one delay, larger delays give higher test error. Note that a NRMSE of 1 would correspond to completely uncorrelated test/teacher signals. Right: average absolute output weights for the various pitches (x-axis) and delays. Larger delays give larger weights.

to the input. In all conditions except for very short motifs, the motif was cued with $r = 2$ repetitions. Depending on k and the amount of noise, interestingly different types of performance were observed.

Motifs of length 6 or 7. In this condition, when the noise is not too strong (amplitude ≤ 0.005), the voting mechanism locks on the appropriate value of k before the second cue motif has ended, that is, the vote for the delay $k - 1$ goes to 1 and the others to 0. A periodic pattern similar to the cue motif is stably reproduced. Figure 5 shows a typical run for $k = 7$, without and with noise. It is apparent that moderate noise does not disrupt the periodic motif reproduction. Figure 6 shows the development of the leaky-integrated errors and the resulting votes. If the noise amplitude is increased to 0.01, the system is driven out of its attractors after every few repetitions of the attractor's loop, whereafter it settles into another periodic attractor, usually of the same period as the previous but distinguished from it by settling on different values on some of the period's time points (figure 7); more rarely or when the noise is further increased, it may jump to different period lengths or become non-periodic altogether.

Motifs of length 8 – 10. If the length of the motif grows into the region where the delay line memory performance of the ESN is poor, the inaccuracies in recalling the input from $k - 1$ steps earlier accumulate to an extent that the motif is not stably retained over time, even when no noise is inserted into the dynamics. Figure 8 shows a typical development for a $k = 9$ cue. Although the cue motif is initially reproduced a few times, the reproduction accuracy is not good enough to retain the pattern. A complex transient dynamics unfolds, which after a much longer time (1000 steps, not shown) would eventually settle in a shorter attractor not related to the cue motif in shape or period.

Motifs of length 4 or 5. Here two mechanisms become superimposed (see figure 9 for an example where $k = 5$, zero noise condition). The voting

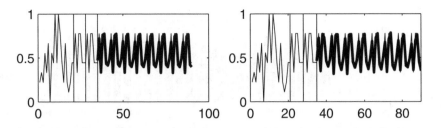

Fig. 5. Cue signal (thin line) and autonomously generated signal (thick line) vs. network cycles (x-axis). Vertical black lines mark the two cue motifs. The correct periodic cue continuation is indicated by the continued thin line (unknown to the system); system output is plotted as a bold line. The unit-coded system output was retransformed to the scalar signal $m(n)$ for plotting. Left panel shows zero noise condition, right panel with a noise amplitude of 0.005.

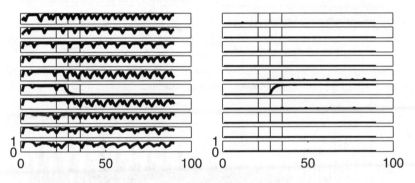

Fig. 6. Development of integrated errors (left panel) and votes (right panel) in the run with added noise rendered in the right panel of figure 5. Each plot corresponds to one delay; top plot corresponds to shortest delay $k = 1$.

mechanism correctly determines the period length k by the time the second cue motif ends, and the motif is initially correctly reproduced. However, because a k-periodic signal is also $2k$-periodic, the vote for delay $2k$ also rises soon after the system starts to produce the pattern autonomously, leading to a shared vote between k and $2k$. Because the $2k$-delay output channel has a poor reproduction performance, errors accumulate and the reproduced pattern wanders away from the original. The long-term behaviour is unpredictable; often the systems settles in a k-periodic attractor unrelated in its shape to the cue, or (more rarely) settles into an attractor with a different period. Notice that this behaviour could be remedied by implementing a winner-take-all mechanism between the votes which would prevent the $2k$ vote from rising. We would then obtain a stable reproduction of the cue motif.

Motifs of length 2 or 3. If the motif is very short, the voting mechanism needs more time than is afforded by a double presentation of the cue to

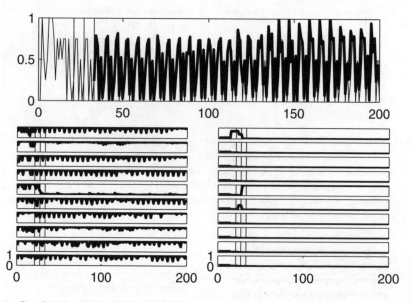

Fig. 7. Similar conditions as in figures 5 and 6, but with medium noise (here of size 0.06), leading to "hopping" between attractor variants.

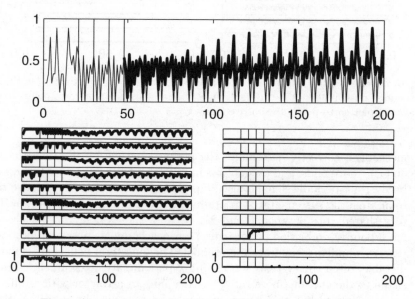

Fig. 8. A run on a cue of length 9, under a zero noise condition

rise toward 1 for the correct period length k. In our simulations, three instead of two successive presentations were needed. Similar to the case of motif length 4 or 5, after the reproduction sets in, the votes for multiples of

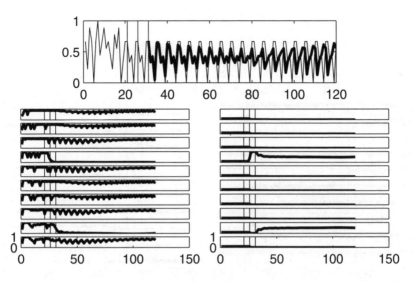

Fig. 9. Performance on a cue motif with length $k = 5$, zero noise condition. Panels show network output, integrated error, and votes, respectively.

k rise, too. For example, if the motif has period 3 (this case is shown in figure 10), the votes for $2k$ and $3k$ subsequently share their saying with the vote for k. Unlike the case of motif length 4 or 5, however, here we have two voted channels (k and $2k$) with a sufficient accuracy of recall, which outweigh the detrimental influence from the inaccurate channel $3k$. In the end, a stable reproduction of the original motif is ensured even in the presence of noise.

7.2   Study 2: Hosting Exponentially Many Periodic Attractors

Again, all details of this study can be found in Appendix C. Here we present an intuitive overview of the setup and the findings.

We created CAPAS architectures using ESN reservoirs whose size was increased from $N = 800$ in increments of 800 to $N = 4000$ (which is about the largest size that could be accomodated by the available 2 GB main memory computer that we used). Each of these was first trained as a delay line memory in a setup with $p = 5$ input units and $d = 0.6N$ delays, that is, with delays ranging from 30 in increments of 30 to 150. For each size N, ten ESNs were randomly created and trained. Figure 11 shows the delay line recall accuracies achieved.

After this training step, each ESN delay line module was planted into an architecture like in figure 3 and submitted to the CAPAS task. Specifically, a network of size N would be tested for periodic motifs of length $k = N/40$, that is, $k = 20, 40, \ldots, 100$ for the models of increasing size. The test setup was similar to the first suite of experiments. The cues consisted of an initial random "melody" sequence of length $M_0 = 20 + 2k$, followed by three repetitions of a random motif

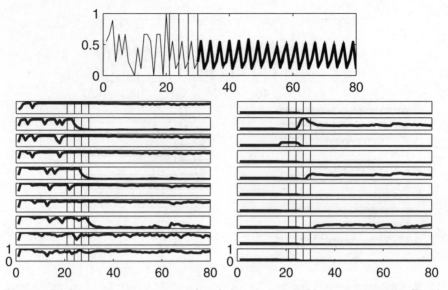

Fig. 10. Performance on a cue motif with length $k = 3$. Noise size is 0.005. Panels show again network output, integrated error, and votes, respectively.

of length k. In order to check whether the system stably locked into the required periodic pattern, it was ran after the end of the cue for 25 repetitions of the period, while noise was added to the fed-back input to challenge stability. After the 25th repetition, the noise was turned off and the system run for another 5 period cycles, of which the last was used for error measurements. The feedback noise was uniform of amplitude $0.01 \cdot 2^{-k/10}$, that is, the noise was scaled inverse exponentially with the the period length (which means inversely proportional to the number of attractors). The control parameters for the leaky integration were optimized by hand for the objective to yield a stable motif detection and reproduction (see Appendix C). Each trained system was tested on ten randomly generated periodic motifs, yielding 100 tests altogether for each network size. Figure 12 summarizes the findings.

The gist of these experiments is that

- the proposed architecture with the hand-tuned control parameters indeed was fit to produce systems hosting in the order of p^k periodic attractors, where $p = 5$ and $k = 20, \ldots, 100$;
- however, the stability and the accuracy of the attractors degraded with period length k, and the attractor length 100 marks about the longest that appeared feasible with networks sized $40\,k$ and the chosen noise levels.

The source of the decline in stability and accuracy of the periodic attractors is the decrease in accuracy of the underlying delay line memory (figure 11, left) and the simultaneous reduction of noise resistance in the delay line memory (see figure 11 right; larger output weights imply increased susceptibility to noise). The

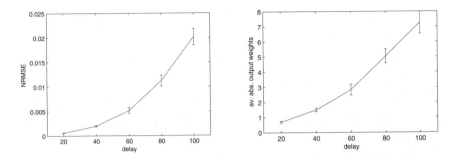

Fig. 11. Left: test NRMSEs of ESNs sized $N = 800, 1200, \ldots, 4000$ in the delay line memory of $p = 5$-dimensional data for delays $d = 20, 40, \ldots, 100$. Each plot point gives an average over ten trained networks. Right: corresponding average absolute output weights.

question of whether it could be possible, by an improved design, to host periodic attractors in numbers exponential in network size, *for unlimited network sizes*, amounts to the question of finding a connectionist model of a delay line memory whose memory span grows linearly with the network size, without bounds. This question has a rather mathematical-theoretical flavour; given the finiteness of biological neural systems it is in our opinion not crucial for purposes of cognitive or neural modelling.

We would like to conclude by pointing out that interesting types of break-downs of performance can be induced when the global control parameters of this CAPAS architecture are changed. Seen reversely, such findings indicate that certain control parameters should be actively adapted if these breakdowns are to be prevented. One example concerns the control of "garden path" periods. When we did the 20-to-100 period survey experiment with faster leaky integra-tion settings (higher leaking rates implying less temporal smoothing; details in Appendix C), we found that about ten percent of the test patterns were not correctly locked into. A closer inspection revealed that these patterns featured repetitions of subpatterns at intevals shorter than the total period length, which raised votes for delays corresponding to the distance of these "garden path" subpattern repetitions. Figure 13 shows one such example.

8   Discussion

We have presented a connectionist architecture for a cue-addressable periodic at-tractor system (CAPAS). It is capable of hosting periodic attractors ("motifs") which are made from arbitrary discrete "pitch" sequences. Within the experi-mental range accessible by the available computing resources, we demonstrated that 5^k attractors can be embedded in the dynamics of a system whose core is a recurrent neural network of $40\,k$ units (tested for $k \leq 100$; beyond this size, there are indications of accumulating inaccuracies and instabilities). The

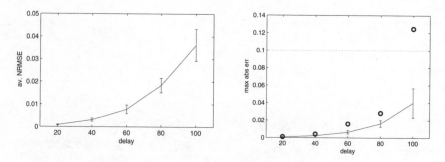

Fig. 12. Left: average test NRMSEs of ESNs sized $N = 800, 1200, \ldots, 4000$ of 100 trials per size N (10 networks tested with 10 random motifs each). The NRMSEs were computed from the last of 30 autonomous repetitions of the motif. Right: maximum absolute difference between CAPAS-produced 30th repetition and the correct target motif. For each trial, the maximum over the k points of the period was taken; these values were then averaged across the 100 trials per network size (solid line). The circles show the maximal maxima. One trial out of 100 in the longest period condition ($k = 100$) brought a maximal deviation greater than 0.1 – note that with $p = 5$ pitches and a pitch range from 0 to 1, an accuracy of better than 0.1 is the critical size needed to uniquely identify a pattern from a degraded replica.

attractors are addressable by cue presentations consisting of two or three repetitions of the periodic target pattern. To our knowledge, this system is the first connectionist architecture capable of being able to lock into any of a combinatorially large number of periodic cues quickly and stably.

We do not claim a close match between our model and biological neural circuits. There are two reasons why such a match cannot be expected. On the one hand, the error-monitoring and voting mechanisms in our model are clearly ad hoc. On the other hand, biological brains need the functionality to pick up periodic motifs in various contexts and modes, and it should be expected that differently structured neural circuitry is used in different instantiations.

The potential interest that our system might have for congnitive and neural modelling resides on a more basic and abstract level than our concrete design. A

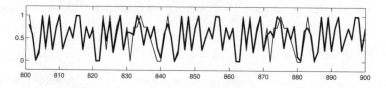

Fig. 13. A section from the last few test cycles of a period-40 test pattern with a "garden path" period of length. Thin line: target pattern, bold line: system output. The target pattern has a length-7 subpattern which repeats at a distance of 18 steps. The CAPAS system response at this time (30th repetition after end of cue) has not fully stabilized; one could say that it still "tries" to find a compromise between the conflicting periods of 40 and 18.

mathematical stability analysis (carried out in [17]) revealed that three aspects of our model are crucial for its capabilities:

1. a delay line memory with a nonlinearity (here: the output unit's sigmoid squashing function) for dynamical stability,
2. the space coding of discrete sequence values by neurons, for yielding a combinatorial mechanism to host very large numbers of attractors, and
3. an error integration and voting mechanism.

This mixture of ingredients mediates between previous models which, when based on attractor entrainment, were too slow to entrain to periodic cues within only very few presentations, or when based on (linear) delay lines, were not dynamically stable.

We conclude by emphasizing that, at least at higher cognitive levels of processing such as music understanding, the dynamics of human periodic pattern processing is certainly more intricate and richer than our simple model. Taking again music processing as an example, human-level processing has at least the following two characteristics which the presented model does not capture:

1. Real-life temporal patterns are often structured in time (multiple timescales, rhythmic structures), and they are modulated in more than just one dimension (of pitch) - for instance, music input would be modulated in timbre, loudness, etc. In sum, real-life dynamical patterns can be much more complex than symbol sequences.
2. Human processing of temporal information certainly often involves accessing long-term memory. In music processing, for instance, it is certainly easier to pick up a periodic pattern that was known beforehand, than to lock into a novel pattern.

We conclude with remarks on music modelling. The current model does not take advantage of the hierarchical nature of musical temporal structure. Music is periodic and repetitive, two qualities accounted for by the current model. But music, at least most Wester music, is also governed by the hierarchical structure seen in meter. Furthermore this structure is generally quite simple, usually a tree having mostly binary divisions with a single beat-level division of some integer ratio (e.g. 3 for a waltz). This hierarchy has a profound impact on how music is performed [27] and perceived [21]. One future direction is to design an explicitly hierarchical ESN-based model which is able to take advantage of such metrical structure. In fact we have taken a first step toward such a model; see [9].

Finally, the way in which the model represents pitch could be expanded. By using simple spatial pitch coding, the model treats all pitches as having equal similarity. In reality (e.g.) a C is more similar to a G than it is to an F# in the key of C. That is, in almost all cases it would sound better to substitute a C with a G than it would to substitute a C with an F#. Having such low-level similarity encoded in the representation is both more human realistic and also more efficient. Given that these effects are relatively well understood [20], it should be relatively straight-forward to represent pitch for the ESN such that these similarities are easy for the network to discover.

Acknowledgement. The authors would like to thank two anonymous reviewers whose acute observations helped to reshape and improve this contribution quite substantially.

References

1. Baddeley, A.: Working memory: looking back and looking forward. Nature Reviews: Neuroscience 4(10), 829–839 (2003)
2. Bengio, Y., Simard, P., Frasconi, P.: Learning long-term dependencies with gradient descent is difficult. IEEE Transactions on Neural Networks 5(2), 157–166 (1994)
3. Buonomano, D.V.: A learning rule for the emergence of stable dynamics and timing in recurrent networks. Journal of Neurophysiology 94, 2275–2283 (2005), http://www.neurobio.ucla.edu/~dbuono/BuonoJNphy05.pdf
4. Cariani, P.: Temporal codes, timing nets, and music perception. Journal of New Music Research 30(2), 107–135 (2001)
5. Cooper, G., Meyer, L.B.: The Rhythmic Structure of Music. The Univ. of Chicago Press, Chicago (1960)
6. Daucé, E., Quoy, M., Doyon, B.: Resonant spatiotemporal learning in large random recurrent networks. Bological Cybernetics 87, 185–198 (2002)
7. Eck, D.: Finding downbeats with a relaxation oscillator. Psychological Research 66(1), 18–25 (2002), http://www.iro.umontreal.ca/~eckdoug/papers/2002_psyres.pdf
8. Eck, D.: Finding long-timescale musical structure with an autocorrelation phase matrix. Music Perception 24(2), 167–176 (2006)
9. Eck, D.: Generating music sequences with an echo state network. In: NIPS 2006 Workshop on Echo State Networks and Liquid State Machines, Whistler, British Columbia (2006)
10. Eck, D., Schmidhuber, J.: Finding temporal structure in music: Blues improvisation with LSTM recurrent networks. In: Bourlard, H. (ed.) Neural Networks for Signal Processing XII, Proceedings of the 2002 IEEE Workshop, pp. 747–756. IEEE, New York (2002)
11. Gouyon, F.: A computational approach to rhythm detection. Phd thesis, Dpt. of Technology of the University Pompeu Fabra, Barcelona (2005), http://www.iua.upf.edu/mtg/publications/9d0455-PhD-Gouyon.pdf
12. Hickok, G., Buchsbaum, B., Humphries, C., Muftuler, T.: Auditory-motor interaction revealed by fMRI: Speech, music, and working memory in area spt. Journal of Cognitive Neuroscience 15(5), 673–682 (2003)
13. Hochreiter, S., Schmidhuber, J.: Long Short-Term Memory. Neural Computation 9(8), 1735–1780 (1997)
14. Jaeger, H.: The "echo state" approach to analysing and training recurrent neural networks. GMD Report 148, GMD - German National Research Institute for Computer Science (2001), http://www.faculty.jacobs-university.de/hjaeger/pubs/EchoStatesTechRep.pdf

15. Jaeger, H.: Short term memory in echo state networks. GMD-Report 152, GMD - German National Research Institute for Computer Science (2002),
    http://www.faculty.jacobs-university.de/hjaeger/pubs/STMEchoStatesTechRep.pdf
16. Jaeger, H.: Tutorial on training recurrent neural networks, covering BPPT, RTRL, EKF and the echo state network approach. GMD Report 159, Fraunhofer Institute AIS (2002),
    http://www.faculty.jacobs-university.de/hjaeger/pubs/ESNTutorial.pdf
17. Jaeger, H.: Generating exponentially many periodic attractors with linearly growing echo state networks. IUB Technical Report 3, International University Bremen (2006),
    http://www.faculty.jacobs-university.de/hjaeger/pubs/techrep3.pdf
18. Jaeger, H., Haas, H.: Harnessing nonlinearity: Predicting chaotic systems and saving energy in wireless communication. Science 304, 78–80 (2004),
    http://www.faculty.jacobs-university.de/hjaeger/pubs/ESNScience04.pdf
19. Kaske, A., Maass, W.: A model for the interaction of oscillations and pattern generation with real-time computing in generic microcircuit models. Neural Networks 19(5), 600–609 (2006)
20. Krumhansl, C.: Cognitive Foundations of Muiscal Pitch. Oxford University Press, Oxford (1990)
21. Large, E., Palmer, C.: Perceiving temporal regularity in music. Cognitive Science 26, 1–37 (2002)
22. Large, E., Kolen, J.: Resonance and the perception of musical meter. Connection Science 6(2/3), 177–208 (1994)
23. Maass, W., Joshi, P., Sontag, E.: Computational aspects of feedback in neural circuits. PLOS Computational Biology 3(1), 1–20 (2007)
24. Maass, W., Natschläger, T., Markram, H.: Real-time computing without stable states: A new framework for neural computation based on perturbations. Neural Computation 14(11), 2531–2560 (2002),
    http://www.lsm.tugraz.at/papers/lsm-nc-130.pdf
25. Mauk, M., Buonomano, D.: The neural basis of temporal processing. Annu. Rev. Neurosci. 27, 307–340 (2004)
26. Mozer, M.C.: Neural network composition by prediction: Exploring the benefits of psychophysical constraints and multiscale processing. Cognitive Science 6, 247–280 (1994)
27. Palmer, C., Pfordresher, P.: Incremental planning in sequence production. Psychological Review 110, 683–712 (2003)
28. Pasemann, F.: Characterization of periodic attractors in neural ring networks. Neural Networks 8(3), 421–429 (1995)
29. Pongas, D., Billard, A., Schaal, S.: Rapid synchronization and accurate phase-locking of rhythmic motor primitives. In: Proc. of 2005 IEEE Conf. on Intelligent Robotics and Systems (IROS 2005), pp. 2911–2916 (2005)
30. Stevens, C., Wiles, J.: Representations of tonal music: A case study in the development of temporal relationship. In: Mozer, M., Smolensky, P., Touretsky, D., Elman, J., Weigend, A.S. (eds.) Proceedings of the 1993 Connectionist Models Summer School, pp. 228–235. Erlbaum, Hillsdale (1994)
31. Thaut, M., Kenyon, G., Schauer, M., McIntosh, G.: The connection between rhythmicity and brain function. IEEE Engineering in Medicine and Biology Magazine 18(2), 101–108 (1999)
32. Todd, P.M.: A connectionist approach to algorithmic composition. Computer Music Journal 13(4), 27–43 (1989)

332   H. Jaeger and D. Eck

33. van Gelder, T.: The dynamical hypothesis in cognitive science. Behavioural and Brain Sciences 21(5), 615–628 (1998)
34. van Gelder, T., Port, R. (eds.): Mind as Motion: Explorations in the Dynamics of Cognition. Bradford/MIT Press (1995)
35. White, O.L., Lee, D.D., Sompolinsky, H.S.: Short-term memory in orthogonal neural networks. Phys. Rev. Lett. 92(14), 102–148 (2004)
36. Widrow, B., Lehr, M.A.: Perceptrons, adalines, and backpropagation. In: Arbib, M. (ed.) The Handbook of Brain Theory and Neural Networks, pp. 719–724. MIT Press/Bradford Books (1995)
37. Williams, R.J., Zipser, D.: Gradient-based learning algorithms for recurrent networks and their computational complexity. In: Chauvin, Y., Rumelhart, D.E. (eds.) Back-propagation: Theory, Architectures and Applications, pp. 433–486. Erlbaum, Hillsdale (1992)
38. Yang, W., Chong, N.Y.: Goal-directed imitation with self-adjusting adaptor based on a neural oscillator network. In: Proceedings, 12th International Conference on Advanced Robotics, ICAR 2005, pp. 404–410 (2005)

Appendix A: Details of the CAPAS Architecture

Error Integration and Voting

The measuring and integration of prediction error is done by a leaky integration scheme. For each delay j ($j = 1, \ldots, d$), in each update cycle n the average $\mathrm{MSE}_j(n)$ across the p components of the jth pitch coding vector is computed:

$$\mathrm{MSE}_j(n) = \|\mathbf{y}_i(n-1) - \mathbf{u}(n)\|^2/p, \qquad (6)$$

where $\mathbf{y}_j(n-1)$ is the previous network output for delay j (a vector of size p) and $\mathbf{u}(n)$ is the current input to the ESN. These MSE_j are leaky-integrated according to

$$\mathrm{MSE\text{-}int}_j(n) = \tanh((1-\gamma_1)\,\mathrm{MSE\text{-}int}_j(n-1) + \alpha_1\,\mathrm{MSE}_j(n)), \qquad (7)$$

where γ_1 is a leaking rate and α_1 is an accumulation weight. The tanh wrapper makes the integrated prediction error saturate at 1.

The d integrated error signals thus obtained will evolve towards zero on all delays that are a multiple of the period length k for a k-periodic input. Likewise, for delays which are not multiples of k, the integrated errors will grow away from 0 and toward 1.

An obvious mechanism to "vote" for outputs which should be fed back into the input channel would be to weigh outputs by prediction confidences $C_j(n) = 1 - \mathrm{MSE\text{-}int}_j(n)$, average across the weighted outputs, and feed the resulting mixture back to the input. In this way, only those ouputs whose delays are multiples of k – i.e., replicas of the periodic target – would be chosen.

However, the integrated errors in the delay channels not commensurate with k will not in general evolve towards 1, because within the periodic input motif there may be time points with spurious good matches between the current motif signal and incommensurable delays (e.g., if a 10-periodic cue is made up from three identical repetitions of a length-3 pattern followed by a singleton point, the delay-3 outputs will have zero error during 6 out of 10 times per 10-period, and the integrated error for the 3-delay outputs will be lower than for other delays). Thus, before becoming useful for guiding the combination of outputs into new fed-back inputs, some further cleaning of the integrated errors is necessary. We do this by two operations. First, the predict confidences $C_j(n) = 1 - \text{MSE-int}_j(n)$ are thresholded at their lower end such that confidences falling below a threshold ε will be zeroed, that is, instead of $C_j(n) = 1 - \text{MSE-int}_j(n)$ we use

$$C_j(n) = s(1 - \text{MSE-int}_j(n)), \qquad (8)$$

where $s : \mathbb{R} \to [0,1]$ maps any number smaller than ε to zero, any number greater or equal to 1 to 1, and linearly interpolates in between. Finally, a further leaky integration and subsequent normalization smoothes $C_j(n)$ to obtain the final votes V_j:

$$\tilde{V}_j(n) = (1 - \gamma_2)\, V_j(n-1) + \alpha_2\, C_j(n)$$
$$V_j(n) = \tilde{V}_j(n) / \sum_{j=1,\ldots,d} \tilde{V}_j(n) \qquad (9)$$

where again γ_2, α_2 are forgetting / accumulation factors.

Feeding Back the Vote-Combined Output

The second phase of the cueing input consists of a small number of repetitions of a motif of period length k. During the presentation of the second and all subsequent repeats, the network outputs match with the k-step previous input and the vote $V_{k-1}(n)$ will grow toward 1, while the other votes move toward zero (it is not $V_k(n)$ that will grow toward 1 due to the unit delay in the feedback circle, see figure 3). When the cue period ends after the second or third motif repetition, the external input is switched off and the network receives instead an input which is essentially made from a weighted combination of the network outputs:

$$\tilde{\mathbf{u}}(n) = \sum_{j=1,\ldots,d} V_j(n-1)\, \mathbf{y}_j(n-1). \qquad (10)$$

A normalization is needed to help stabilizing this feedback loop. Specifically, we ensure that the space coding vectors $\mathbf{b}(n)$ (if they were to be recomputed from the scaled versions $\mathbf{u}(n)$) sum to 1. To effect this, we first retransform $\tilde{\mathbf{u}}(n)$ to the binary format of $\mathbf{b}(n)$, then normalize to unit component sum, and then scale/shift back to the format generated by the ESN:

$$\tilde{\tilde{\mathbf{u}}}(n) = (\tilde{\mathbf{u}}(n) - [0.1...0.1]^\mathsf{T})/0.8$$
$$\tilde{\tilde{\tilde{\mathbf{u}}}}(n) = \tilde{\tilde{\mathbf{u}}}(n)/\text{component sum of } \tilde{\tilde{\mathbf{u}}}(n)$$
$$\mathbf{u}(n) = 0.8\,\tilde{\tilde{\tilde{\mathbf{u}}}}(n) + 0.1 \qquad (11)$$

In order to check the stability of the periodic pattern reproduction, we added uniform noise to the (fed-back) input $\mathbf{u}(n)$ in the simulations.

Appendix B: Details of the First Simulation Study

The learning task is that the trained network, on an input sequence $\mathbf{u}(n)$, outputs d vectors $[\mathbf{u}(n-d)\mathbf{u}(n-d+1)\ldots\mathbf{u}(n-1)]$. For convencience we arrange the target vectors $\mathbf{u}(n-d), \mathbf{u}(n-d+1), \ldots, \mathbf{u}(n-1)$ into a $p \times d$ array $\mathbf{y}(n)$. The training data are thus generated as follows:

1. To make the input data, produce a random space-coded "melody" sequence $\mathbf{u}(n)$ of length $n_{\max}$.
2. For each $n > d$, assemble $\mathbf{y}(n)$ from the previous d instances of $\mathbf{u}(n)$. For the first $n \le d$, use dummies (initial transients of the network will be discarded anyway).
3. The training data consist of $n_{\max}$ input – teacher output pairs $(\mathbf{u}(n), \mathbf{y}(n))$.
4. Create a similar pair sequence for the purpose of testing the delay memory performance.

We use an ESN with a reservoir of $N = 100$ units, with $p = 10$ input units and $d = 10$ delays, resulting in 100 output units. The internal weights $\mathbf{W}$ are drawn from a uniform distribution over $[-1, 1]$, with approximately 90% of the connection weights becoming nulled, resulting in an average connectivity of 10%. The sparse weight matrix is then rescaled to yield a spectral radius of 0.8. The input weights $\mathbf{W}^{\mathrm{in}}$ are drawn from a uniform distribution over $[-1, 1]$.

The ESN was trained on the delay-line memory task in the standard fashion described, for instance, in [15]. The length of the training sequence was 1000, from which the first 200 points were discarded to wash out initial transients. The result of the training are d output weight matrices $\mathbf{W}_j^{\mathrm{in}}$. To prevent overfitting, a regularizer was implemented in the form of uniform noise from $[-0.0005, 0.0005]$ added to the network states harvested while the ESN is driven by the training input.

The various control parameters for the voting dynamics were set to $\gamma_1 = .4$, $\alpha_1 = 4, \gamma_2 = .2, \alpha_2 = 4, \varepsilon = 0.3$.

Appendix C: Details of the Second Simulation Study

In the second study, for training a network of size $N = 800, 1600, \ldots, 4000$ we used training sequences of length $n_{\max} = 2.25 \cdot N$ and testing sequences of length $1.5 \cdot N$.

The reservoir weight matrices $\mathbf{W}$ were sparse with a connectivity that made one neuron connect to ten on average. The nonzero weights were sampled from a uniform distribution centered at 0, and the resulting matrix was rescaled such that the resulting spectral radius was 0.995 (spectral radii close to unity are beneficial for long short-term memories, see [15]). Each input unit was connected to all reservoir units with weights sampled from a uniform distribution over $[0, 1]$.

The ESN was trained using the standard procedure which is variously documented in the literature (e.g., [15]). Data from the first N time steps were discarded to account for initial transients. The linear regression was computed using the Wiener-Hopf equation, which was regularized with a Tikhonov (also known as ridge regression) regularizer of size $\alpha = 0.0001$.

Using Matlab for the computations, we encountered spurious problems when the inverses of the Tikhonov-regularized reservoir state correlation matrices were computed for the Wiener-Hopf solution of the linear regression. The correlation matrices were generally not very well conditioned (Matlab's inverse condition indicator rcond was about 1.0e-14) but still suffienct for a reliable inversion. However, especially for the larger matrices (of sizes 2400×2400 to 4000×4000), Matlab sometimes issued a warning that the matrix was ill-conditioned, and reported rcond's of much smaller size (dozens of orders of magnitude smaller). Given that these matrices were Tikhonov-regularized with $\alpha = 0.0001$, we could not explain this phenomenon, and must assume some instability in the implementation of matrix inverses. When this situation was encountered, the trial was re-started with a freshly created ESN.

The control parameters for the voting dynamics were set to $\gamma_1 = 0.05, \alpha_1 = 2, \gamma_2 = 0.1, \alpha_2 = 2, \varepsilon = 0.2$ for all networks. In the "garden path" example, the settings were $\gamma_1 = 0.2, \alpha_1 = 4, \gamma_2 = 0.1, \alpha_2 = 4, \varepsilon = 0.2$.

Author Index

Printing: Mercedes-Druck, Berlin
Binding: Stein+Lehmann, Berlin

Lecture Notes in Artificial Intelligence (LNAI)